NEW YORK CITY
2007

AN inside GUIDEBOOK
NEW YORK

PUBLISHER, EDITOR-IN-CHIEF	Justin Belmont
ASSISTANT PUBLISHER	Dmitry Shevelenko
GRAPHIC DESIGNER	Michelle Legro
ASSISTANT GRAPHIC DESIGNER	Ellen Marrone

EDITORIAL STAFF

Neighborhoods Editor	Shannon Donnelly
Dining Editor	Andrew Avorn
Nightlife Editor	Orlee Maimon
Shopping Editor	Anna German
LGBT Editor	Jim McCormick
Copy Editor	Tanveer Ali
Copy Editor	Jill Colvin

STAFF WRITERS/EDITORS

Emily Austin, Downing Bray, Adam Brickman, Anshu Budhrani, Nicole Goldstein, Adam Katz, Mike Harvkey, Mary Kate Johnson, Alexis Korman, Johanna Lane, Katherine McMahon, Jamie Peck, Rosanna Platzer, Luis Rodriguez, Laura Regensdorf, Tiara Winter-Schorr

CONTRIBUTORS

Jamila-Khanom Allidina, Thom Blaylock, Abby Caran, Rebecca Dunnan, Jennifer Grossbard, Daniel Heyman, Cindy Horowitz, Julia Kite, John Klopfer, Saki Knafo, Jenna Krajeski, Greta Levy, Elyse Lightman, Julia LoFaso, Laura Nevison, Chris Radcliff, Stephanie Shieh, Isaac Silverman, Aaron Snyder, Cheryl Teran, Mariel Villeré, Josh Weil, Alex Wolff, Richard Wong, Annabelle Yoo, Noah Youngs

MAPS AND ILLUSTRATIONS Ellen Marrone

---

www.insidenewyork.com

2960 Broadway MC 5727 • New York, NY 10027
Phone: 212-854-2804 •Fax: 212-663-9398

Manhattan Subway Map © Metropolitian Transportation Authority, used with permission.

We wish to extend a special thanks to our wonderful interns: Downing Bray, Anshu Budhrani, Jill Colvin, Shannon Donnelly, Adam Katz, Jim McCormick, Katherine McMahon, and Rosanna Platzer. Thanks also to Darrell Russell, Dan Taeyoung Lee, Brian Belmont, Rebecca Rodriguez, Bernadette Maxwell, Yuri Shane, David Seidman, AEPi, the Center for Career Education staff, our advertisers, and the stellar staff of INY 2007.

Sales and Advertising
For information regarding bulk sales, customized editions and advertising, please call 212-854-2804, e-mail sales@insidenewyork.com, or visit www.insidenewyork.com.

Special Note
For dining reviews, we have used dollar signs to designate prices according to the following scale, which is based on the average cost per entrée.
$ inexpensive (under $15)
$$ moderate (between $15 and $25)
$$$ expensive (over $25)

This is a publication of the Student Enterprises Division of Columbia University
PRINTED IN THE USA

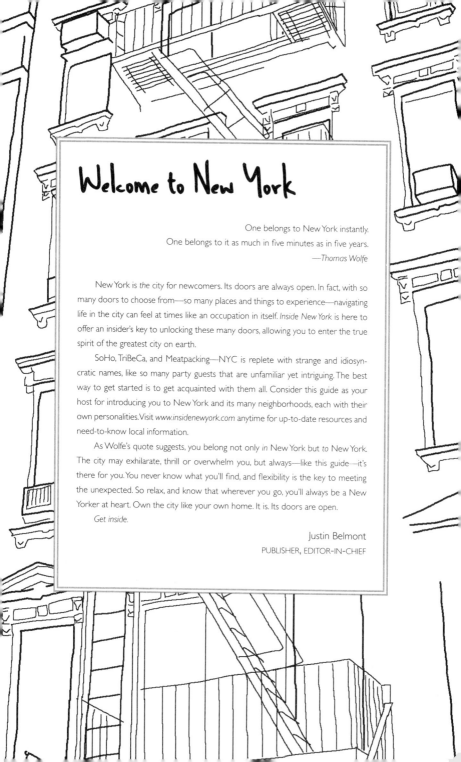

Welcome to New York

One belongs to New York instantly.
One belongs to it as much in five minutes as in five years.
—*Thomas Wolfe*

New York is *the* city for newcomers. Its doors are always open. In fact, with so many doors to choose from—so many places and things to experience—navigating life in the city can feel at times like an occupation in itself. *Inside New York* is here to offer an insider's key to unlocking these many doors, allowing you to enter the true spirit of the greatest city on earth.

SoHo, TriBeCa, and Meatpacking—NYC is replete with strange and idiosyncratic names, like so many party guests that are unfamiliar yet intriguing. The best way to get started is to get acquainted with them all. Consider this guide as your host for introducing you to New York and its many neighborhoods, each with their own personalities. Visit *www.insidenewyork.com* anytime for up-to-date resources and need-to-know local information.

As Wolfe's quote suggests, you belong not only *in* New York but *to* New York. The city may exhilarate, thrill or overwhelm you, but always—like this guide—it's there for you. You never know what you'll find, and flexibility is the key to meeting the unexpected. So relax, and know that wherever you go, you'll always be a New Yorker at heart. Own the city like your own home. It is. Its doors are open.

Get inside.

Justin Belmont
PUBLISHER, EDITOR-IN-CHIEF

Contents

City Living

Getting Around

SUBWAYS

GETTING STARTED
>> New York's subways are the great equalizer. For $2, the system will take anyone just about anywhere. There are no lines and no assigned seating, just a healthy dose of barely organized chaos. If you're good at worming your way into a crowd, you've got as good a chance at snagging a seat as some hotshot Wall Street executive.

The first thing you need to do in order to ride the subway is purchase a MetroCard. Don't let the dispenser machines intimidate you——they're actually quite simple, even idiot-proof, as long as you know the dif-ference between the types of cards offered. A Regular Metro-Card allows you to put enough money for a certain amount of rides ($2 per ride) on the card. If you buy the $10 version, you get six rides for the price of five. (The $20 Metrocard gives you 12 for the price of 10.) Using exact cash or a debit/credit card is recommended as the machines can dispense only a limited number of dollar coins as change.

Alternatively, Unlimited Me-troCards allow you unlimited rides within a fixed amount of time for a flat fee. You can purchase a one-day Fun Pass for $7, a 7-day pass for $24, and a 30-day for $76. These cards are a good value if you plan on taking the subway at least twice a day. But don't try to cheat the system: after swiping in one station, the card cannot be swiped again for another 18 minutes in that same station. Also, know that unlimited cards expire at 3 a.m. the morning after the expiration date, so don't worry about leaving a club or bar early because your card is set to run out that night.

Seniors (65 and older) and disabled persons can qualify for a half-price Reduced Fare after completing an application. Children 44 inches tall and under ride for free. Students at New York City public schools are given a special "Student MetroCard," which allows them to travel for a discounted rate. Subway transit information is available at mta.info.

GETTING AROUND
>>Even native New Yorkers occasionally get lost in the labyrinthine subway system. Stay calm if you get lost: just find the nearest open MTA booth and ask the attendant. You may lose your $2 exiting the turnstile to get to the booth, but it beats accidentally ending up in an unfamiliar neighborhood.

Take some time and double-check your route before you leave your apartment or hotel. Check with the MTA website (mta.info/nyct/subway) for directions and changes to the lines due to repairs. Since most of the colors are attributed to multiple lines, knowing which line to take is essential. For example, the **Ⓐ**, **Ⓒ**, and **Ⓔ** trains are all blue, but the **Ⓐ** train runs express and the uptown **Ⓔ** train heads east after 50th St. Also, know in advance whether your stop is express or local-only, and get on the appropriate train. When in doubt, take the local. Most express stops offer free transfers, so if you miss your stop or get on a train going the wrong direction, sit tight until you get to an express stop and transfer there.

After you use a MetroCard on a subway, you have two hours to use a free transfer for a bus. The same is true for bus-to-subway and bus-to-bus transfers; when transferring from bus to bus, you will receive a transfer only if you are using two different lines. So if you're just headed out for a quick errand, take the subway one-way and the bus the other and you'll save one fare.

The 42nd St–Times Square Station is the main hub of the subway system. At this station, you can pick up the **❶ ❷ ❸ Ⓝ Ⓞ Ⓡ** and **Ⓦ** lines; you can also walk through the tunnel to Port Authority and pick up the **Ⓐ Ⓒ** or **Ⓔ**, or take the **Ⓢ** or **❼** to Grand Central to pick up the **❹ ❺** or **❻**. If you want to pick up the **Ⓑ Ⓓ Ⓕ** or **Ⓥ**, you'll have to take the **❼** from Times Square over to 42nd St.–Bryant Park. For the **Ⓛ**, you'll have to take any north/

south train downtown to 14th St. and pick it up there.

If you have an address but can't figure out the nearest subway stop from MTA's map, visit hopstop.com, where you can get Mapquest-style directions for subway transit.

GETTING THERE IN ONE PIECE

>> Be very careful when taking the subway alone at night. Try to wait for the train in view of the attendant's booth if possible, and ditch the iPod in favor of being aware of your surroundings. If you really don't feel comfortable for whatever reason, you should trust your instincts and consider springing for a cab.

Keep your belongings with you at all times. Do not put your purse, backpack, or suitcase down for even a second, and maintain a good grip on it. If you're going a long distance and don't want a heavy backpack on your lap the whole time, place it on the floor but loop your leg through one of the straps.

Although few and far between, there have been cases of random attacks where passengers were shoved into the path of an oncoming train. Make sure you stand a few feet away from the edge of the platform. It's better to risk not getting a seat on a train than to end up bisected.

For the most part, New York

City's homeless population is non-violent. Many panhandlers come into the subway cars looking for money. After a while, New Yorkers learn to deliberately put some spare change into their pockets before heading out, as it's often easier to give them money than it is to ignore them. If you don't have any money to spare or simply don't want to give anything, try to avoid direct eye contact. If a homeless person starts becoming belligerent, simply walk away. If necessary, find a police officer or MTA worker should someone begin to follow or harass you. Homeless people are human and deserve to be treated as such; however, it doesn't hurt to remember that many are living on the streets because of mental, drug, or alcohol problems, which can cause unstable or unpredictable behavior.

BUSES

CITY BUSES
>> Buses are definitely slower than the subway, but allow passengers to see much more of the city than they would under-

ground. Most buses stop every few blocks along major streets or avenues. Stops are typically marked by a pole topped with a blue circle bus icon and the names of the buses that stop there. In addition, most stops offer a glass-sheltered waiting area. Be forewarned: posted schedules are not always accurate. Sometimes, most frequently during off hours, buses will not run for a long period of time, and then several will come clumped together.

Paying for fare on buses can be a bit of a pain. If you don't already have a Metro-Card, your best bet is to pay in exact change, using quarters and dollar coins if you have them, and nickels or dimes if you don't.

All buses flash their numbers on the screen above the front windshield. They always begin with a letter, then a number. M is for Manhattan, Q for Queens, B for Brooklyn, and Bx is for the Bronx. Most buses run continuously from 7am to 10pm. After that, service is less frequent. It is not unheard of to wait up to an hour for a bus in the wee hours of the morning. Many bus lines run north or south along avenues; if the avenue you are on does not have bus service, walk one block west or east depending on the direction that you are going and catch a bus on the adjacent avenue. There are also cross-town buses that

cut across Central Park and operate on other major thoroughfares throughout the city (there is usually a cross-town bus every eight blocks or so). To switch bus lines, ask the driver for a transfer if you've paid in coins. If you've paid by MetroCard, the transfer is saved on your card for two hours.

The seats nearest the driver are reserved for the handicapped, so try not to sit there unless the bus is full and no elderly, pregnant, or otherwise child-encumbered passengers are standing. Try to use the back door when exiting to help minimize the time spent at stops. Finally, be courteous and always let passengers off before you board.

Express buses are the buses of choice for most New Yorkers who live further away from the city—they can decrease a typical commute from 90 minutes to 45 minutes. Most run between boroughs, and they are subsequently notated by an upper case "X" in the route number. Fare for these rides costs $5 a pop.

If you plan to use buses, always have a map at hand. Grand Central Terminal and Times Square both have large information booths with detailed maps for subways and buses, and you can always get a general service map from any fare booth operator or bus driver.

NON-NYC BUSES

>> Many bus lines operate out of the Port Authority Bus Terminal, which is easily accessible from the Times Square station. Most of these bus lines offer cheap fairs to Pennsylvania, New Jersey, or Connecticut. Some reliable bus lines include New Jersey Transit, DeCamp, Greyhound, and Peter Pan.

Port Authority Bus terminal at Eighth and Ninth Avenues and 40th to 42nd Sts. Take the Ⓐ Ⓒ Ⓔ to 42nd St.–Port Authority, or Ⓝ Ⓡ Ⓢ Ⓦ ① ② ③ to 42nd Street–Times Square. Visit panynj.gov for more information.

TRAINS

LONG ISLAND RAILROAD

>> The LIRR, or Long Island Railroad, is based out of Penn Station and feeds almost all of Long Island with regular service. Main LIRR stations include Jamaica Station in Queens, and Minneola Station in Nassau. Be sure to buy tickets either at the ticket window or from the automated machines, as a surcharge of over three dollars is

added for onboard purchases. Don't worry if the machine at your LIRR station is broken; if this is the case, then the onboard surcharge is waved. Also be aware that the LIRR considers a train to be "on time" if it is running within five minutes of its stated travel time. Therefore, be sure to arrive at least five minutes before your train is scheduled to depart. Long Island affords Manhattanites many wonderful beaches and lovely destinations. Fares vary depending on the distance that is traveled by a passenger.

Penn Station at 34th St. (at Seventh Ave.), mta.info. 718-217-LIRR, 516-822-LIRR or 631-231-LIRR, Lost Articles 212-643-5228, Ⓐ Ⓒ Ⓔ ❶ ❷ ❸ *to 34th St.-Penn Station.*

NEW JERSEY TRANSIT

>> New Jersey Transit is an extensive rail network that delivers hundreds of thousands of commuters each day into New York from the bedroom communities that are emerging all over New Jersey. The line is based out of Penn Station and departs from the same area as Amtrak. Like the LIRR, trains and their track numbers are listed on the huge board in the middle of the station, and finding the right train can be confusing. The trick here is to listen to the announcements closely, as they usually don't announce a train's track until

minutes before it is set to depart. When purchasing a ticket for an NJ Transit train, always be sure to avoid the long lines that build up around tellers. Most NJ Transit stations have automated machines where you can purchase a ticket with a credit or debit card, alleviating what would otherwise be a long stay in a queue.

Penn Station at 34th St. (bet. 7th and 8th Aves.), 973-762-5100, Lost Articles 212-630-7389, Ⓐ Ⓒ Ⓔ ❶ ❷ ❸ *to 34th St.-Penn Station.*

New Jersey Transit also feeds into SEPTA (South Eastern Pennsylvania Transportation Authority), which is the rail system for Pennsylvania, and the cheapest way to get to Philadelphia. Once you master these rail systems, you will uncover dozens of destinations you can access easily and cheaply.

SEPTA Information 215-580-7800.

PATH

>> The PATH (Port Authority Trans-Hudson) trains are a fast and cheap way to commute to and from New Jersey's major northern cities, such as Hoboken and Newark. The largest portal for PATH trains is now at the Manhattan Mall Station, located at 33rd St. and Sixth Ave., next to Macy's and a block east of Penn Station. The trains also stop at the intersection of 23rd St. and

Sixth Ave., 14th St. and Sixth Ave., 9th St. and Sixth Ave., and Christopher and Hudson Sts. The standard fare is $1.50, but you can save some cash by purchasing Quick-cards, which offer reduced fares when purchased in bulk.

Manhattan Mall Station at 33rd St. and Sixth Ave., www.panynj.gov. 800-234-7284, Lost Articles 201-216-6078, Ⓑ Ⓓ Ⓕ Ⓝ Ⓡ Ⓥ *to 34th St.-Herald Square.*

METRO NORTH

>>Metro North is the most expansive commuter line of northern New York State, with train connections to Westchester, upstate New York, and even Connecticut. These trains are relatively cheap (most destinations cost between $6 and $8 if you leave from NYC), and offer a fairly quiet and comfortable ride. If you live uptown, the 125th St. Station is a convenient way of hopping on Metro North's lines that run up the East Side without trekking all the way down to Grand Central Terminal.

Grand Central Terminal at 42nd Street (at Park Ave.), 125th St. (at Park Ave.), www.mta.info. 212-532-4900 or 800-METRO-INFO, Lost Articles 212-340-2555, ❹ ❺ ❻ ❼ Ⓢ *to 42nd St.-Grand Central or* ❹ ❺ ❻ *to 125th St.*

TAXIS

YELLOW CABS

>> Sliding into a cab can feel like suiting up for a kamikaze mission, especially if your driver is the type that switches lanes sporadically and goes fast enough to make even Dale Earnhardt, Jr. nervous. Know, however, that while the number of near misses is astronomical, taxi drivers get into far fewer accidents than you might imagine.

Hailing a cab is easy. Just step onto the street, maybe half a foot away from the curb, and stick out your arm. If you're at a major transit point, such as Grand Central, Port Authority, or Penn Station, you can either get in line at the taxi station or walk over a couple blocks and try to catch your own. Beware of cab poachers, who will stand half a block away against the grain of traffic to try and scoop up a cab before you, even if you've been waiting longer. In theory, cab hailing should be first-come, first-served, but in reality it's a cutthroat free-for-all. Don't be shy about getting out there or the cabs will pass you by and more ruthless passengers will poach cab after cab from you.

Rates include $2.50 base pay to turn the meter on, then 40¢ for each additional fifth of a mile or 120 seconds of stop time. There is an additional $1 charge between 4 and 8 pm on weekdays, as well as a 50¢ charge between 8 pm and 6 am every day of the week. Legally, the driver can take up to four passengers, although if you charm him or her (and promise to tip well) you can negotiate up to five. Under the Taxi and Limousine Commission guidelines, if you receive bad service, you can take the medallion number of the car (located on the partition and printed on your receipt) and call 212-NYC-TAXI. It's a good idea to note the medallion number at the start of the trip anyway, in case you wind up leaving something behind (cellist Yo-Yo Ma once left his prized cello in the trunk of a cab...and got it back).

Drivers on duty are not allowed to refuse a ride to any destination; nonetheless, always wait until you're firmly seated in the cab before you tell the driver where you are going, as some will refuse to ferry you if they do not feel it is worth their time. Drivers usually know exactly where to go, but it helps if you can supply them with the cross-streets. By giving more detailed directions, you also decrease the chances of them taking advantage of you by taking a longer and more expensive route. To that end, you always have the right to tell them which route to take—if you know, for instance, that taking Broadway would be faster than the West Side Highway.

You are also entitled to a smoke and incense-free environment, a quiet ride (sans music and cell phone conversations), and air conditioning if you ask for it. Tipping 10-15 percent is customary.

Finding an Apartment

>> FINDING AN APARTMENT IN NEW YORK CITY is a dramatic rite of passage, like your first kiss or passing your driver's test—and just as nerve-wracking. If money is no obstacle, landing an apartment will take less time than you think. If you're on a tight budget, be prepared to spend some time finding a place both affordable and inhabitable. Expect to be horrified by much of what you see; learn to adjust your expectations. New York living (recently estimated to cost 40 percent more than much of the country) has rules all its own. Landing an apartment is much like a game, so here are some strategies for how to play and win.

1 BE FRUGAL
Draw up a budget of your salary and monthly expenses. Factor in $50 a month for utilities, $50 to $100 for cable per apartment, and at least $250 for grocery basics. Remember, a higher rent means less cash for fun.

2 BE CLEAR
Decide what you can live with and what you can't live without. The pickier you are, the more you will pay in rent and time. Even brokers lose patience and stop returning calls for apartment hunters who are seeking perfection. Nonetheless, be sure to choose a place you find comfortable. After a long day at school or work, you'll want to return to an apartment you can consider "home."

3 BE REALISTIC
Research the neighborhoods you're interested in and don't waste time looking where you wouldn't want to live. Take into account things like proximity to subways, grocery stores, and your school or work-place. Be realistic about what you can afford so you won't stretch yourself too thin. To get an idea of what apartments are going for, visit broker websites, Craigslist (newyork. craigslist.org), *The Village Voice* or the Sunday *Times* Real Estate Section.

4 BE ADVENTUROUS
Don't discount the outer boroughs. Excluding pricey neighborhoods like Park Slope, most of Brooklyn (and mostly all of Queens) offer better deals than Manhattan, and there's a certain pride that comes along with making fun of your Manhattan-centric friends. Queens is the more in-dustrial of the two, but there's beauty in those apocalyptic views—and fantastic food in Astoria. Other areas, such as Long Island City, are still

"in transition," meaning lower rents are just a subway ride away. Jersey City (NJ) offers another alternative for convenient and affordable housing, while Hoboken (NJ) offers a hip spot for the twentysomething set.

BE FLEXIBLE

 Consider getting an apartment with a convertible dining or living room. Temporary walls are not too expensive and can create livable bedrooms and studies. Often apartments are made more affordable by splitting two rooms into one.

BE SAFE

Before you sign the lease on an apartment, visit the area at night. How safe do you feel? How close is the nearest subway? Is there adequate street lighting? Any foot traffic? Your safety is paramount, and if you don't feel comfortable you'll never be happy. For crime statistics and other information, visit the Compstat page of the NYPD's webpage (nyc.gov/html/nypd/home.html).

BE A ROOMIE

If you're the type who plays well with others, you can save major cash by going the roommate route. Just be sure to check references carefully, as things can get very messy (e.g.,

getting stiffed on rent or bills, having to find someone new, paying to repair damage) if the situation turns sour. Finder services like craigslist.com, roommateclick.com, and roommates.com can help in the search. If you are the leaseholder, consider adding utilities to the rent so that you are not left "holding the bag."

BE BROKERED

 No matter how independent you are, be prepared to enlist the services of a broker. Brokers control access to the vast majority of available housing in the city and charge a percentage of the annual rent for whatever great digs they "find" you. When choosing a broker, be sure to confirm that they are accredited and have multiple listings in your desired neighborhood/s. Ask if they represent properties exclusively. If they don't, even if you say, "I'll take it," someone else could have already said the same thing to their broker about the same apartment. Be prepared for a "neck and neck race" for a good find, and find out about fees up front (if they don't offer this information readily, it's probably a bad sign). The standard finder's fee is one month's rent.

BE A 'REAL' NEW YORKER

Subletting an apart-

ment is likely the cheapest way to live in the city. For one thing, you get to use someone else's furniture and you also have more flexibility on the amount of time you rent. A great place to look for and post sublets is sublet.com or craigslist. Prepare to be flexible and yield to the dates set by the owner of the apartment.

BE QUICK

 If you find a place that you consider a great find, act quickly. In a matter of hours, it may be gone. If you tend to be the slow and deliberate type, this is a good time to work on your fastidious ways!

BE BOLD

Though apartments in NYC are some of the most expensive per square foot in the world, there are always buildings in need of tenants. If you are lucky enough to find a landlord who is impatient, the rent might be slightly negotiable: embrace your inner businessperson and play "let's make a deal." Some landlords offer a free month of rent for moving in right away.

BE AWARE

 Do you know your credit score? You should. You can check your credit report for free once a year at sites like freecreditreport.com. Most brokers will invariably check your credit, charging you upwards of $50 to run the check. Every bad mark affects your rating. Landlords often have dozens of sterling applicants and aren't always sympathetic.

 BE PREPARED Be ready to plunk down cash or wire money on the spot after seeing an apartment. In the city that never stops, five minutes can make or break the deal.

 BE WEALTHY Landlords expect you to make (annually) approximately 30 times your monthly rent. Thus, despite the fact you are striking out on your own, you very well might need your parents to serve as guarantors. Landlords may want to see proof of income, so be ready to furnish a face sheet of tax returns. In fact, bring with you any document that can help your case (bank statements, letters from your employer, etc.).

 BE WILLING TO DO IT YOURSELF Budget how much it will cost you to do the physical move into your apartment, including expenses to get your utilities up and running. Moving to a New York apartment can break the bank, even if you do it yourself. Neighborhoods around NYU, Columbia, or the New School are infamous for their "Man with a Van" fliers, tacked onto every other light pole. These men may be cheap, but they aren't registered or referred, so use your best judgment when trying to save a few bucks. You can always get movers on Craigslist in short order.

{ The Roach Approach }

>> FORGET DEATH AND TAXES; the real certainty of city life is having to share your apartment with cockroaches. You may not have advertised for these extra roommates on craigslist, but you can be sure that a few will pop their creepy antlered-heads in from time to time. Roaches love trash and old buildings, and New York has an overabundance of both. While roaches are nearly impossible to eradicate (one messy tenant can support an entire colony), here are ways to minimize your mutual encounters:

∗ Don't leave out open food, standing water, or let dirty dishes pile up. Clean up any paper or clothing piled on the floor.

∗ Caulk cracks in walls or near windows, where roaches can easily sneak in from next door.

∗ Make roach traps: use boric acid chalk or powder (poisonous to roaches) to place lines along the walls where they emerge. Alternatively, pick up a commercial insecticide like Raid, which can usually be found at a supermarket or drug store.

∗ If you spot more than three critters in a week, talk to the building's super —- and be persistent. If all else fails, hire an exterminator.

In short, don't ignore the problem and wait for a full-scale infestation. Unlike the cute critters from MTV's Joe's Apartment, these suckers won't sing and dance—though they do make a satisfyingly squishy crunch when you smack them with a shoe.

Finding a Job

>> FINDING A JOB IN NEW YORK is definitely tough. The city has a reputation for innovative ideas, unmatched talent, and cutthroat competition. But because it is the country's center of business, commerce, and retail, the Big Apple is also ripe with opportunity. The key is knowing where and how to find these opportunities, and being creative enough to make them happen. Always remain open to things like networking, unpaid internships, open job calls, and the possibility of additional skills training.

If you think your top-notch college degree makes you too good for answering phones, think again: unless one of your parents happens to own the company you work for, don't expect to start at the top. Be prepared to fight your way through the door, but always keep your eye on the prize. After all, that stunning view from your office window on the 33rd floor can make for a pretty sweet reward.

(1) Subscribe to online notification services such as *Village Voice CLASSIFIEDS*. For a fixed fee, they will email new job listings to you as they get posted. *The New York Times* offers a similar notification service. Other helpful online classified listings include *The Daily News* (nydailynews.abracat.com) and Craigslist (newyork.craigslist.org).

(2) Post your resume on online BULLETIN BOARDS. Some people say this is a waste of time, but what do you have to lose? Popular job sites include monster.com, job-hunt.com, vault.com, and hotjobs.com. Also, many universities allow alumni to post their resumes on university-owned websites in attempt to help create an "old boys" network.. Some universities even have clubs where alumni can go to hang out, drink, and network.

(3) Despite their intimidating name, HEADHUNTERS can save you precious time and effort by scouting jobs for you. Check out sites like headhuntersdirectory.com for a listing of local headhunters.

(4) Know the state of your industry and the current JOB MARKET. And remember, be realistic. It's not that you can't make it big here, but it's harder when you have so much competition. Aiming too high at the outset is one common mistake, setting you up for rejection and disappointment. Then again, waking up every day and enjoying your challenging job is a pleasure like no other; so don't aim too low. Try to be aware of your competition and make sure you find out what skills and qualifications are required before applying.

(5) NETWORK LIKE CRAZY. Almost every profession has a formal association; do your best to attend every cocktail, luncheon, and lecture they offer. The same holds true for parties with friends – however uncomfortable, make it a habit to mingle and establish personal contacts. Bring along business cards—you can snag free ones at vistaprint.com. The "I can make it on my own" attitude is appreciated, but you'll soon find that getting jobs through connections is just the accepted practice here. Make the most of any opportunity given to you.

(6) Brush up on your COMPUTER SKILLS. Familiarize yourself with the ins and outs of Microsoft Word, Excel, Power-Point, and any other software you might be called upon to use. The New York Public Library offers free classes on often-used computer programs. Make sure to include technical knowledge on your resume.

(7) SHARPEN YOUR IMAGE. New

Yorkers have a certain look, and you'll have a better shot at landing a job if you don't show up for an interview in khakis and penny loafers. Make yourself presentable. Get an expensive haircut and buy a nice suit, preferably in one of the dark colors favored by New Yorkers. Even if the person or company you're interviewing for doesn't seem to abide by high-end dress codes, you should still dress up as much as possible.

 Consider an UN-PAID INTERNSHIP. If you can afford to do unpaid labor for a while, do it. These gigs are often well worth it, giving you needed experience and building your resume. In addition, it's not uncommon for people to get hired by the firms where they intern. If you absolutely need to make money, try finding a part-time internship that will give you enough time to also work a paying job.

(9) DON'T LIE about your qualifications. If you think your previous experience falls a little short, just emphasize the responsibilities you had during those jobs instead of making stuff up.

 Nothing is more important than

CONFIDENCE. If you don't think you deserve a job, neither will your potential employers. Prepare thoroughly for interviews by researching companies online and brainstorming possible questions you may be asked (as well as some questions you can ask them). Decide beforehand what information you want your interviewer to know and make sure you find a way to tell them. During the interview, remember to maintain eye contact without seeming aggressive, and to let your best qualities shine.

(11) Finally, and most importantly, DON'T GIVE UP. Even if it takes a little longer than expected to land that perfect position, try not to get discouraged. Just remember the classic rhyme that made this city famous: if you can make it here, you'll make it any-where...and if not, New Jersey is just across the river.

Dating

>> EIGHT MILLION PEOPLE live in New York City; about three million of them are single. With these odds, dating might seem like a piece of cake. But most days, getting anything more than a stranger's stiff shoulder can seem as long a shot as finding a rent-controlled apartment in SoHo. With everyone moving to the city's frantic pace, meeting someone can feel like more trouble than it's worth. Don't despair. Armed with a very New York "no pain, no gain" mindset, the following insider tips, and a bit of luck, you should be properly suited up for a dip — or a dive — into New York's dating pool.

If you've heard the old saying "Luck favors the prepared mind," then you probably know the answer to this question: I would be more likely to meet someone new; A) in my apartment, or B) not in my apartment. The point: get out, get active, and get involved. A fantastic way to meet people is through your hobbies or sports. New Yorkers adore Mr. and Ms. Eclectic, so take advantage of the city's endless offerings. The anonymity of New York makes it very easy to try something new, and the constant flux in trendy activities means that you could find yourself learning to striptease one day and trying Middle Eastern cooking the next. Try a painting or drawing class, or add speaking a new foreign language to the list of traits that make you interesting. Join one of New York's gyms, or make a habit out of

Central Park's bike and jogging paths. Some yoga studios even offer sexed-up midnight classes for singles who want to get their 'om' on.

Chances are you will still find yourself (at least occasionally, if not often) exactly where most New Yorkers go to meet other New Yorkers—bars and clubs. Check out "Pickup Tips and Tricks" for gender-specific flirting. It just might come in handy the next time you spot that cute guy/gal ordering another drink that you should be paying for. If you're part of the LGBT community, check out our LGBT section for some specific tips just for you.

PICKUP TIPS AND TRICKS
FOR WOMEN:

1) SMILE AND MAKE EYE CONTACT. Many nervous New Yorkers shy away from locking eyes. But making eye contact is actually the least aggressive way to show your interest and get someone's attention. Once you catch their eye, hold it for a second or two, then smile and coyly look away. Look back a second time a few seconds later and if they're interested, they'll come over.

2) GIVE IT A MINUTE. Don't stare—that's creepy and has the potential to confuse ("Is there something on my face?").

{Online Dating}

Once frowned upon as the digital death of romance, online dating has become an increasingly popular way for people to develop serious relationships. In a city of so much possibility and such limited time, sites like **Match.com** and **JDate** have become an efficient way to screen potential suitors and break the ice. Although sites such as **MySpace** and **Friendster** aren't strictly for dating, they're another great way to hook up with like-minded people. Whether you're shy or just curious, the online dating world could be a great place to initiate contact with someone you find interesting. The jury's out on whether meeting online is any more or less dangerous than meeting in a bar—either way, you know nothing about your suitor (no matter how charming he or she may seem) and thus you should always take sensible measures of precaution. It's probably best to exchange numbers (or e-mail addresses) and then meet up later at a café or a restaurant so you can get to know each other in public—you'll want an easy escape if things get sketchy. And, not to bring up grim possibilities, you should make sure at least one friend knows where you're going, who you're meeting, and what time you expect to be back. This way your friend will know when something might have gone awry and can notify the authorities, or know when to call you and get all the dishy details.

3) TALK TO YOUR FRIENDS. Laugh about something. If you seem happy and relaxed, men will feel less intimidated, and approach more easily. It's always a good idea to go out with a few (but just a few) girlfriends if you're looking to meet a guy. If you go out with a horde of gigglers or a group with men, forget it. Only the man of steel would approach a group like that. Also, if you're going to be drinking, it's safer to be out with friends. Just make sure you slip away from the group once in a while to give your target an opening.

4) Many times, the initial smile and eye contact will be enough for a guy to approach but if he met your gaze the first time, and hasn't come over to talk to you yet, then SMILE AND MAKE EYE CONTACT AGAIN. Sometimes a man needs a little extra encouragement. The prospect of potential rejection is intimidating. If you smile and glance his way a few times, you've let him know you're interested.

5) PAY ATTENTION TO THE RESPONSE. If the guy's just not looking back, not smiling, not approaching, and spends more time with his body angled away from you, then he's just not that into you. End of the world? No way—this is New York City, not Walla Walla, Washington. Look around the room for another intriguing soul. If you don't find one, move on. There might be a lot of men in New York, but there are even more bars.

FOR MEN:

1) DRESS THE PART. Especially in a status-conscious, driven place like New York, men have a leg-up if they appear to have their stuff together. You don't have to run out and buy the most expensive Armani suit, but try to at least look neat and presentable. And lay off the handfuls of hair gel—the '90s are over.

2) SMILE AND MAKE EYE CONTACT—-BUT DON'T STARE, no matter how gorgeous she is. If you smile, it makes you seem more interested

in meeting her than beating her.

3) GIVE IT A MINUTE. She needs time to look back, talk to her friends and get them to agree that you are cute enough, that you don't look creepy (since you're not staring), and finally work up the nerve to smile back invitingly.

4) SMILE AND MAKE EYE CONTACT AGAIN. Smile at her girlfriends like you are a nice guy, not like you are trying to choose between different cuts of beef.

5) GAUGE HER REACTION. By this time she has probably noticed that you were looking. This kind of communication happens fast. It only takes a second to tell an inviting smile from a snigger of rejection.

6) IF SHE HAS SMILED BACK AT YOU/MADE EYE CONTACT, THEN APPROACH HER. Offer to buy her a drink. Some people may disagree, but there's nothing wrong with a little alcohol to ease the nerves. The most tactful way to offer is to say something like "I'm getting a drink. Would you like anything?" While you're waiting, start up a conversation.

7) If she DECLINES the drink…it can mean one of three things: 1) she doesn't want to talk to you; 2) she's already had enough to drink; 3) she doesn't drink (this is the least likely, especially if she's currently in a bar). If she declines but is smiling and making lots of eye contact, then you shouldn't take it as defeat. If she declines and is looking around in an absent-minded way, that's not a good sign.

8) If she ACCEPTS the drink…it's important to note that just because a girl accepts a drink, it does NOT mean she's interested in you. Most girls will accept a drink if it's offered (free!) and will be willing to give you a chance. If you're a truly great guy, the drink buys you time to start up a conversation; you win. If she takes the drink and takes off, it's a good sign that she wasn't worth talking to anyway.

9) MAKE HER FEEL COMFORTABLE. One of the biggest mistakes guys make during bar courtship is to make it painfully obvious that their number one priority is to see the girl's thong on his bedroom floor. Relax a little. Women want to hook up just as much as men do sometimes, but they'll feel more comfortable around a guy who acts like he wants to actually get to know her.

Dining Out

>> NEW YORK HAS OVER 20,000 restaurants, from kosher hot dog stands to museum cafés to five star gourmet icons where you'll have to wait two months for a reservation. That means that even if you eat at a different place for three meals a day, seven days a week, 365 days a year, it will take you more than 18 years to sample all the great (and not so great) food New York has to offer. There's a lot to know about eating out in NYC, but this guide should help you get acquainted with the gastronomic wonderland that has become the food capital of the world.

The best way to find out about New York's myriad of eateries is to read reviews (hence, this guide) and talk to people who know a chanterelle from a shiitake. Everyone eats, so everyone has an opinion on where to eat, whether you're looking for New York's best burger, cheapest falafel, or most likely café to spot the Olsen twins. If you're new to New York and need a conversation starter, try asking your coworkers, peers, or strangers where they like to eat. If all else fails, get a subscription to Zagat.com or *Time Out New York* magazine.

Exploring New York's restaurants is a great entree into New York itself. Sure, you can grab some spring rolls and fried rice pretty much anywhere in Manhattan. But, if you want the good stuff, like the most delicious dumplings and dim sum and duck, head straight to Chinatown. Likewise, Little Italy boasts the best pasta in the city, and Jackson Heights in Queens offers the most authentic Indian.

The most satisfying way to find a great restaurant is by wandering the city. This has the added advantages of giving you an excuse to see the sights and helping you build an appetite during the search. It's risky, but if you find that one hole-in-the-wall patisserie that makes your knees melt when you smell their goods, you'll be the center of attention when you're talking to other gourmands.

Insider Dining Etiquette

DRESSED TO FILL

>> With the new marriage of two long-divorced words—dress jeans—New Yorkers can get away with dressing down when stepping out. Jeans, especially in dark colors, are now acceptable at most restaurants, and even some upscale clubs. But use your judgment. If the waiters are donning tuxes, you might want to step your game up a little. For the fanciest (read: most expensive) restaurants, gentlemen might not get in unless they're wearing a jacket and tie. And sporty sandals are never appropriate for a nice restaurant.

RESERVATIONS

>> Forget the old rule that slipping a Hamilton to the maître d' will land you a table at New York's hottest restaurant. Always call ahead to

see if the restaurant accepts reservations. As a general rule, plan on booking your table a week or two in advance. If the restaurant is in high demand, try a month. Many top-notch restaurants have reservation lines that they either rarely answer, or which require you to leave voicemails. If you call and no one picks up, call again. And again. You'll get through eventually.

Once you have landed your reservation, honor it like a doctor's appointment—call to confirm on the day of your reservation, to avoid embarrassing yourself in front of your date. If you must cancel, call in the afternoon to allow them to rebook. If you're running late, give them a heads-up before you jump into the subway— many places give reserved tables away after 15 minutes, and they'll appreciate the courtesy. Furthermore, many restaurants keep track of reservation-ditchers, so the next time you call you're more likely to get an, "I'm sorry, sir, we're booked that evening," instead of a, "Yes, we have something at 8:30."

New Yorkers tend to eat late; 8 or 9 o'clock might seem absurd in Peoria, but it's the New York norm. In the summer, dinner's even later, because no one likes to dine when the sun's still out.

WILL THAT BE CASH OR...CASH?

>> Before heading out, check the restaurant's payment options. Many boutique-sized restaurants eschew credit card company fees by accepting cash-only. Make sure to you fill your wallet with enough green; an embarrassing dash to the ATM is no way to finish a meal. And no, most restaurants will not let you wash dishes instead of paying—they'd rather have the NYPD sort it out.

TIPPING THE SCALE

>> In New York, leaving a tip isn't just customary—it's mandatory. With an hourly wage far below the federal minimum, the city's servers depend on your gratuity for their sky-high rents and acting classes. Typically, diners leave a tip of 15 to 20 percent of the total check. For easy tip calculation, double the 8.625 percent sales tax at the bottom of the bill. Of course, the tip should be adjusted to reflect the quality of service. To reward top-shelf precision, exceeding 20 percent is good form. For a slow-footed, sour-faced server, feel free to leave less—just don't drop below 10 percent.

At the bar, the general rule is to tip at least a dollar per drink. As you move from dive bar to diva bar, however, consider dropping a couple of bucks for that pricey martini. The bartender will no doubt take note, and your second round will come without the wait.

Useful Dining Info

RESEARCH

>> Insidenewyork.com is constantly being updated with new user and editorial reviews that are custom-tailored to new New Yorkers, but if you want to brave the digital jungle of dining listings, try menupages.com (for online menus), citysearch.com (for restaurants, bars, and nightclubs) or zagat.com (a fee-for-subscription service, with simple, standardized ratings). One up-and-coming site, DiningFever.com, provides a comprehensive list of special offers for restaurants around the city, while sites such as Opentable.com pair up with many restaurants allowing reservations to be made online.

GETTING WHERE YOU'RE GOING

>> Sure, you could put your life and cash in the hands of an irate cabbie with a death wish, but walking's usually more fun. If the distance is too far, go to hopstop.com to find the closest subway or bus stop to your destination.

PRIX FIXE

>> If you're on a student budget, but don't want to deprive yourself of dining out in style every once in a while, a prix fixe meal is a great way to get some bang for your buck. Generally including an appetizer, entrée, and dessert, the prix fixe cost is almost always lower than ordering à la carte. Although prix fixe menus are offered in restaurants throughout Manhattan, they are most abundant in the Theater District, where the establishments on "Restaurant Row" (46th Street, between Eighthth and Ninthth Aves.) try to lure in ticket-holding customers by promising to save them both time and money. Many prix fixe menus are only available earlier in the evening, usually before 7 p.m., so it's a good idea to call ahead to find out a restaurant's policy.

WINES: SWIRL, SNIFF, AND SLURP

>> According to standard wine wisdom, white wine pairs best with poultry, fish, and light pastas, while red normally accompanies beef, lamb, and hearty tomato sauces. Nowadays, however, feel free to order whatever you're in the mood for, regardless of your entrée.

If you'd like to impress your date, try this: read over the wine list carefully and then select the second least expensive wine from your preferred category—you can't go wrong with a Sauvignon blanc for whites or Merlot for red.

When the server brings your selection to the table, follow these steps to look like a true connoisseur:

1) Hold the glass up to the light to check the color and texture.

2) Gently swirl the wine and watch how it drips down the walls of the glass. These streaks are known as the "legs". Generally, a better wine will cling nicely and form distinct lines.

3) Smell the wine, inhaling through your nose for at least three seconds, and then ponder for a moment.

4) Take a slow sip, allowing the wine to roll across the tongue, and swish it around in your mouth. Unless it tastes like Robitussin or vinegar, smile in approval and cry, "Salud!" in your best Tony Soprano voice.

If you'd like to perfect your wine manners in a more formal setting, sign up for one of New York's many wine classes, such as Wine 101 at nycwineclass.com.

RESTAURANT WEEK

>> While there's no hope of New York food ever going on sale, there are still opportunities to experience the finest dining in the city at a discount. Restaurant Week is a citywide event every January and July during which 180 top restaurants offer prix fixe lunches and/or dinners, usually featuring three courses (appetizer, entrée, and dessert) for a discounted price. Drinks, tips, and tax are not included. During Restaurant Week, remember to tip generously because the waiters are working at a discount. It's best to reserve your table(s) early, especially for popular restaurants. For more information, go to nycvisit.com/RestaurantWeek.

Nightlife

>> AS THE OLD SAYING GOES, New York is the city that never sleeps—in part because the entry-level investment bankers work 100+ hours a week, and in part because the nightlife is just that good. No matter what day of the week, there is a scene to fit your mood, be it frat house-style beer pong, trendy cocktails with fashionistas, or underground Goth nights. Clubs and lounges stay open until twilight, tempting partiers to catch a free lift home with the morning delivery trucks. As for happy hours, bars in this city set their own rules. Some start as early as 1 p.m., some run just after work, and still others last all day long.

While New York consistently offers a range of nightlife options, from karaoke haunts to hipster dives, the scene transforms every year. Drink options constantly reflect the tastes of a fickle and jaded party population. Order a Cosmopolitan, and the bartender will know you've been watching too many *Sex and the City* reruns on TBS. Keeping up with the (Samantha) Joneses can be confusing, but trends do have a tendency to repeat themselves—and a Bombay Sapphire and tonic never goes out of style.

For many overworked New Yorkers, the weekend nightlife is motivation enough to last until Friday evening clock-out. Still others pay no attention to the well-worn "school night" rule. As a result, various clubs have scheduled some of their hottest DJs to spin on Mondays, Tuesdays, and Wednesdays, turning even slow nights into slamming ones for tireless partiers.

In this city, people tend to leave work late, eat dinner later, and hit the bar and club scenes well after that. Feel free to warm up with a few beers during happy hour, but most regulars don't venture out until 11 p.m., when neighborhoods like the Meatpacking District and the Lower East Side start to pick up. Remember to honor the artful collegiate practice of pre-gaming: at $10 per well drink and $6 per beer at most bars and clubs, it is wise to down a few before leaving the house.

Students from local universities—and, if their fakes are good enough, prep schools—relish in the city's booming nightlife, and there are plenty of bars and clubs that cater to younger tastes. Classic watering holes like The Bitter End and Café Wha?, sports bars like Off the Wagon and Brother Jimmy's, and jazz dens like Smalls and Smoke allow students to socialize before or after studying—or in lieu of, as the case may be.

In Harlem, old standbys like St. Nick's and the Lenox Lounge keep cranking out the sounds along with stiff drinks. On Amsterdam Avenue in the 80s, the saloons and late night ethnic eateries keep locals out late, while frat-friendly bars like Bourbon Street and Jake's Dilemma pump the booze and the tunes until the early morning light. MacDougal Street, and the adjacent stretch of Bleeker, turns into Bourbon St. North when the temperature is nice—and sometimes when it's not—as tons of downtown denizens bop from bar to bar and mingle on the street.

Every neighborhood of New York feels like a self-contained town, each with its own dry cleaner, bagel shop, and local bar where, if you're lucky, everybody knows your name. Once you find the nightspots that suit you—whether they're the mellow, post-industrial digs of Chelsea or the funky lounges of the Lower East Side—you'll truly come to enjoy the pleasures of this multifaceted city. Only here can salsa dancers swivel next to country western saloons, while hip-hop pulses down the street and folk music plays in the basement. The best feature of nightlife in New York City? No matter how wild you've been, you won't ever need to drive home: many subway lines run around the clock, and cabs roam the streets at all hours.

Hit the Bars

>> New Yorkers aren't like other bar goers. Here, people flock to unexplored terrain— those unmarked bars so veiled in mystery they practically require a secret knock. After a while, though, the quest for the bar that's so-hot-it's-not-even-in-the-guidebooks inevitably grows tiresome, and the nomad drinker longs for a barstool he can put a dimple in, night after night. Whatever an individual's preference, the sheer number of pubs and bars ensures that there's a home away from home for every thirsty New Yorker. And until that perfect match is made, there are a lot of bars to scope out. Trial and error never tasted so good.

Not all bars in the city are for pretty people only. Irish pubs, such as McSorley's Old Ale House, Dublin House, and Paddy Reilly's, welcome any bloke or lass with a kind laugh and a sanguine complexion. Craft beer fans will be pleased with the rare brews on tap at a growing number of New York establishments, including Burp Castle and Heartland Brewery. These cozy dens play host to a motley collection of rowdy fans who gather around flat screens to root for their favorite teams. But the best bars, like Satsko's in the East Village, live in your neighborhood. There, the bartenders join—and beat—patrons in rounds of sake bombs, after which you're happy to stumble only a few steps home.

Cabaret, piano, and hotel bars maintain New York's long tradition of metropolitan elegance. A more affluent bar clientele is usually self-select, and if you don't belong, you'll know it soon enough. For the bourgeois-inclined, there are plenty of classy clubs to choose from, like the tame, relaxed atmosphere of CoZ on E. 6th St.

Take the time to get to know the diverse neighborhoods and their numerous liquor lairs—they might just become as cozy as your home. Besides, as they sing in the Broadway hit, *Avenue Q*, "there is life outside your apartment." Drink it up.

Check out the Clubs

>> To make it past the velvet ropes in this city, you will need the wiles of a coyote, the Ben Franklins of a Rockefeller, or the practiced pout of an Olsen twin. Here are a few club rules that should prepare even the most unseasoned partygoer for New York's sometimes unruly club scene, with some advice on how to get lucky if and when you get in.

HOUSE RULES

• Dress up. Way up. Lose the big hair, the heavy make-up, and the cheap cologne. Don't wear anything that will prevent you from dancing your butt off, because you certainly won't want to be sitting on the side—if you can find a seat to begin with—while everyone else shakes their groove thing. Just remember that some clubs make a point to let only "beautiful people" past the velvet rope, appearance will make the difference.

• If you hand the bouncer a crappy fake, expect him to confiscate it and boot you out of line. Bars may turn a blind eye, but top-tier clubs don't need your underage business: you're a liability, and there are fifty people behind you who aren't.

• Do order "The Drink," or else stick to a simple spirit-and-mixer. You'll blow out a vocal chord trying to explain a complicated concoction to the bartender, and make no friends with impatient patrons in the process. If you and your friends are looking to book a table, do your research to find out whether the venue has bottle service—you don't want to be surprised when the tab comes for a $250 bottle of Ketel One. Penny pinchers be forewarned: water often costs just as much as an alcoholic drink.

• Be ready to start early and end late. It's usually best to show up relatively early to avoid the hour-long lines, but the party won't truly start until midnight on a good night, and things stay crackling until the last call at dawn. That's why they make Red Bull.

• Do a lap, find out where the action is, and keep moving. If you're not getting the right vibe, there's no use waiting until you're bored stiff. But do choose wisely, as most clubs will have a hefty wait outside.

• Be ready for some serious body contact. Most hot clubs are wall-to-wall flesh, and you will have various bodily fluids and drinks rubbed or splashed on you before the night is over. It's rarely anything personal. Smart clubheads use the buddy system to repel unwanted grinders by pre-establishing a hand signal that means, "Help! I've got an octopus on me! Pretend you're my jealous lover and pull me away!" Mean clubheads agree to use the buddy system, then point and laugh when you land yourself in a sticky situation. In this case, just pretend that you have to go look for a friend and slip out of his (or her) grasp.

• Whatever you do, stay cool and out of harm's way. The frat party rumble, though appreciated on campus, doesn't fly in this town.

• Never accept a drink from patrons who have carried it to you themselves. Always get your drinks straight from the bartender, and watch them as they mix. When the evening is over, ride home with friends or go solo. While an escort by that mystery clubber may seem exciting at the time, the risk is not worth it.

• It's easy to get caught up in the moment and shed anything that hinders your crowd-pleasing dance moves. However, don't assume that your Gucci purse or Dolce and Gabbana jacket will be fine if left on the couch, 'cause it'll be gone before you finish your first drink. Try to go out with the least possible number of items, and either store them in coat check or keep them on you at all times.

• Finally, if you're hungry at 4 a.m. after a night of drinking and dancing, snag some chicken fingers or a kebab with your friends. Nothing tastes as good as grease when you're coming off that buzz. Plenty of diners serve food all night long, and street vendors often dish up sizzling nosh into the wee hours.

The Arts

>> THE ASTOUNDING ARRAY of cultural opportunities in New York City is enough to overwhelm even the most ambitious among us. But with a little guidance, you can dive head-first into the best of what New York has to offer: museums, galleries, theaters, concerts, dance performances, films, and readings. It won't be long before you're directing newcomers to the TKTS booth in Times Square, rocking out at the Brooklyn Museum's First Saturday dance party, scoring discounted tickets to performances at Carnegie Hall, ushering at The Joyce for free admission to contemporary dance concerts, watching a cutting-edge documentary at FilmForum, or standing behind the spot-lit mike at the Nuyorican Café's Poetry Slam.

Where to begin? Start by checking out the listings in *The Village Voice* (villagevoice.com), *Time Out New York* (timeout.com/newyork), *The New Yorker* (newyorker.com), *The New York Times* (nytimes.com), *New York Magazine* (nymag.com), and the Brooklyn-based *L Magazine* (thelmagazine.com). These well-known publications are jam-packed with current arts listings and reviews.

If you're a die hard supporter of the arts, consider investing in a fold out or popup New York Arts Map. Many varieties are available in the travel section of your neighborhood bookstore. Of course, the best way to find out-of-the-way, innovative exhibits and performances is through word-of-mouth. Your fellow New Yorkers are already plugged into the city. Ask your artist friends which galleries they haunt; ask your actor friends which theaters they frequent; ask your film geek friends which festivals are the most interesting. You get the idea.

MUSEUMS & GALLERIES

MUSEUMS

>> New York has dozens of museums catering to many different tastes and interests. Like the city itself, these museums encompass a vast range of human expression and experience. New Yorkers and tourists alike love to frequent the mighty four: The Met (metmuseum.org), The Museum of Modern Art (moma.org), The Whitney (whitney.org), and The Guggenheim (guggenheim.org). Museum Mile is the famous section of Fifth Avenue from 82nd to 105th that boasts nine museums, and The American Museum of Natural History (amnh.org) is a wonderful stop for anyone who wants to plumb the depths of the world we inhabit.

There are a number of incredible museums that often get left off the tourist checklist but shouldn't be missed by New Yorkers in the know.

Check out ny.com/museums/all.museums.html for a complete list of the city's museums. Recommended picks include The Cloisters, a beautifully-housed branch of the Met located in Inwood and devoted to medieval art; the fabulous El Museo del Barrio (elmuseo.org), filled with Latin American and Caribbean art; The Brooklyn Museum of Art (brooklynmuseum.org), which hosts wonderful temporary exhibitions and has incredible parties on the first Saturday of each month; The Frick (frick.org), home to a lovely private collection bequeathed to the public; and P.S. 1 (ps1.org), a branch of MoMA devoted entirely to contemporary art.

Although the price of admission to many museums may make you wince, there are plenty of opportunities for discounted or free admission. Most museums offer special student rates, and many also have pay-what-you-want days, which are exactly what they sound like—but beware, these days bring out the crowds and the long lines. If you fall in love with a particular museum, you may want to purchase a yearly membership. If you're a museum junkie, you may want to consider volunteering a few hours a week at a museum nearby—your volunteer pass will get you into any museum in the city free, any time.

GALLERIES

>> Lower Manhattan was the supreme center of the New York gallery scene for years; artists such as Bill Viola, Ross Bleckner and Andy Warhol found their "big break" here. In recent years, rising rents have driven many galleries (and artists) deeper into Manhattan and out to the boroughs. There are still dozens of galleries in Chelsea and SoHo and some in the Village, but Brooklyn (particularly Williamsburg) now boasts many of the best spaces and newest arrivals in contemporary art. In addition to searching the standard New York periodicals for gallery shows, check out thenewyorkartworld.com for comprehensive, well-organized lists of galleries, shows, reviews and openings.

Openings are a fantastic way to check out new art and emerging artists, while scoring free drinks (and sometimes food). Contrary to popular myth, they are open to everyone. Don't be intimidated by the too-cool-for school artistes who are bound to show up at the latest opening.

THEATER

THE HIP-HOORAY AND BALLYHOO

>> Despite its reputation as the be-all and end-all of the theater world, Broadway does not hold the cultural monopoly on stage productions, as residents of London's West End (as well as thousands of regional theaters across America) would be quick to point out. Still, few experiences are as quintessentially "New York" as a trip to a show. Whether you choose a musical or a play, orchestra or balcony, on Broadway or off, you're likely to leave the theater with an unforgettable memory.

Most shows are defined as Broadway, Off-Broadway, and Off-Off-Broadway. Now that Off-Broadway theaters are migrating uptown and opening in the Times Square area (traditionally reserved strictly for Broadway), the best distinction between venues can be found in seating capacity. A Broadway house seats over 500, Off-Broadway 100-499, and Off-Off-Broadway is de-fined as any theater seating 99 people or fewer. Generally speaking, the bigger the theater, the larger the production. Bigger theaters cost more to rent, so the budget—and number of marquee-popping stars—tends to increase accordingly. This inflation also has a practical use. After all, an intimate, O'Neill-style drama would be swallowed up in a theater like the cavernous Gershwin, a venue almost large enough to house the Yankees and the Mets. With everything from splashy Broadway musicals playing to roaring crowds in landmark theaters to quirky Off-Off- plays performing to a group of twenty in a converted attic, there's a show and a venue for everyone.

ANOTHER OP'NIN', ANOTHER SHOW

>> Picking a show can be a daunting task, especially if your time in New York is limited and you can only see one or two. Thankfully, there are several handy guides to shows currently treading the boards. *Time Out New York* (timeoutny.com), available wherever magazines are sold, has comprehensive listings for Broadway and Off-Broadway, as well as selected Off-Off-Broadway theater, including capsule reviews, locations, ticket prices, and even running times. Online, there's Talkin' Broadway (talkinbroadway.com), whose On the Boards section features Broadway and Off-Broadway listings with all of the usual information, plus the bonus of a handy guide to Rush and SRO policies. Playbill (playbill.com) and The New York Theatre Experience (nytheatre.com) also provide reliable listings. Other helpful sites include offbroadwayonline.com, theatermania.com, broadway.com, and livebroadway.com. NYC/Onstage (212-768-1818) is a recording service that provides complete schedules and information for many theater and performing arts events. The Theater Development Fund (tdf.org) is the organization that runs it.

There are numerous theaters in the city, each with its own character. The Delacorte Theater is the outdoor stage in Central Park that hosts Shakespeare in the Park every summer, a famous New York tradition that always boasts star-studded casts and foot-numbing lines (get there early in the morning!). The Public Theater (publictheater.org), in addition to running Shakespeare in the Park, has its own long and illustrious history. The Signature Theater (signaturetheatre.com) devotes each season to producing the work of one masterful playwright, and The Kitchen (thekitchen.org) is an innovative organization that is devoted to interdisciplinary and experimental work of all kinds.

I CAN GET IT FOR YOU WHOLESALE

>> There are a million shows, plays, and concerts to see in New York City—meaning there are a million ways to break the bank. But exploring this performing arts cornucopia doesn't have to cost a fortune. In the following section, we'll look at some of the best (but not the only) ways to see shows on the cheap.

•TKTS (tdf.org/tkts)

>> TKTS (each letter is pronounced individually) has become a New York institution since its opening in 1973. Run by the Theatre Development Fund, TKTS has two Manhattan locations, both of which sell tickets for Broadway, Off-Broadway, dance and music events. Be prepared for extremely long waits, especially at the Times Square location, which is often home to snaking lines of thrifty theatergoers and iconic street performers like The Naked Cowboy. Here, you can snag same-day Broadway and Off-Broadway tickets at 50-70 percent off. A large LED board displays all the current offerings, which vary from day to day and are mostly comprised of older musicals and struggling newer musicals. TKTS is a crapshoot in terms of both shows and seat locations, but it's definitely worth a try. Also, if you're willing to gamble, tickets not posted during the day are often released by the theaters to the TKTS booth one half hour before the show. TKTS Times Square Theatre Center is located in Duffy Square (at Broadway and 47th St.) although it is scheduled to be temporarily moved during 2006, so please check the website for details. Hours: M-Sa, 3 p.m.-8 p.m., for evening performances, W & Sa, 10 a.m.-2 p.m., for matinees, Su 11 a.m.-3 p.m. for matinees and 3 p.m.-closing for evening performances. TKTS Lower Manhattan Theatre Center at South Street Seaport is located on the corner of Front and John Sts., at the rear of the Resnick/Prudential Building at 199 Water St. This location tends to have shorter lines, and sells day-of evening performance tickets and day-before matinees tickets only. To get Wednesday matinee tickets, go on Tuesday, for Saturday matinee tickets, go on Friday. Hours: M-F, 11 a.m.-6 p.m., Sa, 11 a.m.-7 p.m.

{Theater Etiquette}

✴ Arrive approximately THIRTY MINUTES before curtain. You'll have enough time to get situated in your seat, and you won't be stuck outside for an hour waiting for the doors to open with the rest of the over-eager patrons.

✴ Nobody dresses to the nines for the theater anymore. Unless it's opening night, SKIP THE BALLGOWN OR TUX—but don't go too far the other way, either. Avoid man-sandals and shorts for guys, and disco-ready threads for the girls. Theater is becoming casual, but not sloppy.

✴ The line for the ladies' restroom during intermission has to be seen to be believed. TRY TO GO BEFORE THE SHOW, or be prepared to make a mad dash as soon as the curtain falls on the first act.

✴ EAT BEFORE OR AFTER THE SHOW. Don't try to sneak a bucket of chicken wings into the balcony to munch on mid-show. Yes, this has happened, and yes, it's disturbing on several levels.

✴ FOLLOW THE RULES. Don't use recording devices or cameras. Turn off your cell phone; keep quiet and stay still; and when in doubt, be considerate. Most people have shelled out considerable dough for the privilege to attend a show and don't want your actions to distract them from the action onstage.

•RUSH / STUDENT / STANDING ROOM ONLY TICKETS

>> Many shows also offer heavily discounted student tickets, rush tickets (tickets released an hour or two before the performance begins, at a discounted rate), or standing-room-only tickets. Policies and prices vary from venue to venue. For Broadway shows, these tickets cost an average of $25; for Off- and Off-Off-Broadway, you can usually get something in the $10-15 range. Talkin' Broadway (talkinbroadway. com) gives a great rundown of each show's policy, and when in doubt, just phone or stop by the box office and ask. However, keep in mind that SRO tickets are often sold only when the show is actually sold out, something which doesn't happen as often as it did before September 11th.

THEATER DEVELOPMENT FUND (tdf.org)

>> The group that runs TKTS also has another excellent discount program for students, teachers, union members, seniors, civil servant employees, not-for-profit organization staff, members of the armed services, and clergy. As a member, you'll also be eligible for TDF vouchers, which are good for over 400 experimental Off-Off Broadway performances, including dance, music and theater shows. A set of four vouchers is a fantastic $28. For an annual fee of $25, you'll receive notices about all of their discount ticket offers. You can buy up to 9 tickets for each show you attend at only $14-$16 per ticket. For more info, call 212-221-0885; or apply online at tdf.org. Not all current shows make their list.

SUBSCRIPTIONS

>> Many theaters and concert halls offer a major discount if you purchase a full season of tickets. If there's a theater or other venue that you attend often and want to support, this is the way to go. Again, check with each venue for their subscription rates.

If all else fails, you can try to "second act" a show (walking in with the typically thinner crowd after intermission and taking an empty seat). It's certainly not the way Mr. Shakespeare would have wanted you to see Hamlet, but half of something great might be better than none of it. Just be prepared for the trick not to work.

MUSIC

>> New York plays host to every conceivable kind of music, making the music scene as diverse as the city itself. There are guides for every niche market, but *Time Out New York* provides comprehensive coverage for just about every genre. Otherwise, check out newyorker. com/goingson/music for Classical, gothamjazz.com for Jazz, and nyrock.com for Rock (look under "Gig Announcements").

Sometimes, the venue is as big a draw as the artist on its stage. Catching a show at legendary hotspots like CBGB or The Bitter End will help you appreciate rock's roots and give you an inside look at the latest buzz band. Attend an opera at Lincoln Center or The Met and emerge a changed New Yorker (polite, well-mannered, even erudite). But not to worry; ten minutes on the subway could turn even a Duchess into a foul-mouthed sidewalk-spitter.

For a night even your parents would approve of, check out New York's heavy hitters: Madison Square Garden (the-garden.com), Carnegie Hall (carnegiehall.org), and Lincoln Center (lincolncenter.org) host high-profile popular and classical musicians. The Bowery Ballroom (boweryballroom.com) and Williamsburg's Northsix (northsix.com) are two mid-size venues with excellent show lists; the mighty Knitting Factory (knittingfactory.com) always delivers a stellar roster of performers. The jazz scene is alive and well in New York City, with smaller venues clustered around Harlem. While jazz clubs like the Village Vanguard (villagevanguard.com), Blue Note (bluenote.net), Birdland (birdlandjazz.com), and Iridium (iridiumjazzclub.com) still fill their calendars with A-list acts, you should also look into local favorites like Smoke (smokejazz.com), the Lenox Lounge (lenoxlounge.com), or St. Nick's Pub (212/283-9728, 773 St. Nicholas Ave.) for a cozy, low-key (and often cheaper) vibe.

DANCE

>> Traditional forms live comfortably with cutting-edge techniques in New York, ensuring that every flavor of dance gets its place to move. From the Balanchine-choreographed pieces at the New York City Ballet to the Fosse-inspired Broadway shows to the Times Square street performers, it sometimes seems like the whole city's dancing. The New York Times always has current reviews up at nytimes.com/pages/arts/dance, and if you see a show that inspires you, check out ny.com/dance for tons of great classes.

The New York City Ballet (nycballet.com), the American Ballet Theater (abt.org), and The Dance Theater of Harlem (dancetheaterofharlem.com) are probably the three ballet companies with the most sought-after tickets. City Center (nycitycenter. org), the Brooklyn Academy of Music (BAM) (bam.org) and the Joyce Theater (joyce.org) schedule a lot of thrilling modern and contemporary work. Dance Theater Workshop (dtw.org), the Joyce SoHo Theater (joyce.org/soho.html), and P.S. 122 (ps122.org) are known for hosting risky, experimental choreography.

FILM

>> Much has been made of the movies' love affair with New York City. The city's streets, bridges, and buildings have appeared on more silver screens than those of any other city, no doubt adding to the mythology that is the Big Apple. But another love affair, just as faithful but less nostalgic, lingers here: the love New Yorkers have for a great film.

Though certainly not what it was in its legendary heyday, New York's film scene still boasts a few fantastic single screens (like the Paris and the Ziegfeld), many art-house and revival spots (like the superb FilmForum, Sunshine, Angelika, Two Boots Pioneer, and BAM in Brooklyn, some of which offer money-saving memberships), a number of popular Museum series (like MoMA, and of course Museum of the Moving Image), and a sparkling megaplex serving seemingly every neighborhood. If you can manage to keep up with screening schedules, you'll be able to see films in New York you wouldn't be able to see anywhere else.

If all that weren't enough to fill your every evening, New York City also plays host to many big-name film festivals. The most star-studded and popular are the New York Film Festival in the fall; the New Directors/New Films Festival (hosted by MoMA) in the winter; and the TriBeCa Film Festival in the spring, which is fast becoming "the one." These festivals are all rife with expensive galas and über-hyped feature films soon to win distribution, but they also screen an amazing array of smaller pictures vying for attention. There is no specific theme or philosophy guiding the choices, other than the common goal of bringing worthy new films into the spotlight. The centerpiece films sell out quickly, so buffs beware: know when tickets go on sale or you'll be shut out, or worse, at the mercy of scalpers (and you thought ten bucks was steep!). Savvy festival-goers sign up for official newsletters, which have updates about new selections as well as contests and discount offers.t

Of course, not everyone agrees on what constitutes a "worthy" film. Alternative festivals that have sprung up in response to the bigger affairs compete to be the most cutting-edge or non-commercial. The largest and most organized of this category are the staunchly anti-mainstream NY Underground Film Festival (March, Anthology Film Archives, 32 Second Ave., $8.50) and the Arlene's Grocery Picture Show (April, Arlene Grocery, 95 Stanton St., $5), hosted by the popular Lower East Side music venue, which prides itself on taking films that no one else will show. Festival favorites are awarded canned food as prizes. The crowds that gather are much rowdier (and grungier) than those at the mainstream events, and the after-parties are more likely to feature a keg than champagne.

READINGS

>> In a city filled with the famous histories of writers like Langston Hughes, Edith Wharton, Allen Ginsberg, Thomas Wolfe, Edna St. Vincent Millay, Frank O'Hara, and Zora Neale Hurston, it is easy to forget that we share the streets today with people whose voices will be added to that history. On any given night, a vast range of readings occur all over town—poetry, fiction, non-fiction, slam, queer, and works in translation are a few of the many types of work that are read before an audience. Many of the readings are free or student-discounted, and sometimes the cover charge includes a free drink. Check the listings in any of the reliable publications for more information.

Some of the more famous reading series include the Unterberg Poetry Series at the 92nd Street Y (92y.org); the KGB Bar readings (kbgbar.com), which have become so popular they've begun publishing anthologies; the St. Marks Poetry Project (poetryproject.com); Bowery Poetry Club (bowerypoetry.com); and the exhilarating Nuyorican Poetry Slam (nuyorican.org). There are plenty of other gems to uncover in New York's thriving literary scene—bookstores often host events tailored to the stores' market niche, and the many MFA (Master's of Fine Arts) programs calling the city home host regular student readings. If you're a writer yourself, drag your most loyal friends out to an open mike night, take a shot of bourbon, and brave the stage. But remember the advice of P.T. Barnum: always leave 'em wanting more.

Useful Information

AREA CODES

There are four area codes in New York: Manhattan has 212 and 646, while outer boroughs have 718 and 347. In addition, 917 is often assigned to cell phones and pagers.

BUSINESS HOURS

Offices are usually open weekdays from 9 a.m. to 5 p.m., and banks are open weekdays from 9 a.m. to 3 p.m. or later, and sometimes Saturday mornings. Stores typically open between 9 and 10 a.m. and close between 5 and 6 p.m. from Monday through Saturday, though major stores like Macy's or Bloomingdales tend to stay open as late as 9 p.m.

CABLE

If you're a television junkie, DIRECTV (directstartv.com) and Time Warner Cable (timewarnercable.com) are the most reputable dealers in town. Both offer basic packages starting at around $45. If you're fine with getting fuzzy versions of the main networks for free, and willing to risk not being able to tell Hurley apart from Locke on Lost, you can get an antenna to mount on your set for around $30 at Radio Shack.

CELL PHONES

As waves replace wires, many city-dwellers are ditching landlines and making their cell phones their only phones. The big cellular providers (Cingular, Verizon, T-Mobile, Sprint-Nextel) all have shops set up around the city, and you can find more information on their websites. If you're old-fashioned, tech-phobic, or just plain thrifty, you can get a landline through a major telephone company such as AT&T (att.com).

DOGS

Who says you can't buy friendship? For $200 or less, you can adopt a friendly canine companion from your local ASPCA (aspca.org). A dog can be a great addition to city life—but first, you'll have to make sure it's the right addition for you. Dogs, of course, require a great deal of time, care, and responsibility; if you've ever seen an otherwise elegant gentleman scooping up the indelicacies of his fluffy Shitzu, you know that owning a dog requires a certain temperament that not all people have. Furthermore, the costs of food, treats, leashes, and veterinary visits quickly add up, and many landlords will not even allow dogs to live in their buildings. To ease the burden of owning a dog in a city defined by small, enclosed spaces, most dog-owners opt for ankle-biters like poodles or Bichons, though you will occasionally see larger breeds strolling around.

If you do decide to purchase a canine, there are certain rules which must be followed. Never forget to leash your Rex, or clean up after him, as both mistakes carry hefty city fines. It is an unwritten rule, however, that most police officers and park attendants will allow dogs to frolic footloose and leash-free in parks before 8:30 a.m. and after 9 p.m.

If, like many New Yorkers, you have no idea what your apartment looks like when it's lit by sunlight, you'll have to hire a dog-walker. Services start at around $14 per dog for a half-hour jaunt. If you are the type that takes your dogs for "pawdicures" or allows them to drink only Evian, you may feel they require doggy daycare, which runs roughly $60 a day.

If you plan to do the walking yourself, you can locate the nearest dog run by visiting the NYC Parks Department's website (nycgovparks.org). Know that a dog park is not just about rump-sniffing and roughhousing: dogs in this city (as well as their owners) form social groups, meeting regularly to catch up, share advise, and play. Here dogs have the opportunity to develop important social skills with the friends they pass on the sidewalk. Do you really want your dog to grow up socially awkward?

Keeping a dog in the city can be cumbersome and expensive, but most owners find it worthwhile. If nothing else, a dog can come in handy—a cute puppy can serve as an icebreaker for meeting attractive singles, and a fierce Doberman might scare away sketchy potential suitors.

GROCERIES

There are a few unpleasant, albeit unavoidable, facts of life in the big city. Inevitably, your building will sport several varieties of vermin, homeless people will ask you for change on a daily basis, and, perhaps worst of all, you'll have to pay a pretty penny for a bag of groceries. New Yorkers generally cope with the last item by taking a few trips per week to the local market, if only to spread the cost out over time. Aside from the slew of local mom-and-pop grocers scattered throughout the city, there are bigger chains such as Food Emporium (thefoodemporium.com), D'Agostino (dagnyc.com), Gristedes (gristedes.com), C-Town (ctownsupermarkets.com), and Fairway (fairwaymarket.com), as well as gourmet shops like Zabars (zabars.com) and Citarella (citarella.com). Prices between stores are comparable—and high, compared to most non-metro areas—but C-Town and Fairway generally offer the best deals.

Nowadays, you can also save yourself some cash (and a lot of time and effort) by ordering your groceries on-line at either Freshdirect.com or Netgrocer.com. Both deliver right to your door, and offer low delivery fees. You can also get fruits and veggies delivered to your door by the Brooklyn-based Urbanorganic (urbanorganic.net).

If organic or vegetarian is your thing, you might also consider taking the **N** **Q** **R** **W** **4** **5** or **6** to 14th St.–Union Square. There, you'll find Trader Joe's (142 E. 14th St.; traderjoes.com), a quirky West Coast favorite that made its Manhattan debut in early 2006 and quickly won over the crowds with its unusual food selection and rock bottom prices. There's also Whole Foods (4 Union Square South or Columbus Circle; wholefoods.com), which offers a ton of organic options, albeit for a higher price than Trader Joe's. Finally, there's the Union Square Greenmarket, a traditional farmer's market offering fresh produce and other homemade goodies, as well as flowers and crafts. The Greenmarket is open Monday, Wednesday, Friday, and Saturday from 8 am to 6 pm, and all transactions are cash-only.

HOSPITALS
DOWNTOWN
NYU Downtown Hospital, 170 William St. between Beekman and Spruce streets 212-312-5063 or 212-312-5000

St. Vincent's Hospital and Medical Center
153 W. 11th St. at

Seventh Ave.
212-604-7000

Beth Israel Medical Center
First Ave. at 16th St.
212-420-2000.

MIDTOWN
Bellevue Hospital Center
462 First Ave. at 27th St.
212-562-4141

NYU Medical Center
550 First Ave. at 33rd St.
212-263-7300

St. Luke's-Roosevelt Hospital
425 W. 59th St. between 9th
Ave. and 10th Ave.
212-523-4000

UPPER WEST SIDE
St. Luke's Hospital Center,
Amsterdam Ave. and 113th St.,
212-523-3335

**Columbia Presbyterian
Medical Center**
622 W. 168th St. between
Broadway and Fort Washington Ave.
212-305-2500

UPPER EAST SIDE
**New York Presbyterian
Hospital**
525 E. 68th St. at York Ave.
212-472-5454

Lenox Hill Hospital
100 E. 77th St. between Park
and Lexington Ave.
212-434-2000

Mount Sinai Medical Center
Fifth Ave. at 100th St.
212-241-6500

INTERNET

New York has a ton of great
options for getting onto the
internet. Time Warner Cable
(timewarnercable.com) is the
most prevalent cable-internet
company in New York City,
and most monthly packages
will run you around $50. New
York Connect (nyct.net) has
cheaper packages available,
and if you're willing to go the
sluggish modem route you can
get reasonable packages from
both companies.

   If you like your internet
served with a side of caffeine
and people-watching, there
are tons of surfing spots
around the city. Most Starbucks and Barnes and Noble
locations offer wi-fi access for
relatively cheap, and places like
the easyInternetCafé (easyin-
ternetcafe.com) on W. 42nd
St. (between Seventh Ave. and
Eighth Ave.) offer coffee, cake,
and high-speed access. Cyber-
cafe is located at 250 W. 49th
St. between Broadway and
Eighth Ave., (212-333-4109,
cyber-cafe.com) There's also
The Village Copier (villagecop-
ier.com), a local Kinko's-esque
chain with various locations
around the city.

PUBLICATIONS

Newsstands thrive in New
York City. You can find one on
just about every street corner
and subway station, and each
carries a vast selection of local,
national, and international
newspapers and magazines, as
well as munchies and snacks
for that long subway ride
home. Major daily papers
include *The Wall Street Journal*
(wsj.com), a financial paper;
The New York Times (nytimes.
com), one of the most
respected papers in the world;
and the *Daily News* (nydai-
lynews.com) and the *New
York Post* (nypost.com), both
daily tabloid papers. *Metro* (ny.
metro.us), *New York Press* (ny-
press.com) and *amNY* (amny.
com) are all free papers given
out at major subway stops
during the morning commute,
and *The Onion* (theonion.com)
is a free weekly news satire.
Along with the **Times**, the
Village Voice (villagevoice.com),
a free weekly paper, provides
comprehensive listings of
films, concerts, performances,
sporting events, museum and
gallery exhibits, and special
events going on around town.
Magazines are also helpful
sources of need-to-know info:
weekly magazines *Time Out
New York* (timeoutny.com),
New York magazine (newyor-
kmetro.com), and *The New
Yorker* (newyorker.com) are
all invaluable resources for the
city-dweller on-the-go.

RADIO

Tune in to the top radio stations in the city:

1. **WNYC New York Public Radio (AM820 or 93.9 FM)**
The most listened-to public radio station in the United States, WNYC is a member station of National Public Radio (NPR), and provides programming and information that reflects the great cultural depth of the metropolitan area. With a BBC News World Update every weekday morning, The Brian Lehrer Show, The Leonard Lopate Show, and various other news, talk, music, and informational programming, this station is a winner. See wnyc.org for schedules.

2. **WINS (1010 WINS), (AM1010)**
With "All News, All the Time," this station offers up-to-the-minute news, weather, and traffic updates. As their slogan promises, "You give us 10 minutes, we'll give you the world."

3. **WFAN Sports Radio (AM 660)**
Home of the New York Mets among other NY sports teams, tune in to WFAN for sports updates along with popular talk shows with personalities such as Mike and the Mad Dog, whose extensive knowledge of the sports world and interviews with top sports personalities can't be beat.

4. **WPLJ (95.5 FM)**
One of New York's most popular radio stations for Adult Top 40, rock, and pop, WPLJ is great for those who want to hear music from newer groups like The Fray alongside recent favorites by artists like Kelly Clarkson, Coldplay, and Nickelback.

5. **WQHT (HOT97), (97.1 FM)**
The best and most well-known New York station for hip-hop and R&B, Hot 97 plays mostly contemporary beats along with a handful of old school jams. With Angie Martinez and Funkmaster Flex as DJs, programming at this station stays current and hot.

6. **WHTZ (Z100), (100.3 FM)**
"New York's #1 Hit Music Station" offers up all flavors of pop music, from reggaeton and R&B to rock and pop. As a Top 40 station, Z100 has (in theory) music to suit every taste, from Britney to Fall Out Boy to 50 Cent. Unfortunately, the station rarely steps outside of the Top 40-parameter, playing the same singles over and over again. Nonetheless, the playlist accurately reflects the current tastes of the nation.

SMOKING

Thanks to the Clean Indoor Air Act, smoking is prohibited inside most NYC buildings, including bars, restaurants, offices, hotels, and all forms of public transportation including subways, buses, and taxis. You can still light up outdoors, but avoid crowding around building doors unless you want to find yourself the object of evil stares and fake coughs.

TIPPING

Knowing how to tip well in New York is vital if you want to have non-hostile interactions with your fellow man. Follow these tips on tipping, and everyone will be happy. Keep in mind that waiters, who often receive less than minimum wage (sometimes as low as $2 an hour), rely on tips for their incomes. Always tip them 15-20 percent—or more, if you're feeling generous. For bartenders, the standard is a dollar per drink, but throw down a few extra bills if you order complicated and-or frozen drinks. Give cab drivers $1-2 for ride fares under $10 and an extra dollar for each $5 increment, bellhops and skycaps at airports $1 per bag, valets $1, and hairdressers and barbers 15 percent.

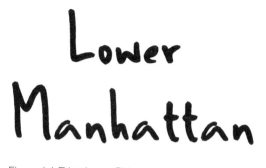

Lower Manhattan

Financial District • Chinatown • Little Italy
TriBeCa • SoHo & Nolita • The Lower East Side

Financial District

THE STATEN ISLAND FERRY DOCKS, the commuter trains pull in and a sea of yellow cabs open their doors. It's another early weekday morning, and the suit-and-briefcase crowds are already on the move to make their first million. Against the backdrop of imposing glass monoliths, the daily feeding frenzy—buying and selling, making and breaking—is about to begin. The morning bell is poised to ring.

Located on the southern tip of Manhattan, the Financial District is the epicenter for the nation's, and the world's, economy. From the opening of the trading floor to the closing of the Japanese market, there's barely time to breathe as brokers rush through office hallways and street-stand falafel lunches, raising the blood pressure and cholesterol of anyone who gets in their way.

The neighborhood revolves around the flow of money, but its activity isn't wholly limited to finances. Also located here are City Hall and the Municipal Building, where Mayor Michael Bloomberg holds court. There are also shoddy discount stores, which celebrate the art of the deal in their own unique way.

The elephant in the room, of course, is Ground Zero. Here, a hole in the ground is all that remains of the World Trade Center and the thousands of lives lost in September, 2001. Plans are underway to build a suitable memorial, and in the meantime, people still flock to the site to pay their respects.

This neighborhood is also home to some of the city's most spectacular parks, from lush Bowling Green to gorgeous Wagner Park. The development of Battery Park City on the west side of southern Manhattan has brought luxury high rises, gourmet delis, and a much-needed residential feel to the area. On Wall Street, downtown becomes a ghost town at night. But soon enough, the cabs will descend, the sun will rise over the skyscrapers, and Wall Street, the center of the capitalist world, will be reborn.

HISTORY

>> ONE OF THE FIRST (and most often misunderstood) real estate scams in American history occurred here in 1626. Legend has it that, for the equivalent of $24, Pieter Minuit, the director general of New Netherlands, bought the island of Manahatta—now Manhattan—from its inhabitants. He encountered little trouble, since to the Native American sellers, private and transferable property was a totally foreign concept. Unfortunately for Minuit, the natives who sold him the land couldn't actually lay claim to that which they sold.

But this swindle came years after an even more brazen land grab. In 1609, the Dutch East India Company hired Henry Hudson to find a passage to India and China. During one of his explorations, Hudson found both the harbor and river that currently bears his name. When news of the harbor reached home, the Netherlands immediately laid claim to it and the rest of the island of Manhattan.

Newamsterdam, as it was called, became New York when the army of the English Duke of York drove away the Dutch in 1664, after which the city grew prosperous from trade and piracy equally. When Washington was defeated at the 1776 Battle of Long Island, in what is now Brooklyn Heights, a seven-year military occupation ensued. Manhattan didn't see American rule until 1783.

Because of its easy access to both the Atlantic and the mainland, Manhattan's downtown harbor flourished, and the island quickly became the biggest center of commerce in North America. Shipping gave way to finance as the neighborhood's driving industry and marinas ceded ground to larger and larger buildings, culminating in the cathedrals of commerce that define today's city skyline.

Downtown has become especially well known following September 11, but Manhattan's southernmost neighborhood is no stranger to tragedy: Dozens died when a bomb devastated the House of Morgan in 1920. The nation collapsed after the New York Stock Exchange crashed in 1929. The World Trade Center was bombed in 1993. And the eerily empty space of Ground Zero serves as a reminder of where the Twin Towers once soared.

WHAT TO SEE

Battery Park

Named after the battery of cannons placed on the site to fend off the British during colonial times, Battery Park's 22 acres are now filled with many important monuments and statues, including the nation's first WWI memorial and an eternal flame to honor the victims of September 11th. The park also has lots of good old-fashioned grass for lazing around and basking in the sun. Come walk the

promenade, toss around a frisbee, and enjoy unmatched views of the New Yo
harbor. ❹ ❺ to Bowling Green, ❶ to South Ferry, ⓃⓇ to Whitehall St.

St. Paul's Chapel

Completed in 1766 when the financial district was nothing but a grassy field,
Paul's Chapel holds the distinction of being Manhattan's oldest public building
continuous use. Notables from George Washington to Bill Clinton to Geor
H.W. Bush have frequented its white-painted pews. But the Church took on
most crucial role in the wake of the terrorist attacks, when it served as a refu
for thousands of rescue and recovery workers who slept and mourned und
its roof throughout the following year. *Church St. (between Fulton St. and Vesey*
212-233-4164, saintpaulschapel.org. Ⓐ Ⓒ Ⓔ *to Chambers St.,* ⓃⓇ *to Cortlandt*

South Street Seaport

Although the famous Fulton Fish Market has relocated north, the Seaport
still the place to check out fish boats and stunning views of the East River. T
cobbled streets and pier of the Seaport have gained some modern additions o
the past few years—clothing stores, boutiques and a mini-mall (with a dece

The New York Stock Exchange

food court) integrate well into established seafood restaurants and the South Street Seaport Museum. The Seaport also hosts many events, including concerts during the summer. *Fulton St at Wall St, 212-732-8257, southstreetseaport.com.* ② ③ ④ ⑤ Ⓐ Ⓒ Ⓙ Ⓜ Ⓩ *at Fulton St.-Broadway–Nassau.*

HANGIN' WITH
THE MAN

The world's largest security exchange and the site of some of the highest-profile financial disasters in world history, the **NEW YORK STOCK EXCHANGE** is a great place to watch the rat race in progress. Tours are given daily. Viva capitalism! *20 Broad St. (bet. Exchange and Wall Sts.), 212-656-5168.* Ⓝ Ⓡ *to Rector St. or* ② ③ ④ ⑤ *to Wall St.*

Tweed Courthouse

Anyone who's seen *Gangs of New York* knows all about Tweed. Rich, politico, beloved by poor immigrants who didn't realize he was huckstering them, this all-around sleazeball wrought underhanded schemes that transformed the Tammany Society into a power-hungry beast. Tweed used this particular construction project to embezzle millions, but all good scams must come to an end, as he was tried in the basement of his own courthouse. *52 Chambers St. (bet. Centre Street and Broadway).* Ⓐ Ⓒ Ⓙ Ⓜ *to Chambers St.,* ④ ⑤ ⑥ Ⓝ Ⓡ *to City Hall.*

Ground Zero

Once, it was called The World Trade Center, those gleaming Twin Towers of commerce that proudly anchored the southern end of New York City's majestic skyline. But the World Trade Center's name change was forced on September 11th, 2001, when the buildings were the sites of the worst foreign attack on American soil in history. Nowadays, everyone calls it Ground Zero, a term the dictionary defines as "the center or origin of rapid, intense, or violent activity or change." *100 Vesey St.* Ⓐ Ⓒ Ⓔ Ⓙ ② ③ *to Chambers St.*

The Wall Street Bull

Also called the "Charging Bull," the 7,000-pound bronze Wall Street statu
has become an icon of New York, money, and power. The statue is the wo
of artist Arturo Di Modica, who was inspired to create the beast after Bla
Monday, the day of the largest stock market losses in history. Di Modica a
tually placed the statue in front of the Stock Exchange building illegally, whe
it quickly attracted attention. But when police tried to haul it away, the pu
lic protested, and the city instead decided to move it to its current loc
tion. *Broadway at Bowling Green.* 🅝 🅡 *to Rector St. or* ❷ ❸ ❹ ❺ *to Wall*

Federal Reserve Bank of New York

There's just something cool about standing on $140-or-so billion dollars. Built
1924, the Federal Reserve is reported to hold roughly one-third of the worl
gold reserve in its subterranean vaults. Take one of the free hour-long tours
visit the gold vault and explore the bank's many informative displays. Note th
reservations must be made at least five business days in advance. *33 Liberty Stre*
between William and Nassau Streets, ny.frb.org. Tours are given Monday through Frid
(except Bank holidays) at 9:30am, 10:30am, 11:30am, 1:30pm, and 2:30pm C
212-720-6130 for reservations. 🅡 *to Rector Street,* 🅐 🅒 🅐 🄢 🄢 🅳 🅕 🄼
to Fulton Street.

Ellis Island

The city's first immigration center, Ellis Island was in use from 1892-1932. Today
single fee covers the ferry ride and admission to both Ellis Island and the Statue
Liberty. Visitors can trace the immigrants' path from the baggage registry roor
and view the American Immigrant Wall of Honor, as well as search for their ov
ancestorsamong the once newly-arrived. Emma Lazarus' "Your tired, your po
your huddled masses" could also apply to the hundreds of bedraggled touri
lugging around kids. *Ferries depart from Castle Clinton in Battery Park every*
minutes during the summer. 212-269-5755, nps.gov/elis. Admission and Ferry $
❹ ❺ *to Bowling Green.*

South Street Seaport

WHERE TO EAT

Bridge Café *American*

Even if you're not a part of the city's political machine, the attentive staff will provide you with reliable standards at this adorable eatery just south of City Hall, one of former mayor Ed Koch's favorite haunts. Mostly a middle-aged crowd of spin doctors and other politicos. *279 Water St. (at Dover St.), 212-227-3344, bridgecafé. com.* ④ ⑤ ⑥ *to Brooklyn Bridge-City Hall.* **$$**

Harbour Lights *Seafood*

After spending a day exploring the South Street Seaport, there is no better place to give your legs a rest and your eyes a treat. Although the food is a bit overpriced and the clientele is touristy, the spectacular view makes it all worthwhile. *South St. Seaport, Pier 17, 3rd fl. (at Fulton St.), 212-227-2800, harbourlts.com.* ② ③ ④ ⑤ ⑥ ⓐ ⓒ ⓘ ⓜ *to Fulton St.* **$$$**

Harry's at Hanover Square *Steakhouse*

If you're in the mood for suits, cigars, and meat, this Wall St. hangout is the place to be. Order a martini and scan the great wine list as you savor one of Harry's sumptuous steaks. Unfortunately, like the stock market, it's closed on weekends. *1 Hanover Sq. (bet. Pearl and Stone Sts.), 212-425-3412.* ⓡ ⓦ *to Whitehall St.* **$$**

Mangia *Mediterranean*

Gourmet Mediterranean cuisine and a friendly waitstaff make Mangia a hot-spot for surrounding businesses, galleries, and museums. Mangia's diverse selection of pastas, sandwiches, and entrées—including an "antipasto table" with an impressive selection ranging from paella to rare tuna—makes for a thrilling meal. In a rush? Stop at the café downstairs for equally delicious take-out dining, or have them deliver right to your door. *40 Wall St. (bet Nassau and Broad Sts.), 212-425-4040.* ⓡ ⓦ *to Rector St.* **$**

BEST BEEF IN
THE LAND OF BEAR
AND BULL

Capitalism sure cooks up an appetite! Serving hearty steaks to a wealthy clientele, **MARK JOSEPH STEAKHOUSE** provides its powerful patrons with a prodigious porterhouse, cooked on the table directly in front of their steely eyes. The food is worth the price and the wait—it's tender and delicious. Their tasty steak sauce is a mixture of horseradish, ketchup, and sugar. For dessert, try the Mark Joseph special, a delectable combination of cheesecake and brownie. *261 Water St. (off Peck Slip), 212-277-0020.* ② ③ *to Wall St.* **$$$**

Seaport Café *American*

The menu at this open-air café includes fresh pastas, sandwiches, wraps, gourmet coffees, and desserts. It's perfect for casual diners who don't want generic fast food or an expensive tab. The outdoor table area is great for people-watching, ensuring that diners won't miss any of the action happening at the lively pier outside. *89 South St. (at Pier 17), 212-964-1120.* ② ③ ④ ⑤ ⑥ ⓐ ⓒ ⓘ ⓜ *to Fulton St.* **$**

ARTS

Irish Hunger Memorial *Museums*

This memorial, which mimics a rural Irish landscape, is meant to raise awareness of the Irish famine of 1845-52. The famine killed many Irish and sent even more fleeing to the States, where they faced widespread discrimination at the hands of more-established American immigrants. *290 Vesey Street.* Ⓐ Ⓒ Ⓔ ❷ ❸ *Chambers St.*

The Skyscraper Museum *Museums*

Elevate your mind in a stylish, intimate space devoted to New York's history and culture as a vertical metropolis. Stainless steel floors and ceilings mirror the display cases to create an impression of towering height in these sleek new galleries. Longstanding exhibits take on the WTC tragedy with the original eleven-foot building model and an outdoor viewing wall of the site that features seventeen historical fiberglass panels. Current exhibits raise high hopes for the future with visual displays exploring the "green" architectural schemes of tomorrow. *39 Battery Place, 212-968-1961, skyscraper.org. Hours: W-Su 12-6pm $2.50 for students with ID.* ❹ ❺ *to Bowling Green,* ❶ Ⓡ Ⓦ *to South Ferry (Whitehall St.) or to Rector St.*

SHOPPING

Abercrombie & Fitch *Clothing : National Chain*

Carrying women's, men's, and children's "rugged, authentic" clothing, this remarkably well-designed flagship offers the same unremarkable clothing and accessories that you can find in their other locations. To many, A&F remains the clothier of choice for preppy coeds who can't live without watered-down, suburban takes on real fashion. *199 Water St. (South Street Seaport), 212-809-9000, abercrombie. com, Hours: M-Sa 10am- 9pm, Su 11am- 8pm* Ⓐ Ⓒ *to Broadway-Nassau St.,* Ⓜ ❷ ❸ ❹ ❺ *to Fulton St.*

CENTURY 21 discount department store, nicknamed "New York's Best Secret," is a dream for any shopper who wants premium designer labels at significantly reduced prices. Just be prepared to battle it out with other bargain hunters over $70 Prada frocks and $25 DKNY jeans. Try to avoid weekend afternoons, when the crowds can be overwhelming. *22 Cortlandt Street between Church and Broadway.* Ⓐ Ⓒ Ⓔ *to Chambers St;* Ⓝ Ⓡ *to Cortlandt St.*

BEST DEAL ON
DESIGNER DUDS

J&R Music World *Music*

Covering an entire block and soaring well into the sky, this store carries everything in video, audio, music, and computers. The staff isn't entirely composed of experts, so ask for multiple opinions before you buy anything. *23 Park Row (bet. Beekman and Ann Sts.), 212-238-9000, jr.com. Hours: M-Sa 9am-7:30pm, Su 10:30am-6:30pm* ❷ ❸ *to Park Pl.,* Ⓐ Ⓒ *to Broadway-Nassau St.,* Ⓔ *to Chambers St.,* ❶ Ⓜ ❷ *Fulton St.,* Ⓡ Ⓦ *to City Hall.*

>> THE ORIGINAL **DUANE READE** was one of three drugstores in downtown Manhattan opened by the Cohen Brothers in 1959. They originally called their stores "Thrift" but, with so many other thrift shops around, that name proved confusing. Their main store was on Broadway between Duane and Reade, and the Cohens noticed many of their workers (mostly immigrants who had great trouble pronouncing "thrift") referring to the main store as "The Duane and Reade shop." The name stuck.

Syms *Clothing : Discount*

Originally a men's suit warehouse, today Syms sells complete lines of men's, women's, and children's designer clothing at heavily discounted prices. With items from over 200 brand labels in stock and a convenient color-coded price tag system to tell you what's in your price range, Syms is a great place for both apparel aficionados who crave the ultimate bargain and novice shoppers who just need a nice, cheap ensemble. *45 Trinity Pl. (at Rector St.), 212-797-1199, syms.com. Hours: M-F 8am-8pm, Sa 10am-6:30pm, Su 12pm-5:30pm* ❹ ❺ *to Bowling Green,* ❶ Ⓡ Ⓦ *to Rector St.*

HOTELS AND HOSTELS

Best Western Seaport Inn

Located near South Street Seaport, this hotel offers clean rooms, good service, and complimentary breakfast. Although it might not be in midtown, a stay in this hotel provides guests with an opportunity to fully experience downtown Manhattan, and Brooklyn is right across the bridge. *33 Peck Slip (Btw Front and Water Sts.) 800-468-3569 or 212-766-6600; bestwestern.com. Single Rooms are $240-$300. Carte Blanche.* ❷ ❸ *to Wall St.*

Chinatown

SHINING FISH EYES. Porcelain tea kettles. Wizened ginseng roots. Tiger-penis aphrodisiacs. Chinatown is a bizarre bazaar, where someone in the know can buy just about anything.

The streets are mostly tiny, and the thick, sweaty crowds are a claustrophobic nightmare. But within this riot of gold and scarlet there are discoveries at every step, whether it's melting red-bean pastries, miniature jade dragons, or the drugstore on Grand Street where deer antlers are still weighed out in brass hand scales.

Chinatown seems caught in perpetual chaos, with too many people doing too much in too small a space—and, indeed, the neighborhood is bursting out of its seams. Having successfully reduced Little Italy to a single street, Chinatown is now gunning for the Lower East Side and even SoHo. The area is also diversifying itself; many of the shops and restaurants now have Thai, Cambodian, Vietnamese, or Korean owners.

The hard sells of the sidewalk knockoff hawkers and the streams of baseball-capped suburbanites ogling roasting ducks in shop windows can make Chinatown feel like a manufactured piece of tourist exotica. Still, while many recent immigrants have favored other, less chaotic Chinese enclaves, like Flushing in Queens or Sunset Park in Brooklyn, Manhattan's Chinatown remains a living, bustling ethnic community with a residential population in the hundreds of thousands. Walk a few blocks from the main drags and you'll find less crowded local spaces complete with video-rental stores, dentists, and unassuming tea shops that make this otherwise commercial spectacle a true neighborhood.

HISTORY

>>CHINATOWN SPRANG UP in the mid-to-late 19th century with the first wave of Chinese immigration to the United States. Prior to then, the area now regarded as Chinatown was part of the Five Points district—a lawless place, notorious for vice, violence, and prostitution. Back then it was home to mostly Irish and some Jewish immigrants.

Migration was not easy for the Chinese. Isolationist leaders had not allowed them to leave their homeland, and immigrants were greeted with fear and even hatred when they arrived in the United States.

The first recorded Chinese resident was a merchant from Kwantung who moved into 8 Mott Street in 1858. By the 1870s, there were almost 2,000 Chinese people living within the boundaries of Canal, Worth, Mulberry, and the Bowery—the area which became Chinatown proper.

The neighborhood grew slowly, largely due to immigration laws which kept men from sending for their families. Business prospects for immigrants were limited. Many opened hand laundries, along with restaurants and shops to attract visitors. The population grew after the Exclusion Act was repealed in 1943, reaching 20,000 residents by 1965. As restrictions and prejudices began to wane in the late '60s, Chinatown expanded into parts of the Lower East Side and Little Italy, thereby becoming the largest Chinese community in the Western world.

WHAT TO SEE

Columbus Park & Five Points

Chinatown's Columbus Park is a community favorite, where the very youngest to the very oldest gather to enjoy summer weather and catch up with friends. On sunny afternoons, watch hordes of kids zip around the playground while the greyer-haired challenge each other to games of Chinese checkers and dominos. Arrive early enough and you'll catch local residents practicing tai chi. In the south end of the park, you'll find the site of the city's first tenements as well as the former center of the infamous Five Points neighborhood, where gangs of Irish and German immigrants fought violently during the 19th century—a conflict depicted in Martin Scorsese's 2002 film *Gangs of New York*. *Mulberry St. (between Bayard and Worth Sts.).* ❹ ❺ ❻ ❶ Ⓜ ❷ *to Brooklyn Bridge.*

MOST INSCRUTABLE
CLAIRVOYANTS

On weekends, the **FORTUNE-TELLERS** in Columbus Park set up shop under red banners advertising "Fortune." Their cards and long reeds promise to uncover buried truths; you imagine them revealing the trail of your future life. This is a dream that's bound to be broken: "Fortune" is the only English word that many of these clairvoyants speak. *Mulberry St. (bet. Bayard and Worth Sts.).* ❶ Ⓜ ❷ ❹ ❺ ❻ *to Brooklyn Bridge.*

Chatham Square

One of the busiest areas in the neighborhood, Chatham Square is a central meeting place, where seven of Chinatown's principle streets—Bowery, East Broadway,

St. James Place, Mott Street, Oliver Street, Worth Street and Park Row—con
verge. The square is home to several important landmarks, including the Kimla
Memorial Arch, erected in 1962 in memory of the numerous Chinese-American
soldiers who died in WWII, and a statue of Lin Tse-hsu, a 19th-century Chines
officer whose anti-drug policies led to the First Opium War against Britain in
1839. to East Broadway.

Confucius Plaza

Standing tall in the shadow of multi-story restaurants and high-rise apartment
you'll find the 15-foot granite statue of one of East Asia's most famous think
ers, the Chinese philosopher Confucius. The statue's inscription, an excerpt from
Confucius's *Chapter of Great Harmony*, describes a perfect society where all cit
zens' needs are fulfilled. *Corner of Bowery and Division Sts.* ⬤ ⓜ ⓝ ⓡ ⓦ ⓩ ⬤
to Canal St.

Mahayana Buddhist Temple

For an escape from Chinatown's colorful, crowded chaos, pass between the two golden lions that guard the entrance of the Mahayana Buddhist Temple, and enter a world of neon spirituality, where the pungent smell of seafood is overcome by the stifling sweetness of incense. Stand for a moment in the small, ornate lobby, where incense burns in golden urns and worshippers bow in prayer. Then, pass through to the back room, where a giant, sixteen-foot golden statue of the Buddha sits atop a lotus, framed by the glow of blue neon rings. Buy a fortune scroll for $1 or visit on a weekend and attend an elaborate public service, featuring drums and bells and other traditional ceremonies. *133 Canal Street, directly across from the Manhattan Bridge, 212-925-8787.* **N R Q W J M Z 6** *to Canal St.*

MOST MILES
PER DOLLAR

The infamous **CHINATOWN BUS** services can get you from Canal Street to Boston for an incredible fifteen bucks. They also go to D.C., Philadelphia, Baltimore, and several other East Coast cities. Yeah, the seats can be cramped and uncomfortable. Okay, so the driver will rarely speak English. True, Boston/New York buses sometimes use routes creative enough to include Providence. And sure, there are apparently documented ties to organized crime. None of this seems to matter when your ticket costs less than an airport sandwich. But be warned, buses frequently break down and are late, so plan for extra time. *staticleap.com/chinatownbus*

WHERE TO EAT

Bo Ky *Chinese*

Seafood variations served over rice and noodles are the staples of the Chinese menu. The central location attracts tourists and locals on their lunch breaks. Efficient service moves patrons in and out in a hurry. *80 Bayard St. (at Mott St.), 212-406-2292. Cash Only.* **J M N R W Z 6** *to Canal St.* **$**

Golden Unicorn *Chinese*

Cleaner and more polished than most Chinatown dim sum houses, this chandeliered restaurant has become especially popular among tourists and local businessmen hosting lunch meetings. Delicious dim sum (seven days a week, 9am-3:30pm) is served Hong-Kong style, stacked on metal carts piloted by vigorous employees. Many claim it's dim sum and then some. *18 East Broadway (at Catherine St.), 212-941-0911. Cash Only.* **B D** *to Grand St.* **$**

Great New York Noodletown *Chinese*

Away from the touristy center of Chinatown, you'll stumble on this affordable and cozy restaurant where you're guaranteed to find a dish to excite your taste buds. In-season seafood specials, the crab in particular, are must-trys, as is the barbecued chicken/duck/pork combo. The ultra-accommodating service will make sure that you leave satisfied. *28 Bowery (at Bayard St.), 212-349-0923. Cash Only.* **B D** *to Grand St.* **$**

Joe's Shanghai *Chinese*

Joe's crabmeat buns are deservingly famous; tourists and locals flock here **t**
them year-round. Friendly service and savory fare keep customers coming ba
for more. Try the soup dumplings, filled with juicy crabmeat and pork in a flavor
broth. *9 Pell St. (at Mott St.), 212-233-8888. Cash Only.* **❶ Ⓜ Ⓝ Ⓡ Ⓦ Ⓩ ➏**
Canal St. **$**

MOST FUN-
FLAVORED DESERT

One of the oldest shops in Chinatown, **The Original Chinatown I**
Cream Factory has been serving yummy frozen treats in flavors like lych
ginger and red bean for almost 20 years. You'll find plain chocolate or vanilla list
under "exotic flavors" along with mint chip, Oreo cookie and peach. The ginge
divine. There's usually a line around the block on weekends. *65 Bayard Street (I*
tween Elizabeth and Mott St.), 212-608-4170, chinatownicecreamfactory.com. Hou
Su-Sa 11am-11pm Cash only. **❶ Ⓜ Ⓝ Ⓡ Ⓞ Ⓦ Ⓩ ➏** *to Canal St.*

Tai Pan Bakery *Desserts*

The pastries at this popular bakery merit its long weekend lines. Custard ta
and pearl milk tea drinks are sure to please, while the Fish burgers are only **t**
the adventurous. *194 Canal St. 212-732-2222, taipan-bakery.com. Hours: Su-*
7:30am-8:30pm Cash only. **❶ Ⓜ Ⓝ Ⓡ Ⓦ Ⓩ ➏** *to Canal St.* **$**

NIGHTLIFE

Happy Ending *Club*

Previously a massage parlor (and suspected brothel), this bar/club has becom
far less risqué. Now the unique features include private white tile rooms a
slight spa scents. In addition to the amazing atmosphere, the people are you
and attractive, and the bartenders are friendly. The music is great for dancing a
lounging. The fact that there is no cover is the icing on the cake of this literal hap
ending. *302 Broome St. (bet. Forsyth and Eldridge Sts.), 212-334-9676, happyenc*
glounge.com. **Ⓡ ❶ Ⓜ Ⓝ Ⓡ Ⓦ Ⓩ ➏** *to Canal St.*

Winnie's Karaoke Bar *Bar*

After the vendors have closed their shops and the carts of vegetables and sme
fish have been packed away, a different Chinatown emerges, as the city's nig
owls head to this neighborhood icon for a late-night snack, a lychee martini,
some good old fashioned Karaoke fun. The eclectic crowd belts out everythi
from classic rock to Mandarin pop, but be careful not to butcher those class
too badly—the Manhattan Criminal Courthouse is right next door. *104 Bayd*
St. (bet. Baxter and Mulberry Sts.), 212-732-2384. M-Su 12pm-4am, Cash only, tw
drink minimum. **Ⓝ Ⓡ Ⓞ Ⓦ ❶ Ⓜ Ⓩ ➏** *to Canal St.*

ARTS

Museum of the Chinese in the Americas *Museums*

If you have any interest in Chinese-American culture or immigration history,
sure to check out this museum, which features one of the most thorough natio

archives of Chinese history in America, with endless documents, oral histories, art, and other artifacts. The museum also hosts film screenings and runs top-notch Chinatown walking tours. Recent favorites include *Have You Eaten Yet?: The Chinese Restaurant in America* and *Godzilla's Yellow Pearl*. *70 Mulberry Street (corner Bayard Street), 212-619-4785, moca-nyc.org. Hours: Sa-R 12pm-6pm, F 12pm-7pm, $3 adult/$1 student.* **N R Q W J M Z 6** *to Canal St.*

SHOPPING

Dynasty Supermarket *Groceries*
One of Chinatown's largest supermarkets, Dynasty boasts a full herb and medi-cine counter, an in-house butcher and fishmonger, a beef-jerky...bar, and, best of all, weekly sales. *68 Elizabeth St. (at Hester St.), 212-966-4943, Hours: M-Su 9:30am-8:30pm* **N R W** *to Prince St.,* **B D** *to Grand St.*

Pearl River Mart *Department Stores*
Magazine editors and bargain hunters alike love the enormous collection of Asian imports found here. The two-floor emporium stocks all the staples that five-and-dimes used to, with a twist: bamboo mats, bedding supplies, electronics, video rentals, a mini grocery section, and traditional cookware. *477 Broadway (at Grand St.), 212-431-4770, pearlriver.com. Hours: M-Su 10am-7pm.* **J M N R W 6** *to Canal St.*

KING OF THE
ART STORES

Art students are often seen toting around huge canvases to and from the Canal Street subway stop. They're all coming from the same place: **PEARL PAINT**. This popular store boasts an astounding six full floors of high-quality arts supplies. Looking for oil paints, brushes, pastels, imported Belgian canvases, gold leaf, or the best paper? Head here, and make sure to give yourself enough time to browse. *308 Canal St., (at Third Ave.), 212-431-7932, pearlpaint.com. Hours: M-F 9am-7pm, Sa 10am-6:30pm, Su 10am-6pm* **J M N R W Z 6** *to Canal St.*

Ten Ren Tea and Ginseng Co. *Groceries*
Masters of the ancient but still sophisticated Chinese ritual of tea preparation, the folks at Ten Ren not only sell teas (ranging from $8 to $125 per lb.) but also provide lessons on the proper brewing and savoring of the venerated green leaf. Superb black teas, jasmine teas, and ginger are also sold here. *75 Mott St. (bet. Canal and Bayard Sts.), 212-349-2286, tenrenstea.com. Hours: M-Su 10am-8pm* **J M N R W Z 6** *to Canal St.*

Little Italy

ON A SEPTEMBER EVENING during the Feast of San Gennaro, Mulberry just might be the world's most color-coordinated street. Red, white, and green banners hang from every shop. Men in red, white, and green bandannas cajole you to play their carnival games: "Win something for your girlfriend. C'mon!" In front of one vendor, a speaker painted red, white, and green belts out classic Sinatra.

Over the years, Little Italy has turned into Very Little Italy: walk south for a couple of blocks and the marinara sauce becomes duck sauce, the espresso replaced with Chinatown's famous bubble tea. The biting line is that the last people you'll find in Little Italy are real Italians, and it's mostly true. In a sense, the old "authentic" Italian community has been pushed aside in favor of a tourist-driven theme park.

Of course, there's nothing wrong with a good theme park. Only the most reckless of sightseers would have freely wandered these streets in the 1920s, when the heavily Italian community was tightly in the grip of the Mob. While today's Cannoliland is a safe, pleasant, and bustling place to stop for an espresso and admire the handsome brick buildings and cobbled streets.

And when San Gennaro rolls around in September, it's still a great party. Italians flock in from the outer boroughs, where Bensonhurst, Bay Ridge, and Belmont remain living ethnic enclaves. The sidewalk food stands smell as enticing as anything you can imagine, and recordings of Ol' Blue Eyes presides over it all, crooning over the crowds as if it were still the old days.

HISTORY

>> BEGINNING WITH THE EXPLORER Giovanni da Verrazzano's 1524 arrival in Manhattan's bay, Italians have played an important role in New York City's history. Immigrants from Northern Italy first arrived in the early 17th century, but their numbers were dwarfed by the larger waves of Southern Italian and Sicilian immigrants who came to New York in the late 19th century.

From 1880 to 1900, the number of Italians in New York rose from 12,000 to almost 220,000 and doubled to 545,000 by 1910. Most of the Italian immigrants settled in lower Manhattan, an area packed with poor immigrant families forced to live in crowded, unsanitary tenements. They tended to cluster according to their relations in the Old World, with Genoans, Calabrians, and Sicilians living on the East Side, and Piedmontese, Tuscans, and Neopolitans on the west. This was the era chronicled by Francis Ford Coppola in The Godfather: Part I, where Sicilian Vito Corleone establishes himself as the benefactor of his community.

By the mid-20th century, most Italians, like the fictional Corleone, had moved out of the old neighborhood to greener places like Staten Island, Brooklyn, Long Island, and New Jersey.

WHAT TO SEE

Feast of San Gennaro

For one week each September, the narrow Mulberry Street is transformed into a colorful carnival, as one million visitors pour into the neighborhood to celebrate the feast of San Gennaro, the Patron Saint of Naples. Food booths line the streets and music plays from every direction. Catch the annual parade or take a ride on the ferris wheel. With games, vendors, drinks, and top knotch Italian food in every direction, there's bound to be something to satisfy everyone. *Mulberry Street between Houston and Canal.* ⑥ ❶ Ⓜ Ⓝ Ⓞ Ⓡ Ⓦ ❼ *to Canal St.*

Christmas Lights

It may be best known for Feast of San Gennaro and summer patio dining, but just after the first snow has fallen, Little Italy becomes a winter wonderland, as the restaurants along Mulberry Street put up some of the most elaborate Christmas decorations in the city. Past years' favorites include a giant, ten-foot snow globe, complete with blowing snow, and more rooftop Santas and Reindeers than the neighborhood has rooftops. Once you've had your fill of glowing lights, tuck into any of the area's warm cafés for a steaming cup of cappuccino or creamy hot chocolate. ⑥ ❶ Ⓜ Ⓝ Ⓞ Ⓡ Ⓦ ❼ *to Canal St.*

The Police Building

Serving as the NYCPD headquarters from 1909-1973, the austere appearance of this Renaissance revival structure, with a commanding copper dome crafted by the same Frenchies who restored the Statue of Liberty's flame, was intended to "impress both the officer and the prisoner with the majesty of the law." It is now a ritzy condominium complex, star-studded with residents like Cindy Crawford,

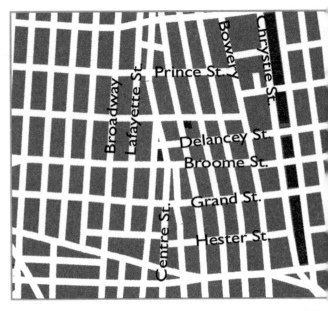

Winona Ryder, and Steffi Graf. *240 Centre St. (bet. Broome and Grand Sts.)* Ⓝ Ⓡ Ⓦ ➏ *to Canal St.*

The Holy Crucifix Church

The Holy Crucifix Church is stately and sedate stone Roman Catholic churc It's in the heart of Little Italy—smack up against an irreverent art gallery. Wh it doesn't offer Sunday mass in Italian or Latin, it does do English, Chinese, ar Spanish—even the Church knows when to give in to the forces of the city. *3ⁿ Broome St. (bet. Mott and Mulberry Sts.).* ➏ *to Spring St.*

WHERE TO EAT

Buona Notte *Italian*

Seating in the front, dining room, or garden provides a variety of options at th charming spot. Plenty of mirrors allow you to detect the fettuccine between yo teeth before your date does. Nice presentation and delicately seasoned dish *Molto bene! 120 Mulberry St. (bet. Canal and Hester Sts.), 212-965-1111.* Ⓙ Ⓜ Ⓡ Ⓦ Ⓩ ➏ *to Canal St.* **$$**

OLDEST
PASTICCERIA IN
AMERICA

FERRARA has been indulging sweet tooths since 1892 with their enormous sele tion of cannoli, tarts, tiramisu, sfogliatella, cream-filled lobster tails, a dozen types biscotti, cheesecake, and other Italian treats. Their gelato is of the creamy, delect ble variety, and is available in more than a dozen flavors. You can get table servi and linger over dessert with a fine cup of Italian cappuccino or take your pastri to go. The cashiers smartly tie pastry boxes tight with red and white string, insu

Ferrara

ing that the dessert will survive for more than a block before you "sample" one, and then all of it. *195 Grand St. (bet. Mott and Mulberry Sts.).* Ⓖ Ⓙ Ⓜ Ⓝ Ⓠ Ⓡ Ⓦ Ⓩ *to Canal St.;* Ⓑ Ⓓ *to Grand St.*

Luna's Ristorante *Italian*

This neighborhood hide-away is still one of the best buys in Little Italy. But come for the food—not the décor. The aroma of fresh garlic sizzling in olive oil more than compensates for the perfunctory service. *112 Mulberry St. (bet. Canal and Hester Sts.), 212-226-8657.* Ⓙ Ⓜ Ⓝ Ⓡ Ⓦ Ⓩ Ⓖ *to Canal St.-Broadway.* **$$**

Pellegrino's *Italian*

Setting itself apart from the mostly mediocre Italian fare on Mulberry St, Pellegrino's is a standout. The informed, old school staff manages both the intimate dining room and breezy sidewalk seating with charm and class. The food is superb—creamy, flavorful sauces, tender meat, and fresh seafood are all served in generous portions. *138 Mulberry St. (bet. Hester and Grand Sts.), 212-226-3177,* Ⓖ Ⓙ Ⓜ Ⓝ Ⓠ Ⓡ Ⓦ Ⓩ *to Canal St.* **$$**

Positano Ristorante *Italian*

The slender space and subdued décor make Positano seem less raucous than its neighbors on Mulberry Street. A peaceful meal in the heart of Little Italy. *122 Mulberry St. (bet. Canal and Hester Sts.), 212-334-9808.* Ⓙ Ⓜ Ⓝ Ⓡ Ⓦ Ⓩ Ⓖ *to Canal St.-Broadway.* **$$**

Puglia *Italian*

Like pasta? Like Elvis? Then you're in luck—spend your meal at large communal tables, chugging wine with new friends as an Italian Elvis works his magic on a little Casio keyboard in the corner. By the time you leave, you'll feel less lonely. *189 Hester St. (bet. Mott and Mulberry Sts.), 212-226-891.* Ⓙ Ⓜ Ⓝ Ⓡ Ⓦ Ⓩ Ⓖ *to Canal St.-Broadway.* **$**

MARINARA
AND MURDER

While **UMBERTO'S CLAM HOUSE** does have a reputation for great Italian se
food dishes, its association with the murder of an infamous mobster is what real
makes this restaurant a topic of conversation. Shortly after opening its doors
1972, Crazy Joe Gallo was killed at Umberto's as he celebrated his 43rd birthd
Visit during the early hours of the morning (it's open until 4am) to enjoy som
succulent clam sauce while thinking back to the forgone days when the mob co
trolled many of New York's streets. *178 Mulberry St. (bet. Mott and Mulberry Sts*
212-431-7545, umbertosclamhouse.com. Hours: M-Su 11am-4am. ❶ ⓜ *to Bowe*
❸ ⓓ ⓕ *to Grand St.,* ❻ *to Spring St.*

NIGHTLIFE

Mulberry Street Bar *Bar*
Gape at the huge photo of Frank Sinatra, then go get yourself a drink at one
Little Italy's last genuine bars. Also known as "Tony's," in case you want to feel li
a real local. *176 Mulberry St. (bet. Grand and Broome Sts.), 212-226-9345. Ca*
Only. ❻ *to Spring St.*

SHOPPING

Di Palos' Fine Foods *Groceries*
Don't be fooled by the corner store size of this Italian specialty gem. Everythi
on the well-stocked shelves of DiPalo's Dairy is of superior quality. Olive o
pasta and traditional Italian breads sit alongside more exotic, but just as delicio
imports like Spanish Marcona almonds. And then there's the cheese—the be
selection of Italian cheeses in the city, period. Browse, sample, and feel free to a
questions, especially if the welcoming owner, Louis DiPalo, is behind the count
Be prepared to take a number and wait in line—but oh how worth it that w
will be. *200 Grand St. (at Mott St.), 212-226-1033, Hours: M-Sa 9am-6:30pm,*
9am-4pm. ❻ *to Spring St.*

Tribeca

AFTER ANGRY OBJECTIONS, near-brawls at community board meetings, and plenty of melodramatic pouting, the artists who pioneered Tribeca's minimalist, neo-industrial aesthetic have been forced to throw in their well-decorated towels. Another iteration of the classic New York story, the chic restaurants and luxury co-ops are in, and the bohemians are out.

During the '90s, this handful of city blocks kicked and scratched its way into the Manhattan elite. Unlike other once-industrial neighborhoods like SoHo and Chelsea, Tribeca had a healthy dose of celebrity to help it on its way. John F. Kennedy, Jr. lived here in the years before his death. Harvey Keitel, M. Night Shyamalan, Tim Robbins, and Susan Sarandon are fixtures at the local bars and bistros. And then there's Robert De Niro, who not only moved to the area but also launched the Tribeca Film Center and Tribeca Grill in hopes of revitalizing the neighborhood and local businesses following September 11. Not that everyone around here has an agent—young Wall Streeters with thick wallets are drawn to the neighborhood for its proximity to the Financial District and abundance ofamazing apartments.

As Tribeca is not yet an insular, overpriced playspace like SoHo, its residents tend to avoid excessive showiness. The side streets can be foreboding and dimly-lit after dark, and the swanky restaurants and bistros are likely to be tucked away in converted storage spaces.

Though Tribeca businesses are still struggling in the wake of decreased downtown tourism post-September 11, the concentrated ef-

forts of city-business improvement organizations are putting this funk
neighborhood back on the map as something other than just a neighbo
to tragedy.

HISTORY

>> TWENTY YEARS BEFORE the last bucketful of sludge was drained fro
the swamp now known as Gramercy Park, Tribeca's parks were already steppi
grounds for genteel young ladies wielding parasols.

Beginning modestly in 1813 as produce-based Bear Market, Tribeca was a maj
point of transfer for the increased shipping and commerce moving through Low
Manhattan by the mid-19th century. Its cast-iron facades and spacious five- an
six-story buildings were factories and storage facilities, as Tribeca joined SoHo
becoming an extensive light-manufacturing zone. By 1939, Bear Market and th
surrounding area were renamed Washington Market; the market itself sustained
greater volume of business than all other venues of its kind combined. It remaine
a vital part of the city's produce industry until most companies left the area in th
early '60s and were quickly replaced by real-estate developers.

The Washington Market Urban Renewal Project was launched almost imme
ately, paving the way for office buildings, institutions like the Borough of Manhatt
Community College, and public parks in the neighborhood. In the '70s alone, th
area's population jumped from 243 to more than 5,000. Development continue
into the '90s: Construction of Stuyvesant High School, the city's most competiti
public high school, was completed in 1993 at a cost of over $150 million. Illeg
lofts were quickly converted into luxury residences, but with the important d
tinction that, unlike those in SoHo, these lofts were open to non-artists as well
those of the creative class.

At the peak of its re-development, Washington Market area was dubbed Trib
ca for "the Triangle below Canal Street"—the previous name was deemed to
uncouth for the loft-living crowd. Ironically, the area, roughly bounded by Car
Broadway, Warren, and West, is really more of a trapezoid.

WHAT TO SEE

Washington Market Park

More than just an area of greenery, this Tribeca green spot offers a wide variety
community events. among these: the Easter egg hunt, Halloween party, Christm
and Chanukah parties. And it doesn't end with holiday festivities—the park offe
a series of summer concerts every Thursday night, and all free for everyone.
beautiful gazebo on the southern perimeter can be rented out for birthday p
ties and the like, as even the ice-cream shaped sprinkler system seems to beg
the presence of little kids. *Greenwich Street and Chambers Street, 212-964-11.
washingtonmarketpark.org.* ❶ ❷ ❸ *to Chambers St.*

Tribeca Film Center

Robert De Niro's presence in Tribeca has always been commanding, and the fi

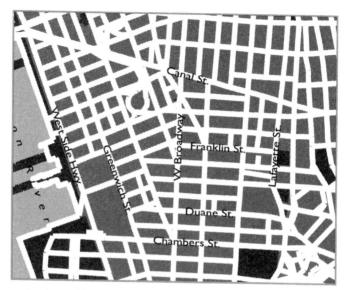

center, , is certainly one way that he has left a resonant fingerprint on the area. Located in the old Coffee Building (a former factory), this complex houses editing and production rooms as well as the Tribeca Grill Restaurant on the bottom floor. This might be a great celebrity watch point, as many of America's biggest directors have their offices right here. *375 Greenwich Street (between North Moore and Franklin Streets), 212-941-2000, tribecafilm.com.* ❶ *to Franklin St.*

Come to Tribeca's **GREENWICH STREET** in hopes of seeing some of New York's famous faces, including Robert DeNiro, Christopher Walken, Mick Jagger, and Sarah Jessica Parker. Admission is free, so bring a friend! *1 Greenwich St. (bet. Duane and Reade Sts.).* ❶ *to Franklin St.*

STALK IN STYLE

Duane Park

The Trapeze School of New York

This small triangular plot of land is the second oldest park in New York. Its history goes way back, having once been part of a Dutch farm settlement that King James II seized in 1674. The royal family then gave it over to Trinity Church in 1705, but the city later bought it in 1797 for a mere $5 to turn it into a park. By 1886, the park had become unkempt, and the city commissioned architect Calvert Vaux, who collaborated with Fredrick Law Olmstead on Central Park, to refashion it to its current tree-shaded and flower-filled splendor. *Bordered by Hudson, Duane and Staple Sts.* ❶ ❷ ❸ Ⓐ Ⓒ *to Chambers St.*

Trapeze School of New York

If you've ever dreamed of being a superhero soaring above the New York skyline, here's your chance—well, at least for the flying part. Quite possibly one of Manhattan's randomest attractions, the Trapeze School of New York offers individual and group classes for anyone who has ever developed a craving for

wings. Anyone age 6 and up is welcome to try their hand at a variety of airbor
circus activities, including fly-trap, static-trap, and ropes, all overlooking the beau
ful skyline from the Hudson River Waterfront. *Hudson River Park, between Ves*
and Debrosses St. ❶ Ⓐ Ⓒ Ⓔ *at Canal St.*

WHERE TO EAT

Bubby's Pie Co. *American*
Bubby's is all about homemade comfort food. Entrées range from burgers
slow cooked barbeque and buttermilk fried chicken, but its their macaroni a
cheese that was voted Best in New York. The milkshake menu includes a seaso
ice cream shake, depending on what homemade flavor is in season. And gu
what…they also have pie! In fact, Bubby's opened as a pie company, serving fre
pies topped with their homemade ice cream. Watch out for the artsy-tren
Tribeca loft-dwellers that populate the place. Once in a while, you may see a s
but most likely it's a wannabe. *120 Hudson St. (at North Moore St.), 212-219-06*
bubbys.com. ❶ *to Franklin St.* **$$**

Café Noir *Café*
A hot spot for late-night dining, Noir's is decidedly Spanish-Moroccan, but the
is generally inundated with well-dressed hipsters on the prowl. Eschew the mo
expensive entrées in favor of lighter treats like tapas, which skillfully comb
simple ingredients. Take advantage of the cheap entrées and splurge on a go
bottle of wine from their extensive list of French vintages. *32 Grand St. (at Thom*
son St.), 212-431-7910. Ⓐ Ⓒ Ⓔ *to Canal St.* **$$**

Chanterelle *French*
Dining is art at this manhattan icon. Everything about chanterelle speaks to its e
quence; the seats are big and comfortable, the silverwear divine, and theambiar
soothing. A meal here is not just a meal, but an event. The tasting menu allo
diners to experience a wide berth of excellent dishes. Although chanterelle
bit pricey for students, make sure to stop by at least once during your time
new york—you won't soon forget it. *2 Harrison st. (At hudson st.), 212-966-69*
Chanterellenyc.Com. ❶ *To franklin st.* **$$$**

BEST TRIBECA
BREAKFAST

Low-for-these-parts prices and the cute setting keep all-American **KITCHENET**
hopping, and the breakfasts are large and luscious. For lunch, try the Soup
across the street, owned and operated by the same team. *80 W. Broadway*
Warren St.), 212-267-6740. ❶ ❷ ❸ *to Chambers.* **$$**

F. Illi Ponte Ristorante *Italian*
Down the river, a demure dining experience awaits. Live jazz, dim lighting, a wo
burning stove, a cigar room, a lounge, and definitive brick décor frame a bea
ful sunset over the Hudson. The service isamiable, the environment relaxed a
pleasant. With a fine selection of wine and a great menu, you cannot go wro

39 Desbrosses St. (at Washington St.), 212-226-4621, filliponte. com. ❹ ❻ ❸ ❶ *to Canal St.* **$$$**

The Harrison *American*

In a dining room that evokes an old wooden ship's, the seafood at this Tribeca classic is delectable and all dishes are well-presented. The service is well-choreographed and runs like clockwork, with a variety of servers attending to their own individual roles in the presentation of the meal. The staff is knowledgeable and eager to advise diners on the freshest, most seasonable choices to suit their wants. A large banquet room in the basement with a wine cellar makes this restaurant a fine choice for large groups, while the cozy atmosphere upstairs and the outdoor seating make it perfect for intimate parties as well. *355 Greenwich St. (at Harrison St.), 212-274-9310, theharrison. com.* ❶ *to Franklin St.* **$$$**

Ninja New York *Sushi*

When you've finally cleared the dark maze at the entrance, and emerged into this simulation of a Japanese feudal village, you'll know you're in for a treat. Ninja New York is a themed Japanese restaurant whose theme was built around the food, not the other way around. The exquisite Japanese-fusion food is filled with surprises that will knock your Ninja slippers off, from a smoke-pouring grapefruit (after you pull out the katana) to a flame-spitting conch. The waiters, dressed as ninjas, of course, are incredibly knowledgeable and friendly, preparing a few dishes at your table. Although Ninja is very pricey, it makes the perfect choice for a special occasion. *Hiyah! 25 Hudson St. (bet. Duane & Reade Sts.), 212-274-8500. ninjanewyork.com.* ❶ ❷ ❸ *to Chambers.* **$$$**

Tribeca Grill *American*

This flagship of the DeNiro restaurant empire is a haven for those who like to enjoy a little celebrity watching with their meal. Movie big shots from the nearby Tribeca Film Center can be found sharing the spacious, darkwood and brick dining room with plenty of other notables and some commoners, all there to enjoy the Grill's New American cuisine. And oh yeah, if you ever manage to finish star-gazing, the food here also happens to be superb. *375 Greenwich St. (at Franklin St 212-941-3900, myriadrestaurantgroup.com/tribecagrill.* ❶ *to Franklin St.* **$$**

Yaffa's Tea Room *Desserts*

Alice in Wonderland stumbles out of the rabbit hole and finds herself in Ne York. Burgundy velvet and antique crystal chandeliers make you feel like a co mopolitan Queen of Hearts while sipping your tea. Reservations are required f high tea ($20), served Monday through Saturday 2pm-5pm *353 Greenwich S 212-274-9403.* ❶ *to Franklin St.* **$$**

NIGHTLIFE

Brandy Library *Bar*

Similar to other specialty lounges that serve only wine, vodka or champagne, th spot is strictly brandy. The liquor is placed like books on shelves, and waitress climb ladders in order to get your drink. The deep leather chairs and availat cigars bring in a neighborhood crowd as well as tired businessmen looking f a little solace. Good for both the person who enjoys a stiff drink as well as th cocktail-loving lightweights. *25 N. Moore St. (at Varick St.), 212-226-5545; brand brary.com.* ❶ *to Franklin St.*

Church Lounge *Lounge*

One bartender described the Tribeca Grand Hotel's bar confidently as the cu tural, sexual, cocktail center of Tribeca. Yet, it seems more like a tourist stop "I'm cool, I Swearville." Ironically, you'll be laughed at if you order a Cosmopolit (they're so over!). Drinks are expensive, too: martinis cost $12. *2 Sixth Ave. (White St., in the Tribeca Grand Hotel), 212-519-6678.* ❶ ❶ ❶ ❶ *to Canal St.*

COOLEST
LOCAL MUSIC

The **KNITTING FACTORY** has long been one of New York City's cool mus havens, and the tradition continues there today. One can kick back with a drink two and listen to eclectic music from the likes of artists such as Ashlee Simps and Dead Meadow. Bring your hipster gear or feel out of place. *81 Franklin 212-219-3006, knittingfactory.com.* ❶ *to Franklin St.*

Liquor Store Bar *Bar*

Huge front windows, an oak bar, and sidewalk seating render this bar irresi ible. The charming, slightly motley group of locals welcomes newcomers as fre victims for their stale jokes. Heaven for any true bar lover. *235 W. Broadw (at White St.), 212-226-7121, liquorstore.net. Cash Only.* ❶ ❶ ❶ *to Canal*

ARTS

Apex Art *Galleries*

Off the beaten path of art and offering a fresh perspective, this is one of the b places to find innovative work. Appreciating it comes easily also, since the staff are far less aloof than most of their SoHo counterparts. Shows tend to featu a combination of efforts by a few different artists and include both painting and sculpture. *291 Church St. (bet. Walker and White Sts.), 212-431-5270, apexart.org. Hours: T-Sa I I am-6pm* ❶ *to Franklin St.*

Collective Unconscious *Performance Space*
Every possible configuration of campy art and anti-art event takes place at this downtown performance space. The hip, tongue-in-cheek crowd doesn't take anything very seriously, especially the art world. Look out though, they're in the process of raising money to move into new digs. *279 Church St. (at White St.). 212-254-5277, weird.org.* ❶ *to Franklin St.,* ❶ Ⓜ Ⓝ Ⓡ Ⓦ Ⓩ ❻ *to Canal St..*

The Flea Theater *Theater*
The home of the Bat Theater Company, you'll be pleased to find both experimental productions of classics and recent, more avant-garde plays. Plays usually run for a week or two, so catch them while you can. You'll also find poetry readings at the theater. *41 White St. (bet. Broadway and Church St.), 212-226-2407, theflea.org.* ❶ *to Franklin St.,* ❶ Ⓜ Ⓝ Ⓡ Ⓦ Ⓩ ❻ *to Canal St..*

SoHo Repertory *Theater*
Home for anything new and compelling, from freshly adapted literary works to personal dramas. Well known for excellent casting choices, the theater generally offers several overlapping runs from which to choose. *46 Walker St. (bet. Broadway and Church Sts.), 212-941-8632, sohorep.org. Cash Only.* ❶ Ⓜ Ⓩ Ⓡ Ⓦ *to Canal St.,* ❶ *to Franklin St.*

TriBeCa Performing Arts Center *Theater*
Inconspicuously housed in the main building of the Borough of Manhattan Community College, this large venue is easy to miss. That would be a shame since the programming is excellent, offering multicultural music, dance, theater from around the world, and urban youth-themed performances consistent with the diverse student population. The college connection means cheap student-rate tickets. *199 Chambers St. (at Greenwich St.), 212-220-1460, tribecapac.org.* ❶ ❷ ❸ *to Chambers St.*

HOPPING

ISSEYMIYAKE *Clothing : Designer*
Designed by Frank Gehry, Tribeca ISSEYMIYAKE—yes, that's how the staff insists you spell the name of experimental Japanese fashion designer Issey Miyake's boutique—looks like the world's most exclusive robot clothing store. There are odd, android-like mannequins, anime murals, and a giant titanium tornado in the middle, and that's just the beginning. Also awesome is Miyake's A-POC line; it stands for A Piece of Cloth, with dotted lines along which you can cut out your clothes. *119 Hudson St. (at N. Moore St.), 212-226-0100.* ❶ *to Franklin St.*

Sufi *Books*

If there were such a thing as a neighborhood spiritual bookshop, this bookst
would hold that place in Tribeca. With a quiet atmosphere and a soft-spoken s
the selection contains a wealth of Eastern religion resources along with sma
sections on Judaism and Christianity. No matter what your spiritual persuas
is, there's something to feed your quest. There's also a large space next door
meditation and yoga classes. *227 W. Broadway (bet. Franklin and White Sts.), 2*
334-5212, sufibooks.com. Hours: T-Sa 1pm-7:30pm ❶ to Franklin St.

HOTELS AND HOSTELS

Cosmopolitan Hotel

Located in the heart of Tribeca, this hotel is perfect for exploring the exc
ment of Lower Manhattan. With comfortable, newly-renovated rooms
are small but boast a private bathroom and a Starbucks on the first floor,
hotel will send you off well-rested and ready to discover the best the city
to offer. *95 W Broadway (at Chambers Street). 888-895-9400 or 212-566-1*
cosmohotel.com, Rooms are $119-$149 for a double. ❶ ❷ ❸ to Chamber

Soho & Nolita

FAMED FASHION MAG *Vogue* may keep its office in Times Square, but it clearly draws inspiration from the streets of SoHo. The narrow, often cobblestone streets are choked with rail-thin models sporting the latest fashions and street vendors hawking the hottest accessories. This isn't the place to score cheap (or fake) Louis Vuittons—that's a few more downtown subway stops away, in Chinatown. No, the buys here are the real deal, with most flagship designers represented at dedicated stores. Fashion aside, the area also offers a number of chi-chi bars, indie cinemas, and spacious galleries.

SoHo—short for South of Houston Street (and don't pronounce the latter like a Texas town unless you want your inner-tourist showing)—was once a haven for struggling artists who couldn't make the midtown rent. Now, 5pm sees a changing of the guard at the Prince Street subway station, as those who work (but could never afford to live) in the area pass by the Wall Street raiders returning home.

Despite the reign of haute couture, bargain buys can still be found, especially with the street vendors lining Canal, Prince, and Broadway. Just make sure to sacrifice fashion for comfort and wear sneakers: the streets and sidewalks of SoHo aren't always well maintained.

Mott, Mulberry, and Elizabeth Streets comprise the area just north of Little Italy, affectionately called NoLita. With its quiet streets, tiny shops, and little cafés, NoLita has a charming, almost dainty, flavor. It's not as crowded as SoHo (yet), so enjoy peacefully strolling through the tree-lined streets while you can. You'd be hard-pressed to find prettier scenery in the city.

HISTORY

>>SOHO FIRST DREW widespread attention after Mayor John V. Lindsay a[nd] Jane Jacobs succeeded in striking down one of Robert Moses' notorious urb[an] renewal projects—a proposal to link the East River bridges and the Holla[nd] Tunnel by carving an east-west expressway through Broome Street. Voters, a[ca]demics, and politicians all eventually agreed that tax revenue from the garme[nt] industries on Broome was essential, and the Renaissance-style buildings of wh[at] many began to call SoHo were sturdy, handsome, and ultimately habitable.

SoHo's low rents and spacious lofts initially attracted artists searching for a[m]ple workspaces, and they began discreetly moving into the area. Although res[id]ing in a light-manufacturing zone was illegal, landlords turned a blind eye. [As] as more and more "illegal" lofts materialized, legalization became inevitable [in] the area with the greatest number of resident artists, laws slowly changed [to] accommodate more and more of them legally. At first, only those working [in] the visual fine arts were eligible; in 1968, eligibility was extended to those in t[he] performing and creative arts. Finally, in 1971, a series of legal solutions result[ed] in SoHo's designation as the first mixed-use zone for artist housing.

Concurrently, an Artist Certification Committee was formed to ensure th[at] SoHo housing went only to artists; thus, the reflexive element of the law [be]gan to reinforce SoHo's privileged status. Overseen by the Department [of] Cultural Affairs, this 20-person committee demanded hard proof that prosp[ec]tive residents were artists, often examining slides or other work samples. T[he] committee still operates today, though it has no enforcement power and bo[th] residents and landlords now routinely ignore the old artists-only policies.

WHAT TO SEE

Haughwout Building

Besides being a fine demonstration of SoHo architecture—its nickname is [the] Parthenon of Cast Iron—this building, which was built in 1897, was once ho[me] to the very first commercial passenger elevator, which was steam-powe[red] back in those days. *488-492 Broadway (at Broome St.)*, ❶ ❻ ❼ ❽ *to Cana[l]*

Prada

This is possibly one of the coolest shopping experiences you will ever co[me] across. The Prada store in SoHo is really more like a high-tech museum - [in] fact, before it was revamped by hip Dutch architect Rem Koolhass of OM[A] housed the SoHo branch of the Guggenheim. You walk in and a huge ro[und] glass elevator lowers you to the bottom floor. In lieu of the elevator, you [can] take the wooden staircase down to the room where most of the merchan[dise] is located. Here, Prada purses and sunglasses are on display museum-styl[e in] glass cases, moveable vertical metal display cages can be rolled back and fo[rth] to change around the configuration of the room, and high-tech gadgets [to] entertain you all day. The changing rooms have sliding glass doors with [an] electric current running through that allows the doors to act like a two-w[ay]

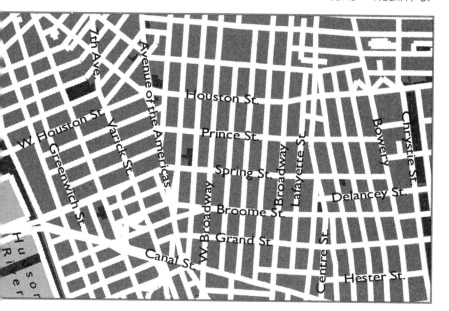

person changing can see the customers outside, but they can't see the person stripping down. *575 Broadway (at Prince St.), 212- 334-8888, prada.com. Hours: M-Sa 11am -7pm, Su 12pm–6pm*  *to Prince St.*

New York City Fire Museum

If you were one of those kids who dreamt of becoming a firefighter, this is the place to go. Real firefighters guide visitors through the museum, where you can look at old firefighting tools and observe the memorial exhibit in honor of the brave New York firemen who risked their lives on September 11. The museum is also located in the former headquarters of Engine 30, a beautiful building dating from 1904. *278 Spring Street (between Varick and Hudson), 212-691-1303, nycfiremuseum.org. Hours: T-Sa 10am – 5pm, Su 10am – 4pm* **C** **E** *to Spring St.* **1** *to Houston.*

Charlton Street

See this historic SoHo street, which is occupied by redbrick town houses dating from the 1820's and 30's. Nearby King and Vandam streets were once the grounds for an estate called Richmond Hill, which was once the pad of historical heroes George Washington, John and Abigail Adams, and Aaron Burr. *West of 6th and south of West Houston.* **C** **E** *to Spring St.*

Little Singer Building

A masterpiece of famous architect Ernest Flagg, this 1904 building is one of the last built in the cast-iron style. Nearby on Broadway is the Singer Tower, which was once the tallest building in the world. *561 Broadway.* **N** **R** **W** *to Prince St.*

Prada

BEST SOHO STROLL

Between Grand and Houston Streets, **WEST BROADWAY** is quite the scene. Local artists and jewelry makers set up stands opposite designer Europea imports. The streets are wide and beautiful, making for a fun window-shoppir and vendor browsing experience. The scene here is more international, so e pect to hear some sexy accents, especially at Broome Street where Downtow Cipriani is still a favorite italiano hang out. ⓒ ⓔ *to Spring St*

WHERE TO EAT

Bistrot Margot *French*

A French treasure hidden in SoHo, Bistrot Margot is gourmet enough to satis its upper-crust older patrons who don't mind the bloated prices. A surpl of two-person tables and seductive lighting emphasize its potential as a da restaurant. *26 Prince St. (bet Mott and Elizabeth St.), 212-274-1027.* ⓑ ⓓ ⓥ *to Broadway-Lafayette St.,* ⓺ *to Bleecker St..* **$**

Blue Ribbon Sushi *Sushi*

Let the simple yet elegant modern Japanese decor draw you into this fashio able SoHo sushi haven and you shall be rewarded with yellowtail and tu of so fresh they'll melt in your mouth. The restaurant is open for dinner ur 2am but accepts no reservations, so weekend waits can be long because of diminutive dimensions. Closed Mondays. *119 Sullivan St. (bet. Prince and Spr Sts.), 212-343-0404.* ⓒ ⓔ *to Spring St.* **$$$**

Café Habana *Latin*

A great spot for watching the SoHo crowd outside. Come for the shockin good grilled corn and delicious plantains, or a Cuban sandwich. Avoid the lc wait by heading next door to Habana's sister takeout café. *17 Prince St. Elizabeth St.), 212-625-2001.* ⓕ ⓥ *to Broadway-Lafayette St.* **$**

Ceci-Cela *Desserts*

Homemade sorbet and café au lait evoke Cote d'Azur at this charming pat

Café Habana

serie perched on the edge of Little Italy. The chat room in back is oh-so-perfect for nibbling on petit-fours and playing salon and the chocolate gateau and croissants are famous all over the city. *55 Spring St. (bet. Mulberry and Lafayette Sts.), 212-274-9179.* ⑥ *to Spring St.,* ⓝ ⓡ ⓦ *to Prince St.* **$**

Fanelli's *American*

One of the last remnants of pre-gentrification SoHo, everything about Fanelli's is unpretentious, from the spare decor to the sturdy pub-style food. Its modesty keeps it going strong as an alternative to all the chic and trendy restaurants in the neighborhood, but be prepared to wait. On weekends they're often packed for hours. *94 Prince St. (at Mercer St.), 212-226-9412.* ⓝ ⓡ ⓦ *to Prince St.* **$**

Kin Khao *Thai*

Don't be surprised to see a supermodel sitting down the bench from you at this trendy Thai eatery. However, the atmosphere isn't prohibitive to normal people—once you get inside, the wait staff is unpretentious and the décor is both beautiful and comfortable. Stick to one of the noodle dishes, which are always appetizing. *171 Spring St. (bet. W. Broadway and Thompson St.), 212-966-3939.* ⓒ ⓔ ⑥ *to Spring St.* **$$**

The Kitchen Club *American*

Turquoise curtains, a huge checkered tile floor, and French doors that open out to the street give Kitchen Club its unique atmosphere. Serving up Continental cuisine with a Japanese twist, this "friendly little place" is as eccentric in your mouth as it is on your eyes. *30 Prince St. (at Mott St.) 212-274-0025.* ⓝ ⓡ ⓦ *to Prince St.,* ⓑ ⓓ ⓕ ⓥ *to Broadway-Lafayette St.* **$$$**

SEXIEST SERVING OF COUSCOUS

Optimally located near the corner of Prince and Mott Sts., the French Moroccan **CAFÉ GITANE** is the place to check out the fashion set while lingering over a citron presse. This small but stylish space is always buzzing with beautiful people. The food is simple, flavorful and inexpensive. So grab a French magazine (their collection is extensive), get some couscous, and savor the view. *242 Mott St. (at Prince St.), 212-334-9552. Cash only.* ⑥ *to Spring St.,* ⓑ ⓓ ⓕ ⓥ *to Broadway-Lafayette St.*

Mae Mae Café *American*

Although it shares a street with storage units and sketchy warehouses, this SoHo gem is cozy, romantic, and friendly. Mae Mae's folk art and candle-lit wall sconces create a homey feel. Thursday night jazz from 6-9 makes Mae Mae a great dating spot, especially for people who need something to focus on besides each other. (No worries, the music is not too loud to prevent conversation if your date is interesting.) The food is light and reasonably priced, though not terribly creative. The periodic drink specials (blueberry lemonade and white wine sangria in the summer) compliment the reliable fare. *68 Vandam (bet. Hudson and Varick), 212-924-5109.* ① *to Houston.* **$**

Fanelli's

The Mercer Kitchen *American*

At this café specializing in American provincial food, you can sit under the side
walk on a SoHo street in a glass-encased dining room and watch people wal
ing above. The celebrity-spotting is fabulous, while the prices are impressiv
99 Prince St. (at Mercer St.), 212-966-5454. Ⓝ Ⓡ Ⓦ *to Prince St.* **$$$**

Nolita House Restaurant & Bar *American*

This appropriately titled restaurant is located in the newest "hippest-place-to
be" in the city. Nolita House serves comfort food with high-quality ingre
ents. The entrées are delicious, particularly the tuna. The real star of the men
though, is the artisinal cheeses that can serve as appetizer or dessert. 7
Houston St. (bet. Mulberry and Mott St.), 212-625-1712, nolitahouse.com. Ⓑ
Ⓕ Ⓥ *to Broadway-Lafayette St.,* Ⓥ *to Bleecker St.* **$$**

Once Upon A Tart *Bakery*

Delectable pastries, both savory and sweet, are much cheaper than the sta
dard coffeecakes in Manhattan's corporate espresso bars...and much tastier. E
erything is made in their own bakery. The crowd here is very loyal, and brun
is always packed. *135 Sullivan St. (bet. Houston and Prince Sts.), 212-387-88*
Ⓒ Ⓔ *to Spring St.* **$**

Penang *International*

This lively, decked out Malaysian eatery is usually packed on weekends, an
rightfully so; the food is innovative and tasty, the crowd young and hip. To avo
a wait, try eating at the bar downstairs, which features a lounge and live mus
109 Spring St. (bet. Greene and Mercer Sts.), 212-274-8883, penangnyc.com.
to Spring St. Additional Locations: 1596 Second Ave. (at 83rd St.), 212-585-38
240 Columbus Ave. (at 71st St.), 212-769-3988. **$$**

Public *American*

Part restaurant, part bar, part heaven on steroids, Public is the future of re
taurant style. With an exotic, satisfying menu, you will not leave hungry. Be su

to visit the bar for unusual, refreshing, and tasty concoctions. This restaurant is sure to impress both yourself and any guest. *210 Elizabeth St., 212-343-7011.* ⑥ *to Spring St.,* Ⓝ Ⓡ Ⓦ *to Prince St.,* Ⓕ Ⓥ *to Broadway-Lafayette,* ① Ⓜ Ⓩ *to Bowery.* **$$$**

Rice *Asian Fusion*

A line around the block means that something good is going on in this cramped, healthy Asian joint. It's cheap and takes cash only but is worth the wait. Light on both your wallet and waistline. *227 Mott St. (bet. Prince and Spring Sts.), 212-226-5775.* Ⓝ Ⓡ Ⓦ *to Prince St.,* ⑥ *to Spring St. Additional location in Brooklyn.* **$**

Salt *American*

In honor of its name, Salt offers three different varieties of the mineral on its communal tables: Hawaiian pink and French grey sea salts next to plain old Morton's. Salt is all about refined simplicity and comfortable elegance. If you come with a date, hope for a two-top window seat, order a smooth wine, and enjoy a fantastic meal. The asparagus and sweet pea risotto, monkish with artichoke puree, and chocolate cake with almond olive oil ice cream make a hearty, delicious meal. *58 Macdougal St, (bet. Houston and Prince), 212-674-4968.* ① *to Houston St.* Ⓑ Ⓓ Ⓕ Ⓥ *at Broadway-Lafayette St.,* ⑥ *to Bleecker St.* **$$$**

Spring Street Natural *Vegetarian*

Its wide windows are perfect for people watching. Despite the copious offerings of twigs and figs on the menu, there's plenty of chicken and fish to offer diners who aren't too health-conscious. The breads are unusual, the water get-it-yourself, and the staff somnolent, but the food is worth the wait and the prices are good. *62 Spring St. (at Lafayette St.), 212-966-0290.* ⑥ *to Spring St.* **$$**

Sui *Sushi*

With aqua colored walls, a mini waterfall at one end of the seating area, and tanks of exotic fish everywhere, the décor of this stellar sushi spot is cheerily oceanic. The underwater theme prevails in the atmosphere as well as in the food, but terrestrial treats make their way into the sushi as well; one of Sui's special sushi rolls come wrapped in prosciutto. Some other unique amalgamations have the raw fish slathered with Thai peanut sauce or drizzled with salsa. This place is great for sushi devotees and culinary adventurers alike. *54 Spring St., (bet. Lafayette and Mulberry St.), 212-965-9838.* ① Ⓜ Ⓩ *to Bowery,* ⑥ *to Spring St.* **$$**

CHEAPEST
PEACE OF MIND

No doubt the ten-dollar sandwiches finance the rent at high-ceilinged **SPACE UNTITLED**, but dorm-room dwellers can take advantage of this capacious café and gallery for the price of a cup of coffee. *133 Greene St. (bet. Houston and Prince Sts.), 212-260-8962.* Ⓡ Ⓦ *to Prince St.* **$**

Woo Lae Oak *Korean*

This Korean import's barbecue is to die for. You know you're not in Benihana

when Kate Hudson, Edward Norton, or Kevin Spacey drift by your table. Tr
the filet mignon, black tail shrimp, or ostrich – all grilled tableside – or order th
delicious cod in a spicy garlic sauce. It tastes like sugar was caramelized on to
of it, creating perfect harmony in taste and texture. Every dish looks and taste
like a million bucks, establishing it as one of the city's best Asian restaurants. Fc
desert, the homemade sorbets prove that Woo Lae Oak's expertise covers a
the bases. *148 Mercer St. (bet. Houston and Prince Sts.), 212-925-8200.* **Ⓝ Ⓡ**
Ⓦ *to Prince St.* **$$**

Zoë *American*

The elegant décor and beautiful tables make it an appealing stop after walkir
the streets of SoHo. Booths line the walls and tables are set in the middle, o
fering an ideal level of privacy – perfect for a first date. Zoë offers a seasonal
menu with colorfully arranged dishes that thrill the taste buds and the eye
alike. The entrées are good, and the attentive, well-timed wait staff is happy t
suggest its favorites. *90 Prince St. (bet. Broadway and Mercer St.), 212-966-672*
Ⓝ Ⓡ Ⓦ *to Prince St.* **$$**

NIGHTLIFE

Botanica *Bar*

Botanica's Afro-Cuban decor and snappy but friendly bartenders make th
one of the neighborhood's most comfortable places to get sloppy. There's a fu
bar and a decent selection of draft beers, but don't ask for anything too con
plicated or silly unless you're prepared to take the heat. *47 E. Houston St. (be
Mulberry and Mott Sts.), 212-343-7251.* **Ⓑ Ⓓ Ⓕ Ⓥ** *to Broadway-Lafayette St*

PEE AND BE SEEN

The main attraction at stylish **BAR 89** is the fabulous unisex bathroom. Late
the glass doors ever so precisely and they become opaque; fumble, and you
be exposing everyone in the room to things better kept private. *89 Mercer*
(bet. Spring and Broome Sts.), 212-274-0989. **Ⓡ Ⓦ** *to Prince St.*

The Cub Room *Lounge*

Business attire is the unwritten dress code for the young and affluent wh
enjoy expensive cocktails and a serious pick-up scene, while lounging on th
comfy furniture. *131 Sullivan St. (at Prince St.), 212-677-4100; cubroom.com.*
Ⓔ *to Spring St.*

Culture Club *Club*

This is the place for the ultimate '80s escape, with Reagan-era pop served
in this two-story club. It boasts a casual atmosphere, murals of your favori
'80s artists, and even a Delorean that Michael J. Fox would envy. *179 Varr*
St. (bet. King and Charlton Sts.), 212-243-1999, nerveana.com. **Ⓘ** *to Houston*

Don Hill's *Club*

This clubhouse is consistently crowded with crazy college kids, especially

Wednesday nights for the Beauty Party, when kids come out to groove '80s style, and Hot Fudge Sundays, which features soul and hip hop music, and the Famous Squeeze Box on Friday nights, a gay rock drag queen party. *511 Greenwich St. (at Spring St.), 212-219-2850, donhills.com.* Ⓒ Ⓔ *to Spring St.,* ❶ *to Canal St.*

Ear Inn *Bar*

This place used to be a brothel. These days it's just a homey bar that attracts a hip, yuppie crowd. Ask about their seasonal poetry readings. *326 Spring St. (bet. Greenwich and Washington Sts.), 212-226-9060, earinn.com.* ❶ *to Houston St.*

Madame X *Lounge*

This two floor cozy lounge sets the mood with bright red decorations and comfy antique couches. The lounge-y feel is representative of the weeknights, while it turns into a packed club spot on the weekend, but a DJ spins all week. You might want to come early if you want to get drinks and a spot. The specialty beverages are tasty and the bartenders are very friendly. The outside garden area is a great little treat for a New York bar. It used to be a place where you got away from smoke but with the new laws its a great alternative to the crowded interior. Check out the art exhibits. Cover charge of $5 on weekends. *94 W. Houston St. (bet. LaGuardia Pl. and Thompson St.), 212-539-0808, mada-mexnyc.com.* ❶ *to Houston St.,* Ⓝ Ⓡ *to Prince St.*

ñ *Lounge*

Savor pitchers of sangría while admiring the Wednesday night flamenco dancers, and don't even try to resist the tapas. It's tiny, though, so stake out a place early and camp out all night. *33 Crosby St. (bet. Broome and Grand Sts.), 212-219-8856.* ❶ Ⓜ Ⓝ Ⓡ Ⓦ Ⓩ ❻ *to Canal St.*

Pravda *Lounge*

Pravda embodies neither post-Soviet mayhem nor hard-core proletariat boozing. Still, the 80 flavors of vodka (including the bourgeois mango and raspberry), caviar, and rust-tinted decor almost justify the name. High-class SoHo-ites eschew communism for black market prices. *281 Lafayette (bet. Prince and Houston Sts.), 212-226-4696.* ❻ *to Bleecker St.*

The Room *Bar*

The Room's bar is made up of two rooms with very different vibes. Room #1 is very narrow and the bar is illuminated with candles. Room #2 also has candles, but they are scattered alongside plush velvet couches, creating a more relaxed atmosphere. By foregoing the hard liquor, the bar focuses on extensive beer and wine options. *144 Sullivan St. (bet. Houston and Prince Sts.), 212-477-2120.* Ⓝ Ⓡ *to Prince St.,* ❶ *to Houston St.*

SoHo:323 *Lounge*

Once you find the unmarked lounge and get past the velvet rope, you'll find the brick walls and dim lighting enticing. The DJ's play loud music both upstair and down. In the upper level, comfortable couches and stools line the wall while bombshell waitresses bring you $9 till your wallet runs dry. *323 W Broad way, (bet. Grand and Canal). 212-334-2232, soho323.com.* Ⓐ Ⓒ Ⓔ *to Canal St.*

The SoHo Grand Bar *Bar*

This hotel bar is growing ever more popular for their martinis, yet sophisticate neighborhooders head here for their "nightcaps." *310 W. Broadway (bet. Cano and Grand Sts.), 212-965-3588, sohogrand.com.* Ⓐ Ⓒ Ⓔ *to Canal St.*

Sweet and Vicious *Lounge*

This Nolita hot spot lives up to its contradictory name. Austere brick an plenty of wood combine with pink bar lights and odd chandeliers, creatin a hip and comfortable vibe. Patrons pack into this trendy bar sipping G&T and shooting tequila like it's their job. If it's not raining, check out the smoker garden. Guaranteed to be a good time for small or large groups. *5 Spring S (bet. Bowery and Elizabeth Sts.), 212-334-7915, sweetandvicious.com.* Ⓖ *to Sprin St.,* Ⓝ Ⓡ *to Prince St.*

Temple Bar *Bar*

Leather seating and thick curtains make this bar a perfect place for an intimat gathering. Offers a wide selection of vodkas, wines and cocktails, includin their signature apple martini. The prices are a bit high but the drinks and foo pairings are very satisfying. *332 Lafayette St. (bet. Bleecker and Houston Sts. 212-925-4242, templebarnyc.com.* Ⓑ Ⓓ Ⓕ Ⓥ *to Broadway-Lafayette St.,* Ⓒ *to Bleecker St.*

ARTS

Deitch Projects *Galleries*

No stranger to the art world, this gallery has featured the works of Georg Condo, Keith Haring, and Yoko Ono, to name a few. Look for the installatio pieces and the precise attention paid to balancing the quirky exhibits with th more serious and mysterious ones. *76 Grand St. (bet. Wooster and Greene Sts. 212-343-7300, deitch.com. Hours: M-F 12pm-6pm.* Ⓝ Ⓡ *to Canal St.,* Ⓒ Ⓔ t *Spring St.*

New World Art Center *Galleries*

This "New Renaissance" gallery has an ambitious agenda, as it seeks to unit fine, graphic, literary, film, video, photographic, designing, and performing ar ists under one roof. The splintered focus keeps exhibitions turnover high an banishes stagnation. *250 Lafayette St. (bet. Prince and Spring Sts.), 212-966-436 Hours: M-Su 11am-6pm* Ⓒ Ⓔ *to Spring St.,* Ⓖ *to Spring St.,* Ⓝ Ⓡ *to Prince St.,* Ⓒ Ⓓ Ⓕ Ⓥ *to Broadway-Lafayette St.*

Peter Blum *Galleries*

Generally on the beaten path in terms of content, with frequent swerves int the odd and obscure. In addition to paintings and sculptures by known artists, architectural sketches and non-Western archeological artifacts have been known to make an appearance in this large, rectangular room. *99 Wooster St. (bet. Prince and Spring), 212-343-0441, peterblumgallery.com. Hours: T-F 10am-6pm* **C** **E** *to Spring St.*

Joyce SoHo *Dance*
All professional and aspiring dancers are familiar with this branch of the Joyce, the venue of choice for seeing all genres in a setting that's not stiflingly formal. Performances are on Friday and Saturday nights with tickets available 30 minutes before curtain. *155 Mercer St. (bet. Houston and Prince Sts.), 212-431-9233, joyce. org/soho.html. Cash only.* **N** **R** *to Prince St.,* **B** **D** **F** **V** *to Broadway-Lafayette St.*

The Ohio Theater *Theater*
Anything goes here, since the stage is rented out to various freelance performance groups. *66 Wooster St. (bet. Spring and Broome Sts.), 212-966-4844.* **N** **R** *to Prince St.,* **C** **E** **6** *to Spring St.*

Angelika Film Center *Film*
This independent film multiplex offers cappuccino and gelato from the well-stocked café, and there is always the possibility of running into celebrities like Bono or Brad Pitt. *18 W. Houston St. (at Mercer St.), 212-995-2000, angelikafilmcenter.com.* **B** **D** **F** **V** *to Broadway-Lafayette St.,* **N** **R** *to Prince St.,* **6** *to Bleecker St.*

SHOPPING

agnès b. *Clothing : Boutiques*
This superior French brand offers the finest in smart, up-to-date women's wear with a touch that makes you feel like Ingrid Bergman. The intimate space and wearability of the clothes makes for fun, stylish, and stress-free shopping. *79 Greene St. (bet. Spring and Prince Sts.), 212-431-4339, agnesb.com. Hours: M-Su 11am-7pm.* **N** **1** **R** *to Prince St.*

Anna Sui *Clothing : Designer*
Rock-n-roll style meets the runway and boutique world in this small designer outpost. Leather pants hang alongside sequined camouflage dresses, and the atmosphere is relaxed enough to allow for trying it all on without feeling conspicuous. It's expensive, but markdowns are often cheap enough for a splurge. *113 Greene St. (bet. Spring and Prince Sts.), 212- 941-8406, annasui.com, Hours: M-Sa 11:30am-7pm, Su 12pm-6pm* **N** **R** *to Prince St.,* **C** **E** *to Spring St.*

Anthropologie *Clothing : National Chain*
A grown-up version of Urban Outfitters, this shop offers a similar blend of housewares and clothing. Ceramics, embellished jewelry boxes, and fancy doorknobs sit alongside circle skirts and sweaters with sweet and funky details

like bows and eyelet trim. The shop provides both basics and fancier pieces th
are good quality, but a bit pricey, at around $70 and up. The clearance rac
generally yield good finds, though, and paying full price is worth it for piec
that you absolutely love, since the classic (and classy) clothes will unlikely go o
of style quickly. *375 W. Broadway (at Spring St.), 212-343-7070, anthropolog*
com. Hours: M-Sa 11am-8pm, Su 11am-6pm ⓒ ⓔ *to Spring St.,* ⑥ *to Spring .*
Additional location at 85 Fifth Ave.

Apple Store *Miscellaneous*

You can see how popular Mac has become in the past few years just by coun
ing the number of people plugged into iPods on the subway. The two Ma
stores in the city are nothing short of impressive with their chic white desig
and interactive approach to shopping. There are several stations where you ca
play around with the actual products as well as a helpful tech support cent
called the "Genius Bar." The SoHo location is a spacious, two-story store wi
a theater for workshops and presentations. *103 Prince Street, 212-226-312*
Hours: Su 9:30am-7pm, M-W & Sa: 9:30am-8pm, R-F 9:30am-9pm Addition
location in Midtown East. ⓝ ⓡ *to Prince St.*

A.P.C. *Clothing : Boutiques*

The clothes here are so simple and perfect that you wonder both why the
cost so much and how you've lived without them for so long. Classics like jea
and button-down shirts hover around the $100 range, so clasp your credit ca
tightly. It's hard to resist such flawless incarnations of old standards, no matt
what the price. *131 Mercer St. (bet. Prince and Spring Sts.), 212-966-9685, apc*
Hours: M-Sa 11am-7pm, Su 12pm-6pm ⓝ ⓡ *to Prince St.*

Aveda *Salons*

Haircuts that would normally set you back $65 are free in the training cla
Expect to wait a month. No coloring. *233 Spring St. (bet. Varick and Prince St.*
call for an appointment, 212-807-1492. ⓒ ⓔ *to Spring St.*

Betsey Johnson *Clothing : National Chain*

In-your-face girly chic means not being afraid to wear lace alongside faux leat
er or to pair zebra stripes with pink fishnets. Straightforward, sexy slip dress
are surprisingly affordable. The store itself looks like some funky teenagers to
a paintbrush to mom's boudoir. *138 Wooster St. (at Prince St.), 212-995-50*
betseyjohnson.com. Hours: M-Sa 11am-8pm, Su 12pm-7pm ⓝ ⓡ *to Prince*
Additional Locations in 248 Columbus Ave., 251 60th St., and 1060 Madison A

Dean & Deluca *Groceries*

One of New York's most revered specialty food stores, Dean & Deluca is t
Zabar's of downtown. Stop by for a caffeine break at the stand-up espres
bar, pick up some paté for your next dinner party, and ogle the produce se
tion, full of fruits and vegetables suitable for a still-life. They also offer specia
breads, meats, cheeses, desserts, and quality-packaged foods. *560 Broadway (*

Dean & Deluca

Prince St.), 212-226-6800. Hours: M-Sa 10am-8pm, Su 10am-7pm ® to Prince St., ❻ to Spring St.

Dorm USA *Housewares*

Need some inflatable furniture for your new pad? Have a fondness for housewares made of neon-colored plastic? You'll find all that and plenty more (from pens to pillboxes), most of it inexpensive and practical. And great for gifts. *382 W. Broadway (bet. Spring and Broome Sts.), 212-334-5580. Hours: M-Sa 11am-8pm, Su 11am-7pm* ❹ ❻ ❺ *to Spring St.,* ❶ ® *to Prince St.*

Face Stockholm *Beauty*

This Swedish based company excels at beauty basics. Personal attention is easy to come by in this airy boutique and the $9 nail polish selection makes you wish you had more fingers. A favored stop for fashionistas and actresses, you might even spot a celeb or two. *110 Prince St. (at Greene St.), 212-334-3900, facestockholm.com, Hours: M-W, F-Sa 11am-7pm, R 11am-8 p.m, Su 12pm-6pm* ❶ ® *to Prince St. Additional locations at 1263 Madison Ave. (at 90th St.) and 226 Columbus Ave. (at 70th St.).*

Housing Works Used Book Café *Books*

Housing Works is a minority-controlled organization dedicated to serving those living with and affected by AIDS in New York City. In this impressive space, with soaring ceilings and spiral staircases, one can browse over 45,000 new, used, and rare books, records, and CDs. Read at the café with a cup of coffee, attend an author reading or a concert (UBC has just launched its Live from Home Acoustic Music Series), or just ogle the hipster clientele. *126 Crosby St. (bet. Houston and Prince Sts.), 212-334-3324. Hours: M-F 10am-9pm, Sa 12pm-9pm, Su 12pm-7pm* ❶ ® *to Prince St.,* ❻ *to Bleecker St.*

INA *Clothing : Vintage & Consignment*

This Nolita standout store features fabulous designer vintage for both men and women. While the shop is known for its well-edited selection of gently worn

current pieces, the real treasures are vintage designer items. *21 Prince St. (be*
Mott and Elizabeth Sts.), 212-334-9048. Hours: Su-R 12pm-7pm, F-Sa 12pm-8p
 to Prince St., *to Spring St. Additional locations at 208 E. 73rd St., 10*
Thompson St.

Kate Spade *Accessories*
While Kate Spade started to attract followers with her fashionable handba
and luggage, her cult has grown as she expanded her Hamptons-chic line t
shoes, journals, paper, hats, and even some clothing. The sale items on the lowe
level are a good bet. Check out Jack Spade, the male counterpart to this stor
around the corner. *454 Broome St. (at Mercer St.), 212-274-1991, katespad*
com. Hours: M-Sa 11am-7pm, Su 12pm-6pm *to Prince St.*

Kidrobot *Miscellaneous*
The hipster mothership has landed in the heart of SoHo. Kidrobot is the adu
answer to FAO Schwartz, a place where you can placate your inner child with
out losing any cool points. The funky toys at this tiny store range from ine
pensive knick-knacks like adorable bear zipper pulls to pricier large pieces tha
would brighten up even the dreariest apartment. Kitsch and Japanese style
rule here, and even the most jaded ironist will want to take home one of th
cute Be@rbricks. *126 Prince St. (near Wooster St.), 212-966-6688, kidrobot.cor*
Hours: Su-R 11 a.m-8pm, F-Sa 11am-9pm *to Prince St.*

L'Occitane *Beauty*
This French favorite has an impressive selection of natural, effective skincar
products. And they smell great too—think verbena, lavender, rose, olive, ar
green tea. The standout Shea Butter line is a dry skin saver. They also have
great selection of their own perfumes and candles. *146 Spring St. (at Wooste*
St.), 212-343-0109, loccitane.com, Hours: M-Sa 11am-7pm, Su 11pm-7pm.
to Spring St. Additional locations at 247 Bleecker St. (at Leroy St.), 101 Universi
Pl. (at 12th St.), Grand Central Terminal, Lexington Passage, and 510 Madison Av
(at 52nd St.)

BEST FOR
UNDER THERE

MIXONA is one-stop luxe shopping for your lingerie drawer. A well-edite
mostly European selection of all things sexy—everything from mesh thong
to lacy corsets to hot bathing suits line the white walls of this large space. Th
store has a breezy vibe, cool music, and fun décor, so take your time browsin
The friendly staff and posh dressing rooms top it off and make shopping her
an absolute delight. *262 Mott St (bet Prince and Houston Sts.), 646-613-0100.*
 at Broadway-Lafayette St.

Opening Ceremony *Clothing : Boutiques*
Away from the frantic pace of lower Broadway, this independent boutique
full of sleek, hip clothes, which are a bit dressy, but not fussy, giving the store
clubby atmosphere without being snobbish. It's full of people genuinely inte
ested in design; every season they showcase unknown labels from a differen

country, so there's plenty of stuff on the racks and in the shoeboxes from Hong Kong all the way to Brazil. There are also very well priced in-house geometric sweaters, for those with slimmer means. *35 Howard St. (at Broadway), 212-219-2688. Hours: M-Sa 11am-8pm, Su 12pm-7pm* ❶ Ⓜ Ⓝ Ⓡ Ⓦ Ⓩ Ⓖ *to Canal St.*

SoHo Antiques Fair and Flea Market *Flea Markets*
It's not as large or as great for people-watching as the more famous Annex market, but that's an advantage if you are strapped for time or are not a flea-market veteran. Find everything from clothing to collectibles and furniture. *Broadway at Grand St., Hours: Sa-Su 9am-5pm* Ⓝ Ⓡ Ⓦ *to Canal St.*

Swatch *Accessories*
Everyone's favorite purveyor of wrist eye-candy is a sweet shop for those interested in checking the time and for people obsessed with the constantly evolving selection of the collect-'em-all series. Of course, there are also more serious styles for those interested in making a statement without going over the top. Prices run from inexpensive to "you-want-how-much-for-that-chunk-of-plastic?" *438 W. Broadway (at Prince St.), 212-613-0160, swatch.com. Hours: M-Sa 10am-8pm, Su 11am-7pm* Ⓒ Ⓔ *to Spring St. Additional locations at 100 W. 72nd St., 640 Broadway, and 1528 Broadway.*

Unis *Clothing : Boutiques*
This boutique targets the man who isn't interested in screaming his label affili-ation from down the street. The subtle, mostly mod, in-store designed clothing combines a reserved palette with relaxed but neat cuts, making clothes that aren't glittery or gutsy, but resemble those pieces you feel like throwing on any day in any mood, like they've been in your wardrobe forever. Not cheap, but reasonable for the neighborhood. *226 Elizabeth St. (at Prince St.), 212-431-5533, Hours: M-Sa 12pm-7pm, Su 12pm-6pm* Ⓖ *to Spring St.,* Ⓝ Ⓡ *to Prince St.*

What Comes Around Goes Around *Clothing : Vintage*
This is quite possibly the largest and most famous vintage store in all of New York, so be prepared to spend a lot of time scouring the store in search of that perfect faded baseball jersey. They have the largest selection of vintage jeans and leather and will make special orders so that you get exactly what you're looking for. Though it may be slightly overpriced, it is a worthwhile trip for the serious shopper. Don't be intimidated by their appointment-only policy; just be sure to phone in advance. *351 W. Broadway (bet. Grand and Broome Sts.), 212-343-9303, nyvintage.com. Hours: M-Sa 11am-8pm, Su 12pm- 7pm* Ⓝ Ⓡ *to Prince St.,* Ⓒ Ⓔ *to Spring St.*

RTS

Poets House
This free reading room and resource center houses the largest collection of poetry books in the country. Call for information about their programs. *72*

Spring St. (bet. Crosby and Lafayette Sts.), 212-431-7920, poetshouse.orgHours: ⑦ 11am-7pm, Sa 11am-4pm. ❻ *to Spring St*

HOTELS AND HOSTELS

Holiday Inn Downtown

With a friendly staff and newly renovated, clean rooms that offer HBO, th Holiday Inn sits serenely in the midst of all the action. Nearby is the incredib shopping of SoHo and a multitude of dining choices. Century 21, as seen c Sex in the City, is just downtown. At this hotel, location is what you are payir for. *138 Lafayette St (Near Canal St.) 800-465-4329 or 212-966-8898, holida inn-nyc.com. Rooms $179-$215.* ❶ Ⓜ Ⓝ Ⓡ Ⓞ Ⓦ ❷ *to Canal St.*

Howard Johnson's Express Inn

With AAA and AARP discounts available, this hotel is a good deal for the pric Because of its ideal SoHo location, it provides clean, but small, rooms to com back to after a day of sightseeing. While accommodations may not be five st its friendly staff is good enough to make your stay a pleasant one. Noise mig be a problem though, so make sure to request a room that does not face th main street. *135 E. Houston St. (at Forsyth St.) 800-446-4656 or 212-358-884 hojo.com. Rooms are $200-$250.* ❺ Ⓥ *to 2nd Ave.*

SoHo Grand Hotel

Everything about the Grand is in-sync with the neighborhood: artsy, avar garde types walk through the cutting-edge industrial lobby to their digs. Yc can even request a black goldfish to accompany you during your stay. In kee ing with the cyber-sexy image, you can make reservations on their websi *310 West Broadway (at Canal St.), 212-965-3000, sohogrand.com. Rooms start $250.* Ⓐ Ⓒ Ⓔ ❶ *to Canal St.*

Lower East Side

ROCK MUSIC BLARES out of bar windows, setting the beat for foot traffic along Ludlow Street. Young locals contend for sidewalk space on Orchard and Rivington Streets, past designer boutiques and ramshackle shops crammed with wedding dresses and roasting pans. Once one of the most overpopulated neighborhoods in the world, the narrow Lower East Side streets can at times feel cluttered and claustrophobic. It is still an area in continual transition, but make no mistake: unless you live in the projects, the smallest apartment in this vibrant and funky neighborhood will still cost you.

Until recently, a glance at the shifting demographics of this cacophonous corner of downtown read like a barometer of economic and political disempowerment in the city. With its dirt-cheap tenement housing, the Lower East Side was the first stop for free black farmers, 19th century immigrants of Irish, German and, most famously, Eastern European Jewish descent. Even now, the cultural tides continue to shift. The Puerto Rican and Dominican presence is still there, but it is waning as crowds of young professionals and black-clad creative types rush east from SoHo and Tribeca. Still, the shtetl remains immortalized by many of the neighborhood's most august institutions, from Katz's Delicatessen to the Lower East Side Tenement Museum to the Yiddish theaters and old-timers who still ply their wares on Orchard St. on Sundays.

Even if the character of Loisaida—the Spanish pronunciation of "Lower East Side"—is fading, it doesn't seem headed for extinction. Artists and political radicals have been finding solace in this easygoing area since the 1920s. Today, the mix of backgrounds is less aggressively hip and more comfortably heterogeneous than that in regions to the north. Walk east of Suffolk St. and the trendy boutiques and bars give way to home cooking, colorful murals, and salsa music.

HISTORY

>> FOR IMMIGRANTS TRAVELING from the provincial areas of Europe, the tenements that dominated the landscapes of the Lower East Side must have been a chilling sight. Infamous for providing the worst housing conditions in the city, these five-story firetraps absorbed most of the first major wave of immigrants that passed through Ellis Island and could not afford anything better. While the Lower East Side might have been cramped, it was beloved as the introduction to America by its inhabitants. During the late 19th century, the largely Irish population was joined by thousands of Italians and Eastern European Jews. Saturated by 1920, the Jewish population alone exceeded 400,000. New laws and housing plans failed to alleviate the crowdedness; as a result, the city's first housing project was built in 1936.

But great spirit arose out of poverty, and the neighborhood soon became as well known for its wealth of intellectual and artistic life as for its overcrowding. During the early part of this century, Yiddish theater flourished along Second Ave., area newspapers grew into forums for academic debate, and performers like George Gershwin, Irving Berlin, and the Marx Brothers cut their teeth in front of their first paying audiences.

The '50s and '60s saw revolutionaries, writers, and musicians populating the northern boundaries, an area that later expanded and became known as the East Village. The Lower East Side fell into decline as rents once again decreased while crime, drugs, and dilapidated housing became prominent neighborhood features. In the '80s, the area stabilized somewhat after an influx of Latinos arrived, causing many to dub the area "Loisaida."

WHAT TO SEE

The Lower East Side Tenement Museum

Long before hipsters struggled with important decisions like whether to hit up The Magician or Rothko on Tuesday night, scores of immigrants struggled to put food on the table and make their way in a new world. A visit to the Tenement Museum may put problems into perspective and give you a newfound appreciation for your seemingly cramped apartment or dorm. *108 Orchard (bet. Delancey and Broome), 212-431-0233, tenement.org.* **F** *to Delancey St.,* **M Z** *to Essex St.*

The Bowery Ballroom

You probably haven't heard of the bands treading the boards at this cozy music venue, but rest assured—you will a few months after their Bowery gig. This music staple is notorious for booking tomorrow's next big thing, so pop in and catch the next Death Cab For Cutie or Clap Your Hands Say Yeah before they

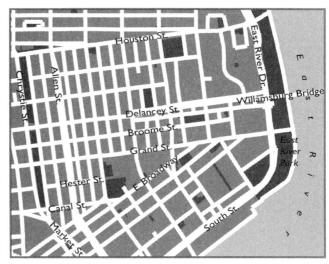

you know, sell out. *6 Delancey St., 212-533-2111, boweryballroom.com.* ⚫ ⓜ *to Bowery,* ⚫ *to Delancey St.* ⓙ ⓜ ❷ *to Essex St.*

WHERE TO EAT

Congee Village *Chinese*

This restaurant the outskirts of Chinatown is a bargain, serving congee (a savory Chinese porridge) in an astounding number of varieties. Get it plain or with chicken and duck, or be adventurous and try abalone and frog or the mysteriously named "thousand-year-old egg." There are hundreds of other dishes available, but congee is clearly the star. It reappears for dessert, sweet and deliciously gingery. *100 Allen St. (at Delancey St.), 212-941-1818.* ⚫ ⓙ ⓜ ❷ *to Delancey St.* **$**

El Maguey Y La Tuna *Mexican*

El Maguey's down-home decor breaks with the East Side upper crust, crumbling its neighborhood's pretensions into flaky forkfuls of banana piñata pastry. Try their signature enchiladas covered in a homemade mole sauce thick with ground nuts, spiced cocoa, and subtle fruit flavors. Traditional family recipes evoke the aromas and hues of Puebla, Mexico, the owners' hometown. The brilliant flags that festoon the ceiling and the Vírgen de Guadalupe watching from the wall complete the transformation, while sizeable crowds sip on smooth tequila cocktails. *321 E. Houston St. (bet. Ridge and Attorney), 212-473-3744, elmagueyylatuna. com.* ⚫ Ⓥ *to Second Ave.* **$**

Frankie's Spuntino *Italian*

Located on an unlikely Lower East Side block, Frankie's serves up spuntinos (snacks) in a friendly, romantic atmosphere. Even better, Frankie's provides Upper East Side quality without the stuffiness of other area restaurants. The dishes

are small, so order a little bit of everything: fresh and hearty soups, ecle[
salads, and any one of their great variety of cheeses. Be sure to check out
assortment of crostini—roasted slices of Italian bread piled high with m[
rooms and truffle oil, or with cannelini, capers, and lemon. In case you're
enamored yet, they buy local and organic produce. Frankie's is all heart, and
think we're in love. *17 Clinton St. (bet. Houston and Stanton Sts.), 212-253-23[*
F **J** **M** **Z** *to Delancey St.* **$$**

Grilled Cheese NYC *American*

All kinds of combinations of grilled cheese imaginable here, all ready for ta[
out. The place is very small, but how long does it take to eat a grilled che[
anyway? Answer: Four minutes. *168 Ludlow St. (bet. Houston and Stanton S[*
212-982-6600. Cash only. **F** **V** *to Second Ave.* **$**

BEST PASTRAMI IN THE
CITY (AND PERHAPS
THE WORLD)

Steaming pastrami, corned beef sandwiches and other artery-clogging del[
cies await at **KATZ'S DELICATESSEN,** where yellowing paint and curling p[
ers tell patrons to "Send a salami to your boy in the army." If you're not i[
pastrami, you can still come to reenact the famous "O" scene from *When H[*
Met Sally. Nothing much has changed here in the last 50 years. A dollar tip
one of the gruff, portly attendants behind the counter will score you a sa[
wich big enough for a family of five. Take a ticket when you go in, and don't l[
it: the consequences are dire. *205 E. Houston St. (at Ludlow St.), 212-254-22[
katzdeli.com.* **F** **V** *to Second Ave.* **$**

Kuma Inn *Asian Fusion*

At the top of a flight of steep, unassuming stairs, enter an intimate and tr[
quil dining area. Choose from a menu of 30 small plates (perfect for shari[
and three to five nightly specials that chef and owner King Phojanakong
designed with a unique fusion of Filipino and Thai flavors. The signature dis[
steal the show: astonishingly fresh bigeye tuna tartare, pan-fried pork tonka[

Katz's Delicatessen

with watercress salad and lime butter, and tamarind glazed Atlantic salmon in Thai coconut curry. Pair these with a flight of three sakes for $15 and the result is a diverse and savory experience. *113 Ludlow St., Second Fl. (bet. Rivington and Delancey Sts.), 212-353-8866. Cash only.* ❺ ❶ Ⓜ Ⓩ *to Delancey St.* **$**

Le Père Pinard *French*

Bare wooden tables and eclectically decorated stucco walls combine for a rustic Frenchambience, and so the sophisticated cuisine with an occasional Asian flair will come as a delicious surprise. Our favorites: Raw Tuna and Ginger Soy Sauce, the Shrimp, Mango, and Asparagus Salad, and the delightfully gooey Chocolate Valrhona Cake with coconut sorbet. *175 Ludlow St. (bet. Houston and Stanton Sts.), 212-777-4917.* ❺ Ⓥ *to Second Ave.* **$$**

Little Giant *American*

Little Giant pairs fresh seasonal ingredients with interesting variations on American classics to craft healthy hearty cuisine on the Lower East Side. Although the menu changes often, the scallops and artichokes are perfect examples of how Little Giant lets their quality ingredients speak for themselves: seasoned just enough to enhance the natural goodness of their foods. The sauces sometimes edge towards sour and the drinks were probably better at the idea stage, but the desserts (such as fresh-baked cookies and spiked hot chocolate) make up for any shortcomings. *85 Orchard St. (at Broome St.), 212-226-5047.* ❺ *to Delancey St.,* Ⓑ Ⓓ *to Grand St.* **$$**

CHEAPEST
ACTION MOVIE

On the ground floor of **ALCHEMY 106** is a welcoming but hip Internet café, where the WiFi is strong and clear and a purchase from their wide selection of coffees bides you half an hour at a terminal. Walk upstairs and you're in a virtual underworld, where twitching men hooked up to X-boxes and plasma TVs blast each other to bits to loud house music. *106 Delancey St. (bet. Essex and Ludlow Sts.), 212-358-8574.* ❺ ❶ Ⓜ Ⓩ *to Delancey St.* **$**

Oliva *Spanish*

Waiters at this Spanish gem greet regulars with a peck on the cheek, helping to make Oliva's the perfect spot to dine with a date or an intimate friend…if you're weird like that. Expect romanticambience with slow groovy music chosen by the manager (a local DJ). The food is impeccably presented and savory; choose from an excellent daily selection of seafood and paella on Sundays and Mondays, as well as the sweet dessert wines. You might leave with your wallet a bit lighter, but you'll be *muy contento*. *161 E. Houston St. (at Allen St.), 212-228-4143.* ❺ Ⓥ *to Second Ave.* **$$**

The Stanton Social *American*

With swanky wood tables and dim lighting, this modern three-story Lower East Side spot makes you feel a like a socialite the moment you open the door. Though its name may sound strange at first, by the time you leave you'll understand that dining here truly is a social experience. The menu is crafted especially

Teany

for table-sharing so that each person can order two to three appetizer ite
which are served continuously throughout the meal. Dishes are miniaturiz
versions of both classic and innovative foods; the Kobe Beef Burgers, Red Sn
per Tacos, and Crab Cake Corn Dogs are so cute you almost don't want to
them. (Almost.) Take one bite and you'll be sure to devour the whole thing. I
don't be fooled. Though the dishes may be small, they're deliciously rich and e
easily add up to a full meal before you know it. *99 Stanton St. (bet. Orchard e*
Ludlow Sts.). 212-995-0099, thestantonsocial.com. ● ⓥ *to Second Ave.* $

Teany *Café / Vegan*

Who knew faux chicken could be so convincing? A small crowd at an unassu
ing little café on the LES, it turns out. Here the stroller mom crowd mixes w
young gay professionals and too-cool hipsters in search of a Moby sighting e
sometimes works the tables). Co-owned by the famous DJ and his girlfrie
the atmosphere matches the food: fresh and fun. As the name suggests,
is the focal point of the dining experience, and they have 98 different ty
available for whatever ails you. The goat cheese salad, one of a few aber
tions on an almost only vegan menu, is light and makes for a perfect snack. T
vegan quicheamazes more in its contradicting terms than in taste. The desse
however, affirm a belief that a vegan diet can be quite an enticing one; try
cheesecake. *90 Rivington St., 212-475-9190, teany.com. Cash only.* ● ❶ Ⓜ
at Delancey St. $

NIGHTLIFE

ABC No Rio *Music*

ABC No Rio has been fusing politics with artistic expression since 1979. Fc
Not Bombs is a great program for those wishing to volunteer a helping hand
this organization helps feed the city's homeless. Also check out Books Throu
Bars, which brings books to people in prison. The Lower East Side Biograp
Project records the stories of the area's long-term residents, and for the arti
cally inclined, there are art classes and gallery shows. If you just want to ro
out, you can catch both local and touring bands at weekly Hardcore Matine

Arlene's Grocery *Music*

Arlene's has established itself as one of the premiere showcases for many New York-based independent labels. Local bands play for free here to build a fan base, and the sound is great, whether the day's music acoustic, pop, rock, or ska. *95 Stanton St. (bet. Ludlow and Orchard Sts.), 212-358-1633, arlenesgrocery.com. Cash only.* 🄵 🅅 *to Second Ave.*

Identity *Club*

This sexy clean-cut dive thumps techno and house music, and sits in the heart of the Lower East Side. A glittery disco ball rotating overhead and the bartenders chatting in French give this place an exotic *je ne sais quoi* quality. The excellent caiphroska blends the caipirinha of Brazil with vodka, using blond sugar cane, fresh orange juice and lime. For eats, try the Cypriot sausage and smoked kasseri cheese, which just might make you want to pack your bags and head for the Mediterranean. *511 E. 6th St. (bet. Aves. A and B), 212-995-8889.* 🄿 *to Astor Pl.*

'inoteca *Bar*

A three-year-old offshoot of its West Village counterpart, this popular Italian wine and tapas bar is perfect for a pretentious night out on the town. With thousands of bottles decking the walls and an eight-page wine list, they take their wine seriously. Yet the staff is more than friendly, as accommodating to non-connoisseurs as to wine snobs, and the open atmosphere (think wall to wall windows) makes this a perfect place for passing the hours with a bottle or two. The eclectic music is perfect for the East Village location, an odd mix between artsy and working class. The crowd is a notch above casual, and in their late twenties, but ideal for a college student looking for a place to sit and talk. *98 Rivington St. (at Ludlow St.), 212-614-0473, inotecanyc.com.* 🄵 🄾 🄼 🄹 *to Delancey St.*

MOST MEYER
FOR YOUR BUCK

The '20s gangster theme starts as you enter the door to the **LANSKY LOUNGE** and are greeted by a zoot-suited bouncer who could knock an average Gus out with his right-hand and steal the man's dame with his left. Named after Jewish gangster Meyer Lansky, the Lounge offers gigantic martinis and good food, all in honor of Meyer, Bugsy, and the rest of Murder, Inc. *104 Norfolk St (bet. Delancey and Rivington Sts.), 212-677-9489.* 🄵 🄹 🄼 🄾 *to Delancey St.*

Lolita *Bar*

A place that used to be a neighborhood secret has been disclosed. On weekends expect to find many stylish Lower East Siders at the bar and looking for someone to love. Fortunately, on weekdays Lolita remains fairly empty and an excellent place to go for happy hour, which occurs daily from 4pm-8pm and offersamazing drink specials. *266 Broome St. (near Allen St.), 212-966-7223.* 🄵 🄹 🄼 🄾 *to Delancey St.*

Max Fish *Bar*

Hipsters live it up at this bright and lively Ludlow standard, once a hotspot, now comfortably cool. Play pool with the regulars or spend a week's wages on pinball while enjoying the local artists' work that line the walls. *178 Ludlow (bet. Houston and Stanton Sts.), 212-529-3959, maxfish.com.* ❻ ❤ *to Second A*

Mercury Lounge *Music*
Once a headstone shop, the Mercury Lounge has established itself as a p miere venue for "just-breaking" bands. A high stage, excellent sound syst and standing room only for three to five acts per night, featuring acous alternative, and rock shows. 217 E. Houston St. (bet. Essex and Ludlow S 212-260-1214, mercuryloungenyc.com. ❻ ❤ *to Second Ave.*

LEAST ATTITUDE BELOW 14TH STREET

If you're looking for a respite from the usually pretentious LES bar scene, **THE MAGICIAN.** This neighborhood haunt is the kind of place where you get your beer served to you by a burly, un-sneering man, then gulp it while ting in big green chairs around a big wooden table. A jukebox full of solid r songs and hanging overhead lights set at just the right wattage make this p complete. Contrary to its name, this place needs no flashy tricks to please patrons. *118 Rivington St. (at Essex), 212-673-7851,* ❻ ❶ Ⓜ ❷ *to Delancey*

People Lounge *Lounge*
The crowd varies on any given night, as People often hosts large parties. T floors of lounge space provideample room for mingling and meeting, as w as comfortable couches and upholstered stools for hanging out with a gro of friends. Dim but warm lighting and high ceilings create the perfect social mosphere. The DJ's eclectic hip-hop mix and the delicious infused vodka dri will have you and your crew meeting and greeting like there's no tomorrow sure to order at least one People-People from the knowledgeable barten 163 Allen St., 212-254-2668, peoplelounge.com. ❻ ❤ *to Second Ave.*

Tuts *Bar*
A brand new Lower East Side dig, this chic yet cozy hookah bar serves gr food and delicious cocktails. Luxuriously decorated, with belly dancing p formances on the weekend and music playing on the big screen, the bar lounge also serves authentic North Africa-tinged Middle Eastern food. W over 15 flavors of deliciously smooth hookah, you'll be puffing away well i the night. 196 Orchard St. (bet. Houston and Stanton Sts.), 212-961-7507, tut com. ❻ Ⓜ ❷ ❶ *to Delancey St.*

Whiskey Ward *Bar*
Cheap beer, a jukebox blasting rock-and-roll, and a refreshingly mixed cro attract a growing group of regulars ranging from hipsters and college stude to the older sort who actually drink whiskey. Decked out in exposed brick w and handmade furnishings, the bar stocks dozens of whiskeys, six taps, and bottled beers. While not ideal for dancing, a friendly staff and a bustling v make this a great place to catch up with some friends and shoot some p 121 Essex St. (bet. Rivington and Delancey Sts.), ❻ Ⓜ ❷ ❶ *to Delancey St.*

Guitar store on Ludlow

Welcome to the Johnsons *Bar*
WTTJ's is where the shabby and chic go to meet each other. The décor is like the Brady Bunch's living room, but there are strong drinks at the bar and the jukebox blares classic rock and funk. *123 Rivington St. (bet. Essex and Suffolk Sts.), 212-420-9911.* 🅕 🅙 🅜 🅩 *to Delancey St.*

RTS

Participant, Inc. *Galleries*
The gigantic lines ever-present outside this shoebox-sized gallery attest to its increasing popularity with more than just an in-the-know art crowd. The space is devoted to live performances that blur the line between audience and performer, sometimes with a comic intent. Just don't forget to sign the ominous legal release wavers before entering. *95 Rivington St. (at Essex St.), 212-254-4334, participantinc.org. Hours: W-Su 12pm-7pm* 🅕 🅥 *to Second Ave.*

HOPPING

Alife Rivington Club *Clothing : Boutiques*
Part "Members Only" Club, part athletic-shoe heaven, this speakeasy-style shop is worth the time it takes to find. Offering a limited assortment of one-of-a-kind kicks in retro styles and crazy color combos, the shop is geared mostly to men with a serious addiction to shoes. *58 Rivington St. (Clinton and Suffolk Sts.), 212-375-8128, rivingtonclub.com. Hours: M-R 11am-7pm, Fri, Sat 11am-8pm, Sun 12pm-7pm* 🅕 🅥 *to Second Ave.*

American Apparel *Clothing : National Chain*
The draw here is a wide variety of tees and other cotton basics made in the USA to ensure fair labor and a living wage, without passing the expense onto the customer. As a rule, every piece seems to come in an assortment of colors that are easy on the eyes and mix effortlessly into your casual drawer. *198 Houston St. (at Orchard St.), 212-598-4600,americanapparelstore.com. Hours: M-R 11am-10pm, F-Sa 11am-12am, Su 12pm-9pm* 🅕 🅥 *to Second Ave.*

FRESHEST BREATH
OF AIR

Fresh air. Dear jaded New Yorker, do you even remember what fresh air
Refresh your memory with a trip to **VITALITY**, which offers up organic bev
ages, yoga classes, free wifi, and yes, an oxygen bar. Enjoy a deep breath of
that has more appealing flavors than the usual taxi exhaust fumes. *169 Lud
St. (between Houston and Stanton), 212-358-9822, vitalitynyc.com.* 🄵 🅥 *to S
ond Ave.*

Bluestockings *Books*

Pop into this volunteer run bookshop/activist center for queer camarade
unusual literary recommendations and a damn good almond butter brow
The store hosts or organizes events like movie nights, book readings, rant s
sions, and open mic performances. *172 Allen St. (at Stanton St.), 212-777-6C
bluestockings.com.* 🄴 🄵 🄼 🅩 *to Delancey St.*

TG-170 *Clothing : Boutiques*

The most sophisticated of the small boutiques on the Ludlow strip featu
simple dresses, skirts, and tops in subtle but fashionably retro designs, as wel
Freitag bags and wallets. *170 Ludlow St. (bet. Houston and Stanton Sts.), 212-9
8660, tg170.com. Hours: M-Sa 11am-8pm, Su 12pm-7pm* 🄵 🅥 *to Second A*

HOTELS AND HOSTELS

Howard Johnson's Express Inn

With AAA and AARP discounts available, this hotel is a good deal for the pr
Because of its ideal SoHo location, it provides clean, but small, rooms to co
back to after a long day of sightseeing. While accommodations may not be fi
star, the friendly staff is good enough to make your stay a pleasant one. No
might be a problem though, so make sure to request a room that does not f
the main street. *135 E. Houston St. (at Forsyth St.), 800-446-4656 or 212-3
8844, hojo.com. Rooms are $200-$250.* 🄵 🅥 *to Second Ave.*

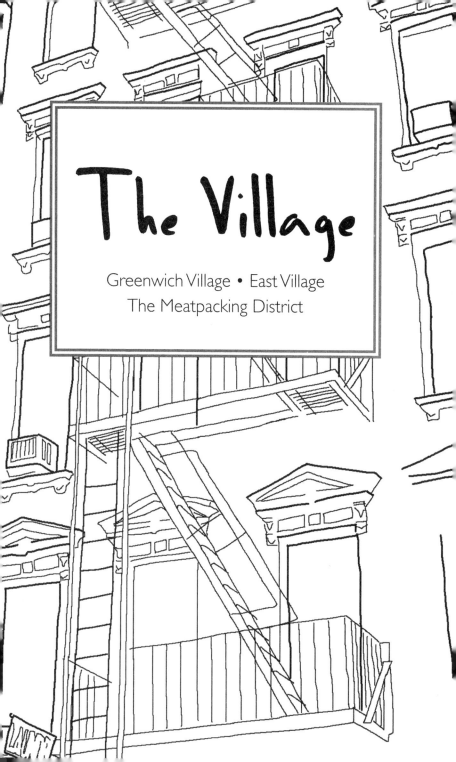

The Village

Greenwich Village • East Village
The Meatpacking District

Greenwich Village

POPPING UP FROM the subway and into the Village, you'll find yours
delivered to a neighborhood of crooked criss-crossing streets brimmi
with charm, far away from the gridded streets and industrial atmosphe
of midtown Manhattan. The landscape here is dotted with countless ba
restaurants, bakeries, boutiques, and unique shops, and the meander
streets are teeming with promise and culture. Having sheltered gene
tions of artists, writers, and revolutionaries, Greenwich Village holds cou
in New York as the elder statesman of hip.

Despite current critics accusing the neighborhood of having sold c
today it still preserves its tradition of artsy allure. The Village is home
a mélange of people. Here, well-to-do professionals and families live si
by side with bohemian residents, and everyone is surrounded by a sea
tourists. Both historically and today, the Village supports a strong gay co
munity, and it is also NYU territory, housing the university's vast stude
population.

The central axis of Bleeker and MacDougal Streets—a.k.a. Bourb
Street North—hosts a cluster of cafés by day, and by night transforms in
a bustling thoroughfare of bars and cheap eats. Stray from the main dra
and you'll stumble upon quieter streets, like Waverly Place and Bedfo
Street, with their quaint restaurants and shops. On the residential stret
es, you can admire the beautiful brownstones while under leafy shade
tree-lined sidewalks. Up and coming Greenwich Avenue boasts a mu
tude of small bars and cafés set back from the broad street and off
beaten path. Take a break at Sheridan Square (Christopher and Seve
Avenue), and then explore corner jazz clubs, trendy gay bars, and N
dorm parties. Here, anything goes—from pink hair to size 13 stilettos.

ISTORY

>> DURING NEW YORK'S 19th-century explosion, Greenwich Village thrived. Its residents commissioned famous architects and artists for their buildings, beautiful churches sprang up, and literary salons, art clubs, and private galleries soon clogged lower Broadway.

As the art scene increased in importance early in the 20th century, the Village's distance from the financial constraints of Midtown's Broadway theaters and publishing powerhouses resulted in the development of a phenomenon for which the neighborhood would become famous: bohemian lifestyle. Experimental theater, galleries specializing in avant-garde art, and irreverent "little magazines," the forerunners of today's zines, exploded onto the scene. Wild parties, candlelit tearooms, novelty nightclubs, and bizarre boutiques soon followed.

Just prior to the Depression, "artistic flats" became the era's local euphemism for what we'd now call gentrification, as luxury apartments displaced many of the long-term residents who had spawned the artistic ferment that first put the neighborhood on the map.

Following the Depression's end, the Beat Generation arrived and the Village saw the first stirrings of gay culture. Once again, writers and artists of all kinds congregated here, fueling the divergent but intimately connected genesis of the hippie movement and the gay revolution. Near Sheridan Square, a 1969 police raid on a local gay bar resulted in the Stonewall Rebellion, a seminal moment in the developing movement for gay and lesbian rights. With the '80s came the AIDS epidemic, which hit the community hard and sparked increased activism that continues today. Now the neighborhood is just as exciting as it was at any point in its history, just bit prettier, and sporting a good coffeehouse or two.

VHAT TO SEE

Washington Square Park

Known more for the sights than the serenity, Washington Square Park captures the city's energy as well as any location on the island. In good weather the park is packed with vendors, performers and onlookers. Hippies happily strum their guitars as NYU studentsamble to class, weaving through the pigeon feeders, chess players, jugglers, and skateboarders. The Stanford White-designed Big Arch marked the 100-year anniversary of George Washington coming to New York. For a more morbid tour of the park, be sure to stop by the "hanging elm," where public executions were held in the 1800's. *washingtonsquarepark.org.* Ⓐ Ⓒ Ⓔ Ⓑ Ⓓ Ⓕ Ⓥ *to W 4th St.*

Chumley's

This old tavern is practically hidden—as it was in the days of old. This former speakeasy of the Prohibition Era still retains its original under-cover atmosphere, furnished with oak booths and an old blacksmith's fireplace. This hangout is about as authentic as you can get. To top it all off, Chumley's was a frequent hangout of such literary clientele as John Steinbeck, Ernest Hemingway, Edna Ferber, Simone

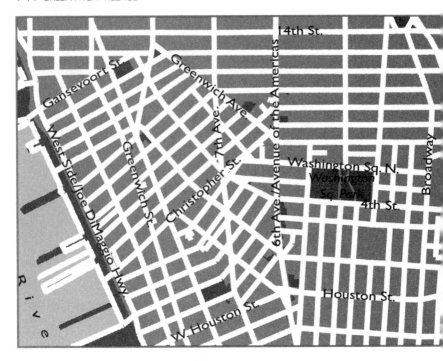

de Beauvoir, and Jack Kerouac. So sit back with a pint and let your creative ge flow like the beer from the tap. *86 Bedford St. (at Barrow St.).* **A C E B D V** *to W. 4th St.,* **1** *to Christopher St.*

Village Halloween Parade

This is probably one of the most fun and outrageous public events you can wit in the city. Starting on Sixth Avenue south of Spring Street and continuing thro 21st St., this parade—which includes dancers, music, floats, and puppets—dr hordes of people each year. Dressed-up New Yorkers make for quite a spect. You'll see costumes ranging from scary to sexy, serious to silly, and quite a few will make you wonder if the wearer of the get-up is male or female. It's almost to determine what you're supposed to be watching, the parade or its specta *halloween-nyc.com*

The Strand

How many books can you fit into one bookstore? A lot, apparently. The Str boasts to hold "18 miles of books" on and around its shelves. In this famous ir pendent store, you could spend all day browsing its never-ending collection of new, used, and out-of-print books. There is always a small crowd of people bro ing the $1.00 stacks outside. Decisions, decisions... *828 Broadway (at 12th St.), 473-1452, strandbooks.com.* **N R O W 4 5 6 L** *to 14th St.-Union Square*

WHERE TO EAT

A Salt & Battery *International*

Homesick Brits rub shoulders with New York's young Anglophiles at this West Village sizzler, where expats fry fish and chips to greasy, golden perfection. If cod and haddock aren't your fancy, eclectic choices like battered banger, deep-fried beets, and pickled onions should do the trick. Forget for a moment that Scotland is the heart attack capital of Europe and try the decadent deep-fried Mars bar, a national delicacy. A meal will cost you more than popping into your local chippie in London, but you won't leave hungry. *112 Greenwich Ave. (between 12th and 13th Sts.), 212-671-2713, asaltandbattery.com.* **A** **C** **E** *to 14th St.* **$**

Blue Ribbon Bakery *American*

The baked goods are the highlight here, but Blue Ribbon is a full-fledged American comfort food gem. Each table is given a heaping basket full of fresh breads, but pace yourself; the portions are huge and you'll definitely want to save room for dessert. The moist chocolate chip bread pudding is a meal in itself. Be prepared to leave with your stomach full and your wallet, well, slightly more empty. *33 Bedford St. (at Downing St.), 212-337-0404, blueribbonrestaurants.com. Reservations not accepted.* **1** *to Houston St,* **A** **B** **C** **D** **E** **F** **V** *to 4th St. Washington Sq.* **$$**

Café Condesa *Latin*

Like most new restaurants, Café Condesa still needs time find its stride, but already it shows promise. Take contemporary American fare, inject some adventure à la Françaises y Español and you've got Café Condesa. The tortellini comes stuffed with succulent crab meat and crowned with thin artichoke slices. Piquant tomatillo sauce smothers the salmon. Snag a window seat in the wide, airy storefront and watch the beautiful Village people stroll by as you sip your Spanish wine. But be

The fish and chip shop A Salt & Battery

forewarned: Tapas-style portions make the Café better for a quick bite than a fu
on feast. *183 W. 10th Street (at 7th Ave), 212-352-0050, cafécondesa.com.* ➊
Christopher St. **$**

Cornelia Street Café *Café*

A village landmark for good reason, Cornelia Street Café offers one of the mo
authentic unique New York experiences you may have. Every night features
lineup of avant-garde performance art. Whether it's the Arab-American poet
reading, storytelling (sans notes—that's the rule), Latin Jazz, or one of their summ
festivals, Cornelia St. Café, the original home of *The Vagina Monologues*, has bee
entertaining, and shocking, for over 29 years. Although the crowd reflects this join
long history, current college students will be as entertained as the Beat generatic
was. *29 Cornelia St. (bet. Bleecker and W. 4th Sts.), 212-989-9318, corneliastreetca
com.* ➍ ➌ ➌ ➍ ➌ ➏ ➐ *to W. 4th St.* ➊ *to Christopher St.* **$$**

Corner Bistro *American*

Locals lament the marathon waits at this immensely popular burger-and-beer jo
Here you'll find a basic, effortlessly funky version of the neighborhood haunt ma
palatable to yuppie Villagers, mostly by virtue of its enduring cachet and stea
stream of ball games on TV. Tables long ago marked by penknives crowd the midc
of the restaurant, though intimate space can be found in back. *331 W. 4th St.
Eighth Ave.), 212-242-9502.* ➍ ➌ ➌ ➊ *to 14th St.* **$**

Cowgirl Hall of Fame *American*

Before riot-girls there were cowgirls, a fact that owner Sherry Delamarter wc
let gringos forget. Come for the history lesson and eclectic Chuckwagon disl
like Eggplant Fritters and Frito Pie. The predominately lesbian clientele revel in 1
place's unabashed homage to the cowgirls of yesteryear, right down to the gift sh
full of cowgirly souvenirs. Check out the suit of armor as you go through the doc
519 Hudson St. (at 10th St.), 212-633-1133, cowgirlnyc.com. ➊ *to Christopher St.*

Cuba *Cuban*

It's nothing if not atmosphere at this two-year-old village restaurant and bar. Exc
mojitos and sangrias decorate the menu and the tapas aim for authenticity. Wl
Cuba is really about is the culture, though; as a handmade cigar roller sits in
window, salsa dancing happens in between tables, and the desserts, especially tc
de tres leches, are to die for. The more-than-attentive staff and live salsa band cc
plete this authentic Cuban experience. The live band four days a week is fanta
but check out the rooms in the back and underground for a slightly quieter di
experience. *224 Thompson St. (at Bleecker St.). 212-420-7878, cubanyc.com.* ➍
➌ ➊ ➏ ➐ *to W. 4t St.* **$$**

Ditch Plains *Seafood*

Simply put—great seafood. The atmosphere evokes its namesake, the popular
spot in Montauk, as its riveted steel wall décor stretches across the back of

restaurant and surfing videos loop on the TVs. Open from breakfast until 2am, and serving specials all day, there's not a bad time to dine here. Every seafood dish, from tuna tartare to curried mussels, is a treat. The Bloody Marys are delicious and complement the oyster shooters perfectly. Half bottles of wine, many only slightly more expensive than the average glass at other restaurants, are a steal, which takes some of the sting off the bill—as does the saltwater taffy. *29 Bedford St (at Downing St.), 212-633-0202, ditch-plains.com.* ❶ *to Houston St.* **$$**

Do-Hwa *Korean*

Even squares can feel hip at Do-Hwa. The details are what make this eatery's environment exceptional, from stylized carvings to polished metal chopsticks to indie artists playing just loud enough not to encumber conversation. The fare ranges from Korean favorites like BBQ beef (bulgogi) to seafood specials that change nightly. If you love ginger, begin your meal with a ginger kamikaze cocktail and finish it with ginger tea. The portions are sufficient but not huge, so order an appetizer if you've brought your appetite. Do-Hwa's prime location makes it perfect for a date or special celebration. *55 Carmine Street (at Bedford), 212-414-1224.* ❶ *to Houston St.* **$$**

Dublin 6 Wine and Dine *International*

You can't escape who you are. Neither can Dublin 6, but that's something to be proud of—it's a fun Irish bar-restaurant where everyone seems to be having a great time. The cool modern décor and attention to detail make D6 a cleaner and more comfortable alternative to its drunken cousins down the street. The food is a mix of spiced-up, gourmet versions of barroom classics—beer battered Maui Onion Rings, French Onion soup—and some solid but unimagined New American entrées like Oysters with Frite and grilled Mahi Mahi. *575 Hudson St. (bet. Bank & W. 11th Sts.) 646-638-2900.* ❶ ❷ ❸ Ⓐ Ⓒ Ⓔ ❶ *to 14th Street.* **$$**

Dragonfly *Asian Fusion*

With a menu fusing Malasian, Chinese, Vietnamese and Thai influences, this restaurant should satisfy just about every Asian food craving. It's fresh and authentic, right down to the fried spring roll banana dessert, and the cocktails are made and tested in a recurrent American Idol-esque contest by owner and bartender every once in a while, meaning they're always...creative. The bar area behind the aquarium proves a nice alternative to the wall of windows lining the Seventh Avenue dining spaces; only the rumble of the subway underneath distracts from people-watching and the distinctive food. *47-49 7th Ave. S. (at Morton St.). 212-255-2848, dfly-nyc.com.* ❶ ❾ *to Christopher St..* Ⓑ Ⓓ Ⓕ Ⓞ Ⓐ Ⓒ Ⓔ *to W. 4th St.* **$$**

EN Japanese Brasserie *Japanese*

EN's menu features small dishes of upscale but home-style izakaya dishes that are best sharedamong friends. Be sure to order their delicate, cloud-like tofu—a new batch is prepared fresh every 90 minutes. Other good choices include succulent chu-toro sashimi and a variety of fried and grilled dishes, such as the sake-grilled

black cod, sea-bass tempura, and crispy fried chicken seasoned with rock salt. Wh
EN isn't cheap, each dish is a micro-masterpiece. For a relaxed and classy expe
ence, try pairing one of their fine sakes with the intricate tasting menu. 435 Huds
St. (at Leroy St.), 212-647-9196, enjb.com. ❶ ❾ to Houston. **$$**

Famous Joe's Pizza *Pizza*

Arguably the best pizza joint in the city—at least, according to Ben Affleck. Th
not-too-greasy, perfectly-baked thin-crust pies are topped with a sweet tom
sauce and just enough cheese. Don't expect a place to sit, but don't worry;
active Bleecker sidewalk provides a great place to polish off your slice. 7 Carmine
(at Bleecker St.), 212-255-3946. Ⓐ Ⓒ Ⓔ Ⓑ Ⓓ Ⓕ Ⓥ to W 4th St. **$**

Garage Restaurant & Café *Steakhouse*

Suburban steakhouse meets Greenwich Village panache at this sprawling multi-
eled local favorite. Its famous weekend jazz brunch offers top-notch music an
mean eggs benedict. During the week, come for the music but stay for the un
gettable mussels, hearty sandwiches, and raw bar. 99 Seventh Ave. S. (at Grove
212-645-0600, garagerest.com. ❶ to Christopher St. **$$**

Gotham Bar and Grill *American*

Everything is high at the Gotham Bar and Grill: the acclaim for chef Alfred Por
the ceilings; the sail-like cream cloth chandeliers; the garden-view windows;
glass carafes of grappa on the bar; and the pyramid of exquisite food that balan
precariously on your plate. Oh yeah, and the prices. You probably won't beco
friends with your waiter, but Gotham's theatrical setting is done to perfection
the elegantly attired clientele. Try the tuna tartare, their delicately flavored salm
or a chocolate cake that sums it all up: warm, inviting, divinely prepared, and
After your meal, you'll be low on cash but high on life. 12 E 12th St. (bet. Unive
Pl. and Fifth Ave.), 212-620-4020, gothambarandgrill.com. ❹ ❺ ❻ ❶ Ⓝ Ⓞ Ⓡ
to Union Square. **$$$**

Gyu-Kaku *Japanese*

Formerly a fast-food joint in Japan, Gyu Kaku has taken New York by storm. Em
lished with white leather couches, a modern bar, and a metallic Japanese the
the restaurant makes a great place for dates or after-work drinks. Show off y
culinary skills by cooking your own food at a grill at the center of your table. Ea
elegance and style at one of New York's best-kept secrets. 34 Cooper Sq. (bet. A
Pl. & E. 4th St.). 212-475-2989, gyu-kaku.com. ❻ to Astor Place. **$$**

Knickerbocker Bar and Grill *Steakhouse*

One of the quieter names in New York steakhouses, Knickerbocker boasts a
history of success. Burgundy walls, warm lighting, and Americana knickknacks c
bine to create a friendly and relaxing mix where diners share delicious sa
meats, and desserts. The chef recommends the lamb sirloin frisee salad, ser
warm. The house-special T-Bone for two is an absolute must, with creamed spin

and garlic mashed potatoes. For dessert, try the peach cake, and do not leave without ordering the churros. *33 University Pl., 212-228-8490.* **6** *to Astor Pl.,* **N** **R** **W** *to 8th St.* **$$$**

La Lanterna de Vittorio *Italian*

Head back to the covered garden, where the wrought iron balustrade and backlit foliage almost make you forget you're in New York. The best wine, thin crust pizzas, and delicious cocktails converge for a truly remarkable experience. Only a block from NYU, this restaurant is alternately chic and relaxed, with a splash of real Italian vigor thrown in the mix. A sampling of cheese plates is necessary, but be sure to end your meal with the city's best espresso-laden tiramisu. *Mangia ! 129 MacDougal St. (bet. 3rd and 4th Sts.). 212-529-5945; lalanternacaffe.com.* **A** **B** **C** **D** **E** **F** **V** *to W. 4th St..* **$$**

Leela *Indian*

Leela's ultra-chic Indian décor and aesthetically charged interior outdoes both its food and service. Leela stirs up delicious unique cocktails like their signature Leela Tonic and trendy guests sip drinks from plush, modern sofas in the dim candlelit lounge. To sop up the booze, sample Leela's variety of artisan breads; they're the best showcase of India's myriad flavors. *1 W. 3rd St (bet. Broadway and Mercer Sts.), 212-529-2059.* **A** **C** **E** **B** **D** **F** **V** *to W. 4th St.* **$$**

Lupa Osteria Romana *Italian*

When in Rome, do as the Romans do. When in New York, follow fellow New Yorkers to this Roman trattoria-style restaurant, part of the successful culinary empire of Mario Batali. The menu changes often to highlight seasonal ingredients, with Brussel sprouts and pecorino in the fall and heirloom tomatoes in the summer. Try the Bucatini All'amatriciana for a classic Roman primi piatti, and be sure to save room for the Lupa tartufo, a rich composition of hazelnut gelato, pistachio biscotti crumbles, and chocolate. *170 Thompson Street (bet. Houston and Bleecker Sts.), 212-982-5089, luparestaurant.com.* **A** **B** **D** **E** **F** *to W. 4th St.* **$$**

Mary's Fish Camp *Seafood*

This small, open-kitchen seafood diner fills up fast, so arrive extra early. The lobster roll (in limited supply) is the main attraction, which includes an ungodly mound of fresh lobster piled into a disproportionately small hot dog bun. Portions are generous and the service is supreme. *64 Charles St. (at W. 4th St.), 646-486-2185, maryfishcamp.com.* **A** **B** **C** **D** **E** **F** **V** *at West 4th St.-Washington Sq.,* **1** *at Christopher St.-Sheridan Sq.* **$$**

Negril Village *International*

Imagine the hottest spot in Kingston airlifted to New York and you've got Negril Village. The menu, featuring goat-stew, jerk chicken, and delicious conch fritters, is full of spicy island classics with modern accents. The drinks include creative Caribbean concoctions such as the "Dark and Stormy," with home-brewed ginger beer, and rum from New York's widest selection of the spirit. Upstairs is a chill Carib-bean-accented lounge where energetic urbanites party, date, or celebrate. Flip por de riddim, mon. *70 W. 3rd St.; (bet. Thompson and LaGuardia Sts.), 212-477-2804 negrilvillage.com.* ❶ *to Houston St.,* Ⓐ Ⓒ Ⓔ Ⓕ Ⓥ *to W. 4th St.* **$$**

One if by Land, Two if by Sea *American*

Don't be fooled by the unassuming exterior of this converted 200-year-old car-riage house, once owned by Aaron Burr. With an extensive wine list and an exqui-site tasting menu, this gem of colonial history provides for the ultimate in roman-tic dining. The Bluefin Tartare is great and the superb Beef Wellington is rightfull-called the house specialty. The knowledgeable wait staff is more than happy to talk about the restaurant's history or unassumingly help you choose which utensil is appropriate for the next course. *17 Barrow St. (bet. Seventh Ave. and W. 4th St., 212-228-0822, oneifbyland.com.* Ⓐ Ⓑ Ⓒ Ⓓ Ⓔ Ⓕ Ⓥ *to W. 4th St.,* ❶ *to Christophe St.* **$$$**

EAT LIKE A
KID AGAIN

PEANUT BUTTER AND CO., a nostalgic little sandwich shop, puts peanut butte on a pedestal with an entire menu devoted to the stuff—the menu offers regula old PB & J and more adventurous bites like the Elvis, which is jazzed up with ba nanas, honey, and bacon. Flavored peanut butter, from a spicy The Heat Is On to rich Dark Chocolate Dreams, is trademarked. Top it off with a dessert like Deat by Peanut Butter and you're on your way to peanut butter heaven. Just don't forg to order a glass of milk. *240 Sullivan Street, 212-677-3995, ilovepeanutbutter.com.* Ⓒ Ⓔ Ⓑ Ⓓ Ⓕ Ⓥ *to W. 4th St.* **$**

Pó *Italian*

So popular that you might need to make reservations a month in advance, th charming Italian restaurant draws in customers with its warm atmosphere, reaso able prices and generous portions. Whether the quality of the food lives up to th restaurant's reputation is up for debate, but one thing's for sure: Pó makes for trendy evening out. *31 Cornelia St. (bet. Bleecker and W. 4th Sts.), 212-645-21 8 porestaurant.com.* Ⓐ Ⓑ Ⓒ Ⓓ Ⓔ Ⓕ Ⓥ *to W. 4th St.,* ❶ *to Christopher St.* **$$**

Red Bamboo and
Vegetarian's Paradise 2 *Vegetarian*

Always packed early for dinner, these strictly vegetarian restaurants (with quite few vegan options) do things with tofu you'd swear were impossible. From veg Fried Calamari to Spaghetti and Meatballs (soy meatballs, of course), selectio are sold in stores as specialty vegetarian foods. If you're tired of the same bla vegetarian options, head over to this West Village bastion of healthy soul food. *1 W. 4th St. (at Ave. of theamericas). 212-260-1212, redbamboo-nyc.com.* Ⓐ Ⓒ Ⓔ Ⓥ *to W. 4th St.* **$$**

Sacred Chow *Vegetarian / Kosher*

This twelve-table vegan and kosher sanctuary sits in peaceful, passive protest to ❶ carnivorous bars and Italian joints near Washington Square. Owner and founder Cliff Preefer prepares an under-priced medley of meatless and organic heroes, hot dogs, noodles and desserts. Deals abound at Sacred Chow: tapas are $12 for three dishes; and during happy hour from 3-6, a pint of beer and two "Hot Diggity Dogs" make it into your hand for a measly $8. The wheat- and gluten-free chocolate brownies will leave dessert-lovers saying, "I can't believe it's not gluten!" Think New York flavor, with a Gandhi state of mind. *227 Sullivan (at W. 3rd St.) , 212-337-0863, sacredchow.com.* Ⓐ Ⓑ Ⓒ Ⓓ Ⓔ Ⓕ Ⓥ *at W. 4th St.,* ⑥ *at Bleeker St.* **$**

Strip House *Steakhouse*

Strip House has an atmosphere that is decidedly less male-oriented than your typical steakhouse, making this a great place to bring a date. The filet is fantastic, the swordfish is soothing, and the desserts are gigantic; no human may be able to finish Strip House's 24-layer Chocolate Cake, though it's worth a shot. *13 E. 12th St. (bet University Pl. and Fifth Ave.), 212-328-0000, theglaziergroup.com.* Ⓛ Ⓝ Ⓡ Ⓦ ④ ⑤ ⑥ *to 14th St.-Union Sq.* **$$$**

Sushi Mambo *Sushi*

A Village Gem. Reasonable prices for tasty, very fresh sushi, and pages upon pages of options. A fantastic location, inviting décor, and wall-to-wall windows make Sushi Mambo as excellent for people watching as those sharing with friends. The fried ice cream cannot be missed. Nor can this spot itself—one of the few Village places worth its reputation and its bill. *255 Bleecker St. (at Leroy), 212-675-5885, sushi-mambo.com.* Ⓑ Ⓓ Ⓕ Ⓥ *to W 4th St.* **$$**

Tavern on Jane *American*

This tavern serves much more than pub food, but still charges typical pub food prices. While the fish and chips are a reliable delight, customers go crazy for the grilled leg-of-lamb with sour cherry sauce, potatoes au gratin, and garlic spinach with Moroccan tuna, served with saffron, lemon and garlic couscous, and wilted watercress. The atmosphere is cozy and inviting—regulars are bound to strike up a friendly conversation over a pint of beer. You know a place is great when the staff hangs out there on their nights off. *31 Eighth Ave. (at Jane St.), 212-675-2526, tavernonjane.com.* Ⓐ Ⓒ Ⓔ Ⓛ *to 14th St.* **$$**

Village Restaurant *French*

The 1920's décor and elegant open dining room are topped only by the freshness and quality of the entrées. The knowledgeable and friendly wait staff is happy to recommend a dish or a wine, and you will rarely be disappointed with their sugges-tions. Swing by for Sunday Brunch and enjoy live jazz played under the huge trans-lucent skylight in the back—it's a treat. *62 W. 9th St. (at 6th Ave.), 212-505-3355, villagerestaurant.com.* Ⓕ *to W. 4th St.,* ① ② *to Christopher St.,* Ⓝ Ⓡ *to 8th St.* **$$$**

Waverly at IFC Center *Café*

Though it was born of the renovations that brought Villagers the new IFC Cen-

ter, this slick downtown restaurant is poised to become a hot destination on
own. The Waverly is conveniently located for a pre-movie-or-pub crawl dinner, b
the expansive spread of affordable gourmet items like artisan cheese, cured me
plates, and unusual entrées like the Vietnamese Tofu Panini. The well-stocked b
features several specialty drinks, and the dessert menu includes a homemade bu
terscotch pudding that's a rich throwback to simpler times. *327 6th Ave. (at W. 3*
St.), 212-924-8866, ifccenter.com/restaurant. Ⓐ Ⓒ Ⓔ Ⓑ Ⓓ Ⓕ Ⓥ *at W. 4th St.* $

NIGHTLIFE

55 Bar *Music*

Live jazz, blues, and funk every night. This bar books good names in jazz along w
some regulars. The intimate atmosphere makes it difficult for anything larger th
a quintet to get on stage—typical acts are trios. This speakeasy-type bar evok
the prohibition era that spawned it. *55 Christopher St (at 7th Ave.), 212-929-98*
55bar.com. ① *to Christopher St.*

Absolutely 4th *Lounge*

Tried and tested "Pop"-tails glitter the menu at this plush Village lounge. Anir
prints enhance the luxurious black leather, as the DJ spins Thursday through Sat
day. Karaoke Wednesdays are an attraction in themselves, but the real specialt
are the drinks. The cocktails and martinis are wholly original creations: the keyli
pie martini tastes like its namesake, and the watermelon martini, served with
chunk of watermelon, is the freshest Jolly Rancher you'll ever have. A perfect pla
for a night out with the girls. *228 W. 4th St. (bet. 7th Ave. South and W. 10th St.), 2*
989-9444, absolutely4th.com. ① *to Christopher St.-Sheridan Sq.,* Ⓐ Ⓑ Ⓒ Ⓓ Ⓔ
Ⓥ *to W. 4th St.-Washington Sq.*

Alibi *Lounge*

Bouncing beats and powerful drinks make this underground lounge worth a v
There's not much room to dance to the DJ-spun music, but that doesn't stop
crowds of fun-seekers who pack the place nightly. If you're not the dancing ty
kick back on the plush couches and let the energetic waitresses bring your dri
to you. *116 Macdougal St. (bet. 3rd and Bleecker St.), 212-254-9996, alibiny.com.*
Ⓒ Ⓔ Ⓑ Ⓓ Ⓕ Ⓥ *to W. 4th St.*

Antarctica *Bar*

Even the artsy crowd needs a sports bar. A place that might be filled with the b
banker set were it in Murray Hill instead finds junior architects and production
sistants gathered around its pool tables and teeming pretzel bowls. A wide ro
flanked by booths and a bar means it's never too crowded, and the rowdy patr
drop names more often than shots. Don't let Antarctica throw you: this isn't a c
for frozen-faced ice queens, just an out of the way local joint where slaves to
kick back like the rest of us. *287 Hudson St. (at Spring St.), 212-352-1666, antarct*
bar.com. ① ② ③ Ⓐ Ⓒ Ⓔ *to Canal St.*

Arte Bar *Bar*

A Village staple. Head straight to the über-cool lounge in the back, perfect for the dual arts of sitting and conversing. The music is varied but hits all the bases, and though the cocktails might not be the freshest, they make great standard well drinks. A spoof on the famous Last Supper painting with Jim Morrison and a bevy of important contemporary apostles hangs on the back wall: it's enough of a con-versation piece to keep you talking all night. *21 E. 9th St. (bet. 5th Ave. and University Pl.), 212-473-0077.* **Ⓝ Ⓡ** *to 8th St.*

Baggot Inn *Pub*

An Irish stronghold in the Village, the location—though not the bar itself—has been in business since the '30s, with the charming old-time cash register to prove it. Dark and hazy, the bartenders are friendly, the live music is entertaining if slightlyamateur, and the drinks are straight-up and served with Irish hospitality. Pop in for a pint and you will be thoroughly entertained. *82 W. 3rd St. (bet. Thompson and Sullivan Sts.), 212-477-0622, baggotinn.com.* **Ⓐ Ⓑ Ⓒ Ⓓ Ⓔ Ⓕ Ⓥ** *to W. 4th St.-Washington Sq.*

Bar 6 *Bar*

Though theambiance in Bar 6 is reminiscent of a 1930's lounge, the drinks are anything but old-fashioned. Come here to casually sip some of the tastiest and most original drinks in the city. For a real treat, try "the Minty," a concoction of melon vodka, mint, and fresh lime. Or, if you're feeling hungry, feast on one of their delicious burgers. *502 6th Ave. (bet. 12th and 13th St.), 212-691-1368.* **Ⓛ Ⓝ Ⓡ ④ ⑤ ⑥** *to 14th St-Union Sq.*

BAR 13 *Bar*

This double-decker dance lounge just might make you nostalgic for your favorite freshman year frat-house scene: couples making out in the corner, girls dancing around them in packs, collar-popping guys chugging beer. The bar boasts two levels: downstairs the music is overbearingly loud, and upstairs is an open-air rooftop deck where actual conversations occur. With a low-key vibe and a mix of tunes ranging from Michael Jackson to early '90s hip-hop, it's hard to fight the urge to join the crowd and get down. Check out the poetry slams, karaoke and open-mic nights during the week. *35 E 13th St. (bet. Broadway and University Pl.), 212-979-6677, bar13.com.* **Ⓛ Ⓝ Ⓡ ④ ⑤ ⑥** *to 14th St-Union Sq.*

Bar Next Door *Music*

What distinguishes this jazz club from all the others in the Village is its inti-macy. The lower level bar offers great jazz so close to you, the musicians (they bring in house trios every night) are practically playing in your lap. Order des-sert (heavenly chocolate cake or the city's best tiramisu) with a meal from the restaurant upstairs and enjoy the romantic setting, the exposed brick walls, and the plush black leather couches. Standout service is another plus. *129 MacDou-gal St. (bet. 3rd and 4th Sts.), 212-529-5945. Cover Charge: $8 Su-Th, $8 per music set F-Sa, one drink minimum.* **Ⓐ Ⓑ Ⓒ Ⓓ Ⓔ Ⓕ Ⓥ** *to W. 4th St.-Washington Sq.*

The Bittter End

The Bitter End *Music*

Opened 40 years ago, The Bitter End has seen countless performers rise to st[]
dom, including Bob Dylan, Joni Mitchell, Tracy Chapman, Jackson Browne, and t[]
Indigo Girls. The drinks are strong and cheap, the music is often free or offer[]
for an affordable cover, and the entire venue is dripping with musical history. *[]
Bleecker St. (bet. Thompson and LaGuardia), 212-673-7030, bitterend.com.* ⑥ []
Bleecker St., ⓝ ⓡ *to Prince St.*

Blue Note *Music*

Though the regular features are an assault on the pocketbook, the five dollar aft[]
hours shows on Fridays and Saturdays are a real bargain. If you have the mor[]
to spend, catch some of the big national jazz acts that you won't be able to s[]
anywhere else. A full bar and continental menu will jazz up your taste buds. *131 []
3rd St. (bet. MacDougal St. and 6th Ave.), 212-475-8592, bluenote.net. Cover: $25 c[]
up.* ⓐ ⓒ ⓔ ⓕ ⓥ ⓞ *to W. 4th St.*

BowlMor Lanes *Bowling*

Bowling isn't just for groups of chain-smoking, middle-aged men in match[]
shirts—anymore. BowlMor Lanes features neon pins under blacklight-lit lanes w[]
a wall of giant screen TVs. The Union Square-area staple pitches bowling to t[]
20-something crowd, with a fully stocked bar and a bowling shirt clad waitress st[]
Come for "Night Strike" on Monday nights, with unlimited bowling from 10[]
– 3am for $20. *110 University Place (bet. 12th and 13th St.), 212-255-8188, bowln[]
com.* ④ ⑤ ⑥ ⓝ ⓞ ⓡ ⓦ ⓛ *at 14th St-Union Sq.*

Café Wha? *Music*

This Greenwich Village hole in the wall features the best and most eclectic ho[]
bands in the area. The musical styling mixes well with the low ceilings, close quart[]
and lack of lighting to create an atmosphere where anything goes. If you're in t[]

audience, be prepared to interact with the band or risk them dropping their funky jazz riff to play a mocking version of "Kumbaya." If you bring the energy, the band will too, and you'll leave wondering just how old that woman who started dancing in the aisles really was. *115 Macdougal St. (at Minetta Lane), 212-254-3706, caféwha. com. Thursday $5 Cover, Fri-Sat $10 Cover.* **Ⓐ Ⓒ Ⓔ Ⓑ Ⓓ Ⓕ Ⓞ Ⓥ** *to W. 4th St.*

Comedy Village *Comedy*

On weekends, it's not uncommon to spot performers from Comedy Central. Three shows occur nightly in this cozy venue, and you'll be hard-pressed to find a spot where the comedian can't spot you (and poke fun at you all night). Pick up the flyers handed out around the corner and the entrance fee is reduced. *82 W. 3rd St. (bet. Thompson and Sullivan St.), 212-477-0130, comedyvillage.com. Cover Charge: up to $25.* **Ⓐ Ⓑ Ⓒ Ⓓ Ⓔ Ⓕ Ⓥ** *to W. 4th St.-Washington Sq.*

Cubbyhole *LGBT*

Favored by friendly college-aged women of various sexual persuasions, this small, dark rendezvous spot lives up to the double entendre in its name. Myriad Christmas lights and quirky jukebox offerings make this small and quiet bar intimate enough for conversation, and an especially good place for women seeking women. *281 W. 12th St. (at 4th St.), 212-243-9041, cubbyholebar.com.* **❶** *to Christopher St.*

Down the Hatch *Bar*

Down the Hatch is pretty straightforward about its essential nature: it's a rowdy, fun college bar with busy foosball tables and Christmas lights. Attracting a lot of NYU students and a few older passersby, it attracts a good mix of people for a fun night out. *179 W. 4th St. (bet. Sixth and Seventh Aves.), 212-627-9747.* **❶** *to Christopher St.*

Fat Cat *Music*

A game room and internet café on the outside, this underground jazz venue makes you feel as though you're the only one that knows its dirty little secret. You're not. Play-by-the-hour pool tables and arcade games line the floor of the basement, while the jazz lies behind a secret door. A motley collection of furniture, pillows, and blacklight set the scene, but the real focus is the music, consistently good time after time. *75 Christopher St. (at 7th Ave.), 212-675-6056, fatcatjazz.com. Cover $10.* **❶** *to Christopher St.*

GYM Sports Bar *LGBT*

The Yanks game is broadcasted on the brick façade, there's a pool table in the back, and everyone's dressed straight as a pencil. But what makes this slightly self-conscious spot a truly authentic sports bar are the excellent drink specials: 4-9pm is happy hour, with draft beer for $1.50 weeknights, $3 weekends, and $5 mixed drinks. The music, surprisingly, is cheesy gay bar fare—but luckily you won't hear it over the after-work din. A laid-back, mixed-age crowd makes it a spot worth checking out. 167 8th Ave. (bet. 18th and 19th Sts.), 212-337-2439, gymsportsbar.com. **Ⓐ Ⓒ Ⓔ** to 14th St.-7th Ave.

Groove *Music*

Groove to sampled hip-hop and R&B: a live band takes the stage seven days [a] week. A diverse crowd adds to the appeal of this Village cornerstone (literall[y]) which stands at the crowded corner of Bleecker and Thompson. Drinks are sm[all] but tasty, and it's as cool to get up and shake your thang on stage as it is to talk [to] your neighbor. 125 MacDougal St. (at W. 3rd St.), 212-254-9393, clubgroovenyc.c[om] $5 cover F-Sa. Ⓐ Ⓑ Ⓒ Ⓓ Ⓔ Ⓕ Ⓥ to W. 4th St.-Washington Sq.

Henrietta Hudson *LGBT*

The bona-fide best bar for women seeking women in all of New York. 'Nuff sa[id] 438 Hudson St. (at Morton St.), 212-924-3347, henriettahudson.com. ❶ to Houston

Kenny's Castaways *Bar*

One of the landmark bars in the West Village, Kenny's is the ideal spot to grab [a] beer and see some up-and-coming local bands. You can listen to the music fro[m] the cozy upper level if you want to get away from the crowd. Hosts mostly blu[es] and rock. 157 Bleecker St. (bet. Thompson and Sullivan Sts.), 212-979-9762, kenn[y] castaways.net. Cover: $5-$10. Ⓐ Ⓒ Ⓔ Ⓕ Ⓥ ❶ to W. 4th St.

The Other Room *Bar*

Far, far out in the West Village there is a bar that wants to be your living room. O[nly] this one boasts lower lighting, plusher seating, and a beer list to rival Belgium's. Y[ou] get the sense that someone has rifled through your music selection, plucked o[ut] the songs you enjoy but never seem to get on your favorite play lists, and is play[ing] them softly enough so that you can still talk with your friends. While it's probabl[y] larger than your living room, that's not saying much in this city: in apartment-spe[ak] it's what they call cozy. 143 Perry Street (at Washington St.), 212-645-9758, theoth[er] room.com. ❶ to Christopher St.

Pieces *LGBT*

Although the décor is something like a John Waters meth-induced nightmare (dr[ag] queen included), this overwhelmingly over-the-top bar boasts an attractive youn[g] professional crowd. Come Tuesday for a spirited and popular karaoke night, with [all] sorts of guys crooning what you'd expect (Madonna) and the occasional surpr[ise] (Metallica). Saturdays, Sundays, and Mondays host the clever "liquid brunch" start[ing] at 2pm Long Island Iced Tea. 8 Christopher St. (bet. Gay St. & Greenwich Ave.), 2[12] 929-9291, piecesbar.com. Ⓐ Ⓑ Ⓒ Ⓓ Ⓔ Ⓕ Ⓥ to West 4th St..

Red Lion *Music*

For twenty years, NYU students, locals and music lovers have been flocking to t[his] Bleecker Street mainstay to rock out to talented live bands and aspiring sing[er/] songwriters. Even though the bar is on the larger side, it manages to fill up to star[nd-] ing-room only (even on weeknights), so arrive early if you want to grab a seat. T[he] drinks are strong and flowing, and the décor is classy yet comfortable. Think da[rk] wood, velvet drapery, and an old-school red telephone booth in the back. The[re] also a full menu and table service in addition to the bar. *151 Bleecker St, 212-260-9797, redlion-nyc.com.* ❶ *to Christopher St;* ❸ ❹ ❺ ❻ ❼ ❽ *to West 4th St.*

SOB's *Music*
Though the name stands for "Sounds Of Brazil," that doesn't even begin to cover the scope of the first world beat club in New York. A bastion of world rhythm, groove, and hip-hop, it's like stepping into a different country every night as African, Middle Eastern, Celtic, Caribbean, and Latin American artists use this club as a home base for national tours. *204 Varick St. (at W. Houston St.), 212-243-4940, sobs.com. Cover: $10-$25.* ❶ *to Houston St.*

Stonewall *LGBT*
Although this is no longer the place to see-and-be-seen, this West Village mainstay will always be iconic for its 1969 riots that symbolized the beginning of the Gay Rights movement. Stonewall does offer a good Thursday night "Detention" party, one of New York's rarely seen 18-and-older dance parties. You have to hand it to them for trying to keep up the raucous energy of its archetypal groundbreakers. *53 Christopher St. (bet. Waverly Pl and Seventh Ave. S.), 212-463-0950.* ❶ *to Christopher St.*

Sullivan Room *Music*
You'll find nothing but raw energy at this underground Village spot. A pricey entry fee is charged on the weekends, but if you love European house music, there may not be a better place to get your fix. The energy is hypnotic, and the creepiness of the décor only adds to the underground feel. Great rotating DJs make this crowded trance playground a serious dance party. A relatively friendly rope, and completely mixed crowds that know how to dance are major pluses. *218 Sullivan St. (bet. Bleecker and 3rd Sts.), 212-252-2151, sullivanroom.com $5-$15 Cover.* ❹ ❺ ❻ ❼ ❽ ❾ ❿ *to W. 4th St.-Washington Sq.,* ❶ ❷ ❸ *to 8th St.-NYU.*

Terra Blues *Music*
One of the few truly authentic blues clubs left in the city, this place is the real deal. Open for 15 years, Terra Blues attracts a crowd of regulars who appreciate the difference between blues and jazz, and tends to book musicians who have been around the scene for some time. If you're not a blues lover (or if you're not even sure what blues is), Terra will convert you any night of the week. Highly recommended. *149 Bleecker St., 2nd Floor (bet. LaGuardia Pl. and Thompson St.), 212-777-7776, terrablues.com. $5-$15 Cover.* ❹ ❺ ❻ ❼ ❽ ❾ ❿ *to W. 4th St.-Washington Sq.*

Turks and Frogs *Wine Bar*
It sounds impossible, we know, but Turks and Frogs exists in two locations—one in the Village and one in Tribeca—and is an antique store in addition to a Turkish wine bar. Although this is a cool concept, keep in mind that antiques weren't made to absorb sound, so bring either a megaphone or earplugs if you go on a weekend night. Signs claim everything is for sale, but don't be fooled; you can't walk out with the chairs, tables, or impressive bottles of obscure international wines. For a calmer

White Horse Tavern

scene, come on a weeknight. *323 W. 11th St. (bet. Greenwich and Washington S.* *212-691-8875, turksnfrogs.com.* **1** **2** **3** *to 14th St.*

BEST
LOW-KEY JAZZ

VILLAGE VANGUARD is one of the best jazz joints in the city. As a small, und. ground lounge, the Vanguard isn't overwrought with tourists or pretentiousne even though loads of extremely talented and famous musicians come here to p the night away. *178 7th Ave. South (near 11th St.), 212-255-4037, villagevanguc com.* **1** **2** **3** *to 14th St.*

Vol de Nuit *Bar*

Alternatively known as the Belgian Beer Bar, an unmarked red door opens int space with garden lounge, private room, and packed bar. The décor is barely visi regulars come here instead for the high-quality selections of imported beer, incl ing a fantastic raspberry Stella Artois. Although pricey, this is one of the be places to both get in and get served. *148 W. 4th St. (at 6th Ave.), 212-982-33 voldenuitbar.com.* **A** **C** **E** **B** **D** **F** **V** *to W 4th St*

West *Bar*

True to its name, this place is as far west as you can go without bar hopping Jersey. Spectacular sunsets over the Hudson are the daily special here, but if y want actual liquor, the cocktails are refreshing and innovative and the prices are half-bad. The scene is comfortable and chic, but low key. *425 West St. (at 11th A 212-242-4375, west-nyc.com.* **A** **C** **E** *at 14th St.*

White Horse Tavern *Pub*

A Village landmark, reputed to be the place where poet Dylan Thomas drank whiskeys and died on the front step. The poets are long gone, supplanted by a destrian twentysomething crowd. Dinner essentials are served, including really gc burgers. *567 Hudson St. (at W. 11th St.), 212-989-3956.* **A** **C** **E** **1** **2** **3** *to 14th*

ARTS

The National Museum of LGBT History *Museums*

Tapping into the pulse of Greenwich Village gay culture, this archive and library provides a rotating space for the art and photography of both new and established queer artists. Get out of your closet-sized apartment (or the closet) and explore piles of donated photographs, historical articles, and avant-garde art embracing pluralistic points of view. *208 W. 13th St. (bet. Seventh and Eighth Aves.), 212-620-7310, gaycenter.org/resources/museum. Hours: M-Su 9am-11pm.* ❶ ❷ ❸ *to 14th St.-Seventh Ave,* Ⓐ Ⓒ Ⓔ *to 14th St.-Eighth Ave.*

Asian American Arts Centre *Galleries*

The Centre features works by artists of Chinese, Japanese, and Korean backgrounds, ranging from traditional folk-art to photography to post-modern sculptures. It also features an extensive historical archive and plays host to many Asian-American dance performances. *26 Bowery (bet. Bayard and Pell Sts.), 212-233-2154, artspiral. org. Hours: M-W, F 12:30pm.-6:30pm., R 12:30pm.-7:30pm.* Ⓝ Ⓡ Ⓠ Ⓦ Ⓙ Ⓜ Ⓩ ❻ *to Canal St.*

Forbes Galleries *Galleries*

The Forbes family has certainly elevated the pack-rat mentality to an artistic level. Located in the lobby of the *Forbes* magazine's Village headquarters, this gallery is the result of years of collecting rare items (all by the Forbes family), from old Monopoly boards to over 1,000 miniature toy soldiers. Don't miss the Faberge eggs, one of the largest collections in the world (only Queen Elizabeth has more in her possession). *62 Fifth Ave. (at 12th St.), 212-226-5548, forbesgalleries.com. Hours: T-Sa: 10am.—4pm.* ❶ ❷ ❸ *to 14th St.*

Gavin Brown's Enterprise *Galleries*

Join trendy crowds at this ultra-hip, if somewhat pretentious, gallery. Nestled in a chic new spot among old warehouses, Gavin Brown and his "family" of artists have received great press coverage. Stop into the adjoining bar, complete with disco-light floor, after the gallery closes. *620 Greenwich St. (at Leroy St.). 212-627-5528, gavinbrown.biz. Hours: T-Sa 10am-6pm.* ❶ *to Houston.*

Actor's Playhouse *Theater*

Gay-and-lesbian-themed shows command the stage at this unique off-Broadway space. Though the seats may be dingy and worn, and the floor may retain a stickiness from soda spilled ages ago, it's still the best queer theater in town. *100 Seventh Ave. (bet. Christopher and Bleecker Sts.), 212-463-0060.* ❶ *to Christopher St.*

Cherry Lane Theater *Theater*

Founded in the '20s by a literary circle headed by the poet Edna St. Vincent Millay, Cherry Lane features the century's best avant-garde new pieces. *38 Commerce St. (bet. Seventh Ave. and Barrow St.). 212-989-2020, cherrylanetheatre.com.* Ⓐ Ⓑ Ⓒ Ⓓ Ⓔ Ⓕ Ⓥ *to W. 4th St.,* ❶ *to Christopher St.*

Lucille Lortel Theater *Theater*

Cramped between the music-pumping, glitter merchandise shops of Christoph
St. stands this supremely immodest performance space, which claims to be Ne
York's foremost off-Broadway theater. A recent success for the theater has be
the acclaimed *Mrs. Klein*, chronicling the life and times of famed psychoanalyst Me
nie Klein. *121 Christopher St. (bet. Hudson and Bleecker Sts.), 212-279-4200, lor*
org. ❶ *to Christopher St.*

Cinema Village *Film*

This single movie screen may have a reputation for hosting only skin flicks, but
actually accommodates a far wider array of independent films with themes rangi
from gay and lesbian to Kung Fu action to African Diaspora. *22 E. 12th St. (b*
University Pl. and Fifth Ave.), 212-924-3363, cinemavillage.com. Cash only. ❶ ⓝ ⓡ
❹ ❺ ❻ *to 14th St.-Union Sq.*

Film Forum *Film*

Two programs run in this classic setting: Program One offers first-run independe
and foreign feature films along with documentaries, while Program Two scree
revivals including reissues of classics along with stellar film series. *209 W. Houston*
(at Sixth Ave.), 212-727-8110, filmforum.org. ❶ *to Houston St.*

Waverly at IFC Center *Film*

Your basic two-theater movie house, which vacillates between mainstream and a
films. Make sure to check out the café here as well. *323 Sixth Ave. (at 3rd St.), 2* ▮
929-8037, ifccenter.com. Ⓐ Ⓑ Ⓒ Ⓓ Ⓔ Ⓕ Ⓥ ❶ *to W. 4th St.-Christopher St.*

SHOPPING

Alexia Crawford *Accessories*

This jewelry designer made a name for herself when she was featured at Barne
almost ten years ago. Now, she not only has a store of her own, but her acce
sories are also sold in stores all over the country. Crawford creates affordat
jewelry, bags, and scarves that rival the great designers. Despite her low price ta
you won't be able to tell the difference between her pearls and Fortunoff's. Ti
quaint and colorful store deals exclusively in those pieces that you never knew y⊙
couldn't live without. *199 Prince St. (bet. MacDougal and Sullivan Sts.), 212-473-97⊙*
Hours: M-R 11am-7pm, F-Sa 11am-8pm, Su 12pm- 6pm. Ⓒ Ⓔ *to Spring St.*

Andy's Chee-Pees *Clothing : Vintage & Consignment*

Andy's houses a large selection of mostly polyester-influenced vintage men's a
women's clothing at sky high prices, plus a more reasonably priced collection
used jeans. Always in stock: your great-grandpa's cabana wear; but he'd roll ov
in his grave if he saw what they're charging for it. *691 Broadway (bet. 3rd and 4*
Sts.), 212-420-5980, Hours: M-Sa 11am-9pm, Su 12pm-8pm. ⓝ ⓡ *to 8th St.,* ❻
Bleecker St., Ⓑ Ⓓ Ⓕ Ⓥ *to Broadway-Lafayette St.*

Atrium *Clothing : Boutiques*

The shopping experience here is big and loud, with lots of jeans, good club wear, clothes that run tight and tarty for the ladies, loose and bold for the men. All this flash doesn't come cheap, but the wide selection of exclusive shoes and hard-to-find foreign labels make up for the blaring music and crowded floor. *644 Broadway (at Bleecker St.), 212-473-3980, atriumnyc.com, Hours: M-Sa 10am-9pm, Su 11am-8pm.* **D** **N** **R** *to Prince St.,* **6** *to Bleecker St.*

Biography *Books*

Muckrakers, voyeurs, and fan club presidents flock to this high-ceiling and brick-wall store for the latest on their respective beloved celebs. The bookstore also boasts an impressive gay and lesbian section. *400 Bleecker St. (at W. 11th St.), 212-807-8655. Hours: Su-R 11am-10pm, F-Sa 11am-11pm.* **1** **2** **3** *to 14th St.-Eighth Ave.*

Bleecker Bob's Golden Oldies Record Shop *Music*

Packed with a huge vinyl selection, including rare albums, Bob's is a hub for DJs and music collectors alike. Their rock, metal, indie, emo, punk, and hardcore CD selection always draws a crowd. Bonuses include the posters, pieces ("for tobacco only"), and a body piercing/tattoo shop in the back. *118 W. 3rd St. (bet. MacDougal St. and First Ave.), 212-475-9677, bleeckerbobs.com. Hours: M-Su 11am-1am.* **A** **B** **C** **D** **E** **F** **V** **1** *to W. 4th St.*

OLDEST
NEW YORK
PHARMACY

C.O. BIGELOW CHEMISTS (est. 1838) is home to a huge selection of imported drugstore beauty products, its full Alchemy makeup line, C.O. Bigelow oils, tasteful jeweled hair accessories, and funky makeup bags in addition to your regular (and designer) tube of sunscreen or toothpaste. You'll want to leave plenty of time for browsing here and don't forget to ask about beauty goodies that they keep behind the counter. *414 6th Ave. (between 8th St. and 9th St), 212- 473-7324, Hours: M-F 7:30am-9pm; Sat, 8:30am-7pm; Sun, 8:30am-5pm, bigelowchemists.com.* **A** **C** **E** **B** **D** **F** **V** *to W. 4th St.*

Books of Wonder *Books*

The model for Meg Ryan's shop in the film *You've Got Mail,* this children's bookstore is ideal for the young and the curious. With story readings and an extensive collection of new titles and all-time favorites, children (and adults) will not want to leave this lovely store. Call or check the website for reading and storytime schedules. *16 W. 18th St. (bet. 5th and 6th Aves.), 212-989-3270, booksofwonder.net. Hours: M-Sa 10am-7pm. Su 12am-6pm.* **L** **N** **R** **4** **5** **6** *to 14th St.–Union Sq.*

Cheap Jack's Vintage Clothing *Clothing : Vintage & Consignment*

Don't be fooled by the name of this groovy vintage store—this place is anything but cheap. Browse through the vast selection of plain and Hawaiian shirts, one-of-a-kind coats, and vintage-style dresses on the first floor; then head downstairs to find jeans. Patience and a keen eye may be rewarded with a heavenly bargain. *841 Broadway (bet. 13th and 14th Sts.), 212-777-9564, cheapjacks.com, Hours: M-Sa*

11am-8pm, Su 12pm-7pm. ❶ ❻ ❿ ❼ ❹ ❺ ❻ to 14th St.–Union Sq.

Condomania *Erotica*

Prophylactics of all shapes, sizes, and flavors. Merely browsing here can be an amusi
experience. Condomania features the latest technology in condoms, including t
"reservoir tip" that could fit a baseball. *351 Bleecker St. (bet. Christopher and W. 4
Sts.), 212-691-9442, Hours: Su-R 11am-11pm, F-Sa 11am-12am.* ❶ *to Christopher*

Creative Visions *Books*

This neighborhood bookstore has a large selection of what you can't find in t
LGBT section of Barnes and Noble, including a helpful, friendly staff. Items he
range from books by intellectual queer authors to seedy, obscure porn vids. Brow
as long as you'd like among the pleasant book displays, or strike up a conversati
with someone from the neighborhood. *548 Hudson St. (bet. Charles and Perry St
212-645-7573, creativevisionbooks.com. Hours: Su-R 1pm-10pm, F-Sa 12pm-11pm
to Christopher St.-Sheridan Sq.*

DSW *Clothing : Discount*

The DSW store in Union Square is a massive, overwhelming, and exciting sh
emporium. Everything in the store is discounted and the sale racks in the back ha
shoes that are priced up to 80 percent off retail. There is a shoe here for everyo
whether you're looking for casual flats by Nine West or deliriously high Jimr
Choo stilettos. DSW also features a small but solid assortment of accessor
(Prada bags were recently spotted). The men's shoe collection is large enough
make you care what's on your feet. *40 E. 14th St., near University Pl. 212-674-21
dswshoe.com, Hours: M-R, 8am-10pm; Fri-Sat, 8am-11pm; Sun, 9am-9pm.* ❹ ❺ ❻
❻ ❻ ❻ ❻ *at 14th St.-Union Sq.*

East-West Books *Books*

As the name suggests, the emphasis here is on introducing Western readers to t
literature of the East. The store specializes in religious and philosophical traditio
from Mahayana Buddhism to neo-Confucianism. The staff will make special orde
to meet your needs. *78 Fifth Ave. (at 13th St.), 212-243-5994, eastwestnyc.co
Hours: M-Sa 10am-7:30pm, Su 11am-6:30pm.* ❻ ❶ ❽ *to 14th St. -Sixth Ave.,* ❶
❻ ❻ ❹ ❺ ❻ *to 14th St.-Union Sq.*

Filene's Basement *Clothing : Discount*

This bargain superstore carries Calvin Klein, Perry Ellis, Kenar, and other c
signer names. It is worth a look for shoes, lingerie, coats, suits, and ev
ning wear. Check out the occasional clearance sales for the best deals. *6
Sixth Ave. (bet. 18th and 19th Sts.), 212-620-3100, filenesbasement.cc
Hours: M-Sa 9:30am-9pm, Su 11am-7pm. 1 to 18th St..* ❻ ❶ ❽ *to 14th*

Flight 001 *Accessories*

This chain store has been popping up all over Manhattan selling items for t modern traveler. The selection ranges from standard travel bags and books, to more humorous barf bags and anti-motion sickness bracelets. *96 Greenwich Ave. (bet. 12th and 13th Sts.), 212-691-1001, flight001.com. Hours: M–F 11am–8:30pm, Sa 11am–8pm; Su 12pm–6pm.* Ⓐ Ⓒ Ⓔ *to 14th St,* Ⓛ *to Eighth Ave.,* ❶ ❷ *to 14th St.*

Generation Records *Music*
The best selection of punk, hardcore, and underground music in the city. Cheap movie and music posters, T-shirts, used CDs, and an extensive vinyl stock soothe the emotional scars inflicted by the glaring staff. Come here for CDs you can't find anywhere else. *210 Thompson St. (bet. Bleecker and 3rd Sts.), 212-254-1100. Hours: M-R 11am-10pm, F-Sa 11am-1am, Su 12pm-10pm.* Ⓐ Ⓑ Ⓒ Ⓓ Ⓔ Ⓕ Ⓥ *to W. 4th St.,* ❻ *to Bleecker St*

New York University Bookstore *Books*
Lines wind around the block at the beginning of each semester at this academic standard. Alas, students get no special discounts. *18 Washington Pl. (at Washington Sq. Park), 212-998-4667, Hours: M-R 10am.-7pm., F-Sa 10am.-6pm.* Ⓝ Ⓡ *to 8th St.-NYU.*

Orlo *Salons*
The city has a ton of decent salons that will get the job done for a reasonable price. However, if you're in the mood to splurge and get a top-of-the-line hair treatment, consider Orlo Salon. They'll wrap you in blankets and serve you chai tea as they add impeccable highlights to your hair, although you better be willing to sacrifice your year's earnings. *34 Gansevoort Street (at W. 13th St.), 212-242-3266,* Ⓐ Ⓒ Ⓔ Ⓛ *to 14th St.*

Oscar Wilde Memorial Bookshop *Books*
For over twenty-five years, New York City's flagship gay bookstore has been offering books for and by gay men and women, as well as videotapes, music, magnets, T-shirts, and jewelry. Occasional readings by established authors are scheduled. *15 Christopher St. (at Sixth Ave.), 212-255-8097, oscarwildebooks.com. Hours: M-Su 11am.-7pm.* ❶ *to Christopher St.*

The Pink Pussycat *Erotica*
At this Village landmark you can find all manner of erotica, from lingerie and clothing to, well, other things designed to aid your love life. The store isn't known for its service, so come armed with knowledge. A bag bearing its famous name is bound to create the expected reaction from any lover. *167 W. 4th St. (bet. Sixth and Seventh Aves.), 212-243-0077. Hours: Su-R 10am-2am, F-Sa 10am-3am.* Ⓐ Ⓑ Ⓒ Ⓔ Ⓕ Ⓥ *to W. 4th St.,* ❶ *to Christopher St.*

Three Lives & Co. *Books*
Praised by the Greenwich Village Historical Society as a "pocket of civility," this small bookstore boasts one of the city's widest book selections. Its extremely knowledgeable staffers, who have read a fairamount of what the store offers, are espe-

cially good at suggesting new titles. *154 W. 10th St. (at Waverly Pl.), 212-741-20* *threelives.com. Hours: M-T 12pm-8pm, W-Sa 11am-8:30pm, Su 12pm-7pm.* ❶ *Christopher St.*

Urban Outfitters *Clothing : National Chain*
This hipster playground for the post-mall generation packs its industrial-esque terior with racks of multicolored, funky kid fashion, suitable for day or evening ban outings. Weave through aisles of vintage clothing, sassy sundresses, and tren housewares while swaying to the smooth rhythms of ambient music. *374 Si. Ave. (at Waverly Pl.), 212-677-9350, urbanoutfitters.com. Hours: M-Sa 10am-9pm, 12pm-8pm.* ❹ ⓑ ⓒ ⓓ ⓔ ⓕ ⓥ *to W. 4th St.*

Verve *Accessories*
While this store specializes in accessories, Verve is also known for their footw Bags, hats, scarves, and jewelry are available for a wide range of prices. While th do carry some designer products, the knockoff bags and hats are the best deal. T friendly salespeople make this a great place to stop for the finishing touches t great outfit. *353 Bleecker St. (bet. Charles and W. 10th Sts.), 212-691-6516. Ho M-Sa, 11am-8pm, Su 12pm-6pm.* ❶ *to Christopher St.,* ❹ ⓑ ⓒ ⓓ ⓔ ⓕ ⓥ *to 4th St. Additional locations at 282 Columbus St. and 105 Christopher St.*

CLASSES AND WORKSHOPS

Capoeira Angola Center
Mestre João Grande, with over 50 years of experience under his belt, brings t trendy style of Afro-Brazilian dance-fighting to the Village. Classes go for $1! pop, but 10 can be purchased for $120. All levels of experience are welcome, come and find your rhythm. *104 W. 14th St., Third Floor (near 6th Ave.), 212-9! 6975, joaogrande.org. Classes: M-F 6:30-8:30pm, W-F 8-10am, Su 10am-12pm.* ⓛ ⓥ ❶ ❷ ❸ *to 14th St.–7th Ave.*

Edgar M. Bronfman Center for Jewish Student Life at NYU
In a townhouse built for the wealthy exporter Lockwood de Forest, the cen presents free lectures focusing on Jewish religious concerns and Israeli politi De Forest founded workshops in India to revive the art of woodworking, so t center is replete with the fruits of his labor. *7 E. 10th St. (bet. University Pl. and Fi Ave.), 212-998-4123, nyu.edu/bronfman.* ⓛ ⓝ ⓡ ⓦ ❹ ❺ ❻ *to 14th St.-Union*

The Writers Studio
Hailed by the *New York Times* as offering "the most personal of the [writing] p grams," the Studio features classes for all skill levels, with a focus on budding write In addition to their five-tier workshop program, there are classes on advanced p etry and one-on-one tutorials between instructor and student. *78 Charles St. (l Bleecker and W. 4th St.), 212-255-7075, writerstudio.com.* ❶ *to Christopher St.*

OTELS AND HOSTELS

Larchmont Hotel

Located in a residential area of the historic Greenwich Village, this warm and sophisticated European-style hotel offers free continental breakfast as well as access to some of New York's finest shopping and dining. While bathrooms are shared, two per floor, they are kept spotless and the wait is never long. *27 W. 11th St. (bet. 5th and 6th Ave). 212-989-9333, larchmonthotel.com. Rooms are $70-$95 for a single, $90-$125 for a double.* Ⓐ Ⓑ Ⓒ Ⓓ Ⓔ Ⓕ Ⓥ *to W 4th St,* Ⓕ *to 14th St.*

Washington Square Hotel

Right across from Washington Square Park, this hotel offers convenience of location along with a helpful, friendly concierge staff. The newly renovated rooms are recommended, but even the other rooms (though small) are clean, and have well-kept bathrooms. Continental breakfast is included in the price of the room—-a great deal in New York City. *103 Waverly Pl. (bet. 5th and 6th Aves.). 800-222-0418 or 212-777-9515, wshotel.com. Rooms are $155-$160 for a single to $220-$230 for a double.* Ⓐ Ⓑ Ⓒ Ⓓ Ⓔ Ⓕ *to W. 4th St.*

The East Village

MORNINGS IN THE EAST VILLAGE are quiet. With most of Manhatt tunneling to work, the paint-tagged gates of the cafés and bodegas he remain shut, defiantly somnolent. The East Village is all about the nig so if you're looking for the true East Village experience that is the ti to come.

Much of the mythology that hovers over the fourteen blocks and or seven avenues that now make up the East Village centers arou its beatnik past. Colorful characters like Bukowski, Ginsberg and Bar advanced a lifestyle of artistic exploration, radical politics, and anythin goes bohemia that infused the neighborhood with an edgy aura of cc But the hard drug use of literary luminaries like William S. Burroug opened a crack into the neighborhood's dangerous side and, when economic plunge of the '70s pushed downturn into despair, the dr traffic exploded, only to be finally tamped down with the turning of t millennium.

A rich, hedonistic past still attracts artists, punks and radicals to t East Village, but they no longer live here. First priced out of SoHo a Greenwich Village, then countless other spots, they've been priced c of this one, too. But CBGB's and the Mercury Lounge still host lo hopefuls, and La MaMa and P.S. 122 still put on political plays that up debate. And in the last few years, the poetry slam has become ubiquitous as the fruit-fronted bodega.

While entire days could be spent riffling through the typical N York sidewalk stuff (the jewelry table, the used CD bin, the hat/sc combo bench), the East Village of today is known for its trendy design shops and bargain-bin second-hand stores. Home to an endless sea restaurants and bars, the neighborhood at night throbs with New York's favorite sin: indulgence. Every week, a new drinking hotspot rises from the ashes of the old. And it's the same story with the food. You could spend a year here and not use the same fork, or chopstick, twice. So pick an avenue or cross street, hit a sidewalk ATM, and go hop some bars.

HISTORY

>> EVER SINCE THE EARLY 1960s, when the area first emerged as a distinct neighborhood, the East Village has been known as a clearinghouse of revolution and decay. Jump-started into life by intellectuals, artists, musicians, and writers frustrated with the rising rents that were taming the West Village in the late '60s, the area supported a level of political and artistic radicalism for which its western neighbor was a bit too genteel. These pioneers set up coffee shops and poetry houses and opened bookshops, saloons, bars, and jazz clubs. The East Village also sported the first rooftop urban windmill that, thanks to a legal battle in the '70s, was allowed to tie into the city's power supply. Most recently, the neighborhood has absorbed large numbers of Latinos and Ukrainians.

Drugs and their associated ills were largely responsible for the neighborhood crisis of the '70s; residents repeatedly demanded police protection from the dealers and government funding for their dilapidated tenements. But such aid was not sufficient, with locals banding together to reclaim vacant lots and abandoned buildings from urban decay. A large community of squatters took hold of such spaces, and in the '80s they fought both neighborhood bullies and the wave of gentrification that arguably continues to this day.

The conflict came to a head in 1989 as police attempted to impose a curfew at Tompkins Square Park, the cultural and geographical hub of the East Village and one of the city's prime targets for redevelopment. The resulting riot, one of worst in recent memory, was solidly won by the cops, who rode through the park on their city steeds arresting rioters. After that the park was closed. Despite continuing marches and violent protests, it didn't reopen until 1992, but the rupture between the law and the community still remains an open wound.

WHAT TO SEE

St. Mark's Place

The stretch of St. Mark's Place between Third and Second Avenues is filled to unbelievable capacity with shops. Cool vintage clothing stores like Search and Destroy take up top floors and tattoo parlors while specialty shops like St. Mark's Comics inhabit the half-sunken bottom floors, with stands hawking socks and water pipes are jammed in-between. Most of the stores here are cash-only, but you don't need to bring much because most of the goods are cheap, and the rollicking ambiance makes it one of the coolest blocks in the city. ❻ to Astor Pl.

The Community Gardens

The East Village is littered with green space the way the rest of the city is just...

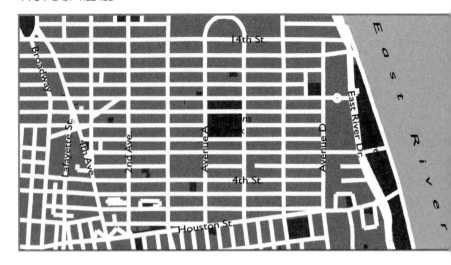

littered. Some of the community gardens, most of which are maintained by vo unteers, are affiliated with New York Parks and Rec. (nyc.gov/parks) With the su filtered through the leaves as you read a book under a tree, you could almo forget you were in New York—if it weren't for the city noise. *Biggest Park: 6th and Ave B Garden. Most Charming: El Sol Brilliante, 12th St between Ave A and B. Be Willow Tree: Creative li'l garden, 6th St between Ave A and B.*

Indian Row

East 6th St, between First and Second Aves, is known as Indian Row, and w good reason. This one block has a concentrated glut of Indian restaurants, rangi from the fancy and expensive to the cheap dives. Not all of it's good, and som is very westernized; but if you crave spicy food, this should be your first stop the island. ❶ ❷ *to Second Ave.*

Japanese Row

In recent years a few of the east-west routes (7th Street in particular, betwee Second and Third) have turned distinctly Japanese with the opening of several a thentic Asian markets and restaurants. At some spots you might just think you in Tokyo; don't look for English on those signs or menus. ❶ ❷ *to Second Ave.*

WHERE TO EAT

Alt.Coffee *Café*

The comfy couches are here because you'll be sitting awhile, checking your em and figuring out your plans for the night. The staff is as handy with the latte mak as they are with any internet questions. *139 Ave. A (at 9th St.), 212-529-2233. Ca only.* ❶ *to First Ave,* ❻ *at Astor Pl.* **$$**

Angelica Kitchen *Vegetarian*

A vegetarian's paradise as well as an intro course for vegphobic carnivores, Angelica offers tangy soups, tofu and pesto sandwiches, and tofu-lemon "cheesecake." Portions are generous and moderately priced. *300 E. 12th St. (bet. First and Second Aves.), 212-228-2909. Cash only.* ● *to First Ave.* **$**

Café Mogador *International*

Weekend brunch is well worth the wait at this Moroccan-themed neighborhood jewel. Traditionalists will find solace in the Eggs Normandy, a smoked salmon spin on the classic Eggs Benedict. If you're looking for more of an adventure, check out the Middle Eastern Eggs—this array of hummus, tabouli, and za'atar pita is not to be missed. Stop by in the evening for a hearty lamb tagine. *101 Saint Marks Pl. (bet. First Ave. and Ave. A), 212-677-2226, cafémogador.com.* ❻ *to Astor Pl.* **$$**

Café Orlin *Café*

Blend in by ordering an espresso, and then quickly whipping out some sort of portfolio. Leave it open on the table and enjoy a smoky omelet or a slice of chocolate cake. Most regulars are artsy East Village chain smokers and aspiring directors, so don't shave that goatee for a few days before you stop by. The low-angle view allows a glimpse of the shoes passing by on St. Marks Place. *41 St. Marks Pl. (bet. First and Second Aves.), 212-777-1447.* ❻ *to Astor Pl.* **$**

Caracas Arepa Bar *Latin*

With only a handful of small two-person tables and some of the most authentically home-cooked Venezuelan food in the big city, this modest taguaria (roadside restaurant) is a popular hotspot among East Villagers. Be sure to sample their arepas—corn flour bread stuffed like pita pockets with traditional meats and sauces. Expect a long line, especially for outside tables during nice weather. This may not be the perfect restaurant for a fancy date or a posh outing, but the food is sure to satisfy those whose patience endures. *93 1/2 E. 7th St. (at 1st Ave.), 212-2529-2314, caracasarepabar.com.* ❻ *at 2nd Ave,* ● *at 1st Ave.* **$**

Caravan of Dreams *Vegetarian*

The décor of this East Village mainstay may be eccentric—a jazz trio playing in the corner complicates the Bedouin-chic—but the food has a clear mission. All dishes are vegan, many are raw, and Rabbi Harry Cohen supervises kosher preparation. Here the dishes are refreshingly innovative both in substance and name—the "Live Love Boat" is an unpredictably delicious plate of live "meatballs" made from almonds and Brazil nuts. An extensive drink list lets you decide whether wine, beer, or "Aqua Fresca"—an electrolyte drink made with Himalayan crystal salt—will best compliment your vegan ravioli alfredo. The restaurant used to host yoga classes in its back room, and you should expect your server to be pretty mellow—but the attitude accounts for what may be the restaurant's greatest idiosyncrasy: a large line of hungry New Yorkers all waiting happily outside. *405 East 6th St. (bet. First Ave. and Avenue A), 212-254-1613, caravanofdreams.net.* ❻ *to 2nd Ave.,* ● *to 1st Ave,* ❷ ❸ *to 8th Street,* ❻ *to Astor Pl.* **$$**

Café Orlin

Casa Adela *International*

This family business has been around for over 20 years. Its cooking is classic
décor clean and bright. Try the chicken and rice, as Adela may be the epitome
boricua cooking. You might feel out of the loop by not speaking Spanish, but
welcome is just as warm in English. *66 Ave. C (bet 4th and 5th Sts.), 212-473-18*
❻ ❼ *to Second Ave.* **$**

Colors *International*

Colors is worker-owned and its staff hails from more than 24 different countr
The menu features exotic cuisine inspired by family recipes. Prepare yourself
a casually elegant atmosphere, attentive service, and a creative blend of in
national tastes, such as charred octopus and pomegranate-glazed scallops. A
don't just eat here once—the menu changes seasonally. *417 Lafayette St. (*
Astor Pl. and E. 4th St.), 212-777-8443, colors-nyc.com. **❻** *to Astor Pl..* **$$$**

Counter *Vegan*

Welcome to the pleasure-dome, vegan style. All the signs forecast that yo
in for a treat: a slick interior, complete with color-changing mood lighting, gi
flower portraits in 3-D, a friendly and helpful wait staff, and a romantic ba
room (think red lighting and Billie Holiday singing in the last stall). Counter's h
chef combines exotic flavors to create unexpectedly comforting dishes, like
bast'eeya, which consists of basmati rice, vegetables, and a hint of citrus baked i
a cinnamon-dusted filo crust. Their caprese is an almost-convincing goat-che
facsimile, all the moreamazing because it's "raw food" (which more often th
not tastes uniformly of ground nuts). By the time the sinfully rich-tasting (the
relatively healthy) desserts arrive, you'll be saying "I can't believe it's vegan!"
First Ave. (at 6th St.), 212-982-5870, **❻** *to Second Ave.* **$$**

Cyclo *International*

You can't miss this East Village eatery, what with the cyclo parked out front. T light, fresh Vietnamese cuisine more than compensates for the noisy atmosphere and cramped tables. The jellyfish and shrimp salad in a chili lime dressing is one of the more unusual appetizers, and the oxtail broth with noodles, sliced beef, scallions, and fresh herbs will fill you up without bogging you down. *203 First Ave. (bet. 12th and 13th Sts.), 212-673-3975.* ⬤ *to First Ave.* **$$**

Friend House *Asian Fusion*

This pan-Asian restaurant serves up a variety of Asian cuisines, including sushi, spicy chicken with peanuts, and steaming preserved-fish hot-pots. The small, elegantly decorated dining room has no air-conditioning, but does boast an outside seating area where patrons can enjoy an occasional breeze (or brutal sun) with their meal. The minimalist concrete interior and forgettable jukebox music make Friendhouse what the industry calls "cuisine driven." *99 3rd Ave. (bet. 12th and 13th Sts.) 212-388-1838.* ⬤ *to Third Ave.* **$$$**

Gnocco Café *Italian*

On a warm night, step through the cozy asymmetrical dining room into the back garden. Tucked in between apartment buildings, the outdoor space has a welcome European feel. Candlelight, ivy, and good wine make this the ideal place for a romantic dinner and quiet conversation. *337 E. 10th St. (bet. Aves. A and B), 212-677-1913, gnocco.com. Cash Only.* ⬤ *to First Ave.* **$**

MOST OLD-SCHOOL SODA

An egg cream, the quintessential turn-of-the-century New York drink, contains no eggs or cream, but rather cold milk, seltzer, and Fox's U-Bet Chocolate Syrup. The countermen at **GEM SPA** newsstand know that the recipe is open to no variation, and their faithful reproductions are yours for two bucks a piece. *131 Second Ave. (at St. Mark's Pl.), 212- 995-1866.* ➏ *to Astor Pl.* **$**

Hedeh *Japanese*

Hedeh stands out from the crowd of New York's hottest Japanese restaurants by focusing on food as their main concern rather than image. This is immediately apparent when you receive your appetizer; who would have known a Japanese restaurant could have some of the best foie gras in the city? The sushi is phenomenal, particularly the Dragon Roll. The entrees are excellently prepared, with the Prime Filet and Black Cod standing out in particular. The desserts are not too sweet, which is a welcome reprieve from the heavy, rich chocolate cakes at most popular steakhouses. Come to Hedeh for cuisine, not to be seen. *57 Great Jones St. (bet. Bowery and Lafayette St.), 212-473-8458.* ➏ *to Bleecker St.* **$$$**

Holy Basil *Thai*

It's hard to decide which is better: the romantic multi-level dining room with exposed brick, stained glass, and candles, or the enclosed porch overlooking the East Village. Either way, the food is a spicy treat in this popular Thai destination. The extensive menu features traditional favorites like mixed-seafood red curry with pineapple, along with a complete vegetarian menu; stand-outs include dishes like

brown soybean sauce, mushrooms and broccoli over wok-seared rice nood
Plates range from sweet to spicy (often leaning toward one of those extrem
with plenty of dipping sauces and arty flair. Although the wait staff seems frazz
at times, they aim to please. *149 Second Ave. (bet. 9th and 10th Sts.), 212-4*
5557. ⑥ *to Astor Place,* ⓡ ⓦ *to 8th St.* **$$**

Indochine *International*

Overtones of imperialism echo throughout this 22-year-old French-Vietname
stronghold. Palm fronds (real and painted) and a marble tiled floor make patr
feel as if they're in the most luxurious hotel in Saigon. The food is French in p
sentation, but also thoroughly Vietnamese; delectable menu classics are served
banana leaves, and the flavors blend exquisitely with delicious results. The cockt
are pleasant, but the chic and willowy waitresses are aloof. An enjoyable expe
ence, and the expensive atmosphere certainly evokes the highbrow feeling
owning a small parcel of land in another continent. *430 Lafayette St. (bet. 4th*
and Astor Pl.). 212-505-511. ⑥ *to Astor Pl.,* ⓝ ⓡ *at 8th St.* **$$$**

Khyber Pass *Middle Eastern*

With Persian rug placemats, subdued red and blue lights, and Arabian ceil
drapery, Khyber Pass creates a unique cultural experience. From Baulanee Ka
(a spiced pumpkin turnover served with yogurt dip) to the Kabuli and Shire
Palow (lamb and Cornish hen dishes), here Afghan cuisine is served at its fin
and best of all, it won't break the bank. *34 St. Mark's Place (bet. Second and Ti*
Ave.), 212-473-2451. ⑥ *to Astor Pl.* **$**

Le Miu *Asian Fusion*

The chefs from Nobu and Megu have come together to create a fusion me
that maintains the integrity of traditional Japanese cuisine in high New York fa
ion. For an adventure, try dinner prix-fixe, as long as you're okay with not know
what you'll get. Don't expect California rolls or tempura; indulge in the out
geous flavor combinations (fluke and espresso, for example) and the abunda
of tender raw fish at this new age restaurant. *107 Avenue A (bet. 6th and 7th S*
212-473-3100. ⓝ ⓡ ⓦ *to Astor Pl.* **$$$**

Le Souk *Middle Eastern*

Enthusiastic staff and loyal customers pack this candle-lit dive outfitted with t
tables and Moroccan lamps. Although patrons are seated a bit too close toget
in Le Souk's small quarters, the experience is worth the mild discomfort. T
three-tiered Mezze appetizer platter offers a sampling of North African flavor
traditional dishes prepared in a giant clay oven. Try the merguez, an authentic
nisian sausage, or the grilled fish prepared with Moroccan spices,. The restaur
grows increasingly lively as the night proceeds. A belly dancer shakes her east
groove while diners sip drinks or smoke hookahs delivered right to their tab
If you seek a rich cultural experience and flavorful meal, you can't go wrong
this small restaurant big on personality. *47 Avenue B (at E. 3rd St.), 212-777-54*
lesoukny.com. ⓥ *or* ⓕ *to Second Avenue.* **$$**

Le Tableau *French*

An unusual reprieve from typical East Village flamboyance, this adorable French restaurant offers high quality food and attentive service to a casual mix of diners. The daily rotating specials menu should encourage you to make repeat visits, but be sure you make a reservation on Friday and Saturday nights for parties of five and more to enjoy the live jazz band. *511 E. 5th St. (bet. Aves. A and B), 212-260-1333.* ❶ ❷ *to Second Ave,* ❻ *to Astor Pl.* **$$**

Life Café *American*

Featured in the musical Rent, this eclectic source of nutritious Cal-Mex platos is an East Village landmark because of its laid-back creativity. Check out the rotating exhibits by local artists, best viewed during the weekday happy hour from 5pm-9pm Even the restrooms provide an unexpected home to innovative artwork. *343 E. 10th St. (at Ave. B), 212-477-8791, lifecaféynyc.com* ❶ *to First Ave.* **$**

Lucky Cheng's and Waikiki Wally's *Asian Fusion*

If you like theme restaurants but are tired of bored service and cruddy décor, head over to Lucky Cheng's for a fun way to freak out your square folks. The food is good, but the impromptu lap dances provide true titillation. Watch as confused tourists get pulled on stage, partially denuded, and subjected to crazed drag queen whimsy. Once tipsy, descend to the karaoke "Jungle Lounge" to join in the fun and embarrass yourself even more. If you want a better meal than Lucky Cheng's can provide, or just less craze, check out the adjacent Waikiki Wally's for Hawaiian kitsch and a fun time. The drag queens are absent, but the cute male waitstaff still pleases the eye with their sarongs and quirky mannerisms. *24 First Ave. (bet. 1st and 2nd Sts.), 212-473-0516, planetluckychengs.com.* ❶ ❷ *to Second Ave.* **$$**

Mama's Food Shop *American*

Mama is, in fact, a man who cooked so much food for his friends that his space evolved into a restaurant. All the food is home-style and the portions are huge. Try the grilled salmon, but don't miss the awesome mac-and-cheese. Across the street, get soup and sandwiches at Step Mama's, a spin-off. *200 E. 3rd St. (bet. Avenues A and B), 212-777-4425, mamasfoodshop.com. Cash only.* ❶ ❷ *to Second Ave.* **$**

Masturbakers *Desserts*

Nothing spices up an office retirement party like a penis-shaped cake. Of course, making such a request at most bakeries will earn you the label of neighborhood weirdo. Thankfully, there's Masturbakers, whose penis and breast cakes (the latter of which bears the words "Breast Wishes") take the guesswork out of finding a baked good that will appropriately appall grandma. With moist devil's food cake, rich frosting, and bawdy details, the bakery lives up to its motto: "Tasty but tasteless." *511 E. 12th St. (bet. Avenues A and B), 212-475-0476.* ❶ *to First Ave.* **$**

Mermaid Inn *Seafood*

Impeccably fresh seafood, a seasonal menu and a wine list studded with glo-

betrotting picks for less than $40 ensure that this prettified clam shack buzz
every night. Their simple but sophisticated takes on New England beach fare, li
crispy calamari and avocado salad, overstuffed lobster sandwiches, and perfec
seasoned old bay fries are beautifully prepared by a gracious staff. A glass
zesty Riesling in the outdoor back garden serves as the perfect counterpoint tc
selection of briny oysters and clams from the raw bar. Be sure to make reserv
tions and request a table in the front room or cozy garden if weather permits,
the back dining hall is rather dark and clamorous when full. *96 Second Ave (b
5th and 6th St.), 212-674-5870, themermaidnyc.com.* **F** **V** *to Second Ave.,* **6**
Astor Pl. **$$**

Mitali *Indian*

The stretch of 6th St. between First and Second Aves. is overrun with medioc
Indian joints—but Mitali isn't one of them. Most of the chicken dishes here a
quite tasty and not too greasy, and they give you a lot of bang for your buck
great place to take a friend and talk. *334 E. 6th St. (bet. First and Second Aves.), 2*
533-2508. **6** *to Astor Pl.,* **F** **V** *to Second Ave.* **$**

Odessa *International*

One of the hippest Eastern European diners in the city, Odessa offers everyth
from standard diner food to potato pancakes and other regional fare. The locati
and 24-hour service makes it perfect for a food break while cruising the Aver
A bar scene. To continue drinking, you need only walk next door to their loun
where the cheapest gin and tonics in Manhattan are served by a surly babush
119 Ave.A (bet. 7th and 8th Sts.), 212-253-1470. **F** **V** *to Second Ave.,* **L** *to First Ave*

JUNK FOOD AS AN
ART FORM

Head down to **POMMES FRITES** for some of the best French Fries this side
the Somme. Choose from tons of sides, including vinegar, mayonnaise, and pl
ole' Ketchup. After enjoying some fries, walk around the area and check out
Mark's place for some debaucherous fun. *123 Second Ave., 212- 674-1234.* **N**
to 8th St.-NYU **$**

Rai Rai Ken *Japanese*

At this 14-seat noodle bar, a bowl of piping-hot ramen is infinitely better than
pre-packaged dorm-kitchen cousin. Fortunately for students, the prices are nea
as cheap, and the speedy cooks may even beat your humble hotplate in a ti
trial. Pair an ice-cold Sapporo with either miso or shio ramens—both win sm
between slurps. Still hungry? The pan-fried gyoza hits the spot every time.
214 E. 10th St. (bet. First and Second Aves.), 212-477-7030. Cash only. **6** *to As*
Pl., **L** *to First Ave.* **$**

Supper *Italian*

The people may be hot, but the pasta's even hotter. Don't miss the Priest Str
glers and the daily risotto special. Stop in on Saturday for the one flavored w
priceyamarone wine. Be prepared to sip a few glasses of wine in the cramped

Yaffa Café

stylish bar next door while you wait for a place at one of the rustic communal tables. *156 E. 2nd St., 212-477-7600. Cash Only.* **F** **V** *to Second Ave.* **$$**

Teresa's *International*

Vegetarians and dieters should steer clear of this stalwart, which is as old-world as it gets. At this Polish standby, middle-aged patrons sit amid thickly-framed oil paintings and happily devour big, meaty dinners. Start with the pierogi, and then order the thin, tender breaded veal cutlet. *103 First Ave. (at 6th St.), 212-228-0604.* **6** *to Astor Pl,* **F** *at Second Ave.* **$**

Two Boots Restaurant *Pizza*

Two Boots specializes in Cajun-Creole fare, such as creative pizzas with kitschy names like "The Divine" and "Mrs. Peel," and lots of vegan options. The restaurant got its name from the fact that both Italy and Louisiana are shaped like boots. Make sure to eye the slices before you buy, as sometimes they hang around a little too long. *37 Avenue A (at 3rd St.), 212-505-2276, twoboots.com.* **F** **V** *to Second Ave. Additional locations in Manhattan.* **$**

JNKIEST FOOD

The 24/7 **YAFFA CAFÉ** epitomizes eclectic taste. The menu is healthy and vegetarian-friendly, the décor ranges from Indian mosaics to Romanesque oil lamps, and the patrons are as diverse as the East Village itself. When it's possible to sit outside without getting hypothemia, go for the outdoor seating in the charming garden out back. There are few better places to wind down a night of drinking with some delicious food that's almost healthy enough to counteract the booze. And when you're paying your bill up at the counter, be sure to ask for the free Yaffa condoms. *97 St Marks Pl. (between Avenue A and 1st Ave.), 212- 674-9302, yaffacafé.com.* **6** *at Astor Pl;* **N** **R** **W** *to 8th St.* **$**

Yuca Bar *Latin*

Whether it's the music or the incredible food, something about this Latin American bistro makes you want to dance like you've never danced before. Every night, the street corner fills with a hipster crowd braving an hour-long wait that is worth it. The food is so top-notch and authentic you'll almost be convinced that you've flown to Southamerica for supper. To remind you that you're still in Manhattan, the menu has a fusion-twist (as do the Latin American cocktails), combining traditional American and South American flavors into great dishes like the guava BBQ short ribs. With a constantly changing menu, you never know what surprises will pop up. But one thing's for sure: Your meal will be a hit. *111 Avenue A (at 7th St.), 212-982-9533.* **6** *to Astor Place,* **F** **V** *to Second Ave.* **$$**

IGHTLIFE

11th Street Bar *Bar*

Locals fleeing the influx of tavern-tourists on Avenue A find asylum here. A cramped front bar opens up in the back with a handful of tables large enough to fit all your roommates or new friends. Incidentally, it's the official home in New

York for fans of the Liverpool Football Club. *510 E. 11th St. (bet. Aves. A and 212-982-3929. ● to First Ave, ● at Astor Pl.*

Angel's Share *Bar*

House rules border on the Draconian: no loud conversation, no parties lar than four, and no standing. But the ambience is intimate, the drinks profession mixed, and the floor-to-ceiling windows offer an excellent view of Stuyvesant Bring a date. *8 Stuyvesant St. (at Third Ave.), 212-777-5415. ● to Astor Pl.*

B Bar and Grill *Bar*

Formerly the Bowery Bar, this gives the impression of a place too cool for own good. It specializes in delightfully strong apple martinis, and the three bar including an outdoor courtyard and a back-room dance floor—keep custom entertained. Tuesday is gay night and Saturday brings in a young Wall St. cro Weekend brunches are generally mellow. *40 E. 4th St. (bet. Bowery and Lafay Sts.), 212-475-2220, bbarandgrill.com. ● ● to 8th St-NYU., ● to Bleecker.*

Baraza *Lounge*

At this dimly lit bar (part tropical bungalow, part industrial warehouse), dre locked waiters serve young couples and trios while a DJ spins reggae beats. C a green steel door opens onto the street—unless you know what to look for, rasta hip-hop spot for Alphabet Citizens may go unnoticed. *133 Ave. C (bet. and 9th Sts.), 212-539-0811, barazany.com. Cash only. ● to First Ave.*

Bar 288 (Tom & Jerry's) *Bar*

Colorful pottery sits behind the bar as a jukebox bangs out country and cla rock. Artists and filmmakers make this a regular drinking hole on weeknig Guinness ranks highly here, and Wisconsin folks are particularly welcome (Pa ers game every Sunday on the TV). *288 Elizabeth St. (at E. Houston), 212-2 5045. Cash only. ● ● to Broadway-Lafayette St., ● to Bleecker St.*

Beauty Bar *Bar*

Sparkling walls glitter and vintage hair dryers function as lounge chairs at beauty salon-turned-bar. The owner's collection of vintage pomade ads and hairpins add to the deliciously kitschy mood. Wednesday afternoon manicure drink specials are a must. *231 E. 14th St. (bet. Second and Third Aves.), 212-5 1389, beautybar.com. ● ● ● ● ● ● to 14th St.- Union Sq.*

Beige at B-Bar on Tuesday *LGBT*

Tuesday hosts one of the city's most reliable gay nights, with a fashionable cro and an outdoor patio during the summer. Predictably steep prices, so you m want to start the night elsewhere. The pick-up scene can get aggressive as night wears on, so it's not the kind of place you'll want to bring your straight friends to. *40 E. 4th St. (bet. Bowery and Lafayette St.), 212-475-2220, bbaran com. 6 to Bleecker St. ● ● ● ● to Broadway-Lafayette St.; ● ● ● at 8th S*

Continental *Music*

Everybody from Patti Smith to The Ramones to Guns N' Roses has played this famous club. Hard rock and ska shows are the main draw. *25 Third Ave. (at St. Mark's Pl.), 212-529-6924, continentalnyc.com.* ⑥ *to Astor Pl.,* ⓝ ⓡ *to 8th St.*

Coyote Ugly Saloon *Bar*

For all those not in the know, a "coyote ugly" is when you get so loaded that you wind up going home with someone and waking up to find that they are singularly unattractive and you would rather chew your arm than wake them up. It's not pretty and neither is this East Village standard. But dive bars are supposed to be ugly—just don't expect Tyra Banks to be dirty dancing on the bar. *153 First Ave. (bet. 9th and 10th Sts.), 212-477-4431, coyoteuglysaloon.com.* ⓛ *to First Ave,* ⑥ *at Astor Pl.*

DBA *Bar*

On Sundays, enjoy complimentary bagels with lox and cream cheese. Every day, enjoy one of the most extensive beer selections in the city. Hand-pumped ales and a wide variety of tequilas make this a popular hangout for regular East Siders, and there's a beer garden in back for those who crave fresh air. *41 First Ave. (bet. 2nd and 3rd Sts.), 212-475-5097, drinkgoodstuff.com.* ⑥ *to Bleecker St.,* ⓑ ⓓ ⓕ ⓥ *to Broadway-Lafayette St.*

Decibel *Bar*

Go early and with a small group, because this tight but beautiful sake bar gets packed fast. Hipsters descend on it because it's cavelike and mellow. Great for dates. If you want something more fast-paced, check out its spawn, Megadecibel. *240 E. 9th St. (bet. Second and Third Aves.), 212-979-2733, sakebardecibel.com.* ⓝ ⓡ ⓦ *to 8th St.-NYU, 6 to Astor Pl.*

Doc Holliday's *Bar*

"I'm trapped in here with the convicts who love me," said one bartender about the regulars. On weekends, this country-western joint swarms with hell-raisers who come to admire the wild animal pelts on the walls and the even wilder staff, who can often be found dancing on the bar. Try the homestyle BBQ food. *141 Ave. A (bet. 8th and 9th Sts.), 212-979-0312, docholllidaybar.com. Cash Only.* ⓛ *to First Ave,* ⑥ *at Astor Pl.*

Esperanto *Bar*

Crowds fill this tropical restaurant-bar on Monday and Wednesday evenings to hear Cuban bands and boleros play. A Pan-Latin menu of food and drinks combines Brazilian with Cuban, Caribbean, and other South American cuisines. Customers choose from items like Paella Bahiana, the standard Brazilian feijoada (bean stew) or seafood ceviche. Meals cost from $13 to $16, and drinks like mojitos run $6 to $8. *145 Ave. C (at 9th St.), 212-505-6559, esperantony.com.* ⓛ *to First Ave.,* ⑥ *to Astor Pl.*

Fish Bar *Bar*

This quaint owner-operated bar is a favorite in the neighborhood. The place
filled with reminders that you are in the Fish Bar, as the walls are painted a de
blue and are covered by fish paintings and sculptures, as well as a few ancho
The easy music soothes you, but feel free to ask the bartender to turn it up—c
tomers occasionally burst into song if the feeling hits them. The drinks are low
and the smaller seating area welcomes dates or small groups. If you have a fr
Monday, check out quiz night and win prizes. *237 E. 5th St. (bet. Astor Pl. and ⋅
St.), 212-475-4949. Cash only.* ⑥ *to Astor Pl.*

Joe's Pub *Bar*

This elegant but cozy lounge hosts some of the city's best live music, from hip-h
to cabaret. Acts are nearly always followed by a DJ. The drinks may be expens
but the waitstaff makes up for the prices by being so genial you want to hug the
Live acts are consistently good, so come by even if you have never heard of ⱃ
musicians. *425 Lafayette St. (bet. E. 4th St. and Astor Pl.), 212-539-8778, joespub.c
Cover: $5-$20.* ⑥ *to Astor Pl.*

KGB *Bar*

Soviet paraphernalia give this small upstairs bar an illicit feel, which is reinforc
by the regular poetry readings and theater downstairs. It's perfect for bringing ⱃ
your inner subversive artist with a good stiff drink. *85 E. 4th St. (bet. Second ⱃ
Third Aves.), 212-505-3360, kgbbar.com. Cash Only.* ⑤ ⑰ *to Second Ave.*

Lakeside Lounge *Music*

Come prepared to wait for your drinks, since this hipster haunt is packed e
on nights the bartender calls "real slow." Lots of live bands play regularly as v
Don't forget to immortalize yourself by stopping at the photobooth before y
leave. *162 Ave. B (at 10th St.), 212-529-8463, lakesidelounge.com.* ⑫ *to First Ave*

Louis 649 *Lounge*

For people who prefer good conversation to yelling over loud music, this Alp
bet City jazz bar is cool and laid-back. Four nights a week you can soak up so
jazz and sip up some inexpensive but carefully selected French and Italian wi
or imported beers. While nibbling on olives and goat cheese at the hand-craf
art deco bar, you can feel at home and out on the town at the same time—
be sure to observe the no cell phone rule. *649 E. 9th St., 212-673-1190, louisé
com.* ⑫ *to First Ave.*

Lunasa *Lounge*

Live Celtic music, a laid-back atmosphere, a warm candlelit interior and ⱦ
charming Irish accents of the staff create a distinctly Irish atmosphere in this l
East Village enclave. There are quiet tables in the back, a performance area in fr
and a large bar in the middle offering a wide selection of beer. Try their spe
the PB&J shots, for an interesting interpretation of the classic sandwich. *126 ⱦ

Ave. (bet. 7th and St. Marks), 212-228-8580, lunasabar.com. ❶ *to First Ave.,* ❻ ⓥ
to Second Ave.

Manitoba's *Music*

Owned and operated by "Handsome" Dick Manitoba, frontman for NYC's legendary punkers, the Dictators. Manitoba's known for pouring some of the East
Village's strongest drinks. Featuring live music 7 night a week, with genres ranging
from country to rock. *99 Ave. B (bet. 6th and 7th Sts.), 212-982-2511, manitobas.
com.* ❻ *to Second Ave.,* ❶ *to First Ave.*

Mannahatta Music *Bar*

A caramel-colored aura absorbs the high-energy vibe of the famed CBGBs across
the street, beckoning Bowery Bar stragglers to this two-level tapas lounge complete with downstairs dance parties and balmy outdoor seating. Upstairs, sleek
inviting couches cradle decadent triple-decker desserts and theamorous couples
ordering them. The dance floor, however, seems like a basement with a direct
line from the NJ Transit. The sometimes stubborn bouncers will let anyone in
willing to pay the gender-blind $10 cover charge. The drinks are strong, but also
small enough to remind you of those juice cups mother served you OJ in as a
kid. Despite the relaxed vibe, you'll find yourself ready to move on after a few
mini-cups. *316 Bowery (bet. Bleecker and Bond), 212-253-8644, mannahatta.us.* ❻
at Bleecker St.

Mars Bar *Bar*

A rowdy and boozy bunch fill this tattered shoebox of a bar at all hours. Possibly
the dumpiest, most disheveled bar on the planet, but charming nevertheless.
25 E. 1st St. (at Second Ave.), No Phone. Cash Only. ❻ *to Second Ave.*

McSorley's Old Ale House *Bar*

The walls reveal the history of this beer-lover haven that opened in 1854. The
photographs that cover the walls show men drinking the legendary dark and
light beers (ale and porter) date as far back as the early 20th century. Steeped
in tradition, the newer management stays true to the legend of the tavern by
continuing to serve only light and dark beers, costing $3.50 each. Patrons can
snack on cheese and crackers until closing. It is rare to find such a friendly tavern
in this city, filled with genuine Irish accents and hospitality that no one can beat.
*15 E. 7th Street (bet. Second and Third Avenues), 212-473-9148, mcsorleysnewyork.
com. Cash only.* ❻ *to Astor Pl.*

Mona's *Bar*

Punk rock lives…in the jukebox at Mona's. It's a favorite place for East Village
squatter kids who come here with their mangy dogs and multiple tattoos and
piercings. *224 Ave. B (bet. 13th and 14th Sts.), 212-353-3780, liveatmonas.com.* ❶
to First Ave.

Mr. Black *LGBT*

Formerly Table 50, this basement disco retains some of the seediness of past li
as a speakeasy and an S&M dungeon; now this establishment is frequent haunt
a fashionable, young crowd. We particularly loved dancing to the superior mu
Stylish, but not uptight, it sells expectedly pricey drinks that complement
$5 cover on weeknights, $10 weekends, but free on Sundays. Though equipp
with the customary shadowy lounge area, the DJ's smart mix of electro, hou
Italo disco, and funk will guarantee you won't be down for long. *643 Broadw
(at Bleecker St.), 212-253-2560, basementnyc.com. Cash only, $10 cover T R a
midnight.* ⓝ ⓡ ⓦ *to 8th St.*

Niagara *Bar*

Niagara puts a hip spin on nostalgia. From the bartenders in their silk, ha
painted ties to the bamboo-walled tiki lounge downstairs, Niagara pays hom
toamerica's innocent years. The tiki lounge features a full range of tropical dri
112 Ave. A (bet. 7th and 8th Sts.), 212-420-9517. ⓕ ⓥ *to Second Ave.*

Nightingale Bar *Bar*

The Nightingale has a reputation for being the favorite late night jam spot
many now-famous acts. You can see local acts here seven nights a week. Ha
hour from 1pm-8pm daily. Mostly pop and rock bands and the occasional sol
*213 Second Ave. (at 13th St.), 212-473-9398, nightingalelounge.com. Cash only. C
er: free-$5.* ⓛ *to Third Ave.*

Orchid Lounge *Lounge*

Red satin pillows and Japanese lanterns fill this bar, a relaxed place to unw
The bartenders are friendly, unlike many of their pretentious Lower East S
colleagues. Try some of their unique drinks, like pumpkin-infused vodka, or cho
from their wide selection of Asian beers. *500 E. 11th St., (bet. Aves. A and B), 2
254-4090, orchidloungenyc.com.* ⓛ *to First Ave.*

Otto's Shrunken Head *Bar*

Formerly the Barmacy Bar, this tiki bar welcomes private functions, film sho
photo shoots, and "anything else you'd like to shoot except drugs." It's not
served on most nights however, when stylish downtowners crowd the place
generously-poured drinks. *538 E. 14th St. (bet. Aves. A and B), 212-228-2240,
tosshrunkenhead.com.* ⓛ *to First Ave.*

Pyramid *LGBT*

Its worn black exterior and neon sign make this East Village dance club a l
off-putting from the outside, but once you step inside, the party is defin
worthwhile. There's typically a $10-or-under cover charge, for only the ga
'80s dance music, and once you're in back dancing to "Ah-Ha" it's very har
pry yourself away from the floor. Drinks are small and slightly overpriced, bu
rare to find a place to dance that's consistently fun. Gay men and gay women
all approachable and eager to get picked up, but the scene is not all meat mar

Mars Bar

Pyramid will please your whole group of party-goers, even the straight ones, because the dance floor is dark enough to hide even the most embarrassing moves. *101 Ave. A (bet. 6th and 7th Sts.), 212-228-4888. Cash only.* *to Astor Pl.*

Sidewalk Café *Café*
Before moving to the backroom of the Sidewalk Café, the Fort was an afterhours club on the Lower East Side. It still retains its underground appeal, centered around manager Lach's Anti-Folk Anti-Hoot on Mondays, which is an open mic. Sidewalk Café features one of the cheapest breakfast specials in NYC, as well as a full menu and bar. Presents folk, anti-folk, and rock shows. *94 Ave. A (at 6th St.), 212-473-7373.* *to Second Ave.*

Starlight *LGBT*
Starlight fits in perfectly with the jam packed East Village party crowd, as it's nearly always full on weekends. The chandelier-lit bar is on the small side but plenty of white vinyl seats up front appease competitive partiers. Getting drinks, finding a seat, and striking up conversation with that cute recent-grad at the next table are more difficult than expected. Nonetheless, Starlight is the center of the East Village gay scene, and is one of the few gay bars that has actually succeeded in attracting both gay men and gay women (Sunday is ladies-only). *167 Ave. A (bet. 10th and 11th Aves.), 212-475-2172, starlightbarlounge.com.* *to Astor Pl.*

Swift Hibernian Lounge *Lounge*
Beneath the dreamlike painting that stretches the length of this long beer hall, drinkers at Swift's encounter sweating mugs of beers imported from all over the world; they toss their drinks down in the loud company of friends from the neighborhood. The dim-lit, cavernous back room has long oak tables and is separated from the bar by a purple velvet curtain. *34 E. 4th St. (bet. Lafayette and Bowery Sts.), 212-260-3600.* *to 8th St.,* *to Astor Pl.*

Tile Bar–WCOU Radio *Bar*

They may serve good martinis, margaritas, and hot sake, but sitting down at [this] old-school bar across from huge wood-framed mirrors, you're gonna want a [cold] cool pint. Looking around at the trappings of old New York, it is no surprise [the] owner is fond of antiques. Check out the vintage black and white photographs [of] the old neighborhood that adorn the walls. Whether your musical taste runs [to]ward Stan Getz or the Beastie Boys, you're sure to find something on the eclec[tic] jukebox glowing against the back wall. Happy Hour 5pm-8pm, seven days a we[ek] and Sundays from midnight to 4am. *115 First Ave. (at 7th St.), 212-254-4317.* [6] *to Astor Pl.,* ● *to First Ave.*

Zum Schneider-Bavarian Bierhaus *Pub*

This essential German-style pub has become a must-drink for locals. The so[c]cer crowd gathers here to watch from a handful of TV screens and drink be[er] from 10-inch-tall liter mugs of Weltenburger Kloster, Kacker Pschorr, Panla[ner] Schneider Weisse, and Spaten. 5 to 7 dollars for pints, double that for liters, a[ll] accompanied by menu items like Wiener Schnitzel ($15), Bratwurst ($12), a[nd] Baked Bavarian Meat Loaf ($10). *107 Ave. C (at 7th St.). 212-598-1098, zums[ch]neider.com.* ● *to First Ave.*

ARTS

Rivington Arms *Galleries*

Fashionistas and Brooklyn hipsters intersect at this gallery run by the children [of] New York society mavens and downtown royalty. With the intent of making [the] Lower East Side into the new Chelsea, evolution has become a byword for [the] diverse installation pieces at this small but creative gallery full of gay guys and g[als]. *4 E. 2nd St., 1st Floor (at Bowery). 646-654-3213; rivingtonarms.com. Hours:* [W] *11am-6pm, Sa-Su 12pm-6pm, Sa-Su 12pm-6pm* ● ● *to Second Ave.*

Astor Place Theater *Theater*

The theater has housed the famous Blue Man Group for many years, allow[ing] people to come and see three bald and blue figures perform before their e[yes]. Although the performance is engaging, the theater is also a good reason to [visit] this venue. Originally built in 1831 in a series of connected buildings, it was de[sig]nated as a historic landmark in 1963. The building is designed in a Greek style [that] incorporates marble columns and once served as a residence to the Vanderb[ilts]. *434 Lafayette St. 212-254-4370.* ● *to Astor Pl.,* ● ● *to 8th St.-NYU.*

Bowery Poetry Club *Theater*

This is the latest project of Bob Holman, poetry popularizer extraordinaire. [He] helped engineer the rejuvenation of the Nuyorican Poets Café in the late '[80s,] guided the People's Poetry Gathering, and teaches at Bard College in upst[ate] New York. Here, in a cozy café and bar with an art gallery on one side and a st[age] in the back, poets and performers of all kinds come for readings, plays, and c[on]certs. The small seating area for the stage is somewhat uncomfortable (with h[ard] seats), but if you go on a good night, you'll forget all about where you're si[tting]

Pearl Theater

as you listen. Acts range from nervous college students reading overly intellectual rambles to acts by Andy Warhol's buddy Taylor Mead; also be sure to check out the interesting off-off-Broadway shows and world music. Poetry chapbooks and CDs for sale give a small taste of the ever-growing scene this venue fosters. *308 Bowery (at 1st St.). 212-614-0505, bowerypoetry.com. Cash only.* ❶ ❶ *to Second Ave.*

The Kraine Theater *Theater*

The Kraine is a fantastic blackbox venue featuring eclectic fare presented by the Horse Trade Theatre Group. Upstairs from the Kraine is the KGB bar, and the third floor houses the intimate Red Room theatre. That's a lot of entertainment packed into one narrow building, and the shows performed at all three locations rarely disappoint. *85 E. 4th St. (at Second Ave.), 212-460-0982, horsetrade.info.* ❶ ❶ ❶ ❶ *to Broadway-Lafayette St.,* ❻ *to Bleecker St.*

New York Theater Workshop *Theater*

Upon entering the pristine, gorgeous New York Theater Workshop, you may find yourself unable to believe you're standing in the birthplace of the legendary rock opera Rent. But Rent did indeed start at the NYTW, along with shows like Bright Lights, Big City, Dirty Blonde, and Homebody-Kabul. The NYTW is a key player in the downtown theatre scene as a nurturing home to new voices, and their productions are often electric and thought-provoking. Rush tickets are available for most performances. *79 E. 4th St. (at Second Ave.), 212-780-9037, nytw.org.* ❶ ❶ ❶ *to Second Ave.*

Pearl Theater *Theater*

This classic repertoire-resident company sticks to a strict pre-WWI itinerary, with conventional productions of Shakespeare, Molière, Sophocles, as well as revived relics. Shows generally run seven weeks. Heterogeneous crowd with plenty of local traffic. *80 St. Mark's Pl. (bet. First and Second Aves.), 212-598-9802, pearltheatre. org.* ❶ ❶ *to 8th St.,* ❻ *to Astor Pl.*

St. Mark's Church

Performance Space 122 *Theater*

This small performance space in a converted church serves as a showplace for cutting-edge dance, theater, and performance art. Artists range from obscure-but-talented newcomers to established members of the downtown scene. Runs tend to be short and very popular, so try to get tickets in advance. *150 First Ave. (at 9th St.), 212-477-5288, ps122.org.* ❶ ❶ *to Second Ave.*

St. Mark's Church in the Bowery *Theater*

A quiet and beautiful cultural oasis in the bustling East Village, this century-old church is home to three excellent arts "projects," including Danspace, Poetry Project, and the Ontological Theater. The Poetry Project offers special literary events and workshops for budding poets; they also offer a forum for both well-known and emerging poets to read their work. *131 E. 10th St. (at Second Ave.), 212-674-6377, stmarkschurch-in-the-bowery.com. Cash only.* ❻ *to Astor Pl.*

Theater for the New City *Theater*

Not to be confused with Theatre for a New Audience, this scrappy East Village outpost of bizarre performance art and radical philosophy holds its own across the street from P.S. 122. The lobby houses ancient, overstuffed sofas where grungy, dazed-looking Bohemians lounge, reading from pamphlets and manifestosamong the books for sale. Flyers and postcards advertising upcoming performances and goings-on elsewhere paper every possible space. Performances in the boxy, high-ceilinged theater range from puppet shows to wildly experimental acts to acrobatics. This is definitely not the place you want to go for a nice, calm evening of theater, especially if you've never been to an off-off Broadway show. But if you enjoy a message with your entertainment, or can handle the extra-wacky and low-budget, drop by. After this, nothing will seem strange. *155 First Ave. (btw 9th and 10th St.), 212-254-1109, theaterforthenewcity.net. Cash only.* 🄵 🅥 *to Second Ave.*

Amato Opera House *Music*

Head downtown to see the divas of tomorrow paying their dues in an intimate setting. Theamato Opera House is an alternative for opera lovers who lack the funds for nosebleed seats at the Met. amato's goal is to foster opera appreciation by making the genre more accessible, so many performances are English translations of Italian classics. *319 Bowery St. (bet. E. 2nd and Bleecker Sts.), 212-228-8200,amato.org. Cash only.* 🄱 🄳 🄵 🅥 *to Lafayette St.*

CBGB *Music*

When CBGB OMFUG—which stands for Country Bluegrass Blues and Other Music For Uplifting Gormandizers—opened in 1973, no one could have guessed this little hole-in-the-wall bar-music venue would become a rock and roll legend.among other things, it showcased The Ramones before they revolutionized American punk, and Debbie Harry before she was the face of Blondie. Now, thanks to a lease dispute, the club's future is in constant danger, so hurry downtown and catch a piece of rock history before it's too late. *315 Bowery (bet. 1st and 2nd Sts.), 212- 982-4052, cbgb.com.* 🄶 *to Bleecker St.*

Anthology Film Archives *Film*

Examining film as an art form on par with that of the hallowed halls of the MoMA, this gallery organizes viewings, reviews, opening parties, and curated exhibitions of their rotating collection. This new approach appeals not just to film buffs already in-the-know, but those of us looking for something more than the current blockbuster can offer. *32 Second Ave. (at 2nd St.), 212-505-5181, anthologyfilmarchives. org. Hours vary. Cash only.* 🄵 🅥 *to Second Ave.*

City Cinemas Village East *Film*

By all indications this seems to be just another multi-screened showplace for big-budget Hollywood productions, but within the nondescript exterior lay the preserved interior of the old Yiddish Theater. It is complete with original adornments and multi-tiered theater-style seating. So for a real treat, buy a ticket to whatever is showing in Theater Number One and get there early to check out

CGBG

this historical landmark. *181 Second Ave. (at 12th St.), 212-529-6998,* 🅛 🅝 🅡 🅦 ❹ ❺ ❻ *to 14th St.-Union Sq.*

Landmark Sunshine Cinema *Film*

Originally an old vaudeville house, this space was redesigned into a new movie theater that is both comfortable and pleasant. Three screens and stadium-style seating give the viewer the variety of movies and comfort needed to enjoy a show—even if a six-foot giant takes the seat in front of you. The theater is very clean, and an excellent espresso bar serves coffee and locally baked cookies and pastries. *143 E. Houston St. (bet. First & Second Ave.), 212-236-5849, landmarktheatres.com.* 🅕 🅥 *to Second Ave.*

HOPPING

Arthur's Invitations and Prints *Miscellaneous*

Eight thousand square feet of custom invitations and exclusive gifts lie in the heart of Union Square. Luxe custom-printed invitations are available for any occasion you can think up. Carries high-end stationary and notepads for all purposes, including names like Crane & Co., Kate Spade, and H. Lalo. Full service printing, designing, and framing is done on-premises. And if that wasn't enough, they also have a live jazz concert in the front once a month, as well as an annual wedding cocktail gala. *13 East 13th St. (5th ave), 212-807-6502; arthursinvitations.com, Hours: M-Th 9am-8pm, Fr 9am-7pm, Sa 10am-7pm, Su noon-7pm.* 🅛 🅝 🅞 🅡 ❹ ❺ ❻ *to Union Sq.-14th St.*

Cronick Valentine *Clothing : Boutiques*

This store's uniqueness comes from its ability to excel at the art of "reusing." At this cute shop, customers can browse the store's patented T-Shirt Graveyard and turn their old tee shirts into everything from new iPod cases, to tote bags and duvet covers. Where else can one turn that Foreigner t-shirt from the 1984

World Tour into something useful? If you do not have personal clothing to spa
Cronick Valentine also sells pre-made items from vintage t-shirts. 324 E. 9th
212-288-7767, cronickvalentine.com. Hours: Su, T-R 12pm-7pm, F-Sa 12pm-9pm
to First Ave.

Kiehl's *Beauty*

The latest and, as many claim, greatest in all-natural skin care and cosmetics,
store has been selling standout products like their #1 lip balm and notoriously r
hand creams since 1851. Service here is exceptional and salespeople are kno
for giving out oodles of samples. The line is a bit pricey, but certainly worth it. A
available at Barney's, Bloomingdales and Saks. 109 Third Ave. (at 13th St.), 212-6
3171, kiehls.com. Hours: M-Sa 10am-7pm **N** **R** **W** **4** **5** **6** to 14th St.-Union

Other Music *Music*

A haven for indie-rock lovers that also offers a full selection of ambient psyche
lia and noise. Keep an eye out for special in-store performances that have alre
featured Yo La Tengo and Jowe Head. 15 E. 4th St. (bet. Broadway and Lafayette
212-477-8150, othermusic.com. Hours: M-F 12pm-9pm, Sa 12pm-8pm, Su 12
7pm **B** **D** **F** **V** to Broadway-Lafayette St., **6** to Astor Pl.

Screaming Mimi's *Clothing : Vintage & Consignment*

It's hard to miss the signature violet flag, visible from anywhere on Lafayette
hanging above the shop's storefront. Inside, you'll find some of the most out
geous vintage clothing in the city: Elvis suits, pink leisure outfits, leather pants, a
neon-colored patched shirts. The excellent condition of the clothing marks
the prices a bit, but the pieces are well worth it—if you dare to wear them.
Lafayette St. (at E. 4th St.), 212-677-6464, screamingmimis.com. Hours: M-Sa 12
8pm, Su 1pm-7pm **B** **D** **F** **V** to Broadway-Lafayette St., **6** to Bleecker St.

St. Mark's Comics *Books*

From *X-Men* to the less conventional *Sexy Sushi*, there's enough here for
comic book connoisseur. Kids (and the young at heart) will love the large se
tion of toys, posters and old comics. 11 St. Mark's Pl. bet. Second and Third Av
212-598-9439. Hours: Su-T 10am-11pm, W-Sa 10am-1am **6** to Astor Pl.

CLASSES AND WORKSHOPS

Time's Up Bike Repair Workshop

Time's Up is best known for their controversial Critical Mass rallies, where hor
of bikers flood city streets in protest of our car-centric society and the problem
presents. The group also sponsors a free bike repair and maintenance worksh
for basic skills such as fixing flats and overhauling wheels. On Monday nights, t
offer a women's class with female mechanics. The space hosts an open skill-sh
workshop and demonstrations on welding and more advanced modificatic
You're also invited to come in and practice on bikes in need of repair; fix two

the third you fix is yours! *49 E. Houston St. (bet. Mott and Mulberry), times-up.org. Hours: M 6:30pm, T 6:30pm, R 6:30pm.* **B D F V 6** *to Bleecker St.-Lafayette St.*

HOTELS AND HOSTELS

Bowery's Whitehouse Hotel of New York

As the newest hostel in the NoHo district of Manhattan, Bowery's Whitehouse Hotel offers clean, but small rooms and a convenient location. Housing is dormitory style, with thin walls that do not reach the ceiling separating beds, but is otherwise as expected for a hostel. *340 Bowery St., whitehousehotelofny.com. Single $27-$30, double $50-$60, triple $70-$80.* **F V** *to Bowery.*

Jazz on the Town

This free-spirited hostel in the heart of the East Village offers small but clean rooms, along with cleaner-than-average bathrooms. The service is friendly and the location is great, with eclectic bars and restaurants only minutes away.amenities include free blankets, pillows, and linens, air-conditioned rooms, and no curfew. *307 E. 14th St (at Secondnd Ave.), 212-228-2780, jazzonthepark.com. Rooms are $29-$39.* **L** *to First or Third Aves.*

Second Home on Second Avenue

A classic, tranquil, European-style bed and breakfast, this hotel is a good choice for low maintenance guests. It boasts clean and functional rooms with comfortable beds, a friendly manager, and a good location. Though the club below can get noisy at times, Second Home is a good choice for those looking to experience down-home comfort while in the big city. *221 Second Ave (bet. 13th and 14th Sts.), 212-677-3161, secondhome.citysearch.com. Rooms $80-$200.* **4 5 6 L N O R W** *to Union Sq.,* **L** *to 3rd Ave.*

Union Square Inn

This boutique hotel offers a great location along with affordability. But with hard beds, noisy neighbors, the constant smell of cigarette smoke, and broken windows, this hotel might not be the best choice for an extended stay in the city for all but the most budget-conscious. *209 E. 14th St. (bet. 2nd and 3rd Ave), 212-614-0500, unionsquareinn.com. Rooms $129-$179.* **L** *to Third Ave*

Meatpacking District

ONCE ONE OF MANHATTAN'S grittiest neighborhoods—thanks
250 meat-processing plants and an underworld of alternative sex lairs
the Meatpacking District is now the premier destination for celebriti
socialites, and convincing poseurs, putting a whole new spin on the ter
"meat market." Formerly known as Gansevoort Market, the neighb
hood stretches from the Hudson River east to Hudson Street, and fro
Gansevoort Street up to about 16th Street.

At night, Jimmy Choo-shod models stumble along the cobblesto
streets, brusque bouncers corral crowds with velvet ropes, and pe
ish after-partiers recharge at the popular French bistro Pastis and
24-hour neighbor, Florent. During the day, after the morning stench h
cleared from the thirty-odd remaining packing plants, the beautiful pe
pleamble from boutique to gallery, often stopping for a late lunch
Spice Market with their Alexander McQueen and La Perla shopping ba
tucked under the table.

Widely regarded as one of the city's most fashionable neighb
hoods, the Meatpacking District has only been a hot spot for a har
ful of years. Following in the footsteps of other renovated grit-to-c
areas like SoHo and Tribeca, the neighborhood changed from butc
to scenester so fast that a coalition of concerned New Yorkers, head
by local restaurateur Florent Morellet, started Save Gansevoort Mark
which successfully lobbied for the area to be designated a historic distr
in 2003.

Juggling three separate economies keeps the district busy round 1
clock. Design stores, boutiques, salons, and galleries operate from 1

morning to late afternoon, just when the area's restaurants start turning tables. Around midnight, the bars and clubs take over, their music thumping until the wee hours of the morning. Finally, as straggling partiers enter waiting cabs, the remaining meatpacking plants come alive.

The result is a vibrant neighborhood in transition, a mix of blue-collar and star-studded industries alike. Day or night, the district piques the senses, whether with packing-plant runoff or designer perfume, rumbling truck motors or booming house music, rustic metal awnings or glittering window displays.

HISTORY

>> THE FIRST PEOPLE to leave their mark on this land were, not surprisingly, Native Americans. Hundreds of years ago, local tribes carved a trail leading to the Hudson River: the Great Kill or Old Kill Road. Years later, amid the first rumbles of the War of 1812 with Britain, the fledgling American military constructed a fort at the end of this road. They called it "Fort Gansevoort" after General Peter Gansevoort, a veteran of the American Revolution. In 1837, the old river trail took the soldier's name as well and became Gansevoort Street.

Gansevoort Market opened in 1884 as an open-air produce market, with meat, poultry and dairy products sold in a nearby building. In 1949, the city built the Gansevoort Meat Center on the market's original site, cementing the meat industry's foothold on the district. Soon the architecture began to reflect the industrial tenants. Characteristic metal awnings jutted from simple, functional building designs. Animal carcasses hung from giant hooks.

The meatpacking plants, usually operating from high moon to high noon, may have provided the neighborhood's most lucrative nightlife, but certainly not its most salacious. Beginning in the late 1960s, the area became home to a motley collection of businesses including gay clubs like Assterisk and Cell Block, as well as after-hours haunts like Jay's Hangout and the infamous Hellfire Club. The members-only club Mineshaft lured clientèle through a clothes check on their way to the dungeons on S&M nights. Most of these have vanished with the neighborhood's redevelopment, as have many of the smaller meatpacking plants; with rising rents and an ever-cleaner image, the neighborhood is slowly sweeping the grit and grind off the block.

WHAT TO SEE

The High Line

Separating the Meatpacking District from the Hudson River, this rusty railroad elevated some thirty feet above the ground hasn't seen a passing train since 1980, but it still keeps the neighbors and city planners abuzz. As recently as 2000, developers and local property owners sought to demolish the site, but concerned preservationists convinced authorities to transform it into a public park. The city

expects to complete the first stage of the project—a verdant swath stretch
from Gansevoort Street to 20th—by Spring 2008. Originally dubbed the "L
Line of New York," the High Line, begun in 1924 and completed a decade lat
once passed straight through dozens of warehouses, supplying West Side indu
trial communities with food and raw materials. *33rd Street (between 11th Ave. c*
the West Side Highway), thehighline.org. Ⓐ Ⓒ Ⓔ *to 34th St.-Penn Station.*

The Little Flatiron Building

Few architectural feats are as visually striking as triangular buildings. Everyon
knows the Flatiron Building, but a similar structure downtown has garnered t
nickname The Little Flatiron Building. The structure was completed in 1849 an
served a myriad of purposes over the years, including the housing of both Ja
Hangout and the Hellfire Club, infamous haunts of the underground gay, lesbi
and S&M scenes. Now, the space houses Vento Trattoria during the daytime an
evening, and Level V, a club that throbs in the building's basement, at night. *669-6*
Hudson Street (between 13th and 14th Sts.). Ⓐ Ⓒ Ⓔ Ⓛ *to 14th St–8th Aven*

Florent

In 1985, when the Meatpacking District was still known for pork shoulders an
prostitutes, restaurateur Florent Morellet opened an all-night bistro on Ga
sevoort Street, drawing local crowds with his staple French fare. Twenty yea
later, his eponymous restaurant, Florent, stands at the heart of this revampe

Maritime Hotel

district, serving the same moules frites to late-night clubbers now as he served to biker chicks decades ago. *69 Gansevoort Street (between Greenwich and Washington Streets), 212/989-5779, restaurantflorent.com.* **A** **C** **E** *to 14th St,* **L** *to Eighth Ave.*

Maritime Hotel

Once the National Maritime Union, in 2003 this glamorous boutique hotel opened as yet another hip addition to the Meatpacking District. Designed by renowned architect Richard Meier, this modern, white-tile 25-story building situated near the Hudson looks like a huge boat beached on the city streets of Manhattan. Unique port-hole windows, along with room accommodations that resemble ship staterooms, truly give it a sea-worthy appearance, and the sleek dining and nightlife facilities make it a hotspot for scenesters. *363 W. 16th St. (at Ninth Ave.), 212-242-4300, themaritimehotel.com.* **A** **C** **E** *to 14th St.,* **L** *to Eighth Ave.*

WHERE TO EAT

5 Ninth *Asian Fusion*

5 Ninth no longer relies on word-of-mouth advertising for being known. Wheras before it hid behind an umarked door, now a glass-covered menu greets passersby. This Asian-inspired restaurant is still well worth a whispered recommendation. On the building's ground floor, the bar offers primly named cocktails, like the White Star Imperial Daisy and the Pompadour. In the main dining room on the second floor, plates of Berkshire pork belly sit alongside red curry duck. The top floor houses a dimly lit lounge, one of the last Manhattan refuges where smokers can light up indoors. *5 Ninth Avenue (bet. Gansevoort and Little West 12th Streets), 212-929-9460, 5ninth.com.* **A** **C** **E** **1** **2** **3** *to 14th St.* **$$$**

BED *French*

Don't worry about getting crumbs in the bed—it's expected at this Miami import, where diners can enjoy a delicious meal while seated upon a luxurious mattress. The cuisine is French-inspired, with a hint of Brazilian influence. The foie gras appetizer is phenomenal; but be sure to try one of the sultry cocktails, like the Red Head in Bed or the Wet Spot. The desserts are also fabulous, particularly the crème brulée. *530 W 27th St, 6th Floor (bet. 10th & 11th Aves.), 212-594-4109.* **C** **E** *to 23rd St.* **$$**

Ono *Asian Fusion*

Located within the Hotel Gansevoort, this snazzy Asian-American fusion delivers unparalleled Eastern delicacies in an interior setting that smacks of Hollywood glam. For a more intimate evening, try Ono's sofa-laden private cabanas. The menu includes an impressive assortment of succulent meats and fish cooked over an open flame robata grill, a signature selection of sushi, and a choice of large plates that are ideal for sharing. Do not neglect their exceptional cocktails: the "Blushing Geisha" is out of this world. *18 Ninth Ave. (at Gansevoort St), 212-660-6766.* **A** **C** **E** **L** *to 14th St.-Eighth Ave.* **$$$**

Little Pie Company

ONLY MODEL–FREE
STORE IN THE
NEIGHBORHOOD

For some, dessert in the Meatpacking District means an espresso and a cigarette. For the rest, a nice slice of homemade cherry pie hits the spot. **LITTLE PIE COMPANY** specializes in decadent pies ranging from sour cream apple walnut to Southern pecan. Stop by for a slice, splurge on a five-inch individual tart, or order a full-sized pie to share with the roommates. Other bakery staples like brownie and coffee cake are also available, as well as assorted savory quiches. If you like old-school vibe, you'll love the retro feel in this bakery, complete with a diner-style counter and swivel stools. *407 West 14th Street (bet. 9th and 10th Aves.), 212-4 2324, littlepiecompany.com.* **Ⓐ Ⓒ Ⓔ Ⓛ** *to 14th St–Eighth Ave.* **$$**

NIGHTLIFE

Guest House *Club*

With wallpaper resembling a Victorian living room, and comfortable couches line ing the walls, this almost feels like your local bed and breakfast— only with pour ing music. Everyone in the crowd is either beautiful, well-connected, or rich, mo often a combination of all three. Dance to your favorite urban beats spanni decades, or elbow your way through those with lots of AmEx Black to burn Guest House. Not just a weekend spot, this place is hopping on Tuesdays. Expe to pay: Grey Goose, even in your mixed drinks, is the norm, and bottle serv will set you back a pretty penny. *542 W. 27th St. (at 10th Ave.), 212-273-37 homeguesthouse.com. No Cover.* **Ⓒ Ⓔ** *to 23rd St.*

BEST REASON TO
BATTLE THE
VELVET ROPE

If you can make it past the bouncer at **CIELO**, you're in for a long and gloric night at one of the District's hottest clubs. Voted Best Deep House Club New York magazine in 2006, Cielo prides itself on being the city's best ver for international dance and electronic music. Inside, linear designs in brown a beige suede create a retro 1970s feel and, with a capacity of only 300 people, t atmosphere is intimate and lively. *18 Little West 12th St (between Ninth Ave. c Washington Street), 212-645-5700, cieloclub.com.* **Ⓒ Ⓔ** *to 23rd St.*

HIRO *Club*

Edgy beauties mix with pre-professionals at this japonais-chic rock-and-roll club. Posh without the pretension, a soft sexy glow emanates from the votive candles cast along the walls as scantily clad ladies serenely swing from the ceilings. Although tables are set up where the dance floor should be, everyone here breaks a sweat. VIPs congregate in the balcony lounge. Drinks can be expensive and tables overpriced; just bring in some girls and tell them it's your birthday. *371 W. 16th St. (at 9th Ave.), 212-242-4300.* Ⓐ Ⓒ Ⓔ Ⓛ *to 14 St-Union Sq.*

Home *Club*

No different from your typical Meatpacking destination, Home is intimate, which means rubbing elbows (or bodies) with everyone on the floor. Hit Home on the weekend for the best crowd, but arrive earlier if you want to beat the crazed rope rush. As expensive as the rest of them, but with a slightly less diverse crowd. Good DJing means some serious dancing—on the floors, on the tables, on the couches…just about anywhere you can find space. *532 W. 27th St. (at 10th Ave.), 212-273-3700, homeguesthouse.com.* Ⓒ Ⓔ *to 23rd St.*

PM *Lounge*

For the moment, pm is still a very trendy lounge. There usually isn't a cover, though it can be difficult to get in if you aren't in a group comprised mostly of beautiful women. The space is divided by a long counterspace down the middle, on which barely-dressed paid dancers occasionally perform. Rows of tables line each side, leaving just enough space for people to dance later in the night. The drinks are well-made, but expensive. *50 Gansevoort St, (bet. Greenwich and Washington), 212-255-6676, pmloungenyc.com.* Ⓐ Ⓒ Ⓔ *to 14th St.*

Sunday at HIRO at the Maritime Hotel *LGBT*

Comprised of an enormous ballroom, sultry lounge, rooftop cabanas and (seasonal) penthouse, all of which are done up in a chic *Kill Bill* style, Sunday nights find the dance floor teeming with gays, their female friends, and the straight guys left picking up the pieces. The club prices, steep with $7 beer and $11 mixed drinks, are justified by the DJ alone. The bronzed go-go dancers are over-the-top but don't detract from the dynamic vibe. Though it features the requisite dark nooks and corners, the club isn't excessively cruisy. Still, you're almost guaranteed a hookup, or just a high-energy night with your friends. *371 W. 16th St. (at 9th Ave.), 212-727-0212, themaritimehotel.com.* Ⓐ Ⓒ Ⓔ Ⓛ *to 14th St.-8th Ave.*

SHOPPING

Bumble and Bumble *Salon*

At the downtown outpost of Bumble and Bumble, the stylists all sport hipster hair-dos and rockstar tattoos and the result is always buzz-worthy. While waiting for your appointment at this well-known salon, sip a complimentary beverage and take in the sweeping vista of the Hudson River from the 8th floor loft lobby. If you don't want to fork over the dough, check out their website for information on

their free model calls. Be forewarned that your hair may be in the hands of styl
short of professional; if you can, try to score a slot as a demo model to ensu
that a practiced instructor snips your mane. *415 West 13th St. (bet. 9th Ave. c
Washington St.), 212-521-6500, bumbleandbumble.com.* Ⓐ Ⓒ Ⓔ Ⓛ *to 14th St.*

Catriona MacKechnie *Clothing : Boutique*

The secret to a confident and successful job interview, as everyone knows
a dynamite set of undergarments. Before heading off to that hedge fund—
Vogue magazine—meet-and-greet, pick up a gorgeous Dolce & Gabbana bra a
matching underwear at Catriona MacKechnie. You'll adore the wide selection
designers and the super-chic décor, but cross your fingers that you land the job
you'll need it to pay off your credit card bill. *400 West 14th St. (at 9th Ave.), 2
242-3200, catrionamackechnie.com. Hours: M-Sa 11am-7:30pm, Su 12pm-6pm.*
Ⓒ Ⓔ *to 14th St.,* Ⓛ *to Eighth Ave.*

Jeffrey New York *Designer*

The astonishingly selected styles by the leading designers from around the wo
make Jeffrey the leader of the pack when it comes to posh clothing for m
and women. Unfortunately, the prices are as breathtaking as the designs—
to many, it's worth a visit just to see the "best of the best" and consult with t
fashion oracle. *449 W. 14th St. (at Tenth Ave.), 212-206-1272, jeffreynewyork.c
Hours: M-W, F 10am-8pm. R 10am-9pm, Sa 10am-7pm, Su 12pm-6pm.* Ⓐ Ⓒ
to 14th St.

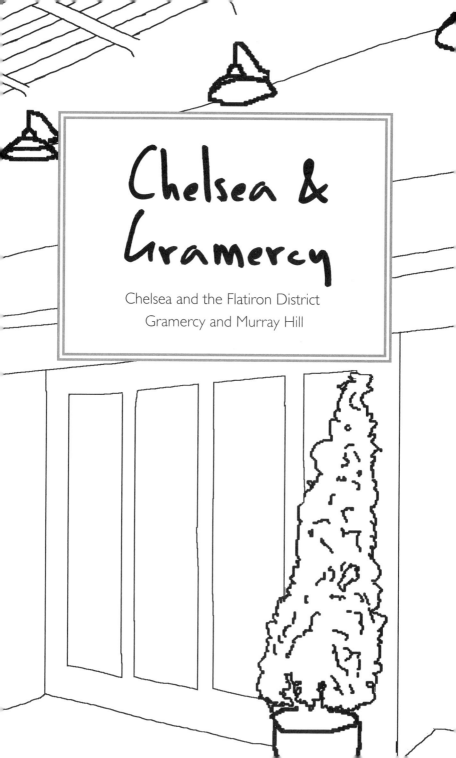

Chelsea & Gramercy

Chelsea and the Flatiron District
Gramercy and Murray Hill

Chelsea and Flatiron

GORGEOUS BROWNSTONES line one side of a street, and towe
ing projects occupy the other. Upscale boutiques nestle between u
tidy bodegas. Beautiful, bronzed gods descend to walk amongst me
Welcome to Chelsea, home to the largest gay population this side
West Hollywood.

Unlike the relatively laid-back LGBT community in the Village, th
Chelsea scene is very…shiny. Shiny, snazzy clothes cover shiny, ha
bodies. If you want to fit in this neighborhood's street scene, hit th
gym first, and be prepared to bring your A-game, because arour
here, it's all about seeing and being seen.

There's a lot to do in Chelsea. Wine, dine and unwind in the ma
coffee shops, chic lounges and restaurants that line Seventh, Eighth ar
Ninth Avenues, or update your apartment with a little something fro
one of the posh furniture and housewares stores on the same stretc
Walk a little west past Tenth Avenue and peruse the ultra-sleek, ultr
hip art galleries, all the cooler for their industrial surroundings. For
more natural setting, wander the leafy streets of Chelsea's histo
district (between 19th and 23rd streets), which developed in the ea
nineteenth century and stand as a peaceful alternative to the *sper
spend, spend* attitude of the avenues.

A relatively new addition to the neighborhood is Chelsea Mark
Once part of the complex where Oreo cookies were first bak
the area has become a food mecca of a different kind. These da

expect more gourmet finds: upscale bakeries, flower-merchants, butchers, fishmongers, ethnic restaurants, and an Italian market complete with espresso bar…and an indoor waterfall.

ISTORY

>> CHELSEA PIERS OPENED in 1910 with much pomp and circumstance after stewing in development hell for several decades. Designed by the same team responsible for Grand Central Terminal, the piers soon became the prime docking space for both passenger and military ships. Chelsea Piers bore witness to many tearful departures and happy reunions between the soldiers of both World Wars and their loved ones left behind. During the 1950s and 60s, it served as a cargo terminal, but soon thereafter fell into disrepair and decay. It wasn't until the 1990s that the pier was overhauled and rebuilt, saving it from joining the ranks of other forgotten New York relics.

Chelsea also boasts a rich history of artistic movements. As one of the stops on the theater district's uptown crawl from SoHo to Times Square, it enjoyed a brief tenure as the premier place to catch a live performance of classics new and old. The 1990s art boom saw an influx of studios and galleries move into the neighborhood, as artists were priced out of more traditional visual art enclaves such as SoHo. And before motion pictures became talkies, Chelsea served as an East Coast outpost for Hollywood production centers—some of Mary Pickford's earliest films were shot here.

VHAT TO SEE

The Flatiron Building

While 21 stories barely constitute a skyscraper in modern New York City, this triangular office building, standing at the intersection of Fifth Avenue and Broadway, certainly impressed turn-of-the-century tourists. The limestone façade and steel frame of the building are still seen by many as representing the dawn of the skyscraper era. The Flatiron Building has also been the star of several movies, the most recent being *Spider-Man*, in which it was home to Peter Parker's *Daily Bugle*. *175 Fifth Ave. (bet. 23rd St. and Broadway).* **N** **R** *to 23rd St.*

SEEDIEST HOTEL
IN THE CITY

THE CHELSEA HOTEL has spent most of the last century playing host to tragedy. In 1912, Titanic survivors dried off at the Chelsea. Before poet Dylan Thomas went gentle into that good night after knocking back too many at the White Horse Tavern, he was a long-term resident here as well. And most infamously, Room 100 played host to the brutal slaying of groupie Nancy Spungen; Spungen was killed by her boyfriend, the notoriously unhinged ex-Sex Pistols bassist Sid Vicious. Thankfully, not every Chelsea story is so grim. Leonard Cohen, Mark Twain, Tom Wolfe, O. Henry, Andy Warhol, and Arthur C. Clarke all lived here, and none the worse for the wear. Still, you can't blame the owners for changing the name to The Hotel Chelsea. *222 W. 23rd St., 212-243-3700, hotelchelsea.com.* **1** **C** **E** *to 23rd St.*

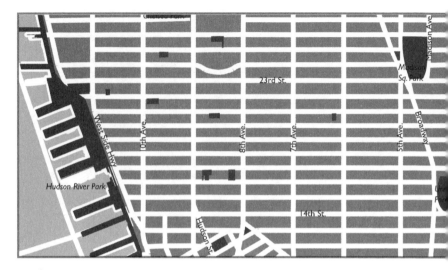

Chelsea Market

The Chelsea Market was formerly the site of the National Biscuit Company, Nabisco, which manufactured the first Oreo on the premises in 1898. It open as Chelsea Market in 1997, and has rapidly expanded ever since. Today, it's fill with loads of gourmet restaurants and specialty food shops, chic boutiques, a art galleries. It's also home to the Food Network. *75 Ninth Ave. (bet. 15th and 1 Sts.), chelseamarket.com.* ❹ ❻ ❺ *to 14th St;* ❶ *to Eighth Ave.*

Chelsea Piers

Pick a sport. Any sport. Choose between golf, swimming, roller-skating, tenn hockey, basketball, gymnastics, soccer, rock climbing, baseball…the list is endle This famous 30-acre complex on the Hudson River features activities you'd hard-pressed to find elsewhere in the city. Including Piers 59, 60, 61 and 62 contains a golf club, health club, roller rink, ice rink, paintball facilities, extrem sports park, and even a bowling alley. *West Side Highway (bet. 18th and 23rd St 212-336-6666, chelseapiers.com.* ❶ *to 23rd St.*

WHERE TO EAT

Amin Indian Restaurant *Indian*

This low-key restaurant is a welcome diversion from Chelsea's typically bustl' dining scene. Curries, kebabs, and kormas are spicy enough to satisfy natives a will only set you back about $10. Combo platters pair gluttony with variety. *1 Eighth Ave. (bet. 17th and 18th Sts.), 212-929-7020.* ❹ ❻ ❺ ❶ *to 14th St.* **$$**

Artisanal Fromagerie and Bistro *French*

This lively, spacious, and densely-packed bistro is a cheese-lover's paradise a caters to an upscale crowd. But have no fear, Artisinal's knowledgeable and atten-tive waitstaff gives diners the full treatment and has the dish on any cheese you can imagine. Try one of four creamy fondues with an assortment of baigneuses available for dipping, like kielbasa or crudités, though the hearty breads do just fine. A basket of addictive gougeres (puffed cheese bread) is an absolute must. Other favorites include the parmesan gnocchi with wild mushrooms and spring vegetables. Call ahead to reserve a table in "the cave," a temperature- and humid-ity-controlled room that literally surrounds you with cheese. *2 Park Ave. (on 32nd, bet. Park and Madison Aves.), 212-725-8585, artisanalcheese.com.* **⑥** *to 33rd St.* **$$**

Aspen *American*

The frosted glass and deer heads mounted above the bar of this luxe ski-lodge style restaurant might make you feel like you've returned from a day swooshing down the slopes instead of a day tromping through the urban jungle. Take your cue from the trendy twenty-somethings and professional types with money to burn and gather around the fire pit. The small plates are meant for sharing, and include everything from juicy bison sliders to elk sausage and trout tacos. The cuisine is decidedly American but the wine list covers the globe, including afford-able selections from Austria and Slovenia. Finish off the meal with snow-capped cupcakes or the warm chocolate cake and get away from it all. *30 W. 22nd St (bet. Fifth and Sixth Aves), 212-645-5040.* **❶ ❷ ❸ ❹ ❺ ❶** *to 23rd Street.* **$$**

Big Cup *Café*

This gay coffee haunt is a good alternative to the bar scene, offering quite a bit more than just a cup of coffee. Although the coffee and tea selection is good, the eye candy is this hot spot's main draw. Quite a few men come here to sit with a cup, but an equal number of young bucks are cruising for action. Tip: those on the market often sit alone with a book. *228 Eighth Ave. (at 22nd St.), 212-206-0059, bigcupcoffee.com.* **❸ ❹ ❶** *to 23rd St.* **$**

Bolo *International*

The Food Network's own Bobby Flay turns out his own version of "Fantasy Span-ish" at this relaxed Flatiron restaurant. Sangria, rabbit on roasted pea risotto, and sautéed wild mushrooms with chile oil are only a few of Flay's playful creations. A comprehensive selection of fine wines and ports make perfect complements to a meal that is the stuff of dreams. *23 E. 22nd St. (bet. Broadway and Park Ave.), 212-228-2200.* **❶ ❷ ❸** *to 23rd St.* **$$$**

Caféteria *American*

Don't let the name, menu, and 24/7 service fool you: this ultra-hip Chelsea spot is anything but a lowbrow caféteria. The chic dining spot is always crowded with good-looking, trendy young people who are too cool for school (and many men who are too cool for women). Caféteria's urban minimalist design employs clean pat-terns, white walls, and chrome tables. After a long night of clubbing, come eat some waffles, mac and cheese, or fried chicken at any time of day, and feel really modish while doing it. *119 Seventh Ave. (at 17th Street), 212-414-1717.* **❶** *to 18th St.* **$$**

Caféteria

Devi *Indian*

Painted glass lanterns float in this dimly-lit space, lending an air of old-world ex
cism to this modern Indian restaurant. There are plenty of options for vegetar
and meat-eaters alike—the $55 tasting menus will give you a broad sweep of
liberally spiced, inventive cuisine with not a drop of common curry in sight.
presentation and service make up for the saltiness of the dishes (be prepared
drink a lot of water). Relief comes from their homemade sorbet and ice cream
E. 18th St. (bet. 5th Ave. and Broadway), 212-691-1300, devinyc.com. ❻ ❼ *to* 1
St, ❶ *to 6th Ave.* **$$**

Duvet *Sushi*

The perfect place to get your date into bed before you even pay for dinn
Unlike most conventional restaurants, the diners sit on beds, grabbing their fo
from a Lazy Susan in the center. Exquisite pillows line the beds, and each di
is given slippers they can don for their meal and bring home. While everyth
tastes excellent, their specialty is seafood, so sample a Dragon roll and enjo
(legal) Purple Haze, a violet-infused Grey Goose cocktail. *45 W. 21st St. (bet. F
and Sixth Ave.), 212-989-2121, duvetny.com.* ❻ ❿ ❽ ❼ *to 23rd St.* **$$$**

Empire Diner *Diner*

Featured in the opening montage of Woody Allen's *Manhattan*, this 24-hour
ery boasts an upscale dinner menu, complemented by a jazz pianist. It's a gr
club-hopping pit stop, and staying up for prix fixe brunch is well worth the sl
deprivation. Don't go à la carte, or else the prices soar. *210 Tenth Ave. (at 22nd
212-243-2736.* ❸ ❸ *to 23rd St.* **$**

Markt *International*

There's a saying that the Belgians eat as well as the French and as much as
Germans. Diners at Markt will eat like Belgians. Large, loud, and delicious,
authentic bistro is as good as any in Brussels. Rustic dark-wood décor, open
seating, an incredible array of Belgian beers, and a helpful, svelte waitstaff make

restaurant a good choice for a group outing or date. Try the dewy-fresh Belgian endive and mache salad topped with vinaigrette. Mussels with a side of pommes frites is a perfectly inexpensive complement for a cold beer. Take a break, have a French press coffee, then try the warm Belgian chocolate tart with homemade pistachio ice cream. *401 West 14th St. (at 9th Ave.), 212-727-3314. marktrestaurant.com.* **Ⓐ Ⓒ Ⓔ ② ③** *to 14 th St,* **Ⓛ** *to Eighth Ave.* **$$$**

Monster Sushi *Sushi*
With its casual-trendy decor and monster-sized menu (which includes helpful descriptions of each dish) Monster Sushi is perfect for the sushi grasshopper. Groups of students and young professionals settle at tables in the back under posters of Godzilla and kitties dressed in Japanese garb. The food is fresh and light, including the fried items, while the green tea ice cream is the most decadent around. Service at Monster Sushi is fast and friendly, and the prices, while not the cheapest in the city, are far from monstrous. *158 W. 23rd St. (at 7th Avenue), 212-620-9130, monstersushi.com.* **①** *to 23rd St.* **$$**

Morimoto *Japanese*
Iron Chef Masaharu Morimoto competes in NYC with the debut of this secluded spot. Morimoto gets a bow for authenticity, freshness, and well-rounded courses. Choices range from sushi and sashimi to perfectly cooked lobster and Kobe beef. Unlike many other celebrity restaurants, here the Chef makes his presence felt in all aspects, from the flavor and plating of each dish, to his signature sakes served in carafes boasting his own design. The omakase, or chef's tasting menu, is a must for the fearless diner—it's custom-crafted by Morimoto himself to show off all aspects of the spectacular craft of his Japanese cuisine. For a more affordable night out, cocktails, appetizers, and raw bar specials are served in an intimate and modern lounge downstairs. *88 10th Ave. (bet. 15th and 16th Sts.), 212-989-8883.* **Ⓐ Ⓒ Ⓔ** *to 8th Ave.,* **Ⓛ** *to 14th St.* **$$$**

Periyali *Mediterranean*
Peacefully tucked away between two busy avenues, Periyali is a Mediterranean oasis. Dimmed lights illuminate a garden and a glass roof, creating a warm and sophisticated atmosphere. The grilled octopus in a creamy red wine sauce is a house specialty and favorite of the regulars. The rice pudding is rich and creamy; their excellent baklava, made with delicate filo dough and velvety honey, melts in your mouth. Service is friendly, well-informed, and attentive, so bring your appetite. *35 W. 20th St. (bet. Fifth and Sixth Ave), 212-463-7890.* **①** *to 18th St.,* **Ⓡ** *to 23rd St.* **$$**

Shake Shack *American*
In a city where $29 burgers are gussied up with foie gras and black truffles, the most talked-about burger in town—flipped at this stand in Madison Square Park—is surprisingly unassuming. Topped with American cheese, lettuce, tomato, and special "shack sauce," the Shack Burger is unpretentious and utterly satisfying.

Shake Shack

Save room for the delicious frozen custard, available daily in vanilla and chocol
along with a rotating flavor du jour. Enjoy it in a simple cone or cup, slurp it
a shake or creamsicle, or try a Concrete—a formidable tub of custard blend
solid with a slew of toppings. Be prepared to wait in a long line of foodies, su
and chattering 20-somethings before ordering. In the summertime, the Shack
open until 11 pm and serves both draught and bottled beers, as well as wir
by the glass, half-bottle, and bottle. *Madison Square Park (Madison Ave. at 23rd 9
212-889-6600, shakeshacknyc.com.* **Ⓝ Ⓡ Ⓦ ⑥ Ⓕ Ⓥ** *to 23rd St.* **$**

Sueños *Mexican*

Although some culinary newbies may not see how the words "upscale" a
"Mexican food" can go together, one trip to Sueños will surely change their mir
The food here is beautiful, pleasantly and artistically prepared to please bo
palette and eye. The guacamole, made in front of you, is delicious. The margari
are strong, and you'd be *loco* not to try one. If you're feeling crazy, order the $
Double-Secret-Probation Margarita or the higher-end $69 version of it. The a
petizers are delicious, especially the chicken carnitas, but the entrees are sligh
spicy, so make sure you can take the heat. The desserts, especially the Très Lech
cake and the Chocolate-Banana crepes, are excellent. *311 W. 17th St. (bet. Eigh
and Ninth Ave), 212-243-1333.* **Ⓐ Ⓒ Ⓔ** *to 14th St.* **$$**

Yakiniku JuJu *Korean*

Combining the traditional and the innovative, Yakiniku JuJu offers Shabu-Sha
BiBimBop, and Korean BBQ, with a focus on health and nutrition. Their origi
sushi rolls are made with kimchee, chicken, and beef. To make everyone feel mc
at home, the jukebox plays an eclectic mix of hip-hop, jazz, and pop. The all-yo
can-grill BBQ is a great deal at $23 if you bring your appetite, with assorted me
that are freshly sliced rather than sitting around in a buffet bin. Don't bother le
ing room for dessert. *157 E. 28th St., 212-684-7830.* **⑥ Ⓝ ⓇⓌ** *to 28th St.* **$$**

IGHTLIFE

Barracuda *LGBT*

With no sign and a single red light bulb over the entrance, this Chelsea icon has often been mistaken for a bordello. But have no fear, because inside the place is packed with the friendliest New Yorkers you'll ever meet. The vintage-Vegas themed décor is a little seedy, but the gorgeous bartenders and riotously-funny show with Shequida (every night at 2:00) will make you feel right at home—or as homey as you can feel with a drag queen dancing around. While it's never too crowded to get to the rear lounge, there's always a healthy selection of attractive and welcoming folk to please even the most jaded New Yorker. So make like the Flintstones and have a gay old time! *275 W. 22nd St. (at 8th Ave.), 212-645-8613. Cash only.* ❶ *to 23rd St.*

Crobar *Club*

One of New York's reigning megaclubs, Crobar features two rooms (three if you're Very Important) with distinctly different vibes. The Reed Room is cozy, intimate, and sticks with hip-hop dance tracks. The cavernous main dancehall often hosts superstar DJs spinning the latest in house, trance, and progressive, as Chelsea boys and girls try to outdance each other. More often than not, professional go-go dancers perform in barely-there garb on pedestals high above the pulsing masses. The scene is dress to impress, but a lax door policy ensures entrance to anyone willing to fork over money for the steep cover. *530 W 28th St., 212-629-9000.* ❶ ❶ *to 23rd St.*

Chetty Red *Bar*

The red-lit bar is well stocked, and beautifully tendered, and the entire room is infused with ruby light. From a raised section in the back, you can survey the young crowd milling (not dancing) around on the dance floor. Comfy chairs and short tables line the walls in the back, making it a loungy refuge from the loud, crowded bar. The bathroom attendant is a nice touch despite the cramped commode area. *28 E. 23rd St. (bet. Park Ave. and Broadway), 212-254-6117.* ❶ ❶ ❻ *to 23rd St.*

The Cutting Room *Bar*

One of the city's best destinations for a night out. There's live music, an amazing jukebox, attractive patrons, great drinks, and food complete with homemade ketchup for their burgers and fries. There are live performers almost every night, including comedians, musicians, and saxophone players. One of the owners is *Sex and the City*'s Mr. Big himself, actor Chris Noth. Expect to see celebrities here from time to time. *19 W. 24th St. (bet. Broadway and Sixth Ave.), 212-691-1900, thecuttingroomnyc.com.* ❶ *to 23rd St.*

Dusk Lounge *Lounge*

With cracked mirror walls and a bathroom so dark you can't check your make-up, this bar makes it clear that appearances are not the point, so relax and have a drink. The pool table in the front is always busy and the bar further back serves the local crowd killer cosmopolitans and margaritas. *147 W. 24th St. (bet. Sixth and Seventh Aves.), 212-924-4490.* ❶ *to 23rd St.*

Flatiron Lounge *Lounge*

The speakeasy craze has afflicted many a downtown watering hole—you've seen one nameless door and you've pretty much seen them all. But there is a light at the end of Flatiron Lounge's low-tunneled entrance, and it takes its shape in the form of red banquets and bona fide antique cocktails. Recipes range from the 1895 "Corpse Reviver" to a classic New York Sour circa 1930. The original drinks are just as inspired, incorporating flavors such as juniper, lychee, and hibiscus. The décor is subdued and lovely, as are the people, who are content to sip and savor their drinks as if prohibition were still on. *37 W 19th St (at 5th Ave.), 212-727-7741, flatironlounge.com.* ❷ ❸ ❹ *to 23rd St.*

G *LGBT*

Despite some flaws in the decor, G bar is a mainstay of the gay bar scene. A huge circular bar dominates the room, perfect for seeing and being seen, but when the crowd is light it feels empty. Leather ottomans up front interfere with foot traffic and there's rarely a place to sit in the rear lounge when the crowd swells. Stop for a drink to get a feel for the scene, but be aware that the crowd is older than you might expect. *223 W. 19th St. (bet. Seventh and Eighth Aves.), 646-253-2246 glounge.com.* ❶ *to 18th St.*

Heaven *LGBT*

The name just says it all. Heaven is the gayest bar in Chelsea, meaning the music ranges from pop to house and shirts aren't required once inside. Great place for the younger crowd to avoid the ubiquitous chickenhawking of the Chelsea scene. Fridays are for the ladies, while Saturday nights host hundreds of college-age guys (18+) on three dance floors. It can get very, very hot in here, literally, so don't bother with a jacket unless you absolutely need it. The $10 cover price seems steep, but the experience of heaven, hell, and purgatory all in one place will make your night here stand out. *569 Sixth Ave. (bet. 16th and 17th Sts.), 212-243-6100* ❺ *to 14th St. or* ❻ *to Sixth Ave.*

Live Bait *Bar*

Located on Madison Square Park, curious passersby and neighborhood locals find it hard to resist this urban rendition of the Louisiana bayou. Force your way past the boisterous happy hour crowd to the tables in back in order to sample the Cajun shrimp or the mesquite BBQ. *14 E. 23rd St. (bet. Broadway and Madison Ave.), 212-353-2400.* ❷ ❸ *to 23rd St.*

Marquee *Club*

It's one of the hottest clubs in NYC, so the door policy is strict—dress to press. Assuming you get inside, it's pretty much all it's cracked up to be—beautiful people packed into both levels, each of which has a large bar, so it's never too hard to get a drink (though they aren't cheap). The design is simple, but the atmosphere is great. Watch out for Diddy if Marquee (or Diddy) is still hot by the time you read this. *289 10th Ave. (bet 26th and 27th St.), 646-473-0202. marqueeny. com.* ❸ ❺ *to 23rd St.*

Nells *Lounge*

Three rooms on two floors blaze an eclectic mix of music ranging from reggae, hip-hop, jazz, Latin, funk, and disco. The elegance of the spacious upstairs room calls for a sophisticated drink from the well-stocked bar. Downstairs, relax in a more intimate lounge or move to house, R&B or classics aimed at a stylish mix of "tourists, regulars, and DJs." *246 W. 14th St. (bet. Seventh and Eighth Aves.), 212-675-1567, nells.com. Cover: $10-$15.* ❶ ❷ ❸ *to 14th St.*

Old Town Bar

Old Town Bar *Bar*

Don't count it out as just another of the ubiquitous "oldest bars in New York." Old Town doesn't rely on its past as a gimmick to draw a crowd; it's just content to pour you a stiff one after work in the gritty splendor of dusty stained glass and antique booths. Don't call it worn either: this one is a classic, and is just about as much as a dive bar as the young professionals who frequent it are willing to risk. Some call their burgers the best in the city and if you order one, you'll get to see your waitress flex her muscles to haul it from the upstairs kitchen on the oldest dumbwaiter in New York. *45 E. 18th St. (bet. Broadway and Park Ave. S.), 212-529-6732, oldtownbar.com.* ❶ ❻ ❼ ❹ ❺ ❻ *at 14th St.*

The Park *Bar*

This sleek spot in the far west of Manhattan attracts models and upscale 30s and 40s because of its elegant, spacious setting. The outdoor garden has leafy trees, fuel-heated lamps, and yellow light bulbs overhead. The interior feels industrial with Zen accents—with Japanese paper lanterns and brick walls that pad the heavy beat. Special plates include mussels and chorizo, fois gras, steak tartare, and larger numbers such as pan-seared salmon and couscous, paella, and the delicate duck sandwich. *118 Tenth Ave. (bet. 17th and 18th Sts.), 212-352-3313.* ❶ ❸ ❺ ❶ *to 14th St.*

Serena *Lounge*

A low ceiling, red walls, and curious tin chandeliers lend a cozy atmosphere to this subterranean lounge under the Chelsea Hotel. Perch yourself atop one of the seats surrounding the gargantuan U-shaped bar, or sink with drink in hand into a couch lining one of the adjacent rooms and dig the foxy clientele. *222 W. 23rd St. (bet. Seventh and Eighth Aves.), 212-255-4646.* ❸ ❺ *to 23rd St.*

Slate *Billiards*

The former Chelsea Billiards has been revamped as New York's swankiest pool hall, with low blue lights shedding an amniotic glow inside. There's surprisingly little attitude for this part of town, and the new Mediterranean fusion menu is fantastic.

54 W. 21st St. (bet. Fifth and Sixth Aves.), 212-989-0096. ❶ ⓝ ⓡ Ⓦ❹ ❺ Ⓖ *Union Sq.-14th St.*

Strata *Lounge*

Slightly more polished and pricey than the other Chelsea lounges, Strata attra a young early-to-mid-twenties crowd. Feel free to sink into the comfort of t lush decor and kick back with cocktails and appetizers in a unique celebrity-si ing hotspot, but be wary of your bill. On weekends, Strata transforms into a c dominated by thumping hip-hop and house music. *915 Broadway (at 21st 212-505-7400.* ⓝ ⓡ *to 23rd St.*

Wye Bar *Bar*

College kids and yuppies can bond by listening to Top 40 hits and drinking (if slightly overpriced) gin and tonics. The classy red lighting complements numerous couches but large parties provide the majority of the clientele don't expect to meet new people here. Nonetheless, when the faces are pr and the mood is right, there aren't many better places on the West Side to n and sip martinis. *105 W. 27th St. (bet. Sixth and Seventh Aves.), 212-675-7117 to 28th St.*

XL *LGBT*

There's plenty of space to scope the scene here, especially from the sec floor balcony and seating areas. Excellent mood-lighting and thumping tech pop music make this lounge feel like a dance club lacking a dance floor. The co bathroom is famous for the fish tank-separated urinal wall, but it's the fashion and attractive gay men (and the women who love them) that make this b Friday night destination. *357 W. 16th St. (at Ninth Ave.), 646-336-5574, xlnew com. Cash only.* Ⓐ Ⓒ Ⓔ *to 14th St.*

ARTS

Rubin Museum of Art *Museums*

Geometrically positioned flags on the elegant Chelsea façade hint at the we of tapestries and paintings inside. Housing everything from centuries-old n sculpture to contemporary Himalayan art, the Rubin showcases the beau products of countries like India, Tibet, and Nepal. An ongoing exhibit introdu the uninitiated to the fundamentals of the genre while rotating exhibits exp complex themes both uniquely Himalayan and universally human. *150 W. 17th 212-620-5000, rmanyc.org. $7 for students with ID.* ❶ ❶ ❷ ❸ *to 14th St.*

Brent Sikkema *Galleries*

The generic gallery setting with white walls and monotonous lighting belies extremely untraditional artistic works displayed within. Works of contempo artists, such as Burt Barr, Amy Sillman, and Vik Muniz have cast their creative (sometimes creepy) shadows upon these walls, and the quirky curating often prises even the most seasoned New York gallery hound. The crowds may make the space a little stuffy, so visit in the morning or enjoy heavy air as part of the artistic ambiance. *530 W. 22nd St. (bet. Tenth and Eleventh Aves.), 212-929-2262, brentsikkema.com.* Ⓒ Ⓔ *to 23rd St.*

Cheim & Read *Galleries*
At first the grey brick entrance and sunken glass doors are a bit difficult to find, making this gallery a bit of a sleeper. But once inside, the gallery distinguishes itself by selling works by many high-profile pop artists, such as Diane Arbus and Robert Mapplethorpe Goldin, as well as work by lesser-known amateurs. *547 W. 25th St. (bet. Tenth and Eleventh Aves.), 212-242-7727, cheimread.com.* Ⓒ Ⓔ *to 23rd St.*

David Zwirner *Galleries*
First opened in 1993, the gallery focuses on the works of international emerging artists. Hanging lights and the completely white space attract focus to the large, painted works. Along with contemporary artists, the gallery will occasionally exhibit paintings by masters such as Max Ernst, Rene Magritte, and Pablo Picasso, and have catalogues are on hand in case an artist is unfamiliar. *525 W. 19th St. (bet. Tenth and West St.). 212-727-2070, davidzwirner.com.* Ⓒ Ⓔ *to 23rd St.,* ① *to 18th St.*

Pace Wildenstein Gallery *Galleries*
A Manhattan art world standard with several outlets throughout the city, the Chelsea branch is a testament to the quality that sustains its popularity. Housed in a large and accessible street level space, the Chelsea space presents solo shows by some living, established NYC artists (increasingly becoming a rare breed in the art world). *534 W. 25th St. (bet. Houston and Prince Sts.). 212-929-7000, pacewildenstein.com.* Ⓝ Ⓡ *to Prince St.*

Atlantic Theater *Theater*
Theater buffs have long insisted that the stage is hallowed ground, but in this case the metaphor rings true. The Atlantic Theater Company, founded in 1985 by David Mamet and William H. Macy, moved into this renovated church in 1991. For a break from schmaltzy musicals, the company proclaims the Atlantic as a place "where great stories are told." *336 W. 20th St. (bet Eighth and Ninth Aves.). 212-691-5919, atlantictheater.org.* Ⓒ Ⓔ *to 23rd St.*

Joyce Theater

Joyce Theater *Theather*
The Joyce is an unlikely successor to a former porn palace. The large stage and virtually clear sightlines create an ideal setting for performances by top touring companies from around the world. Bookings range from weekly engagements to a month-in-residence with the Feld Ballet and Margie Gillis. The Joyce often subsidizes in-theater production costs. "All Together Different" is a program that promotes the seven most promising up-and-coming companies *175 Eighth Ave. (at 19th St.). 212-242-0800, joyce.org.* ① *to 18th St.*

Elmo *Music*

Downstairs from the famous Elmo restaurant is one of the hottest new live mu
venues in New York. Decorated like the legendary El Morocco, let the palm me
wallpaper and mirror tiles on the walls transport you to 1950s Miami, when 1
music was so good that everyone grooved to the beat. *156 Seventh Ave. (bet. 1*
& 20th Sts.), 212-337-8000. **C** **E** *to 23rd St.*

Dance Theater Workshop *Dance*

Just down the street from the venerable Joyce Theater, this modern dance sp
opened in the Fall of 2002, but has already garnered a great deal of praise.
Artist Resource Media Lab and spacious Bessie Schoenberg Theater showc
modern theater technology and glass-walled rehearsal studios face the street
passersby can watch. Some of the B-list companies that perform are not quite
to the Joyce, but as a newcomer it has the freedom to experiment and does
with aplomb. *219 W. 19th St. (bet. Seventh and Eighth Aves.), 212-691-6500, dtw.*
1 *to 18th St,* **2** **3** **F** **L** **A** **C** **E** *to 14th St.*

New York Theatre Ballet *Dance*

Few of the uninitiated to dance know of this chamber ballet company, of
eclipsed by the fame of the city's larger companies. George Balanchine's chore
raphy has been the touchstone for American ballet for over fifty years—but
ensemble stubbornly sticks to its non-Balanchine roots, adhering to the style
the lesser known Enricho Cecchetti and Antony Tudor. While the dancers' te
nique isn't on par with that of the bigger companies, the repertory is refreshir
different, especially when you can't stomach another Balanchine piece. The co
pany's school, Ballet School New York, offers classes for all levels. *30 E. 31st St.*
Madison Ave.). 212-679-0401, nytb.org. Cash only. **6** *to 33rd St.,* **N** **R** *to 28th S*

SHOPPING

192 Books *Books*

With its high ceilings and numerous reading tables, 192 Books may feel m
like a library than a bookstore. But the collection is extensive, with a speci
art books section. Weekly readings will make you feel more at home than ot
commercialized shops do. *192 Tenth Ave. 212-255-4022, 192books.com. Ho*
T–Sa 11 am-7 pm **C** **E** *to 23rd St.*

ABC Carpet & Home *Housewares*

Expect to find ample mother-daughter pairs ooh-ing and aah-ing their way thro
six floors of housewares, antiques, and knick-knacks. Although fairly expensive,
store is worth a visit for its creative window displays and extraordinary fi
such as a gilded ten-foot bird cage. The Parlour Café on the ground floor all
weary shoppers to lounge and lunch on the furniture that they probably c
afford to buy. *888 Broadway (at 19th St.), 212-473-3000.* **1** **N** **R** **W** **4** **5**
to 14th St.-Union Sq.

ABC Carpet & Home

A.I. Friedman *Miscellaneous*

Ask a salesperson at this gigantic art store to categorize their merchandise, and they will invariably struggle. You can't blame them; the shop's stock ranges from Filofaxes to handbags, office furniture to art supplies, origami to at least thirty variations of tape. They are particularly proud of their Swedish Bookbinders Design section (priced from $3 to $60), colorfully hand-covered albums, notepads, and cards that can't be found anywhere else. *44 W. 18th St. (at Fifth Ave.), 212-243-9000, aifriedman.com.* ① *to 18th St.,* ⑤ ⑦ *to 14th St.*

Annex Antiques Fair and Flea Market *Flea Market*

The "original" and most famous flea market in the city, the Annex gathers over 500 vendors every weekend in a trio of parking lots that stretch along Sixth Avenue. While you try to distinguish between trash and treasure, you might stumble upon a celebrity or two. *Sixth Ave., from 24th St. to 27th St., 212-243-5343.* ⑤ ⑦ *to 23rd St.*

BALDUCCI'S renovated the landmark New York Savings Bank building into this well-stocked supermarket. Grab your groceries under a vast, vaulted ceiling, then order a quick cup of coffee and sip it upstairs in their café-style picnic area. *81 Eighth Avenue (at 14th St.), 212/741-3700, suttongourmet.com. Hours: M-Su 9am-9pm.* ⓐ ⓒ ⓔ *to 14th St.*

FRESHEST FOOD IN A HISTORIC LANDMARK

Barney's Co-Op *Clothing : Designer*

This is the house that denim built. Though the shelves abound with designer look-alike clothes from Barney's more trend-oriented store label, the Co-Op is humming with stylish shoppers in search of this moment's hottest jeans who will almost certainly find their style and size on the massive over-stuffed back wall. *236 W. 18th St. (bet. Seventh and Eighth Aves.), 212-826-8900, barneys.com.* ① *to 18th St.*

Bed Bath and Beyond *Housewares*

This moderately priced emporium of all things domestic is a good bet for stu-

dents in need of supplies like dishes, rugs, and even furniture. The convenienc
everything in one store sometimes makes you forget that all their goods cai
bought cheaper elsewhere. *620 Sixth Ave. (bet. 18th and 19th Sts.), 212-255-3*
bedbathandbeyond.com. **F** **V** *to 14th St. Additional locations in Manhattan at*
61st St. and 1932 Broadway.

Chelsea Market *Groceries*
Once a Nabisco biscuit factory, Manhattan's largest wholesale and retail
concourse offers a multitude of fresh gourmet options from fudge to fish and
erything in between. The building's brick and terracotta arches and wood-bea
walls provide a haven from the typical urban surroundings while satisfying
the most refined palates. *75 Ninth Ave. (bet. 15th and 16th Sts.)* **A** **C** **E**
14th St.

Complete Traveler Antiquarian Bookshop *Books*
Hands down, the best store for new, out-of-print, and antiquarian books. The
lection of books provides information on real trips (though sometimes outda
and fuel for the imagination. The prices reflect the quality and selection. The
is amiable, knowledgeable, and willing to discuss anything from City politi
sub-Saharan travel. *199 Madison Ave. (at 35th St.), 212-685-9007.* **B** **D** **F**
V **W** *to 34th St.-Herald Sq.,* **6** *to 33rd St.*

Filene's Basement *Clothing : Discount*
This bargain superstore carries Calvin Klein, Perry Ellis, Kenar, and other des
names. It is worth a look for shoes, lingerie, coats, suits, and evening wear. C
out the occasional clearance sales for the best deals. *620 Sixth Ave. (bet. 18th*
19th Sts.), 212-620-3100, filenesbasement.com. **1** *to 18th St.,* **4** **5** **6** **L**
R **W** *at 14th St.-Union Sq. Additional location at 2222 Broadway.*

Fishs Eddy *Housewares*
Get all the supplies to set a perfect dinner table, as you mix and match from
stocks of commercial dishes and glasses. Watch the price tags, though, and
leave without checking out the bins in the back for $1 saucers and the shelv
$2 wine glasses. *889 Broadway (at 19th St.), 212-420-9020, fishseddy.com.*
R **4** **5** **6** *to 14th St.-Union Sq.*

Jo Malone *Beauty*
This British-based store specializes in customizable perfume. Inside the
there is a machine that divides up ingredients that can be added to each oth
make the final perfume. As an added bonus, the machine shoots only a little
into the air so customers don't get overwhelmed by the stench. *949 Broa*
212-673-2220. **N** **R** *to 23rd St.*

Tekserve *Miscellaneous*
Tekserve just might be the most famous computer store in the world. The

cialty here is Apple, and they will gladly fix yours or sell you a new one. Beyond basic sales and repairs, Tekserve also deals in professional-quality audio and visual systems. The staff is hip and remarkably friendly. *119 W. 23rd St. (bet. Sixth and Seventh Aves.), 212-929-3645.* ❶ *to 23rd St.*

CLASSES AND WORKSHOPS

Chakrasambara Buddhist Center

Learn to let go in this urban sanctuary, with guided meditation and lectures that integrate Buddha's teachings into everyday life. The center also hosts weekend retreats, meditation for children, and more in-depth course programs for Buddhist study. A single meditation class is $14; an $80 monthly membership is also available. *322 Eight Ave., Suite 502 (entrance on 26th St., bet. 8th and 7th Aves.), 212-924-6706, meditationinnewyork.org.* ❹ ❻ ❶ *to 23rd or 28th Sts.*

Gotham Jiu Jitsu

Self-defense is taught here with an emphasis on realistic situations, incorporating simulations of street encounters into each lesson. Ditch the dojo for Sensei Tay's Central Park classes, including a popular rape prevention class taught at Central Park West and 72nd ($20) *122 W. 27th St., Second Floor (bet. 6th and 7th Aves.), 646-284-1461, gothamjiujitsu.tripod.com.* ❶ *to 28th St.-7th Ave.* ❷ *to 28th St.-Broadway.*

Laughing Lotus Yoga

Not just a yoga studio but a community center and holistic haven for the frazzled New Yorker, with weekly events and musical guests to soothe the soul and build the dharma. The focus is on the vinyasa style, one of the most physically demanding and rewarding forms of yoga. A single class is $15, with cheaper package deals and a donations-only community class. *59 W. 19th St., Third Floor (off 6th Ave.), 212-414-2903, laughinglotus.com.* ❷ ❻ *to 23rd St-6th Ave..,* ❶ *to 18th St.-7th Ave.*

Upright Citizen's Brigade
Theatre Training Center

Learn the ropes from one of the most respected and irreverent sketch comedy troupes in the country. Pick your own teacher from a list of minor celebrities for introductory to intensive courses in "the Harold long-form technique," or get behind the scenes with one of the sketch writing workshops. *307 W. 26th St. (bet. 8th and 9th Aves.), 212-366-9176, ucbtheatre.com/classes.* ❻ ❹ *to 28th St.- 8th Ave.*

West Side Pistol and Rifle Range

A bastion of American masculinity below New York's epicenter of effete. After you've picked up your custom eau de toilette at Jo Malone, and before you head to Barracuda to pick up a Chelsea Boy, why not pick up a rifle? For $55, one of New York's last remaining manly men will show you how to operate a .22 caliber

Ruger rifle, then let you blaze up a paper bad guy with 50 rounds of ammo in th under-ground gun range. Forget yoga: there is simply no better respite from N York's wussy museums and shops than unloading a clip or five with your frier If you have a pistol license, grab your Glock and fire away with ex-cops, secu guards, "sportsmen," and a surprising number of women. *20 W. 20th (bet 5th c 6th). 212-243-9448. westsidepistolrange.com.* ❶ *to 23rd.*

HOTELS AND HOSTELS

Chelsea Lodge

This lodge may be a small in price, but not in size or service. It boasts rooms re vated in a country Americana style that instantly welcome and create a homey fe ing. While each room has its own sink and shower stall, toilets are shared betwe neighbors. With a staff that leaves a Hershey Kiss on your pillow each night, this tel is the perfect choice for those looking for great quality without a huge bill. 3 *W. 20th St. (btw 8th and 9th Ave), 800-373-1116 or 212-243-4499, chelsealoc com. Single room $99, Double $114.* ❸ ❸ *to 23rd & 8th Ave.,* ❶ *to 23rd & 7th*

Chelsea Savoy Hotel

Located in a hip neighborhood, this no-frills hotel provides friendly service clean albeit small rooms for a moderate cost. With the subway simply a bl away, this hotel's location is perfect for the curious tourist looking to expl *204 W 23rd St (at 7th Ave.) 866-929-9353 or 212-929-9353, chelseasavoynyc.c Rooms $99-$275.* ❸ ❶ *to 23rd St.*

Colonial House Inn

Situated in a historic brownstone in Chelsea, this welcoming inn has been the re ient of the *Out and About* Editor's Choice Award for gay-specific accommodati for ten years running. A unique, affordable choice for those travelers intereste really experiencing New York in comfort without resorting to a commercial ch hotel, this inn boasts clean rooms and a complimentary breakfast, including you-can-eat bacon and eggs. *W. 22nd St. (bet. 8th and 9th Ave). 800-689-3779, lonialhouseinn.com. Rooms are $85-318.* ❸ *to 23rd & 8th Ave.,* ❶ *to 23rd & 7th*

Gershwin Hotel

With a view of Fifth Avenue, the Gershwin Hotel is the quirky and artsy to experience New York City. As the location where the venerated names wrote his songs during the '30s and '40s, this hotel's history, will provide you entertainment in and of itself. Problems with the plumbing, cable, and noise common grievances but the price and location are ideal. *7 E. 27th St. (bet.. 5th Madison Ave.), 212-545-8000, gershwinhotel.com. Bunk beds from $40 to Suite $249-$329.* ❶ ❶ ❶ ❶ ❻ *to 28th. St.*

Gramercy & Murray Hill

DON'T BE FOOLED by the stone fountain, perfectly manicured English garden, and rows of carved niches overlooking lush flowerbeds. You're still in Manhattan: Gramercy Park, to be exact. It's one of the city's most beautiful, tranquil spaces—and unless you are one of the select millionaires with keys, you're not allowed in.

This is a neighborhood of low-key modern aristocrats. Its calm attracts aging movie stars and bird-boned models tired of public celebrity. But the true attraction is curb appeal. Take a stroll and you'll see some of the most beautiful homes in Manhattan. They are a mix of Southern-style architecture and posh high-rise apartments, nestled in cool, leafy streets—a welcome oasis from the insanity that is nearby Union Square and Baruch College. The calm is broken only by yaps here and there; dogs, like money, are de rigueur in this neighborhood, where it's not uncommon to pass a harried walker with twenty-five pampered pooches milling about his ankles.

If all the entitlement and money isn't your thing, head down to 16th and Park. There, you'll find Union Square, an area jam-packed with theatres, vegetarian-friendly restaurants, and megastores like DSW, Trader Joe's and Virgin Records. The nightlife scene here is pretty chill compared to other parts of the city, with the legendary handcrafted beers at Heartland Brewery being the biggest draw,. But it's still worth a visit after dark for a relaxing stroll through Union Square Park.

In the last few years, nearby Murray Hill has become the affordable housing choice (affordable because it's a relative trek to the nearby ⬤ ⬤ lines at Lexington Ave.) of middle income hipsters in search of a g deal, but wary of the great leap to Brooklyn or Queens. The neigh hood has become particularly popular with the UN crowd—they walk to work at 46th St. easily from here. That has to make for s interesting conversations in the bars around 5 pm

HISTORY

>> ALTHOUGH ORIGINALLY A SWAMP, the area surrounding Gram Park has long been considered one of the most fashionable addresses in York City. Thanks to its intellectual residents at the turn of the century, his cal Gramercy has been called an "American Bloomsbury." Past residents inc James Harper, founder of the Harper Collins publishing house, Theodore R evelt, Edith Wharton, Eugene O'Neill, and O. Henry, who wrote "The Gift o Magi" in Pete's Tavern, a local restaurant.

In 1831, Samuel Ruggles, long-time trustee of Columbia College, drained swamp and laid out 66 English-style lots around a private park —Gramercy In the 1920s, the development of high-rise apartment buildings, the extensio the Third Avenue elevated train, and the onset of the Depression meant th address around Gramercy Park was no longer as desirable as it once was neighborhood's majestic mansions crumbled a bit, and the turn-of-the-cen elite shopping mecca dubbed Ladies' Mile became a "temple of love" after an of brothels. On the heels of a capital flight came a vibrant population of artis cluding Andy Warhol, who installed his legendary Factory here. Gramercy be an enclave for groups of rebels, ranging in identity from communists to junk vas, with heavy drug traffic and drifters plaguing the area until its regentrific

WHAT TO SEE

The National Arts Club

The National Arts Club is situated on the south side of Gramercy Park. O the most notable things about it (besides the fact that it's been there since is that it still has a dress code. Ladies, if you're wearing "stirrup pants, capri p leggings, spandex or lycra" you just won't get in. Gents, you'll need a jacke none of this matters anyway, because, much like the Park, it's members on *Gramercy Park South, 212-475-3424, nationalartsclub.org.* ⬤ *to 23rd St.*

Gramercy Park

Though Londoners are well used to private urban parks, Gramercy is the one of its kind in New York. When Samuel Ruggles developed the area i 1840s and 50s, he hoped that such an exclusive privilege would draw in pot homebuyers. It did, and 150 years later, a key to the coveted park is still a incentive to those with enough dough to buy here. *20th St. to 21st St. (bet Ave. S. and Third Ave.),* ⬤ *to 23rd St.*

Union Square Greenmarket

The city's flagship outdoor market is a destination for New York's top chefs and foodies. It's also a regular shopping stop for residents and commuters who pass through Union Square on their way home from work. Stand after stand of dairy, jams, flowers, game, seafood, and baked goods, not to mention fruits and vegetables stretch across the entire north side of the square. Even though you can get high-quality fresh produce at the Whole Foods and Trader Joe's nearby, nothing beats the opportunity to personally buy from and chat with farmers, as well as the guarantee that your food is locally grown. *17th St., between Broadway and Park Avenue S. Hours: M W F Sa 8 am-6 pm* ❶ ❺ ❻ ❼ ❽ ❹ ❺ ❻ *to 14th St.-Union Sq.*

BEST SMELLING
CITY BLOCK

Fifth Ave at 28th St. is your usual vaguely ratty office district. At Sixth Ave., it's the Amazon. This is the **FLOWER DISTRICT,** concentrated on 28th between Sixth and Seventh, where dozens of tiny flower shops line the block and fill the sidewalk with their wares all day long. It's mostly a wholesale operation, and it's at its most beautiful in the early mornings, as decorators and shop owners hoist boxes of roses and violets above their heads as they sashay across the sidewalks. ❶ *to 28th St.*

Union Square

WHERE TO EAT

Barça 18 *Latin*

Incredibly authentic Spanish food meets modern décor in Barça 18. It is part
the Steve Hanson restaurant empire and located right above Union Square P
You'll never forget where you are, as the atmosphere evokes the perpetu
fashionable Gramercy area much more than a Barthalonian experience. Yet,
food manages to stay true to its roots—fresher, even, than some dishes in Spair
large selection of Spanish wines complements the abundant fish and ham dish
and you absolutely cannot go wrong with paella. However, the real treats are
desserts: the authentic ones—churros con chocolate and Crèma Catalana ma
with a family recipe—and you'll find yourself in absolute *cielo*. *225 Park Ave. So*
(at 18th St.). *212-533-2500.* **4** **5** **6** **L** **N** **Q** **R** **W** *to 14th St.-Union Sq.* **$$**

Blue Water Grill *Seafood*

With everything from live jazz to an oyster bar, this delightful seafood café
perpetually crowded, beautiful, and hip. Look up, and the high ceilings will rem
you that this was once a bank. The nouveau cuisine is heavy on the seafood a
the quality is consistently solid. Check out the jazz downstairs, and try to rese
a sidewalk table. *31 Union Sq. West (at 16th St.)*, *212-675-9500, brguestrestaura*
com. **L** **N** **R** **W** **4** **5** **6** *to 14th St.-Union Sq.* **$$**

Chango *Mexican*

Pinks, yellows, and blues, couch-style seating, bamboo dividers, and finished te
cotta—if Mexico hits gold, its future will be Chango. From the tri-colored t
tillas, guacamole, and over-sized margaritas, to the cut-away cove-lit ceiling a
the ceramic serving plates, this trendy *Sex and the City* hot-spot is a non-st
fiesta. Bring a date who doesn't mind the sound of chatter or the competiti
of a gorgeous wait staff and you'll find a perfect choice in both taste of food a

stunning décor. *239 Park Ave. South (bet. 19th and 20th Sts.), 212-477-1500.* **6** to 23rd St. **$$**

City Crab & Seafood Co. *Seafood*

Surf your way into City Crab for an enormous selection of underwater delights. Everything on the menu, from steamers to lobster to Alaskan King-Crab, is fresh from the Fulton Fish Market and prime for good hearty eatin'. The service is quick and the small-town feel is a nice contrast to the sophistication of its Park Avenue neighbors. *235 Park Ave. South (at 19th St.), 212-529-3800.* **L N R W 4 5 6** to 14th St.-Union Sq. **$$**

Coffee Shop *Latin*

This shop is not really a coffee shop, but an upscale Brazilian restaurant with a fabulous bar in the back. The drinks and the crowd are consistently gorgeous, and the Brazilian brunch is to die for. Try to get an outside table, and enjoy the views. *29 Union Sq. W. (at 16th St.), 212-243-7969.* **L N R W 4 5 6** to 14th St.-Union Sq. **$**

{Stop Right There!}

CURRY HILL

>>FOR SOUTH ASIANS, or those seeking the South Asian experience without leaving Manhattan, look no further than Lexington Avenue. Located between 26th and 31st Streets, the area known as "Curry Hill" (a part of Murray Hill, also known as Little India) is distinctive from other ethnic neighborhoods, as it maintains a diverse residential population and remains relatively unknown, both to the average tourist and New Yorker. The young neighborhood, which emerged from what was once a crime-ridden area in the 1980s, is sprinkled with restaurants, Bollywood video stores, and Indian grocers, and offers an alternative to the homogenous South Asian neighborhood of Jackson Heights in Queens.

The neighborhood remains viable and continues to attract South Asians to buy and sell distinctively ethnic goods from establishments like the paan shops, which sell everything from chewable leaves, (originally associated with Hindu custom) to the latest Indian fashions.

In terms of restaurants, **CURRY IN A HURRY** on Lexington and 28th Street, which was once proclaimed by founder and former owner Sayedul Alam to be "an exotic alternative to McDonald's," remains the most popular and attracts the most diverse group of diners.

But if you desire a more authentic—and cheaper—experience, and would like to rub elbows with Curry Hill regulars, **HAANDI**, a small and humble restaurant containing a display of South Asian cuisine behind a glass counter and a television showing old Bollywood musicals is the place to go. There are also several vegetarian-only options in the area, from vegetarian curries to dosa.

Ess-A-Bagel *Delis*

Ess (Yiddish for "eat") is the real deal for bagels. Its pumpernickels are chock-
of raisins, its cream cheese is always fresh, and its lines are always long. If you
on a diet, don't bother. *359 First Ave. (21st St.), 212-260-2252, ess-a-bagel.com.*
to 23rd St., ● *to First Ave.* **$**

Friend of a Farmer *American*

Only in Gramercy could you find Vermont coziness more convincing than a
thing south of the Green Mountain State itself. While stick-to-your-ribs din
specialties like shepherd's and chicken pot pies are great anytime, the crowd
brunch is its best feature. Prices are like dining in Montpelier. *77 Irving Pl. (bet. 1*
and 19th Sts.), 212-477-2188. ● Ⓝ Ⓡ Ⓦ ❹ ❺ ❻ *to 14th St.-Union Sq.* **$$**

Galaxy Global Eatery *American*

This dark, cozy, Irving Plaza neighbor has a ceiling spattered with twinkling s
and swirling blue planets. After sampling hemp-infused dishes like soba nood
tiger shrimp, and garden burgers, you might feel like you're dining on cloud ni
15 Irving Pl. (at 15th St.), 212-777-3631, galaxyglobaleatery.com. ● Ⓝ Ⓡ Ⓦ
❺ ❻ *to 14th St.-Union Sq.* **$**

Ixta *Mexican*

This unusually-located modern Mexican haven offers a surprisingly refres
break from midtown madness. Although a lot of the crowd comes for ha
hour, the food is distinct, flavorful, and mixes the best of the old with the bes
the new. Savory cocktails complement delicious twists on the burritos, and
beefsteak atop avocados is one of the richest meals. Desserts aren't worth
trouble, but try the dessert tequila, no salt and lime necessary—this is defin
not the Jose Cuervo you pregamed with last night. *48 E. 29th St. (bet. Madison*
Park), 212-683-4833, ixtarestuarant.com. ❻ *to 28th St.* **$$**

Les Halles *French*

Celebrity chef Anthony Bourdain's bestselling tell-all, *Kitchen Confidential,*
done nothing to hinder the loyalty of the crowd of New York glitterati at thi
French brasserie. A bit expensive, but well worth it, the entrées, from coq au
to steak au poivre will not disappoint. Don't miss the crème brulée, no ma
how full you may be—and you will be, as beautiful French food with Ame
portions are the highlight of this longtime midtown spot. Try brunch here, or
their Tribeca location. *411 Park Ave. South (at 29th St.), 212-679-4111, lesh*
net. ❻ *to 28th St.* **$$**

Olive's NY *Mediterranean*

This place is desperately trendy, and you'll pay for it. Olives has an attractiv
entèle, topped only in beauty by the presentation of the food: modern Ame
cuisine infused with Mediterranean flavor. Todd English's culinary genius is
apparent in his traditional preparation of non traditional meats, like his sp

scallop carpaccio or T-bone steak—of lamb. Mingle with New York's finest (no, not the NYPD) here, and several of your senses will be delighted. Your wallet will not. *201 Park Ave. South (at 17th St.), 212-353-8345.* ❹ ❺ ❻ ⓛ ⓝ ⓞ ⓡ ⓦ *to 14th St.–Union Sq.* **$$**

Park Avalon *Mediterranean*

Sink in and soak up the self-esteem of this crowded gothic hot spot, where the pleasure is in the seeing as much as in the eating. In spite of its popularity, the spacious interior makes crowding unlikely. The Mediterranean-American fare isn't too shabby either. *225 Park Ave. South (bet. 18th and 19th Sts.), 212-533-2500.* ⓛ ⓝ ⓡ ⓦ ❹ ❺ ❻ *to 14th St.-Union Sq.* **$$**

Pinch: Pizza By the Inch *Pizza*

Size really does matter here. Order your pizza by length, from the largest pizza at 36" downwards. The 24" is delicious and big enough for two. Finish your meal with an incredible gelato and savor some of the city's best. *416 Park Ave. South (bet. 28th and 29th St.), 212-686-5222, pizzabytheinch.com.* ❻ *to 28th St.* **$**

Pongal *Indian*

The best Indian restaurant on the strip of some of the best Indian eateries in New York. Pongal's South Indian vegetarian dishes have made it a solid choice for interesting and tasty food. The food is quite a bargain: most of the entrées hover around nine dollars, making an authentic Indian experience easy on the wallet as well. *110 Lexington Ave. (bet 27th and 28th Sts.), 212-696-9458, pongalnyc.com.* ❻ *to 28th St.* **$$**

Pure Food and Wine *Vegetarian / Sushi*

Bringing the California trend of raw food to New York City, everything on the menu is cooked under 118 degrees and elegantly and tastefully prepared. The sushi is particularly delicious, as is the restaurant's famous meatless lasagna (convert your favorite carnivore). As the name suggests, the wines are organic, biodynamic, and just plain high-quality. *54 Irving Pl. (bet. 17th and 18th St.), 212-477-1010, purefoodandwine.com.* ⓛ ⓝ ⓡ ⓦ ❹ ❺ ❻ *to 14th St.-Union Sq.* **$$**

The Turkish Kitchen *Mediterranean*

This reasonably-priced Gramercy restaurant has been in business for over ten years. Its longevity could be due to the intensely hued red walls, a color that the owner confides "makes people hungry." More likely, it's the food, particularly fish entrées such as the Mediterranean Sea Bass dressed with lemon oil, and the satiating grilled meat and veggie dishes. The first floor dining room is cozy enough for a quiet dinner for two, while the brighter upstairs room is ideal for groups. *386 Third Ave. (bet. 27th and 28th Sts.), 212-679-6633, turkishkitchenny.com.* ❻ *to 28th St.* **$$**

Union Square Café *American*

This landmark restaurant has been voted most popular restaurant by critics times for great gourmet food and friendly service that isn't so intimidating think you're holding your fork wrong. The American fare has an Italian slant fresh ingredients are procured from the Greenmarket a block away. *21 E. 16 (bet. Fifth Ave. and Union Sq. West.), 212-243-4020.* **L N R W 4 5 6** *to St.-Union Sq.* **$$$**

Zen Palate *Vegetarian / Asian Fusion*

Zen Palate is a vegetarian restaurant serving Asian and Asian-inspired dishes this shouldn't deter meataholics; the diverse cuisine is filing and delicious. If yo feeling too healthful, have the rich and smooth mushrooms in black bean s and enjoy the guilt trip accompanying your culinary indulgence. The patrons r from students looking for a trendy yet affordable meal at the café-style ta on the first floor, to adventurous families and first dates. The feng shui prese tion, excellent upstairs service, and three-course meal for $30 make Zen P well worth the wait you endured (with great zen) to get in. *34 Union Squa (at 16th St.), 212-614-9345, zenpalate.com.* **4 5 6 L N Q R W** *to St./Union Sq.* **$**

NIGHTLIFE

Belmont Lounge *Lounge*

Like a miniature terrarium of New York City nightlife, the Belmont Lounge r ages to fulfill each required niche of the drinking community. A long bar plenty of schmooze room leads back toward tables and club chairs, which way to a larger room with full service booths and lounging sofas. The back d lead to a small outdoor terrace and a tantalizing bit of green. While none ma to rise above the rest, the simple presence of food, drink, and fresh air is en of a holy trinity. *117 E. 15th St. (at Irving St.), 212-533-0009, belmontloungenyc* **4 5 6 N R L** *to 14th St.*

Failte Irish Whiskey Bar *Bar*

Two floors of classic rock and thirsty people keep the intensity on "high" at sports bar/pub/lounge. Couches upstairs provide patrons respite from the table and televisions in the lower level. With the radio blasting Guns N' Roses Tom Petty, and the bartenders serving up drafts of Guinness and Bodding catch all the games, or drop by after work for a pint. Be warned—the barte actually does have an Irish accent, and the regulars might take offense if some toasts to the Queen. *531 Second Ave. (bet. 29th and 30th Sts.), 212-725-944 to 28th St.*

Maker's Bar *Sports Bar*

A typical city sports bar, Maker's has the big games playing night and night and happily serves up its eponymous drink, the classic Boilermaker. Shoot s

Pete's Tavern

pool in the back, or unwind after work at a reasonable happy hour. Prices are sensible, the crowd is slightly older than college age, and the staff is friendly. *405 3rd Ave. (bet. 28th and 29th Sts.), 212-779-0306, makersbar.com.* 🌀 *to 28th St.*

Paddy Reilly's Music Bar *Music*
The world's first and only all-draught Guinness bar. That's pretty much their deal. They have traditional Irish music seven days a week. Celebrities love the bar, maybe because it's quiet and you can always get a seat. *519 Second Ave. (at 29th St.), 212-686-1210.* 🌀 *to 28th St.*

Patrick Kavanaugh *Pub*
A great place to go after work or for a relaxed night, this classic Irish pub offers a wide selection of beers and is reasonably priced for its midtown locale. It also has great bar food and a full restaurant in the back. The popcorn shrimp is highly recommended. *497 Third Ave. (at 33rd St.), 212-889-4304.* 🌀 *to 33rd St.*

Pete's Tavern *Tavern*
Pete's has been a local hangout for ages. Although it's mostly a bar, the Italian menu is more than adequate. *129 E. 18th St. (at Third Ave.), 212-473-7676.* 🌀 🌀 🌀 🌀 🌀 🌀 *to Union Sq.-14th St.*

Red Sky Bar *Bar*
With three very distinctive floors, this bar can accommodate a host of patrons, from the sports bar enthusiasts on the first floor to loungers and hipsters on the second floor and roof. This flexibility has made Red Sky a popular spot for MTV shoots and celebrity parties, but the reasonably-priced drinks make it a destination for anyone. *47 E. 29th St. (bet. Park & Madison Aves.), 212-447-1820, redskynyc.com.* 🌀 *to 28th St.*

Rocky Sullivan's *Music*

The owner of this bar is the lead singer of an Irish band named Schanechia (Ga[e]
for "storytelling"), which plays here often. This is primarily a Guinness crowd, w[ith]
a hard-core constituency of Irish males that cluster in the simple, brick-wal[l]
beer hall downstairs on Lexington Avenue. *129 Lexington Ave. (at 28th St.), 2[12-]
725-3871.* ❻ *to 28th St.*

Rodeo Bar & Grill *Music*

Don't expect cowboy hats and big belt buckles at this cozy Wild West water[ing]
hole, but then again, don't let the giant stuffed buffalo above the bar surprise y[ou].
The menu is limited, but live rockabilly bands keep the place swingin'. *375 T[hird]
Ave. (at 27th St.), 212-683-6500, rodeobar.com.* ❻ *to 28th St.*

Stone Creek *Bar*

A relatively new establishment, Stone Creek has your standard Murray [Hill]
crowd—young yuppies who moved to New York to work with money to spe[nd]
but not to burn. Catch the game on the TV or host a party in the makeshift b[ack]
room. Expect standard bar food, and inexpensive, minimalist décor. A decent [bet]
on an average night, with a crowd running from mid-twenties to mid-thirties. [140]
E. 27th St. (bet. 3rd and Lexington Aves.), 212-532-1037, stonecreeknyc.com.* ❻ [to]
28th St.*

It's stark. It's minimalist. It's cool. It's the **W HOTEL BAR** on Union Square. Se[ttle]
into one of their comfy round booths and enjoy the show of models, celebs…a[nd]
rich, smarmy-looking businessmen hoping to date them. *201 Park Ave. South. [(at]
17th St.) 212-253-9119, starwoodhotels.com.* ❶ ❶ ❶ ❶ ❶ ❹ ❺ ❻ *to 14[th,]
Union Sq.*

HOTEL BAR
THAT'S WORTH IT

ARTS

Repertorio Español *Theater*

Though just a drop in the sea of New York's overwhelmingly English-langua[ge]
performing arts centers, this venerable institution is a dignified and hard work[ing]
force to be reckoned with. Since 1968, these dancers, actors, and directors h[ave]
aimed to broaden discourse in the performing arts with productions in th[eir]
cozy yet elegant theater. The ensemble stages classic Spanish-language drama[s as]
well as adaptations of novels by the likes of Gabriel Garcia Marquez and Ma[rio]
Vargas Llosa. The company actively fosters young playwrights and commissi[ons]
new works, in addition to hosting top-notch Spanish dance productions. Ev[en]
non-Spanish speakers can enjoy the offerings: headsets that provide simulta[ne]-
ous translation are available. *Gramercy Arts Theater, 138 E. 27th St. 212-889-28[50,]
repertorio.org.* ❻ *to 23rd St.*

Irving Plaza *Music*

This is a surprisingly clean and well laid-out rock venue. With a large wraparou[nd]
balcony and plenty of floor space, there's hardly a bad sightline in the place. Tic[kets]

prices are usually quite affordable, and there's usually a great assortment of acts in each month's lineup. *17 Irving Pl. (corner of 15th Street and Irving Pl.), 212-777-6800, irvingplaza.com.* **4** **5** **6** **L** **N** **O** **R** **W** *to 14th St./Union Sq.*

OTELS AND HOSTELS

The Marcel

For a clean, comfortable, modern experience in New York City, visit The Marcel. Boasting Belgian linens, down comforters, and a complimentary cappuccino bar, this hotel offers many luxurious perks, but without the exorbitant price tag. It's small but adequate rooms are a good choice for the budget-minded traveler who is looking for a touch of modernity. *201 E. 24th St. (at Third Ave.), 888-66-HOTEL or 212-696-3800, nychotels.com. Rooms are $125-$300.* **6** *to 23rd and Park.*

Murray Hill Inn

For the price and location in midtown Manhattan, the budget minded would surely be hard-pressed to find another such deal. Rooms are spacious and clean, with some even boasting plasma TVs, and bathrooms have recently been remodeled. *143 E. 30th St. (bet. Lexington and 3rd Ave.), 888-996-6376 or 212-683-6900, murrayhillinn.com. Rooms are $139-199.* **6** *to 28th St.*

Gramercy Park

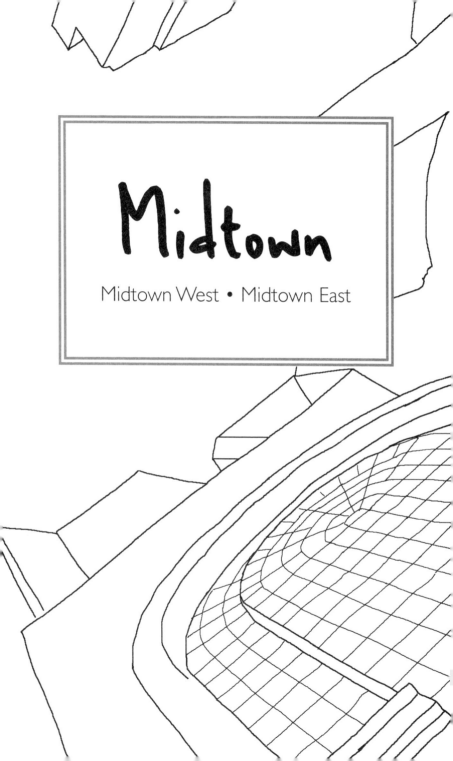

Midtown

Midtown West • Midtown East

Midtown West

TAKE A LOOK AT MIDTOWN late at night and it's easy to see wh Frank Sinatra sang about waking up in "a city that doesn't sleep." Th fluorescent buzz of Times Square, the crowds outside Madison Squa Garden, and the twenty-four hour delis sprinkled throughout Midtow West keep both the locals and the tourists up all night.

The west side of the massive area known as Midtown Manhatta has made a name for itself as an international hub of people ar places. Every morning, commuters from the surrounding suburbs ru through Penn Station, while tourists wake up and decide whether th should rush to the Empire State Building before or after they cat a Wednesday or weekend matinee. Here, you can bask in the gau lights and take in the surreal grandeur of the skyscrapers, but bewa this neighborhood wants your money, and the price of revelry in t nation's most famous urban funhouse doesn't come cheap.

West of the crowds dodging taxis and ogling office buildings is t region known as Hell's Kitchen. The only tourists that pass through t part of the city are the ones who want to see where notorious gar sters of the early 20th century settled their disputes, or where gar of Irish and Puerto Rican immigrants (think *West Side Story*) ruled t streets. Nowadays, Hell's Kitchen is ruled by savvy locals who kno that the area is the best place to grab a plate of pasta above 14 Street and businesspeople who want to knock back a few Boilerma ers at a low-key pub.

South of Times Square is the Fashion/Garment District, but don't look for a lot of practical examples of the hottest trends strutting the streets; you'll have to head downtown for that. Instead, the area is filled with personal shoppers, high-end designers, FIT students, and fashion industry mavens, all scurrying about while looking for the best deals on raw fabrics and disappearing into unmarked doors concealing vast workshops. Unlike other parts of Midtown West, the Fashion District turns into a ghost town come sundown, so don't dally if you're alone.

One of the most overwhelming features of Midtown West is its saturated population density. For decades, throngs have come here both to make a dollar and to spend a paycheck, and as long as they keep coming, don't count on there being much elbow room.

ISTORY

>> BELIEVE IT OR NOT, there was indeed a time (about 400 years ago) when shops and pavement were absent from Midtown's streets. Things have changed. Toward the middle of the 19th century, New Yorkers began to settle down in Midtown as they were migrating northward through Manhattan, some with the intention of leaving behind the squalor of downtown tenements, others just looking for a spot to call home.

It was during this period that the Garment District flourished and Midtown West became a center of industry. North of the factories filled with recent immigrants and sewing machines, however, emerged a new neighborhood known as Longacre Square, which quickly developed a reputation as Manhattan's "red light district," and to the west lingered Irish shanty towns where men found work on the docks or with the railroad. As time went on, the Garment District fell into mob hands and eventually shut down most of its factories. Hell's Kitchen has meanwhile maintained its reputation as a gritty, blue collar place to live, even if it has been attracting more young actors looking to make it big on Broadway than hardened thugs looking to run the city.

In 1904, *The New York Times* moved their offices uptown to Longacre Square, convinced the city to re-name the area, and celebrated with a big fireworks-fueled bash on New Year's Eve, kicking off a tradition which has lasted for over 100 years. Around World War I, the area shook off the remnants of the preceding century's entertainment styles—vaudeville and Ziegfeldesque follies shows—and Times Square became one of the premier areas for legit theater, rivaled only by London's West End.

Show folks, of course, sometimes have a reputation as a bunch of ne'er-do-wells, an image that wasn't helped by Times Square's infestation of flesh peddlers and drug pushers for most of the 20th century. But the area was rid of its more unsavory parts in the 1990s when Mayor Rudolph Giuliani spearheaded a massive clean-up campaign which included forcing all adult stores to convert a percentage of their wares to more innocuous goods. The final uplift coincided with the mouse

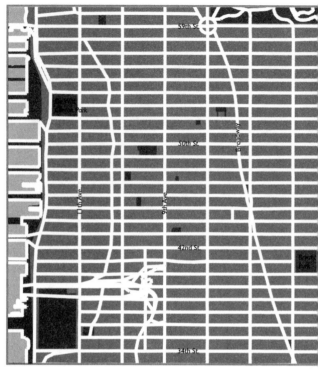

invasion, as Disney set up a (now-gone) store on 42nd Street and renovated Amsterdam Theatre for their production of *The Lion King*. The turning of the lennium signaled the rebirth of Times Square as a buoyant, all-ages urban boa walk, where the only crimes are the inflated prices of kitschy souvenirs.

WHAT TO SEE

Madison Square Garden

One of the world's most famous arenas, this huge 20,000-seat venue, convenie ly located above Penn Station, is home to the New York Knicks and the Ranger holds numerous high-profile events throughout the year, from blowout conce to the Westminster Dog Show. *7th Ave. (bet. 31st and 33rd Sts.), 212-465-MS thegarden.com.* **A C E 1 2 3** *to Penn Station-34th St.*

New York Public Library

Find the answer to any question at the main branch of this renowned libr Here you'll find a world-class repository of knowledge housed in a masterpi of architecture...with a picturesque garden to boot. Come here to do resea read, or gain much-needed peace and quiet. *5th Ave. and 42nd St., 212-930-08 nypl.org.* **F V B D** *to 42nd St–Bryant Park.*

Bryant Park

Bryant Park

Never as quiet or secluded as Central or Riverside, Bryant Park is a small grassy area halfway between Times Square and Grand Central Terminal on 42nd street. Serving as the backyard to the largest branch of the New York Public Library and home to New York's Fashion Week, something is always going on here. Every summer, a free film festival (every Monday at dusk) and concert series draw large crowds. And if you need to use the bathroom, don't fear—it was recently rated "Best in America." *42nd St. (bet 5th and 6th Aves.), bryantpark.org.* **B** **D** **F** **V** *to 42nd St–5th Ave.*

The Museum of Modern Art

Fresh off a 2004 renovation, which you'll either love or hate, MoMA is a must-see for all modern art enthusiasts (and just about every one else, too). Six floors filled with Dalí, Picasso, innovative interior design, captivating photography, and inventions will keep you occupied all day. There's an outdoor terrace with its own café, a restaurant, and two excellent design stores. Visit on Fridays between 4 and 8 pm when admission (otherwise $20) is free. *11 West 53rd St., 212-708-9400, moma.org.* **E** **V** *to 5th Ave.*

Pennsylvania Station

McKim, Mead, and White modeled the original station on the Baths of Carcalla in Rome, intending to upstage Grand Central and put another feather in the City Beautiful movement's cap. The criminal tear-down of this monument to pave the way for Madison Square Garden was a wake up call to New Yorkers to preserve their urban fabric. Today's Penn Station is a low tunnel of magazine kiosks and pizza stands, but the prospect of relocating the station to the Beaux-Arts post office across the street suggests that the glory of old Penn Station might live again. *Between 30th and 34th Sts. (bet. 7th and 8th Aves.)* **1** **2** **3** *to Penn Station.*

Times Square

Like any manic-panic tourist destination—New Orleans' Bourbon Street, Los Angeles' Walk of Fame—Times Square is glitzy, gaudy, crowded…and something everyone has to visit at least once. Be prepared for rowdy crowds and price gouging. Like many city sights, Times Square is best enjoyed at night, when the Broadway theatres are lit up, glittering signs compete for your attention, and the whole place takes on a carnival atmosphere. So go, grab a pretzel, take in the sights, see a show, snap the requisite pictures and then head off to an area of New York with fewer than five people per square foot. **Ⓐ Ⓒ Ⓔ Ⓝ Ⓞ Ⓡ Ⓦ ❶ ❷ ❸ ❼ Ⓢ** *to 42nd St.–Times Sq.*

Home to Radio City Music Hall, where the Rockettes keep on dancing; the NBC studios, where you can watch a broadcast of *Saturday Night Live*; an observation deck for scenic views; a variety of restaurants, stores and Art Deco architecture and the country's most famous Christmas tree, **ROCKEFELLER CENTER** is a bona fide New York icon. *47th-50th Sts. and 5th Ave., rockefellercenter.com.* **❶** *to 50th S* **Ⓕ Ⓓ Ⓑ Ⓞ** *to Rockefeller Center.*

TREE CHEERS

Rockefeller Center ice rink

The James A. Farley Post Office

As passersby whisk around you, take a moment to admire the Beaux-Arts sty columns of this astonishing example of the McKim, Mead, and White architectur firm, which still stands strong near Penn Station. The Post Office must hold a plac in every American's heart for bearing the famous postal worker's slogan—cribbe from a paraphrase of Herodotus' works—known to every school child. *Eighth Av at 30th St.* **Ⓐ Ⓒ Ⓔ ❶ ❷ ❸** *to Penn Station–34th St.*

WHERE TO EAT

44 Restaurant at the Royalton Hotel *American*

Dining at this restaurant is a special treat. Its ultra trendy interior (designed ' Phillip Starck) makes its European-American food seem even better than it is. Th customers are a glamorous, black-clad crowd, often admiring themselves in th restaurant's giant mirrors. It's quite expensive but worth it if you like classic ste and fish dishes served in a fancy spot. *44 W. 44th St. (bet. 5th and 6th Aves.), 21 944-8844, royaltonhotel.com.* **❹ ❺ ❻ ❼ Ⓢ** *to 42nd St.-Grand Central.* **$$$**

Abigael's on Broadway *International*

Whether it's mouth-watering Portobello mushrooms with balsamic drizzles, cedar-plank prepared salmon, or super tender ribs and steak, Abigael's entirely kosher menu will be a hit even if you're not in the tribe. Serving primarily meat dishes, this place will knock you off your feet with great service and terrific food. Abigael's is also known for their fabulous desserts to cap off a fun night of kosher feasting. *1407 Broadway (at 39th St.), 212-575-1407, abigaels.com.* Ⓐ Ⓒ Ⓔ Ⓝ Ⓡ Ⓢ Ⓦ ① ② ③ ⑦ *to 42nd St.-Times Sq.* **$$$**

B. Smith's *Soul Food*

This upscale soul food spot has a soul sister in Union Station, Washington, DC, and is known to be a draw for the expense account crowd. Owner Barbara Smith, once a model, sure knows how to decorate, but the food isn't consistently fabulous. Try the greens and salads, but skip the fried items. *320 W. 46th St. (bet. Eighth and Ninth Aves.), 212-315-1100, bsmith.com.* Ⓐ Ⓒ Ⓔ Ⓝ Ⓡ Ⓢ Ⓦ ① ② ③ ⑦ *to 42nd St.-Times Sq.* **$$**

Ban'n *Korean*

While the closely packed tables full of pre-theatre chatterboxes can make this upscale Korean restaurant a bit noisy, the antique swords and scroll-style menus make up in ambiance for any deficiencies. Can't wait for your Broadway show for some entertainment? Luckily, the built-in grill at your table will keep you busy as you pick from a variety meats to barbeque; don't have too many of their inventive house cocktails, though, or you're in for a charred meal. The hot appetizers are the gems of the menu, especially the light, airy baked scallops, and the crispy Dungeness Crab spring rolls. *350 West 50th St. (bet. 8th and 9th Aves.), 212-582-4446.* ① Ⓒ Ⓔ *to 50th St.* **$$**

Bar Americain *American*

Chef Bobby Flay maxes Southwestern cuisine and fine dining in this vast restaurant. Bar Americain's rich, mahogany décor compliments an American fusion

Bryant Park Grill

menu that includes duck with dirty wild rice and Bourbon, Porterhouse la
chops with green peas, and sweet potato gratin. The recipes are less adven
ous than Flay's famous style, but they reflect a balance between local ingredie
(like Fulton Fish Market cioppino) and Southwest flavors (like Flay's tradem
green chilies). All this topped with a wine list the size of a Mark Twain tome,
Americain makes a lovely choice for a date or business meeting. *152 W. 52n*
(bet. 6th and 7th Aves.), 212-265-9700, baramericain.com. **B D E** *to Seventh A*
E V *to Fifth Ave.-53rd St.* **$$$**

Benihana of Tokyo *Japanese*
This kitschy restaurant, known for its knife-throwing chop-chop chefs who dis
their talents tableside, has impressed several generations. With a reputation
drawing tourists rather than locals, Benihana is an alternative to Manhattan c
So sidle up to Bob and Suzy from Ohio and enjoy the show! *47 W. 56th St. (*
Fifth and Sixth Aves.), 212-581-0930, benihana.com. **N Q R W** *to 57th St.* **$**
Additional Location: 120 E. 56th St. (bet. Lexington and Park Aves.).

Blue Fin *Sushi*
Although it's strategically located for tourists in the heart of the W Hotel in Ti
Square, Blue Fin restaurant is certainly good to please the most selective N
York diners. While its décor is sufficiently ornate to be a midtown crowd-ple
(the 400-seat restaurant is adorned with an abstract rendering of fish that h
in the air between walls engraved with wave patterns), do not let it distract
from what is on your plate: extremely fine sushi and fish entrées that equal
other notable seafood restaurants in the city. *1567 Broadway (at 47th St.), 2*
918-1400. brguestrestaurants.com. **N R W** *to 49th St.,* **1** *to 50th St.* **$$$**

Broadway's Jerusalem II Kosher Pizza *Pizza*
This is the most popular Kosher pizza joint in Manhattan. Lots of students fi
the nearby Stern College for Women drop by for a slice, as do Jewish office wo
ers or tourists heading out to a Broadway show. Delivery is available to alm
anyone, anywhere in the world. *1375 Broadway (bet. 37th and 38th Sts.), 212-3*
1475, flyingpizzas.com. **A C E 1 2 3** *to 34th St.–Penn Station.* **$**

Bryant Park Grill *American*
Nestled up against the backside of the main branch of the Public Library, a res
rant would be hard-pressed to be more picturesque, especially in the spring.
food and service are uneven, the crowds crushing, but the view is fabulous.
bar, particularly when it moves outdoors in the summer, is known as a primo m
market and brunch is excellent. *25 W. 40th St. (bet. Fifth and Sixth Aves.), 212-8*
6500, arkrestaurants.com. **B D F V** *to 42nd St.–Bryant Park,* **7** *to Fifth Ave.*

Burritoville *Mexican*
This Mexican chain has great prices, with food that is low on ambiance and big
quantity. The burritos won't win any awards, but for a quick bite, with or with

heartburn, Burritoville fits the bill. Beware the fresh salsa, it's *muy caliente.* *625 Ninth Ave. (at 44th St.), 212-333-5352, burritoville.com.* **A C E** *to 42nd St.-Port Authority,* **N R Q S W 1 2 3 7** *to 42nd St.-Times Sq.* **$** *Additional locations in Manhattan.*

Café Edison

Café Edison *Diner*

Devotees of charming midtown staple lovingly call it "The Polish Tea Room." It's easy to see why the café has earned both a nickname and a reputation among Broadway insiders as the go-to place for pre- and post-show meals. The service is fast (if occasionally brusque) and you'll be glad of it when you've got only one hour 'til curtain. The food is a mix of authentic Polish and standard deli fare, with big portions and great prices. Also, there's a good chance you'll find yourself dining across from the star of the show you're about to see. If that's not enough to convince you, consider this: Neil Simon, one of the great American playwrights, based an entire play on this restaurant. *228 W. 47th St. (bet. Broadway and 8th Ave.), 212-354-0368.* **C E 1** *to 50th St,* **N R** *to 49th St.* **$**

Café Un Deux Trois *French*

Though a little strenuous on the wallet, this busy, touristy spot is perfect for a bowl of savory French onion soup or a crème brulée. Avoid the high prices by sitting at the bar. If you're up for a full meal, sit table-side for a plate of steak and pommes frites, and let your imagination run wild as you design your own table cloth with a cup full of crayons. *123 W. 44th St. (bet. Sixth Ave. and Broadway), 212-354-4148, caféundeuxtrois.biz.* **A C E N R Q S W 1 2 3 7** *to 42nd St.-Times Sq.* **$$**

Carmine's *Italian*

Come with a group of friends and order up a storm of family-style Italian. Seating is slow, so a visit to this enormous dark wood institution happily mandates a stop at the lovely bar. *200 W. 44th St. (bet. Broadway and Eighth Ave.), 212-221-3800, carminesnyc.com.* **A C E N R S W 1 2 3 7** *to 42nd St.-Times Sq.* **$$**

Cheyenne Diner *Diner*

The short walk from the meatpacking district's mega clubs to Cheyenne Diner will leave you sober enough to get through the door in one piece, but still tipsy enough to devour their perfect plate of scrambled eggs. By night, this 24/7 greasy spoon caters to party animals; by day, workers and commuters stop in looking for a quick bite. The food, which runs the gamut of diner classics from omelets to burgers to pie, isn't amazing but is cheap. The diner is a slice of Americana charm that's rarely found in a city obsessed with chic and hip. *411 Ninth Ave. (at 33rd St.), 212-465-8750.* **1 2 3 A C E** *to 34th St.* **$**

Churrascaria Plataforma *Latin*

Plataforma is New York's swankiest Brazilian barbeque joint, where the all-you-can-eat meatfest will have you dieting for the rest of the week. The lighting and

clientele are beautiful, the lime-based drinks divine, and the salad bar a work
art. The prices aren't cheap, but for a memorable evening, it can't be beat. 316 W
49th St. (bet. 8th and 9th Aves.), 212-245-0505. **V** **C** **E** to 50th St. **$$**

Cupcake Café Bakery

This is a quaint bakery with pink walls on the raunchiest stretch in Hell's Kitche
Great donuts, waffles, and cupcakes, with a few tables to allow for immediate co
sumption. The location is unfashionable for a food pilgrimage, but come for ol
fashioned sweets. 545 Ninth Ave. (at 41st St.), 212-465-1530, cupcakecafé.com.
C **E** to 42nd St.-Port Authority, **N** **R** **S** **W** **1** **2** **3** **7** to 42nd St.-Times Sq. **$**

Del Frisco's Steakhouse

High ceilings and dark mahogany walls give this midtown steakhouse an ove
whelmingly classy appeal. The mixed crowd is made up mainly of dashing you
professionals and businessmen out on the town. The Double Eagle Dallas stea
house specializes in exceedingly tender and flavorful meats seared in pepper a
spices, served on piping hot plates which keep the meat warm throughout yo
meal. Sommeliers traverse the two-floor dining area, to help you choose fro
the extensive wine list. Try the porterhouse or the filet accompanied by delicio
creamed spinach and garlic mashed potato sides, but don't forget to start w
the world-famous crabcakes in a lobster bisque sauce. The hardest part of eati
at Del Frisco's is leaving room for the wonderful desserts. 1221 Sixth Ave (at 49
St.), 212-575-5129, delfriscos.com. **B** **D** **F** to 47-50th Sts.-Rockefeller Ctr. **$$**

Dimple Indian

Situated in the middle of midtown's wholesale district, Dimple is a surprising
comfy hole-in-the-wall catering to both Indian wholesalers and savvy suits. Ch
Manaan lovingly imbues his South Indian dishes with enough spice to satisfy eve
the most maniacal of heat seekers. Paper thin dosas, air-filled pooris, and a wi
array of rice dishes are perfect for soaking up a rotating selection of delectab
curries from the lunch buffet, topped, of course, with tamarind sauce and cocor
chutney. At $7 for unlimited buffet access, or $6.50 for their "take out thali" (tw
curries with rice, naan, raiita, and dessert), their lunch special is one of the be
deals in midtown. 11 W 30th St. (bet. Fifth Ave. and Broadway), 212-643-9464.
R to 28th St. **$**

Don Giovanni Italian

For a slice of the neighborhood, sit outside at a table and enjoy a pie at Do
Giovanni. Made in a brick oven, with thin crust, fresh mozzarella, and a swe
tomato sauce, this pizza is bound to please. Be forewarned: delivery takes at lea
an hour. 358 W. 44th St. (bet. 8th and 9th Aves.), 212-581-4939, dongiovanni-ny.cc
A **C** **E** **N** **R** **S** **W** **1** **2** **3** **7** to 42nd St.-Times Sq. **$$**

Estiatorio Milos Mediterranean

The fish are displayed fresh for you to select from at this Greek piscatory/resta rant that features by-the-pound pricing and fresh fish cooked in Mediterranean sauces. Nothing compares to the seafood at Milos; it floats somewhere above, an ideal not to be touched. *125 W. 55th St. (bet. 6th and 7th Aves.), 212-245-7400.* **N** **Q** **R** **W** **F** *to 57th St.* **$$$**

The Flame *Diner*
Better known as a neighborhood icon than for its food, The Flame nonetheless ably serves up the expected diner menu, from omelets to burgers to gyros. The business crowd converges around 1 pm for lunch, but otherwise there is ample seating and rarely a wait. This is a good place to chat without having to fork over lots of dough. *893 Ninth Ave. (at 58th St.), 212-765-7962.* **A** **B** **C** **D** **1** *to 59th St.-Columbus Circle.* **$**

Havana Central *Latin*
Havana Central is a stylish place to stop after a long day of work or for a pre- or post-theatre respite. With an extensive drink menu featuring classic and fruit-flavored mojitos, many varieties of sangria, and an incredible summer cocktails menu, your friends can all find something to suit their tastes. The melt-in-your-mouth churros are a must-have to finish off your meal, especially with the chocolate and butterscotch dipping sauces. Havana Central's Cuban sabor makes it an affordable spot with a lot to offer and fantastic drinks. For Columbia students who want to replace their West End crawls with Havana nights, check out Havana Central at the West End, where you can get a classic pitcher of beer along with the student-friendly Cuban fare. *151 W. 46th St. (bet. 6th & 7th Aves.), 212-414-4999, havana-central.com.* **N** **Q** **R** **W** **S** **1** **2** **3** **7** *to 42nd St.-Times Square.* **$$** *Additional location across from Columbia University at 2909 Broadway (bet. 113 & 114).*

Joe Allen *American*
Upscale thespians, including bonafide Broadway celebs in search of some post-performance relaxation, come to this dark and elegant but unpretentious eatery to fill up on gourmet meatloaf and hot fudge pudding cake. On Sunday nights, 8pm to closing, fifteen percent of every check goes to Broadway Cares/Equity Fights AIDS. *326 W. 46th St. (bet. Eighth and Ninth Aves.), 212-581-6464, joeallen-orso.com.* **A** **C** **E** *to 42nd St.-Port Authority.* **$$**

Joe's Shanghai *Chinese*
This is an authentic Chinese restaurant for a crowd that knows its Asian food. Try the soup dumplings, filled with delectable crab and pork. The service won't bowl you over, but the food will. The prices are good, too. *24 W. 56th St. (bet. 5th and 6th Aves.), 212-333-3868.* **E** **V** *to Fifth Ave.-53rd St.,* **6** *to 51st St.,* **F** *to 57th St.* **$$**

Kashkaval *Middle Eastern*
Between Hell's Kitchen and Columbus Circle, Kashkaval is an affordable oasis in the City's desert of pricey dining. A gourmet food market (touting over 100 international cheeses, imported olives, cured salamis and meats) fills the front. In

Joe Allen

back is a cosy, candle-lit restaurant packed with rowdy locals, even on weeknigh
Kashkaval is named after a salty, sharp Bulgarian goat cheese. Order a bubbl
cauldron of the stuff, served with big hunks of French bread, and pair it with
couple of European beers. *856 9th Ave. (bet. 55th and 56th Streets), 212-58
8282.* **Ⓐ Ⓑ Ⓒ Ⓓ Ⓘ** *to Columbus Circle.* **$$**

Kiiroi Hana *Sushi*

This sushi joint is big on authenticity, small on imagination and décor. Try sor
inside out rolls or the eggplant appetizer in miso sauce. *20 W. 56th St. (bet. Fi
and Sixth Aves.), 212-956-0127.* **Ⓔ Ⓥ Ⓖ** *to 51st–Lexington Ave.* **$$**

Koi *Japanese*

L.A. meets New York in this fine Japanese dining experience. Koi is a welcor
burst of shallow air in a city obsessed with its integrity. Nonetheless, this is n
to say that the food at Koi is anything less than excellent. The house Dragon R
is one of the tastiest in New York, and both the Kobe Filet and Chilean Sea B
were tender and delicious, with the former being exactly as buttery as it shou
be. The desserts, while standard, are very tasty, making them a welcome cap
any meal. *40 W. 40th St. (bet. Fifth and Sixth Aves.), 212-921-3330, koirestaurant.co*
Ⓑ Ⓓ Ⓕ Ⓥ Ⓥ *to 42nd St.-Bryant Park.* **$$**

La Bonne Soupe *French*

An authentic French bistro, right down to the waiters' thick accents and
creamy chocolate mousse. Red-checkered tablecloths and colorful paintings a
to the homey, rural atmosphere. Start with a glass of wine and some fond
or the Paysanne soup, then try the duck platters, and end the meal with crè
caramel. *48 W. 55th St. (bet. 5th and 6th Aves.), 212-586-7650, labonnesoupe.co*
Ⓝ Ⓡ *to 57th,* **Ⓔ Ⓥ** *to 53rd St.,* **Ⓖ** *to 51st St.* **$$**

Le Bernardin *French*

There is nothing we can write here to adequately describe this fantasy o restaurant. Simply surrender yourself to the magic of Chef Eric Ripert, and the charms of owner and co-creator Maguy Le Coze, and cherish the exhilarating sensation of eating a perfectly elegant meal. You may only get to do this once, but savor every minute. There is only one thing we can really say: any New Yorker who appreciates culinary miracles should come here to have a religious experience. Never mind your wallet; this meal is priceless. *155 W. 51st St. (bet. 6th and 7th Aves.), 212-554-1515, le-bernadin.com.* ❶ *to 49th 50th St.,* ❷ ❶ ❶ ❶ *to 47-50 Sts.–Rockefeller Ctr.* **$$$**

Le Rivage *French*

Le Rivage's cuisine consistently ranks with NYC's top tier French restaurants. Only a short walk from the Theatre District, Le Rivage is an ideal place for a pre-theatre dinner. After 8:00 pm, They offer a $22 prix fixe three-course meal, which is an excellent value considering the twenty entrees available, ranging from duck à l'orange and steak to monkfish and sole. The garlic-infused baked mussels, sautéed frog legs, poire hélène, and peche melba are all highly recommended. *340 W 46th St. (bet. Eighth and Ninth Aves.), 212-765-7374. lerivagenyc.com* ❶ ❷ ❸ ❼ ❶ ❶ ❶ ❶ ❶ *to Times Sq.-42nd St.* **$$$**

Marseilles *French*

Take a seat and let your mouth enjoy a trip through the Mediterranean's many different regions with each new course. Making a selection from the elegant offerings is challenging—everything sounds as delicious on the menu as it tastes on the plate. Marseilles' intimate location, removed from the midtown buzz, features a spacious, decadent interior. It is an ideal spot for dating and one of New York's best French-inspired bistros. *630 9th Ave (at 44th St.), 212-333-2323, marseillenyc. com.* ❶ ❶ *to 50th St.* **$$**

Norma's *American*

You would never expect to find this refreshingly low-key restaurant serving brunch all day long nestled in Le Parker Meridien Hotel. With fabulous chocolate or Rice Krispy French Toast "for kids," as well as adult specialties like Wa Zaa (a waffle smothered in berry brulee) alongside traditional brunch items such as smothered eggs or eggs benedict, Norma's has been pleasing for years. Even Martha Stewart has dined here. On weekends, come early. *118 W. 57th St. (bet. 6th and 7th Aves.), 212-708-7460. parkermeridien.com.* ❶ ❶ ❶ ❶ ❶ *to 59th St.* **$$**

Osteria del Circo *Italian*

Tuscany goes to the circus in this Italian offshoot of Le Cirque 2000, but unlike its upscale French cousin, Osteria just wants to have fun. The circus theme runs from the trapeze ladders draped from wall to wall or the flame-colored metal juggler and musician sculptures perched on the back wall. A beautiful restaurant, with fabulous food and a ideal location. One must try the donut dessert; it is fantastic. *120 W. 55th St. (bet. 6th and 7th Aves.), 212-265-3636, osteriadelcircio.com.* ❶ ❶ ❶ ❶ *to 57th St.* **$$$**

Pietrasanta *Italian*

This is a Hell's Kitchen neighborhood secret, where the chef sometimes leaves
kitchen to ask how customers are enjoying their meals. For an appetizer, try
succulent scallops in a rich pesto sauce, and order the pumpkin ravioli in sw
pepper sauce as an entrée. *683 9th Ave (at 47th St.), 212-265-9471.* **C** **E** to !
St., R to 49th St. **$$**

Pigalle *French*

In French cooking, the line between rich and fatty is often blurred. Pigalle is
exception. The rich appetizers and desserts begin and finish the meal on a
note, but it seems that the chef spends more time creating these amuse bou
creations than on the mains. The décor, a pleasant mix of outdoor Parisian
and American diner, and the charming French wait staff make this late-night :
a fun experience. But be advised: whether you're a young dater or an old thea
goer, you'll still spend a pretty penny. *790 Eighth Ave. (at 48th St.), 212-489-2*
Tourdefrancenyc.com. **C** **E** *to 50th St.* **$$**

Ruby Foo's *Asian Fusion*

Fun, cool, hip pan-Asian food offering everything from dim sum to sushi...a
popular Sunday brunch! Ruby Foo's is known for its over-the-top and ostenta
decor and sometimes snooty service. *1626 Broadway (at 49th St.), 212-489-5*
brguestrestaurants.com. **1** **C** **E** *to 50th St.* **$$$**

San Domenico *Italian*

If the location right near Central Park's horse-drawn carriages doesn't gi
away already, this romantic Tony May restaurant epitomizes upscale Italian
ing. Stringed curtains shelter the restaurant from city traffic, yielding an intir
luxurious dining space. Expect perfectly crafted courses like egg yolk-filled ra
in truffle butter or veal fillet with risotto "al salto,"—a memorable culinary ad
ture. For a special treat, come during truffle season (September-December)
sample recipes that highlight the truffles brought directly from Italy throug
the season's harvest. *240 Central Park South (bet. Broadway and Seventh Aves),*
265-5959. **1** **A** **B** **C** **D** *to 59th St.-Columbus Circle.* **$$$**

Seppi's *French*

Despite the Italian name, Seppi's offers traditional French cuisine. While the n
is not incredibly creative, the chef prepares high-quality French classics tha
sure to satisfy picky theatre-goers. Contributing to its classy, romantic atmosp
Seppi's features jazz every night. The décor's a bit odd, with a wide rang
French paraphernalia crowding the walls, but the rose on each table and
cushions in the booths focus diners' attention on each other, not the walls
service is fast and food is generous and filling, but only the desserts have
creative flare that separates the *mezza mezza* from the *magnifique. 123 W. 5*
(bet. 6th & 7th Aves.), 212-708-7444. **N** **Q** **R** **W** *to 57th St.–7th Ave.* **$$**

Soup Kitchen International *American*

While *Seinfeld* fanatics are bemoaning the end of an era, one remnant lives on. The lines at this pop-culture landmark are unreal at lunchtime, but have you noticed how smoothly it moves along? Patrons have made up their minds what to order by the time they reach the counter of this famous take-out. Otherwise it's "No soup for you!" *259-A W. 55th St. (bet. Eighth Ave. and Broadway), 212-757-7730, soupkitchenintl.com.* Ⓐ Ⓑ Ⓒ Ⓓ Ⓘ *to 59th St.-Columbus Circle.* **$**

Thalia *American*

Chef Paul Nelson puts such enthusiasm into the presentation and composition of every dish on the menu that to choose only a few to mention would be insulting to the rest. His finely-crafted sophisticated flavors and texture combinations smack of careful planning and playful experimentation. The meticulous décor and extensive wine list enrich the meal and ensure that this spacious restaurant stays packed. (If you get a chance, ask charismatic co-owner Avi Camchi for an earful about his current favorites on the menu). *828 Eighth Avenue (at 50th), 212-399-4444, restaurantthalia.com.* Ⓘ Ⓒ Ⓔ *to 50th St.,* Ⓝ Ⓡ Ⓦ *to 49th St.* **$$**

Topaz Thai Restaurant *Thai*

This spot may be cramped and a bit hard to find, but the food's tasty and, judging by the constant flux of diners, easy on the budget. Upon your arrival, a smiling, speedy waiter will seat you at a table three inches from your neighbors on all sides. However, the delicious curried entrées and Thai iced tea will make you forget the cramped quarters. *127 W. 56th St. (bet. Sixth and Seventh Aves.), 212-957-8020.* Ⓝ Ⓠ Ⓡ Ⓦ Ⓕ *to 57th St.,* Ⓐ Ⓑ Ⓒ Ⓓ Ⓘ *to 59th St.-Columbus Circle.* **$$**

Uncle Nick's Greek Cuisine *Mediterranean*

Serving enormous kebabs, salads brimming with stuffed grape leaves and olives, and huge wedges of flaming saganaki cheese, Uncle Nick's won't leave you hungry. The bustling atmosphere, attentive wait staff, and speedy service make this restaurant great for pre-theater dining. *747 Ninth Ave. (bet. 50th and 51st Sts.), 212-245-7992.* Ⓒ Ⓔ *to 50th St.* **$**

Via Brasil *Latin*

This Little Brazil fave is full of jazz, palms and fabulous food. The waiters are nice, and the appetizers as good as the entrées. Try the lime drinks, fish casserole, and piping hot coffee. Lots of Brazilians come here too, so you know it's legit. *34 W. 46th St. (bet. Fifth and Sixth Aves.), 212-997-1158.* Ⓑ Ⓓ Ⓕ Ⓥ *to 47-50th Sts.-Rockefeller Center.* **$$**

West Bank Café *American*

The West Bank Café, conveniently located near the theater district, is an up and coming eatery that offers comfort food with an interesting twist. The ambiance is relaxed enough for families and casual pre-show dinners, while offering just enough sophistication for a first date or cosmopolitan night out. While the entrees are well-crafted and hearty, the adventurous appetizers prepared by ambitious chef are not to be missed. Also features downstairs cabaret and excellent wine and cognac selection. *407 W. 42nd St. (bet. 9th & 10th Aves.), 2* *695-6909.* ❶ ❷ ❸ Ⓐ Ⓒ Ⓔ *to 42nd St.* **$$**

NIGHTLIFE

Albion *Club*
Quickly emerging as a trailblazer in the advancement of the Gothic, Industrial, Electronic music scenes, this club is one of the best "underground" clubs in city. Plenty of seating at the bar and at tables makes this a comfortable room listen to the unique sounds of New York's alternative bands. *251 W. 30th St. Seventh and Eighth Aves.), 212-695-2747. albionnyc.com.* ❶ *to 28th St.*

Barrage *LGBT*
Comfortable, if a little awkwardly decorated, Barrage hosts some regulars w also catering to the spillover from Therapy a few blocks up. Excellent servic the bar, with several beer selections (usually anathema to gay bars) on tap. an especially hip place for the 25-30 crowd, there's a lot to like about this lou though not a meat-market, it's a great place to get picked up. Just don't put it on the night's agenda, as the crowd begins to thin out around 2am *401 W. St. (at Ninth Ave.), 212-586-9390.* ❶ *to 50th St.*

B.B. King Blues Club & Grill *Music*
Lodged between Broadway's theaters, this prestigious venue for New York m cians combines a restaurant with a music hall and attracts both locals and tou Music ranges from blues, jazz, and rock to soul and hip hop, featuring big-n artists like B.B. King himself. Some 500 people can pack this luxurious music ha enjoy good American food and drink over a wonderful evening of live music. Sunday gospel brunch is a neighborhood favorite, with soul food and even m soulful sounds. *237 W. 42nd St. (bet. Seventh and Eighth Aves.), 212-997-414* Ⓒ Ⓔ Ⓝ Ⓡ Ⓢ Ⓦ ❶ ❷ ❸ ❼ *to 42nd St.-Times Sq.*

Connolly's *Music*
You can't be Irish in New York if you haven't heard of Black 47, the Dublin band. Black 47 plays at Connolly's every Saturday, with other acts occasio taking stage as well. Full menu and full bar (of course). *14 E. 47th St. (bet. and Madison Aves.), 212-867-3767, connollyspubandrestaurant.com.* Ⓔ Ⓥ *to Ave-53rd St.*

Dizzy's Club Coca Cola *Music*
A jazz club at the Time Warner Center? While this ambiguous identity can s a little off-putting to lovers of the NYC jazz scene, Dizzy's can serve as a g introduction to Gotham's jazz universe. With gorgeous views of Central Dizzy's dishes out three sets a night that even the most casual of jazz fans revel in. From jazz legends to NYC up-and-comers, Dizzy's has a diverse

delicious musical lineup. The cocktails are a bit too ambitious, so stick to the solid wine list. While the quality of the southern-inspired food does not compare with the beats, Dizzy's specialties, the gumbo and the mac and cheese, will ensure a solid dining experience. *10 Columbus Circle, 5th Floor (at 8th Ave.), 212-258-9595.* Ⓐ Ⓑ Ⓒ Ⓓ ❶ *to Columbus Circle.*

Fashion Forty Lounge *Lounge*
The Fashion Forty Lounge is a smooth nightspot perfect for a connoisseur of fine drinks and finger foods. The small assortment of paninis and salads are tasty, provided you can see the menu through the dim lighting. Sit back in the comfortable chairs, curl up with a pillow and enjoy the laid back atmosphere of high-class lounging. *202 W. 40th St. (at Seventh Ave.). 212-221-3628.* Ⓐ Ⓒ Ⓔ Ⓝ Ⓡ Ⓢ Ⓦ ❶ ❷ ❸ ❼ *to 42nd St.-Times Sq.*

Flute *Bar*
Champagne afficianados, look no further—bubbly heaven has been found at this cozy, romantic lounge. You can order by the bottle or the flute, and do not miss out on the exotic spring rolls (the Sateri is especially tasty, made of tuna, rice vermicelli, avocado, and fresh mint). The champagne cocktails are inventive and refreshing, and will cost you around $10. If you'd like to have a sampling of a few types of champagne, the Magic Flutes provides a tasting of three. *205 W. 54th St. (bet. Seventh Ave. and Broadway), 212-265-5169.* Ⓑ Ⓓ Ⓔ *to Seventh Ave.,* ❶ *to 50th St.*

Hammerstein Ballroom *Music*
Opened in 1906 by Oscar Hammerstein, this venue is the setting for many national touring acts as well as television broadcasts and corporate events. Music is an eclectic roster, from Hanson to Manson. No food, but several bars. *311 W. 34th St. (bet. 8th and 9th Aves.), 212-279-7740. Cash Only. Tickets: $20-$60.* Ⓐ Ⓒ Ⓔ ❶ ❷ ❸ *to 34th St.-Penn Station*

Hudson Bar *Bar*
Take the fluorescent green escalator in the Hudson Hotel to reach this trendy bar with shiny floors, bright lights, translucent gel cushions on Louis XV chairs, and a main bar that glows from within. This hip place also has overpriced drinks and a pretentious staff. Guys coming alone will have a difficult time making it past the velvet rope—unless you're Leonardo DiCaprio, of course. *356 W. 58th St. (bet. Eighth and Ninth Aves.), 212- 554-6343.* Ⓐ Ⓑ Ⓒ Ⓓ ❶ *to 59th St.-Columbus Circle*

Iridium *Lounge*
This large music lounge has been relocated from the Lincoln Center to the heart of the tourist area in Midtown. Big-name bands play here every week, bringing in both the local hardcore jazz fans and curious foreign tourists. Drinks run $7 to $10, and food entrées average $20. *1650 Broadway (at 51st St.), 212-582-2121.* Ⓐ Ⓒ ❶ *to 50th St.*

Roseland Ballroom

Jimmy's Corner *Bar*

Escape from the giddiness of the Theater District at this easy-going local ⟨ the site of some of the scenes in Raging Bull. Owner Jimmy Glen subsidize⟨ career as a boxing trainer and manager with the revenues from this hopping An eclectic crowd of boxing fanatics, literateurs, grad students and the occasi movie star hang out here. *140 W. 44th St. (bet. Sixth and Seventh Aves.), 212-.* 9510. Ⓐ Ⓒ Ⓔ Ⓝ Ⓡ Ⓢ Ⓦ ❶ ❷ ❸ ❼ *to 42nd St.-Times Sq.*

La Gazelle Lounge *Lounge*

Be prepared to forget about the garish bright lights and touristy crowd of T⟨ Square as soon as you enter the lobby of the Time Hotel. Take the glorious elevator up one floor and find yourself in the midst of a gorgeous lounge s⟨ welcoming after-work professionals as well as other non-hotel guests sea ing for the perfect martini as the evening progresses. Window shades block⟨ everything that might remind you of where you are, while dim candlelight posh couches help you wind down. The menu features delightful martini coc⟨ with names like the Time Bomb and the Bed Time. These martinis are absol⟨ amazing, but prepare yourself to pay about $12. Wine, champagne, and bee⟨ also available. *224 W. 49th St., 2nd Fl. (bet. Broadway and Eighth Ave.), 212- 6236.* ❶ *to 50th St.*

The Oak Room *Lounge*

One of two lounges at the Algonquin Hotel where Dorothy Parker's wit pres⟨ over a legendary circle of writers and critics in the '20s. Dress up to fit in⟨ the stylish crowd soaking up late-night cabaret performances in this stylish Er⟨ tearoom. *59 W. 44th St. (bet. Fifth and Sixth Aves.), 212- 840-6800.* Ⓑ Ⓓ Ⓕ 42nd St., Ⓐ Ⓒ Ⓔ Ⓝ Ⓡ Ⓢ Ⓦ ❶ ❷ ❸ ❼ *to 42nd St.-Times Sq.*

O'Flaherty's Ale House *Pub*

Here, you'll find the only pub in NY with a tree growing right through the m⟨ of the bar. In the back, discover a private garden away from the Midtown b⟨ Live music, great beer and plenty of dancing keep everyone busy. *334 W. 46⟨ (bet. Eighth and Ninth Aves.), 212- 581-9366.* ❶ *to 50th St.,* Ⓝ Ⓡ Ⓦ *to 49th⟨*

Roseland Ballroom *Music*

It started as a popular ballroom in the 1930s, and the newly renovated Ros⟨ is still one of the more frequented venues in town. Large enough to draw a s⟨ crowd, but small enough to retain some of that intimate club charm, these⟨ expect to find the bigger named alternative acts. *239 W. 52nd St. (bet. Broc⟨ and Eighth Ave.), 212- 247-0200, roselandballroom. com. Tickets: $15-$20.* Ⓒ *to 50th St.*

Shelly's New York *Lounge*

Shelly's serves up some of the city's best steaks and seafood. The award-wi⟨ mac and cheese is also a highlight. Shelly's offers jazz solo, duet, and trio jazz⟨

perform every night except Sundays, usually starting at around 8pm. Notable musicians perform regularly, but don't worry about jazz purists getting upset if you have a conversation. *41 W 57th St. (bet. Sixth and Seventh Aves.), 212-245-2422.* Ⓝ Ⓡ Ⓦ *to 57th St.*

Show *Club*

At Show, the crowd is generally young, attractive, and well-dressed, but guys without ladies will have to wait a long time to get in. With scantily clad women swinging from the ceilings and half-naked musclemen dancing up a storm, Show amps the rampant sexual energy to a peak. The dance music is the usual hip-hop and house beats, and the drinks are extremely expensive (and come in a plastic cup, no less). *135 W. 41st St. (bet. Sixth Ave. and Broadway), 212- 278-0988. show-night-club.com.* Ⓐ Ⓒ Ⓔ Ⓝ Ⓡ Ⓢ Ⓦ ① ② ③ ⑦ *to 42nd St.-Times Sq.*

Siberia *Bar*

The proverbial hole in the wall, Siberia is small, dark, and revels in its trashiness. Siberia attracts a diverse crowd, from actor/waiters to yuppies. Their jukebox is among the best in town, and they host DJs and film screenings weekly. *356 W. 40th St. (bet. Eighth and Ninth Aves.), 212- 333-4141. Cash Only.* Ⓐ Ⓒ Ⓔ *to 42nd St.*

The Supper Club *Music / Dance*

As one of New York's more elegant venues, be prepared to dress up for a night of dinner and dancing on the town. Historically a ballroom, The Supper Club is the center of the swing scene every Friday and Saturday night. During the rest of the week, catch a live band under the sparkling chandelier and painted gold stars. French and American Continental food served from 6pm-12:30am. With '40s lindyhop, jump, swing, and occasional private rock and pop concerts. *240 W. 47th St. (bet. Broadway and Eighth Ave.), 212-921-1940, thesupperclub.com.* Ⓒ Ⓔ ① *to 50th St.,* Ⓝ Ⓡ Ⓦ *to 49th St.*

Therapy *LGBT*

The classiest, hippest, coolest gay bar in Manhattan. As Hell's Kitchen gradually steals Chelsea's thunder, this bi-level, greenhouse-inspired bar / lounge attracts downtowners in-the-know, college scenesters, 30+ single finance professionals, and out-of-towners alike. Every now and then a big name stops by and performs on the small 2nd-floor stage, and even if you're not cruising, Therapy is the perfect place for a dry martini and great conversation. The beers may be a little overpriced at $6, so try signature drinks like the "Freudian Sip," "Bi-Polar," or a "Psychotic Episode" to get a taste of Therapy's psychoanalysis. The crowd dies down earlier than expected, so your best bet is to arrive before the clock strikes midnight. *348 W. 52nd St. (bet. Eighth and Ninth Aves.), 212-397-1700, therapy-nyc. com. Su-W 5 pm-2 am, R-Sa 5 pm-4 am* ① *to 50th St.*

Xth Ave. Lounge *LGBT*

Velvet couches, leather armchairs, a slate bar and euphoric-smelling bathrooms are highlights of this Hells Kitchen bar, where the friendly staff pours drinks at re-

freshingly affordable prices. What's most surprising to newcomers is the atti
here—there is none. Whereas most gay bars attract the "see-and-be-seen" cre
the regulars here are much more relaxed. They're chilling with friends, drin
classic cocktails and listening to the festive progressive house that's spun by g
DJs. Off the beaten path for most, this is a classy and welcoming addition to
Hells Kitchen mix and certainly worth a late-night visit. *642 Tenth Ave. (bet.
and 46th Sts.), 212-245-9088. Hours: M-Su 6pm-4am.* Ⓐ Ⓒ Ⓔ Ⓝ Ⓡ Ⓦ
❸ *to 42nd St.—Times Sq.*

ARTS

Madame Tussaud's New York *Museums*
Getting your picture taken with Britney Spears? Difficult. Getting your pic
taken with Oprah? Pretty much impossible…unless you visit Madame Tussa
of course. Sure, it's a little creepy standing in a room filled with perfectly-scul
wax models of famous figures living and dead, but nowhere else can you see
how short most actors really are and pose for pictures with them all. Ah, to
traps. *234 West 42nd St. (between 7th and 8th Ave.), 212-512-9600 and 800/
8872, nycwax.com, Open daily, call ahead for updated opening & closing times.* ●
Ⓔ *to Port Authority,* ❶ ❷ ❸ Ⓝ Ⓡ Ⓑ Ⓓ Ⓕ Ⓠ *to the 42nd St.—Times Squa*

Carnegie Hall *Music*
Still the reigning champ of bourgeois nightlife, this legendary institution is
artist's Valhalla. Concerts usually take place every night of the week except d
July and August, when the Hall is closed. The majority of acts are classical, but
may catch the occasional Joan Baez or David Bowie show (if you're lucky)
adjoining restaurant and bar serves American cuisine. *881 Seventh Ave. (at
St.), 212-247-7800, carnegiehall.org. Tickets: $16-$150.* Ⓝ Ⓡ Ⓦ *to 57th St.*

Christie's *Galleries*
Scope out the goods at free public viewings held five days before auctions a
New York branch of the London legend. Nineteenth and twentieth century
pean art traditionally favored here. *20 Rockefeller Plaza. 212-636-2000; chr
com. Hours: M-F 9:30am–5:30pm* Ⓑ Ⓓ Ⓕ Ⓥ *to 47-50th Sts.-Rockefeller Ce*

Exit Art *Galleries*
A huge upstairs loft space, complete with a shop filled with art trinkets and a
made for lingering when gallery hopping becomes tiresome. Never stodg
gallery favors themed group shows. Past innovations have include having a
move their studios into the gallery and an exhibit of art and paraphernalia
social protest movements. Openings are not to be missed. *475 Tenth Ave. (at
St.). 212-966-7745; exitart.org. Hours: T-Th 10am-6pm, Sat 12pm-8pm Sugg
contribution $2.* Ⓐ Ⓒ Ⓔ *to 34th St.-Penn Station.*

Marlborough *Galleries*
A good place to see works by relatively well known contemporary and mo
artists, this is just one of multiple Marlborough Gallery spaces worldwid

Carnegie Hall

though their focus is on selling big-ticket pieces from the estates of well-known artists such as Jackson Pollock and Franz Kline, the atmosphere in the gallery is laid back and comfortable. *40 W. 57th St. (bet. Fifth and Sixth Aves). 212-541-4900; marlboroughgallery.com. Hours: M-F 10am-5:30pm.* **A** **B** **C** **D** **1** *to 59th St.–Columbus Circle.*

BEFORE THEY
WERE STARS

Both a well-respected theater and a non-profit acting school, **CIRCLE IN THE SQUARE** is an important place for those involved with and excited by the New York theater scene, and its shows are among the many quality alternatives to the larger Broadway spectacles. *1633 Broadway (at 50th St.), 212-307-0388, circlesquare.org.* **1** *to 50th St.*

Manhattan Theater Club *Theater*

Terence McNally, A.R. Gurney, and Richard Greenberg are just a few of the play-wrights whose work has been featured at MTC, one of the oldest subscription-based theater companies in the city. The company presents a broad range of work, mixing audience-pleasers and challenging pieces on its two stages. MTC received a great deal of media attention in 1998 as the site of McNally's contro-versial Corpus Christi. *131 W. 55th St. (bet. Sixth and Seventh Aves.), 212-399-3000, mtc-nyc.org.* **N** **R** **W** *to 57th St.-Seventh Ave.*

MOST
CONVENIENT
CONCERT

It's always a party inside the **TIMES SQUARE SUBWAY STATION** down near the platform for the Grand Central shuttle: the MTA gives the space over to loud, lively, and talented musicians and performers, many of whom you can catch on television on Showtime at the Apollo. The hip-hop dancers always put on a good show and other performers keep the station alive all hours of the night. **A** **C** **E** **N** **Q** **R** **W** **1** **2** **3** **7** **S** *to 42nd St.–Times Sq.*

Mint Theater *Theater*

Broadway and off-Broadway are both awash in revivals these days, as if there weren't thousands of starving playwrights struggling to get their work produced. Yet surprisingly, many audiences stumble out of a revival wondering just why it

Alvin Ailey Dance Theater and School

was revised. Not so with this theater, which stages obscure works by famou[s] writers in addition to revivals of signature works by obscure writers. The sm[all] theater feels intimate rather than cramped because it invites audiences to hav[e] an intense experience as part of the well-crafted action. Despite its convenie[nt] location, shows staged here feel different, like throwbacks to the time when th[e] quality work being performed on stage was contemporary rather than recycle[d] *311 W. 43rd St. (bet. Eighth and Ninth Aves.). 212-315-9434, minttheater.org.* Ⓐ Ⓔ Ⓝ Ⓡ Ⓢ Ⓦ ❶ ❷ ❸ ❼ *to 42nd St.–Port Authority.*

Playwrights Horizons *Theater*
Long the anchor of Theater Row, this theater company has been premiering i[n]novative and new American plays for the past 25 years. The work of Christoph[er] Durang and Wendy Wasserstein was first presented here, as was Stephen Sor[d]heim and James Lapine's Pulitzer Prize-winning musical *Sunday In The Park W[ith] George.* The upstairs Studio Theater presents work by up-and-coming write[rs.] *416 W. 42nd St. (bet. Ninth and Tenth Aves.), 212-279- 4200, playwrightshorizons.c[om]* Ⓐ Ⓒ Ⓔ Ⓝ Ⓡ Ⓢ Ⓦ ❶ ❷ ❸ ❼ *to 42nd St.–Times Square.*

Signature Theatre Company *Theater*
Under the leadership of visionary artistic director James Houghton, the Signat[ure] has carved out a unique mission: highlighting the work of one major playwri[ght] each season. Past seasons have included retrospectives and world premieres fr[om] Arthur Miller, John Guare, Adrienne Kennedy, and Sam Shepard. *555 W. 42n[d] (bet. Tenth and Eleventh Aves.), 212-244-7529, signaturetheatre.org.* Ⓐ Ⓒ Ⓔ Ⓝ Ⓢ Ⓦ ❶ ❷ ❸ ❼ *to 42nd St.–Times Sq.*

St. Clement's Church *Theater*
A working theater for 35 years, this charming little church has hosted some of [the] best off-Broadway theater in the city. Episcopal services are still held here Sund[ay] and Wednesday nights. Conveniently located on Restaurant Row and around [the] corner from the greatest concentration of ethnic restaurants in the city. *42[3] 46th St. (bet. Ninth and Tenth Aves.), 212-246-7277, stclementsnyc.org.* Ⓐ Ⓒ Ⓔ Ⓡ Ⓢ Ⓦ ❶ ❷ ❸ ❼ *to 42nd St.–Times Square.*

Alvin Ailey American Dance Theater *Dance*
"The dance came from the people. It should be given back to the people," [the] theater's namesake once said. Alvin Ailey developed his famous repertoire h[ere,] often set to music by jazz greats such as Duke Ellington and Wynton Mar[salis.] *405 W. 55th St. (bet. Ninth and Tenth Ave.). 212-405-9000, alvinailey.org.* Ⓐ Ⓑ Ⓒ ❶ *to 59th St.–Columbus Circle.*

SHOPPING

Colony Music *Music*
Convenience doesn't come cheap. This midtown staple stocks all sorts of [music,] CDs (especially showtunes and karaoke), rock memorabilia, and sheet m[usic]

You'll find things here that you won't easily find anywhere else, but most items are marked up in standard Times Square fashion. Still, you can't beat the selection or easy location. *1619 Broadway (at 49th St.), 212-265-2050, colonymusic.com, Open daily 9:30 am–midnight.* ❶ *to 50th St.*

H&M *Clothing : National Chain*

Crowded to the point of suffocation, Euro-import H & M draws hordes of fashion-hungry New Yorkers to its Manhattan outlets with its chic clothing at ludicrously cheap prices. Of course, no one ever accused H & M of making their clothes well. But if you want to look like a million bucks and only pay wholesale, follow the Scandinavian lead. *34th St., Herald Sq. (at Sixth Ave.), (646) 473-1164, hm.com, Hours: M-Sa 10am-9pm, Su 11am-8pm.* ❸ ❹ ❺ ❻ ❼ ❽ ❾ *to 34th St.*

Joseph Patelson Music House *Music*

This mecca for music lovers, near Carnegie Hall, boasts over 47,000 pieces of sheet music for the piano and organ, strings, woodwind, and brass, as well as chambers and ensembles. *160 W. 56th St. (bet. 6th and 7th Aves.), 212-582-5840, patelson.com. Hours: M-Sa 9 am-6 pm.* ❻ ❼ ❽ ❾ ❿ *to 57th St.*

Macy's *Department Stores*

The inside of "The Largest Store in the World" often resembles the chaos of the Thanksgiving Day parade that the New York institution sponsors, especially around Christmas time and after work hours. Most items are priced lower than in other department stores, but the service and bathrooms reflect this reduction. *34th St. (at Broadway), 212- 695-4400, macys.com, Hours: M-Sa 10am-8:30pm, Su 11am-7pm.* ❸ ❹ ❺ ❻ ❼ ❽ ❾ *to 34th St.–Herald Sq.*

Manhattan Mall *Malls*

Its dominating presence, highlighted in glass and neon, incites feelings of either veneration or loathing. Elevator rides through this skyscraper of a mall are fun, though the vertical design doesn't allow for much room to stroll. It may not be chic or elegant, but if you're in need of some familiar chain stores and a food court, this is the place for you. *33rd St. and Sixth Ave.* ❸ ❹ ❺ ❻ ❼ ❽ *to 34th St.–Herald Sq.*

Midtown Comics *Books*

This store is a dream-come-true for comic fanatics. From mainstream to alternative, the store offers an extensive selection of back issues to browse through, as well as a helpful staff. *200 W. 40th St., 212-302-8192, midtowncomics.com. Hours: M-Sa 11 am-9 pm, Su 12 pm-7 pm.* ❶ ❷ ❸ ❹ ❺ ❻ ❼ ❽ ❾ ❿ *to Times Sq.*

Mysterious Bookshop *Books*

Serving the city's voracious whodunit lovers, this store stocks out-of-print books as well as a healthy selection of interesting British imports. *129 W. 56th St. (at Sixth Ave.), 212-765-0900. Hours: M-Sa 11 am-7 pm.* ❶ ❷ ❸ *to 57th St.-Seventh Ave.,* ❹ *to 57th St.*

Sam Ash *Music*

Ever want to DJ? Sprawling along 48th St., these four music shops fulfill almo every music-making need, selling everything from acoustic instruments, to cording equipment, to MIDI systems, computers and software, DJ equipm lighting, sheet music, and more. The staff knows its stuff, and all locations (exc for #163) rent and repair instruments and equipment. *155, 160, 159, and W. 48th St. (bet. Sixth and Seventh Aves.), 212- 719-2299, Hours: M-F 10am-8 Sa 10am-7pm, Su 12pm-6pm.* **Ⓝ Ⓡ Ⓦ** *to 49th St.,* **Ⓑ Ⓓ Ⓕ Ⓥ** *to 47-50th Rockefeller Center,* **❶** *to 50th St.*

Virgin Megastore *Music*

Redefining the idea of the megastore, this flashy three-level entertainment co plex boasts movie theaters, over one thousand listening booths, and a wide lection of videos, laser discs, and CD-ROMs. *1540 Broadway (bet. 45th and 4 Sts.), 212- 921-1020.* **Ⓐ Ⓒ Ⓔ Ⓝ Ⓡ Ⓢ ❶ ❷ ❸ ❼** *to 42nd St.–Times Additional location in Manhattan at 52 E.14th St.*

Whole Foods *Groceries*

For gourmet foodies and plebian squares alike, this big market is somewh between a Dean & Deluca and a Fairway, intersecting at the notion of high qu and freshness. All this comes at a price, but the gleaming stocks of natural and ganic produce, flavorful cheeses, and other delicacies offered by equitably-trea employees mean sustainability and community awareness never tasted so go *10 Columbus Circle (basement of Time-Warner Building), 212- 823-9600.* **Ⓐ Ⓑ Ⓓ ❶** *to 59th St.-Columbus Circle.*

CLASSES AND WORKSHOPS

The Acting Studio, Inc.

Deep in the theatre district, the Acting Studio has trained aspiring thespians over 21 years. Offering intensive short- and long-term acting classes specializir a number of different techniques, the Studio also gives courses on a range of t ics, from directing, to monologue workshops, and even one Shakespearean se nar. Tuition ranges from $300-1,500, or $50/hr for a private coach. *244 W. 54 12th Fl. (bet. Broadway & 8th Ave.), 212-580-6600, actingstudio.com.* **❶** *to 50t*

Aikido of Manhattan

In the heart of Manhattan, this dojo offers classes for students of all experie levels in the technique and philosophy of the art of "moving Zen." On Thurs nights, students take up arms in a weapons class, and three times a week pu meet in Central Park. The center also hosts seminars given by esteemed teach from around the world. *60 W. 39th St., Third Floor (on 6th Ave.), 212-575-0 aikidoofmanhattan.com. Hours: M-F 12:15-1 pm, 5:30-7:45 pm, Sa 10-11:30 am* **Ⓒ Ⓔ Ⓝ Ⓞ Ⓡ Ⓢ Ⓦ ❷ ❸ ❼** *to Times Square-42nd St.*

Gotham Writer's Workshop

Workshops in fiction writing, poetry, screenwriting, and a number of other genres are offered at seven locations throughout Manhattan. They even have online classes for your convenience. Classes meet once a week for three hours and cost about $400 for a ten-week semester. The teachers are widely published writers. *1841 Broadway, Suite 809 (bet. 60th and 61st Sts.), 212-974-8377, writingclasses. com. Hours: M-F 9 am-5 pm* **A B C D 1** *to 59th St.-Columbus Circle.*

The Yoga Project in Bryant Park

This popular annual summer yoga series offers free classes, lectures, mats and the joy of practicing outdoors from the beginning of June through the end of August. *Bryant Park (at 40th St. and Sixth Ave.), bryantpark.org.* **B D F V** *to 42nd St-Bryant Park,* **7** *to 5th Ave.*

Midtown East

FEW NEIGHBORHOODS CAN RIVAL the stateliness and old m[ ]
ey clout of Midtown East. It's the place to come when you've g[ ]
hankering for diamonds or the latest Chanel suit. It's also where h[ ]
powered companies hold board meetings amidst the dizzying heig[ ]
of the wall-to-wall "glass box" skyscrapers, and where executives[ ]
lunch at some of the city's ritziest restaurants. Domestic and for[ ]
dignitaries kick back at Park Avenue's Waldorf-Astoria Hotel, stayin[ ]
suites that can go for well over a thousand dollars a night. A few bl[ ]
to the north stands the functional modernist Seagram Building, a m[ ]
el for mid-twentieth century architecture, while classic brownsto[ ]
and apartment buildings line the streets east of Lexington Avenue[ ]

The wealthy residential neighborhood of Turtle Bay boasts [ ]
fashioned town houses and a pleasant view of the East River fr[ ]
Beekman Place. Just to the south, the United Nations Headquar[ ]
sprawls along the shore. Further downtown, the neighborhood[ ]
Kips Bay and Murray Hill are home to a relatively quiet and patri[ ]
population of New Yorkers. Many residents have recently moved th[ ]
to raise children in the comfortable environs carved out between [ ]
heart of Midtown and the East River. Whether one feels exhilar[ ]
or daunted by Midtown East, the center of Manhattan's skyline [ ]
hard to turn one's eyes away from it.

ISTORY

>> IN 1639, THE DUTCH GOVERNOR of New Amsterdam granted a pair of Englishmen 40 acres of land, little suspecting that one day it would turn into some of the most valuable real estate in the world. By the Revolutionary War, the land had become known as Turtle Bay Farm, named after the cove, containing turtles, that lapped at its shores. Turtle Bay soon grew into a thriving wharf area, integral to the island's trading economy.

The bay was bound to last longer than the farm. Throughout the next century the population of Manhattan boomed, and pastoral landscape went the way of the Native Americans who had once hunted in the woods. By the middle of the 19th century, the hills were graded and New York's grid as it's currently known—with its broad avenues and neatly criss-crossing streets—was born. Not long after the Civil War, Turtle Bay disappeared as slaughterhouses and breweries replaced the docks and boats; later, tenement buildings crowded out the post-war brownstones. With the construction of a pair of elevated trains that ran along Second and Third Avenues, the 40 acres that had been Turtle Bay Farm, now called Midtown East, joined the bustling world of a roaring metropolis.

During the 20th century the neighborhood changed again. The area's ideal location spurred a growth in real estate value, as shabby tenements were replaced with office high-rises and luxury condominiums. In 1946, the slaughterhouses were razed and the United Nations Headquarters was built in their place. Residents and office workers, as industrious as ever, were left with a slightly quieter Midtown East, if not quite the pastoral land that had once bordered the bay.

HAT TO SEE

Grand Central Station

Chances are, you'll pass through this station anyway, and when you do, you'll recognize it easily as it has been featured in countless movies. While you're there, take a minute to look closely at the mural of stars painted above the Main Concourse (the zodiac is painted backwards), restored in '98 to resemble the 1913 original; this façade would have disappeared had the Terminal failed to gain National Historic Landmark status in 1976. After you check out the fantastic food court, walk with a friend to the low arches in front of the Oyster Bar; stand in opposite corners, facing the wall, and whisper. Laws of acoustics (or magic) dictate you'll be able to hear each other with startling clarity. *E. 42nd St. and Park Ave., grandcentralterminal. com.* **S ④ ⑤ ⑥ ⑦** *to Grand Central Station.*

Dahesh Museum

Feel so sophisticatedly European when you visit Dahesh, the only museum in the United States dedicated to the collecting and exhibiting of 19th and 20th century European academic art. Admission is free on the first Thursday of every month from 6 to 9 pm, usually accompanied by fantastic gallery talks. *580 Madison Ave., 212-759-0606, daheshmuseum.org.* **Ⓔ Ⓥ** *to Fifth Ave.*

St. Patrick's Cathedral

If you're Catholic, this is a great place for Mass, but even if you're not, the archi
ture and art will astound. The edifice is the largest decorated gothic-style Cath
cathedral in the United States, and the pieta, the Stations of the Cross, and
rose window are only a few features that make a visit here a majestic experie
Fifth Avenue (bet. 50th and 51st Sts..), 212-753-2261, saintpatrickscathedral.or
❶ *to 5th Ave.*

United Nations Headquarters

Leave Manhattan for international territory without ever stepping off the is
You won't need your passport, but you will need to join a guided tour (war.
ing around alone is not allowed) of this famous international government b

Grand Central Station

ing where the 191 member states debate some of the most pressing issues of the day—and sometimes even hammer out agreements. *1 United Nations Plaza, un.org.* ❹ ❺ ❻ ❼ *to 42nd St–Grand Central.*

LAST QUIET SPOT IN MIDTOWN

An oasis replete with a 25-foot waterfall, **GREENACRE PARK** makes the most of its diminutive size with careful, calming landscaping smack in the middle of Manhattan. Leafy trees and café tables make it a soothing respite for restless residents, businesspeople, and visitors alike. *E. 51st St. (bet. 2nd and 3rd Aves.).* ❻ *to 51st St*

WHERE TO EAT

Asia de Cuba *Latin*

If only all New Yorkers were as good looking and stylishly-dressed as this crowd. You might have to wait upwards of an hour for a table at prime time even if you have a reservation, but the delicious food and sophisticated atmosphere make it worth the wait. Enjoy one of their excellent mixed drinks to help fan the burning hole in your wallet. *237 Madison Ave. (bet. 37th and 38th Sts.), 212-726-7755.* ❹ ❺ ❻ ❼ ❺ *to 42nd St.-Grand Central.* **$$$**

Café Centro *French*

Popular with the expense account set, this midtown Mediterranean spot boasts great service and the food is consistently good. With taste to spare, the café is an oasis in midtown. Lunch is jam-packed. *200 Park Ave. (at E. 45th St.), 212-818-1222.* ❺ ❹ ❺ ❻ ❼ *to 42nd St.-Grand Central Terminal.* **$$$**

English is Italian *Italian*

For $39 a person, diners share multiple courses with the rest of their parties. You will certainly not leave hungry. Portions are large and the food is delicious. With its modern décor, the ambiance is brilliant as well. Only in New York will you find a restaurant with this kind of character, experienced chefs, and great service at a reasonable price. Be sure to order a glass of wine from the wine tower. *622 Third*

Ave. (at 40th St.), 212-404-1700. **S** **4** **5** **6** **7** *to 42nd St–Grand Central.* **$**

Felidia *Italian*

Felidia is one of the best, most authentic Northern Italian restaurants in New Y
Lidia Bastianich creates a welcoming ambiance by designing the restauran
resemble a two-tiered Etruscan villa. Don't even bother trying to decide betw
dishes; every item on the menu is distinctive and utterly magnificent. In addi
the menu remains constantly in flux to capture the signature delights of e
particular season. In truth, you have only one option: surrender your appetite
autonomy to the brilliant chef Fortunato Nicotra, who will devise a blissful tas
menu sure to suit your fancy. *243 E. 58th St. (bet. Second and Third Aves.), 212-7
1479.* **4** **5** **6** **N** **R** **W** *to 51st St.-Lexington Ave.* **$$$**

The Four Seasons *American*

If you want to spot Henry Kissinger, Ranan Lurie, or other old school New Y
powerbrokers, the Pool Room is the place. Call it stuffy, call it pretentious,
the Four Seasons is still the place to beat for wheeling and dealing. The foo
fabulous, the wine list spectacular, and the service stellar. They know what
are doing, so know your wines before you go. *Seagram Building, 99 E. 52n
(bet. Lexington and Park Aves.), 212-754-1077.* **6** *to 51st St.* **E** **V** *to Lexin
Ave.-53rd St.* **$$$**

Franchia *Korean*

These people take tea seriously. A tin of their finest first-picked green tea c
$100, while a pot goes for $10. Franchia's terraced pagoda-style interior tr
ports diners to the Korean countryside, blocking the big city bustle on the o
side of the wall. But make sure to sit on the top level where the tea ma
performs ceremonies for the calmest calm. Franchia's dumplings, including gr
tea flavored ones, rival those of New York's finest Chinese restaurants, and
tofu-almond ice cream is truly spectacular. The $25 tea tray sampler is the pe
way to soak up the Zen tranquility and sample Franchia's vegetarian masterpie
12 Park Ave. (bet. 34th and 35th Sts.), 212-213-1001. **6** *to 33rd St.* **$$$**

Hale & Hearty Soups *American*

H&H offers dozens of homemade soups along with salads and other healthy
A favorite with men and women in suits unafraid of spilling their lunch, H&
especially popular in the winter when a warm meal is just the ticket. The p
and lunchtime crush, however, may make some think twice about venturin
side. *849 Lexington Ave. (at 64th and 65th St.) 212-517-7600.* **F** *to Lexington
Additional locations in Manhattan* **$**

Hangawi *Korean*

About half a dozen patrons at a time take off their shoes and settle onto c
ions before wooden tables at this cozy, traditional Korean find. (Don't worry
tables have openings below for those who prefer not to sit the Korean way).
flickering candles, zen music, and antique Korean pottery transport diners

more peaceful time while they nibble tiny treats. Hangawi takes as much care with the food as it does with the ambiance: nuts and berries float in hot tea, pumpkin and cinnamon fill hollowed apples, and patrons fold vegetable slivers into tiny carrot and spinach pancakes. Thanks to the waiters' explanations of the dishes, this restaurant makes foods like mountain root and lotus appealing even to the most devout carnivores. *12 E. 32nd St. (bet. 5th and Madison Aves.), 212-213-0077, hangawirestaurant.com.* **B D F N Q R V W** *to 34th St-Herald Sq.,* **1** *to 34th St.* **$$**

Inagiku *Japanese*

Inagiku combines traditional Japanese cuisine with the stylish interior decoration of Adam Tihany. The waitresses are dressed in classical Japanese kimonos and are very eager to explain all of the delicious dishes created by Chef Haruo Ohbu. You can choose an entrée or combine "classic little dishes" to sample various Japanese specialties. The shrimp and lobster tempura are a must, as is the eel hagata, which is imported from Japan. The restaurant is also known for its wide selection of sakes and a unique array of bar beverages. Make sure to leave room for the many creative desserts such as the Ogura milk crepe. Inagiku also has a Shabu Shabu station and private tatami rooms that seat 4-18 people. *Waldorf-Astoria 111 E. 49th St. (bet. Park and Lexington Aves.). 212-355-0440.* **B D F V** *to 47-50 Sts.-Rockefeller Center,* **E V** *to 53rd St.,* **6** *to 51st St.* **$$**

L'Absinthe *French*

How many restaurants truly make someone feel like they're in a Paris brasserie? L'Absinthe's main appeal—besides the delicious, decidedly French cuisine – is the fact that anyone who dines at this east 60s restaurant feels as if they're in a different country and culture. Both the manager and chef are authentic Frenchmen, and it shows in L'Absinthe's decor and ambience. *227 E. 67th St, (bet. 2nd and 3rd Aves.)., 212-794-4950.* **6** *to 68th St.-Hunter College* **$$$**

Maya *Mexican*

No burritos here. Though the flavors are undeniably Mexican, the cuisine here is far removed from the usual south-of-the-border fare. Along with great guacamole and fiery salsa, the stars of the menu are dishes like the pork tenderloin with roasted corn and pumpkinseed sauce and the chicken breast with cheese dumplings and cilantro pesto. The décor is reminiscent of an Acapulco convention center, but the super-smooth service and uniformly great food justify the high-class price tag. Don't miss the desserts, some of which include chocolate so rich it's almost spicy. *1191 First Ave., at 64th St. 212-585-1818,* **S 4 5 6 7** *to 59th St.-Lexington Ave.* **$$**

Michael Jordan's Steakhouse *Steakhouse*

Amid the hustle-and-bustle of Grand Central Terminal lies the dining legacy of a sports legend. Much like MJ's athletic performances, the atmosphere here is energetic and celebratory. The steak is superb and succulent, so be careful not to fill up on their addictive garlic bread with gorgonzola fondue, or the more-than-complementary sides. After one taste of the 12-layer chocolate cake you'll be happy you were scrupulous with the preceding dishes. *Grand Central Terminal the West balcony), 23 Vanderbilt Ave. (bet. 43rd and 44th Sts.), 212-655-2300.* **S** **5** **6** **7** *to 42nd St.-Grand Central.* **$$$**

Monkey Bar Steakhouse *Steakhouse*

Don't let the long walk through a crowded lounge fool you; the Monkey Bar fers much more than cocktails. Eating in the luxurious dining room with atten service is a pleasure. You'll appreciate the small touches, like the freshly roas garlic with your steak. And don't skip their delicious desserts—they add the fect exclamation to a fantastic feast. *60 E. 54th St. (bet. Madison and Park A 212-838-2600.* **6** *to 51st St.,* **E** **V** *to Lexington Ave.-53rd St.,* **N** **R** **W** **4** **5** *to Fifth Ave.-59th St.* **$$$**

Pampano *Mexican*

Relax in the airy, whitewashed dining room or on the beautiful outdoor terr The tangy seafood dishes, lively salsa music, and enormous variety of margar make it that much easier to pretend you're looking out over the ocean instea a skyscraper on Third Ave. *209 E. 49th St. (bet. Second and Third Aves), 212-7 4545.* **E** **V** *to 53rd St.,* **6** *to 51st St.* **$$**

SWANKIEST SEAFOOD

Those who like to down their oysters amidst ambiance that glows of riches a string of pearls should head to **THE GRAND CENTRAL OYSTER BAR**, wh patrons dine on shellfish and crustaceans beneath impressive vaulted ceili Oyster aficionados can choose from over a dozen varieties. For those who w to soak up the atmosphere without draining their wallets, five dollars buys a b of Manhattan clam chowder—and a seat in the room. *Grand Central Station., 2 490-6650, oysterbarny.com.* **S** **4** **5** **6** **7** *to 42nd St.–Grand Central..* **$$$**

Park Bistro *French*

Recently purchased by its chef of 11 years, Park Bistro carries on with the sa old-school design and French cuisine that made it famous. The design may m young ones feel old, but the service more than makes up for it. This family of s waits on you hand and foot, and makes sure Park Bistro feels like home. W the wild mushroom ravioli has been a specialty of the house here for more th decade, everything on the menu is worth a try. *414 Park Ave South (bet. 28th 29th Sts.), 212-689-1360.* **6** *to 28th St.* **$$**

Prime Grill *Steakhouse*

This is the only steak house in the city where Kosher diners can experie the same business-class steak that dominates the diets of many major New Y power brokers. This centrally located Jewish hot-spot offers a superior select of steaks and kosher red wines that satisfy the observant and non-affiliated a But wine connoisseurs beware: even that $100 Merlot will fall short of y standards because of glatt Kosher preparation. For those who abstain from e non-treif steak, there is an impressive collection of sushi to fill the void. Some the best kosher food you can get (outside of your bubby's kitchen, of course)

E. 49th St, (bet.. Madison and Park Aves.). 212-692-9292, theprimegrill.com. ❸ *to Fifth Ave.,* ❹ ❻ *to 51 St.* **$$$**

Shaburi *Japanese*

If you've ever tasted Kobe beef, you probably think that's as good as meat gets. Think again. At this Japanese-Taiwanese sensation, Kobe beef ranks a distant second to the luscious Matsuzaka. A classic shabu-shabu dish, the Matsuzaka is served raw in very fine slices. Here, all the tables are fully equipped with electric stovetops, and each diner cooks the meat to his liking within seconds. When the Matsuzaka turns a juicy red, it is ready to melt in your mouth. While the shabu-shabu is Shaburi's sexiest dish, the sukiyaki and sushi selections are marvelous in their own right. With only the highest quality of ingredients, this meal is sure to delight. *125 E. 39th St. (bet. Lexington and Park Ave.), 212-867-6999.* ❹ ❺ ❻ ❼ ❺ *to 42nd St.-Grand Central.* **$$$**

Silverleaf Tavern *American*

This pleasant and peaceful eatery channels old-school New York style, while incorporating some bold modern dishes. Silverleaf delivers on old favorites, such as shellfish pan roast, East Coast Halibut, and Long Island Duck. But it also wows with some daring appetizers: the Westfield Chevre French Toast is innovative and exciting. The main attraction is the "bottomless" six-ounce glass of wine, which allows diners to sample seven varieties of the sommelier's handpicked collection. Though the food stands on its own, the wine elevates the experience to a completely different level. *43 E. 38th St. (at Park Ave. South), 212-973-2550.* ❹ ❺ ❻ ❼ ❺ *to 42nd St.-Grand Central.* **$$**

Smorgas Chef *International*

If you like being served succulent Swedish meatballs by a tall Scandinavian waitress, Smorgas Chef is the spot for you. Three of their drinks were finalists in the Sidewalk Café Cocktail Competition, and their innovative mixes of fresh fruit and spices are worth the honors. The recycled blue bottles on the walls and vivid nature photographs (not to mention the live tree growing inside) create a quirky-cool ambiance. Smorgas Chef's Scandinavian fare is fresh, hearty and balanced, particularly its fish. But it's the drinks that are truly spectacular. *924 Second Ave. (at 49th St.), 212-486-1411, smorgaschef.com.* ❸ ❷ *to Lexington Ave.-53rd St.,* ❻ *to 51st St.* **$$**

Taksim *Turkish*

Taksim is undoubtedly one of the best Turkish restaurants in New York City. The laid-back atmosphere and cheaper prices make diners feel completely comfortable and at home (if they live in Istanbul). Because the starters are so cheap, be sure to try a few, especially the falafel and hummus. For entrées, the lamb is a great choice. No visit to Taksim is complete without an order of baklava or kadayif. *1030 Second Ave. (bet. 54th and 55th Sts.), 212-421-3004.* ❸ ❷ ❻ *to 51st St.* **$**

Tao *Asian Fusion*

Tao is the trendy new-age restaurant. If *Entourage*'s Vincent Chase were to re
to his hometown, you can bet that Ari would reserve the "sky-box" private di
room, where VIPs dine hovering above us mere mortals. The decor is a ma
in its own right. After entering through an opulent golden entryway, diners
through an ethereal enclave of cool dominated by a backlit three-story go
Buddha and house music. Be sure to make a reservation far in advance and
there on time: the crowded bar and lack of waiting space can make stan
around for your table in front of the gorgeous crowd humiliating. *42 E. 58t*
(bet. Madison & Park Aves.), 212-888-2288, taorestaurant.com. **N R W 4 5**
to 59th St. **$$**

NIGHTLIFE

Believe *Lounge*

A lounge in every sense of the word, Believe is a warm and inviting space that
udes boudoir chic. Owner Chynna Soul is responsible for the imaginative, po
cocktails and the funky-yet-lush furniture and art. Bring a pack of friends and e
some drinks—the music is smooth and low enough to facilitate conversa
There's no threat of skeezy, cheesy pick-up artists, so feel free to make it a
outing. Believe radiates positive energy, and clever touches, like mini-flashli
that allow you to read the drink menu without using a candle or cell phone, m
this place a must-visit. *1 East 36th (bet. 5th and Madison Aves.), 212-481-4*
believelounge.com. **B D F V N O R W** *to 34th Street-Herald Square.*

Campbell Apartments *Bar*

With lush oriental carpeting, comfy lounge chairs, and a lovely ceiling, Camp
Apartments is more than just a cozy spot for Wall Streeters to throw back a
before hitting the Metro North. Rememer to bring a credit card though, bec
drinks are pricey. *Grand Central Terminal, 15 Vanderbilt Ave. (bet. 42nd and 43rd*
212-953-0409. **S 4 5 6 7** *to 42nd St.-Grand Central.*

Chill Lounge *Lounge*

Down to earth and entertainingly self-aware, Chill Lounge belies its cheesy n
and location. The crowd reflects those working in this area, so the occasi
older male group sits beside the carefree twentysomethings. Serves great n
foods; but the real draw is happy hour, as Midtowners crowd the place from
until well into the night. Sentinels of white and red sangria flank the entrance,
the bar's delicious secret recipe won't disappoint. A live DJ starts at six, so
fun, shake off that workday tension and boogie, salsa, or toss down. *329 Lexin,*
Ave. (bet 38th and 39th Sts.), 212-682-8288, chilloungenyc.com. **4 5 6 7**
to 42nd St.-Grand Central.

Monkey Bar *Bar*

It's hip beyond trendy, and we love the bar Monkey Bar for its chic and classic s
This art deco masterpiece attracts a glamorous older crowd sipping cock

and flaunting Chanel. The bar is named after a '40s actress who once lived at the hotel and always brought her monkey down with her to the bar—the epitome of swank. *60 E. 54th St. (in the Hotel Elysée bet. Madison and Park Aves.), 212-838-2600. ❸ ❤ to Lexington Ave.-53rd St. ❻ to 51st St.*

Parnell's Pub *Pub*

Outfitted with a dark wood bar and plenty of Irish pride, this restaurant-bar serves traditional dishes along with the famous Guinness. *350 E. 53rd St. (at st Ave.), 212- 355-9706. ❸ ❤ to Lexington Ave.-53rd St. ❻ to 51st St.*

Pig 'n Whistle *Pub*

This classic Irish pub features friendly bartenders who are happy to mix with the amiable and unpretentious clientele. Their fine selection of whiskey and beer is an instant stand-out. A guaranteed good time, this is an excellent place to grab a drink after eating at any of Midtown's delicious steakhouses or other restaurants. *922 3rd Ave (bet. 55th and 56th), 212- 688-4646. ❸ ❤ ❻ to 51st.-Lexington Ave.*

Sutton Place Restaurant and Bar *Music / Dance*

This vibrant venue boasts two spacious levels as well as a large rooftop bar. DJs spin current hits, and the ample space accommodates even the most boisterous dancers. Projection screens cover the walls, providing diverse coverage of sporting events. The typical crowd is of the after work variety, but Saturday nights invite twentysomethings looking for a party. *1015 Second Ave. (bet. 53rd and 54th Sts.), 212-207-3777, suttonplacenyc.com. ❸ ❺ to Lexington Ave. ❻ to 51st St.*

RTS

Japan Society *Museums*

As a booming cultural resource, the institute is worth a visit for the gallery alone; it is one of the foremost in America for the exhibition and research of Japanese art. In addition to visual art, the Society also screens Japanese and Japanese-American films and hosts cultural events and lectures by prominent artists, writers, and leaders. The Society also serves as an educational institute, offering Japanese classes at 12 different levels. *333 East 47th St., 212-832-1155, japansociety. org. Hours: M-F 9:30am-5:30pm. ❻ to 51st St. or 42nd St.-Grand Central. ❸ ❤ to Lexington Ave.-53rd St.*

THE MORGAN LIBRARY AND MUSEUM is renowned for its collection of original manuscripts, drawings, and scores by the likes of Dickens, Twain, Rembrandt, and Beethoven. Now a center for research and education, the Italian Renaissance-style palazzo remains a striking monument to the old money of Midtown East. Check out the elegant, albeit pricey, café; they offer a nice selection of wines, and the food portions are small but decadent. *225 Madison Ave. (at 36th St.), 212-685-0008, morganlibrary.org. Hours: T-R 10:30am-5pm, F 10:30am-9pm, Sa 10am-6pm, Su 11am-6pm. ❻ to 33rd St.*

EST GILDED-AGE
HOARD

The Morgan Library

St. Patrick's Cathedral

Mary Boone Gallery *Galleries*

This longtime SoHo staple recently headed for greener pastures up north, a now carries an elegant address on Fifth Avenue. Many artists came along for ride, such as Ross Bleckner (best known for his shows at the Guggenheim). 7 *Fifth Ave., Fourth Floor (at 57th St.). 212-752-2929; marybooñegallery.com. Ho T-Sa 10am-6pm.* Ⓝ Ⓡ Ⓦ *to Fifth Ave.-59th St.*

Urban Center Gallery *Galleries*

A subsidiary of the Municipal Art Society (a nonprofit group involved with urt planning and public art), this is a space that celebrates beautiful spaces. Exhib change at eight-week intervals and canvass topics that include city planning a design, preservation and development, and architectural excellence. Buildings veal their personalities on wide gallery walls the way the pages of a novel expe a character. Be sure to browse the bookstore's 9,000 holdings on your way o 457 Madison Ave. (at E. 51st St.), 212-935-3960, Admission free. 6 to 51st St., E V *Fifth Ave.-53rd St. (at Madison Ave.).* Ⓑ Ⓓ Ⓕ *to Rockefeller Center.*

Sony Wonder Technology Lab *Museums*

Visit this virtual wonderland to play with cutting edge communications techr ogy. Take a trip down the esophagus or skip to the bottom floor, where latest PlayStation games are calling your name—literally. When you log in, y get a card encoded with your picture and voiceprint. What's more, admission free soyou'll leave with a full wallet, unless you succumb to Sony's many obvic marketing ploys. Go during off-hours when the kids (and noise level) are a minimum—after all, you want to hear the music in your brand new MP3 pla *550 Madison Ave. (56th St. bet. Madison and Fifth Aves.), 212-833-8100, sonyw dertechlab.com. Hours: T-Sa 10 am-5 pm, Su 12 pm-5 pm Admission free.* Ⓐ Ⓢ *to 59th St.-Lexington Ave.,* Ⓔ Ⓥ *to Fifth Ave.-53rd St.,* Ⓝ Ⓡ *to Fifth Ave.-60th*

St. Patrick's Cathedral *Music*

St. Pat's serves as the seat of New York's archbishop and is the focal point American Catholicism. The Gothic-style cathedral's white marble sustains a sti ing balance between the grand majesty of its spires and the quiet simplicity the side chapels. Plan your visit carefully, though, because the Cathedral, locat squarely amid the flash floods of midtown tourists, can be a zoo during Chr mastime—but that's no surprise, given the camels and sheep in the traditio crèche display. *460 Madison Ave. (bet. 50th and 51st Sts., across from Rockefe Center), 212-753- 2261, saintpatrickscathedral.org. Hours: M-Su 6:30 am-8:45* Ⓔ Ⓕ *to Fifth Ave.*

SHOPPING

Apple Store *Miscellaneous*

On Fifth Avenue, a luminescent Apple logo hovers within a 32-foot-high gl cube, hinting at the expansive store hidden below. Inside the glass enclosure, v tors will find a retail environment filled with familiar and beloved products, fre the new Macbook to the iPod Nano. Gray stone floors gently diffuse the light coming from the windows above, while an interior of pale wood and brushed aluminum focuses all attention on the sleek products on display. Be forewarned: you'll have to be ready to squeeze your way through the crowd the store is often packed despite the long hours. *767 Fifth Avenue, 212-336-1440, Hours: Open 24 hours.* ❶ ❷ ❸ *to 5th Ave-59 St.*

Bauman Rare Books *Books*

Boasting a vast selection of first editions from the 15th through the 20th centuries, this store is the perfect resource for serious collectors. If you like rare books, it's a worth a visit, but be prepared to shell out big money for immaculate first editions, like Adam Smith's *The Wealth of Nations. 535 Madison Avenue (bet. 54th and 55th Sts.), 212-751-0011, baumanrarebooks.com. Hours: M-Sa 10 am-6 pm 6 to 51st St. Smaller location at the Waldorf-Astoria Hotel, 301 Park Ave. (bet. 49th and 50th Sts.), 212-759-8300.* ❻ *to 51st St.*

Chanel *Clothing : Designer*

Coco would be proud. Complete with uniformed doormen, this sparkling shrine devoted to simple elegance with flair sells clothing, jewelry, shoes, accessories, and perfume. Ladies who lunch can rely on Chanel for the best tweed suits while younger shoppers have recently taken interest in the brand's classic quilted bags and cartoonish jewelry line. *3 W. 57th St. (bet. Fifth and Madison Aves.), 212- 355- 5050, chanel.com.* ❶ ❷ ❸ ❹ *to Fifth Ave.,* ❺ *to Fifth Ave.-59th St.*

Coliseum Books *Books*

This indie bookstore offers a wide selection, with a helpful, and knowledgeable staff. A summer lunchtime reading series at the Bryant Park Reading Room features many well-known authors Wednesday afternoons. *11 W. 42nd St. (bet. 5th and 6th Aves.), 212-803-5890, coliseumbooks.com. Hours: M-F 8 am-8:30 pm, Sa 11 am-8:30 pm, Su Noon-7 pm* ❶ ❷ ❸ ❹ *to 42nd St.*

Emporio Armani *Clothing : Designer*

The store's flawlessly-cut casual suits are a bit more accessible price-wise than Armani's main line. The renovated Stanford White building lends the store a super-chic look. *601 Madison Ave. (at 57th St.), 212-317-0800, emporioarmani.com. Hours: M-Sa 11am-8pm, Su 12pm-6pm.* ❹ ❺ ❻ *to 59th St.,* ❶ ❷ ❸ W *to Fifth Ave.*

At the **NEW WORLD AQUARIUM,** you can see what is perhaps the city's finest collection of exotic fish. But if you also happen to be looking for that rare species of catfish, or maybe an African Cichlid, to liven up your apartment then you've come to the right place: *New York* magazine has voted this Pisces-lover paradise the "Best Aquarium Store" year after year. *204 E. 38th St. (bet. 2nd and 3rd Aves.), 646-865-9604, newworldaquarium.com. Hours: M-F 11am-9pm, Sa-Su 11am-8pm.* ❻ *to 33rd St.*

Gotham Book Mart *Books*

A sign proclaiming "Wise Men Fish Here" greets you upon entering this bib
phile's haven. Founded in 1920 by a woman named Francis Steloff, the Goth
Book Mart was (and still is) notorious for defending the *First Amendment* rig
of authors. Steloff championed James Joyce's *Ulysses* and was also a noted fan
D.H. Lawrence and Henry Miller. *16 E. 46th St. (bet. 5th and Madison Aves.), 2*
719-4448, gothambookmart.com. Hours: M-F 9:30 am-6:30 pm, Sa 9:30 am-6
B **D** **F** **V** *to 47th-50th Sts.-Rockefeller Center.*

Kinokuniya Bookstore *Books*

Located directly across from the Rockefeller Skating Rink, Kinokuniya offers Ja
nese books, English translations, as well as a diverse selection of stationery a
gifts. *10 W. 49th St. (at Fifth Ave.), 212-765-7766, kinokuniya.com/newyork. Ho*
M-Su 10 am-7:30 pm. **B** **D** **F** **V** *to 47-50th Sts.-Rockefeller Center.*

Posman Books *Books*

The last remaining Posman store in the city is strategically located in Grand C
tral Terminal, making it a vital stop for those embarking on long journeys
of the city. It carries a wide selection of bestsellers and new releases, often
discounted prices. *9 Grand Central Terminal (at Vanderbilt Ave. and E. 42nd St.), 2*
983-1111, posmanbooks.com. Hours: M-F 8 am-9 pm, Sa 10 am-7 pm, Su 10 a
pm. **4** **5** **6** **7** **S** *to 42nd St.-Grand Central.*

Saks Fifth Avenue *Department Stores*

Browsing through this high-end store is sure to you leave you amazed and d
Although Saks targets the older shopper, the fifth floor houses an impressive
sortment of younger brands—Marc by Marc Jacobs, Joie, Catherine Malandr
Juicy and many others. Their men's collection is extensive, but more busin
minded than the youthful look found at Barney's. *11 Fifth Ave. (bet. 49th and 5*
Sts.), 212-753-4000, saksfifthavenue.com, Hours: M-W, F-Sa 10am-7pm, R 10
8pm, Su 12pm-6 pm. **B** **D** **F** **V** **6** *to 47th-50th Sts.-Rockefeller Center.*

Takashimaya *Department Stores*

An experience in itself, this Japanese import is synonymous with elegance a
ambiance. A kind of Barney's-from-the -East, there's no better place to find a r
gift or splurge item. The Asian tea and delicacies department is to die for, and
fresh flower department is a favorite of urbanites craving greenery. This midtc
oasis leaves shoppers with a lighter spirit, not to mention a lighter wallet. *693 F*
Avenue (at 54th St.), 212- 350-0100, Hours: M-Sa 10am-7pm, Su 12pm-5pm. **F**
57th St., **E** **V** *to Fifth Ave.-53rd St.*

CLASSES AND WORKSHOPS

New York Institute of Photography

NYIP is almost as old as the art form itself. Today, they embrace both traditic and modern photography. The Institute offers courses for the casual shutterbug and the aspiring professional alike, and classes work with both 35mm film and digital technology. Regardless of skill level or degree of interest, all who enroll are guaranteed to improve their photography skills. *211 E. 43rd St., Suite 2402 (bet. 2nd and 3rd Aves.), 212-867-8260, nyip.com. Call for schedule.* ❺ ❹ ❺ ❻ ❼ *to 42nd St.–Grand Central.*

❜ORTS AND LEISURE

Mang'Oh Yoga

This yoga and pilates center offers a wealth of varied classes, including cardio belly dance and tai-chi. $16 for a single class, $29 for one week of unlimited classes for first timers. Check website for additional specials. *322 E. 39th St. (bet. First and Second Aves.), 212-661-6655, mangohstudio.com.* ❹ ❺ ❻ ❼ *to 42nd St.-Grand Central.*

Yoga Sutra

First classes are free at this enormous, elegant midtown studio designed by renowned architect Deborah Gans. Yoga Sutra resembles an Indian temple, complete with relics and artwork from South India. Senior/Student discounts are available. *501 Fifth Ave., Second Floor (at 42nd St), 212-490-1443, yogasutranyc.com.* ❶ ❷ ❸ *to 42nd St-Times Sq.,* ❸ ❶ ❶ ❷ *to 42nd St.–Bryant Park.*

❜OTELS AND HOSTELS

Pickwick Arms Hotel

This is the best bet for savvy budget travelers who will appreciate the warm lobby and the safe neighborhood – as long as they don't mind no frills accommodations and forgettable rooms. The rooftop garden overlooking the city's skyscrapers makes this place a relaxing find at a great price. *230 East 51st Street (bet. Second and Third Aves.), 212-355-0300; pickwickarms.com. Rooms start at $60.* ❸ ❷ ❻ *to Lexington-51st St.*

UN Plaza-Millennium Hotel

Often overlooked by tourists, this pleasant Hyatt outpost is a sure bet in East Midtown. Located directly across from the United Nations and the East River, all of the rooms have incredible views. With an abundance of mirrors and marquee lights, the mood is a bit subdued. Don't be surprised if you find yourself rooming next-door to the Ambassador of Uzbekistan and his entourage as patrons are often guests of the United Nations. *1 UN Plaza 43rd St. (bet. First and Second Aves.), 212-758-1234; Rooms start at $225.* ❺ ❹ ❺ ❻ ❼ *to 42nd St.-Grand Central.*

Uptown

The Upper West Side • The Upper East Side
Morningside Heights • Harlem
Washington Heights

Upper West Side

THOUGH IT DOESN'T HAVE the moneyed prestige of its twin neig borhood across the island, the Upper West Side does have someth. the Upper East Side doesn't: accessibility. Three major subway lines through the area, making it a popular choice for tourists daunted cross-town buses and residents who like having easy access to the re of the city. The Westside vibe is distinctly laid-back, aided in part by t constant influx of aspiring artists and students from the numerous hi schools and universities nearby.

More than any New York neighborhood, the Upper West Side impossible to classify in a few simple words. Its residents include p formers who often grace the stage of the famed Lincoln Center, loc whose families go back several generations living in the same apa ments, and businesspeople who appreciate a quiet night at home aft a frantic day downtown. The Upper West Side also includes every et nic and religious background imaginable. This isn't to say that the ent area looks like a walking Benetton ad, but it's still a nice break from t homogeneity that occasionally plagues other neighborhoods.

The thriving arts scene (particularly surrounding Lincoln Cente the impressive run of bars and restaurants along Amsterdam and C lumbus Aves., and the proximity to some of the prettiest parts Central Park make the Upper West Side an obvious choice for venturous visitors or smart New Yorkers who want to benefit from small town feeling in this otherwise crowded metropolis.

HISTORY

>> THOUGH IT MAY BE DIFFICULT to imagine now, the Upper West Side was once viewed as a distant suburb of what is now downtown Manhattan. Before the completion of the Ninth Avenue elevated train in 1879, the area known as Bloomingdale was a largely undeveloped pastoral refuge from the crowded city. The Dakota, once the backdrop for *Rosemary's Baby* and the site of John Lennon's assassination, was christened so because residents felt it was such a distance from the city's hub that it might as well have been out in the Dakotas.

Before the development of Frederick Law Olmsted's visionary Central Park (from 1858 to 1873), this area was comprised of small and independently operated villages. The completion of the park spurred a wave of construction and by the turn of the century, cultural institutions such as the American Museum of Natural History became part of the neighborhood. The real boom came when the Inter-Borough Rapid Transit subway opened its first line in 1904 (the first of its kind in the country), which ran from Harlem to City Hall. A few years later, the Upper West Side finally was part of the city.

The area between Columbus and Amsterdam Avenues is still home to a lively Latino community. This part of the neighborhood underwent a cultural facelift of sorts in the 1960s when Lincoln Center was built. While people still debate the aesthetic merits of the Center—many argue that it's an ugly blot on the landscape—few deny its significant contribution to the arts.

WHAT TO SEE

Columbus Circle

Surrounding an 1892 statue of Christopher Columbus (hence, its name) is this busy center on W. 59th where midtown ends and the Upper West Side begins. If you tire of the car exhaust smell as you shop, duck into the comparatively quiet Time Warner Center, housing a variety of shops and elegant restaurants in a glamorous and well-maintained space. Check out the huge Whole Foods in the basement; there is almost always a long line at checkout, but it moves quickly and the delicious organic food is worth the wait. Towering nearby are the Trump International Hotel and Towers, which offers some of the best views of Central Park. *59th and Broadway.* ❶ ❷ ❸ ❹ ❶ *to 59th Street–Columbus Circle.*

DON'T JUST
IMAGINE IT

STRAWBERRY FIELDS is a sanctuary all its own within Central Park, and is also a tribute to John Lennon, who was fatally shot at the nearby Dakota apartment building in 1980. Steadfast fans place flowers daily around the sentimental IMAGINE mosaic to commemorate the great musician. ❶ ❷ ❸ ❸ ❸ *to 72nd St.*

Lincoln Center

Rockefeller once said, "The arts are not for the privileged few, but for the many." The Lincoln Center for the Performing Arts pays homage to his words: The 16-acre complex holds 12 different facilities, including The Metropolitan Opera, New York Opera, New York Philharmonic, the Juilliard School, and Jazz at Lincoln Center. Besides checking out the famous Revlon fountain that has been featured in

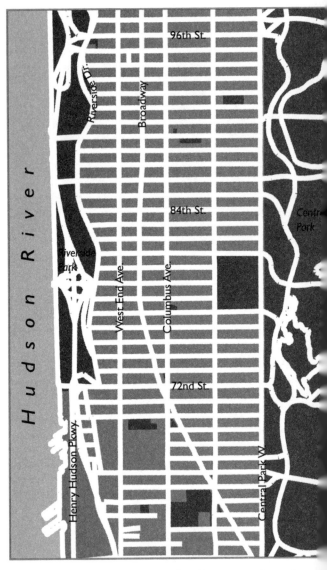

many a movie (think Cher in *Moonstruck*), make sure to catch a performa
Whether it's opera or jazz, orchestra or ballet that meets your fancy, it's all h
and students can often get discounted tickets. *62nd to 65th Sts. (between Colum
and Amsterdam Aves.), 212-875-5456, lincolncenter.org.* ❶ *to 66th–Lincoln Cen*

Belvedere Castle

It's pretty startling to stumble upon this Gothic / Romanesque / Moorish cast
you're strolling through Central Park. Built in 1872, Belvedere Castle is now

site of a U.S. Weather Bureau station, as well as the Henry Luce Nature Observatory with nature exhibits and workshops for children. As if being a castle wasn't cool enough. *Mid-park at 79th St., 212-772-0210. Hours: T-Su 10am–5 p.m, Closed Monday.* ❶ *to 79th St.*

SEE THE SEA (WITHOUT GETTING WET)

Sit under the massive blue whale hovering from the ceiling with a whale song in the background and watch colorful schools of fish flash across the larger-than-life video screen: you will truly feel as if you suddenly emerged underwater (and yet miraculously can still breathe) in this very special room in the Museum of Natural History. While the **HALL OF OCEAN LIFE** is not an aquarium with live fish or ocean-inhabiting animals, it's about as close as you can get. Don't miss the exhibit of the imitation squid attacking a whale (which you might recognize from the movie *The Squid and the Whale*). *79th St. and Central Park West, 212-313-7278, amnh.org. Hours: 10am-5:45pm.* ❻ *to 81st,* ❶ *to 79th*

American Museum of Natural History

This is the world's largest museum of natural history; you could spend eons visiting the 45 exhibition halls and observing over 32 million artifacts and specimens.

{Stop Right There!}

RIVERSIDE PARK

>> RIVERSIDE PARK STRETCHES FROM 72nd to 158th Street along the western edge of Manhattan, overlooking the Hudson and providing dazzling views for runners, bikers and dog-walkers alike. Another design by Frederick Law Olmstead (the mastermind behind Central Park), Riverside is a community-minded park complete with tennis, volleyball, and basketball courts. It also features a newly renovated complex at 110th Street, which includes a skate park and an artificial grass field for soccer and baseball. During spring and summer months, take a stroll through the lovely **91ST STREET GARDENS**. While perfectly safe during the day, exercise caution when walking through the park at night.

The **JOAN OF ARC** statue, the **SOLDIERS AND SAILOR MONUMENT,** and the **ELEANOR ROOSEVELT MEMORIAL** are all must-sees on any Riverside Park walking tour. Above all, make sure to check out Grant's Tomb at 122nd Street, an impressive, austere structure which stands in contrast to surrounding local folk art.

A beautiful rotunda and **BOAT BASIN** mark the park at 79th Street. During the summer months this area is abuzz with activity, both on land and in the water with a series of events, classes, and exhibits dot Riverside Park. Currently open but under development is **RIVERSIDE PARK SOUTH,** a 27.5-acre addition to the park ranging from 59th Street up to 72nd. Be sure to hit Pier 1, a 715-foot recreational peninsula built directly on top of an old shipping pier, which juts directly into the Hudson River.

Whether jogging along as the sun sets on the Hudson or watching boats pass at 79th, Riverside Park is well worth the exercise. *For more information, visit nycgovparks.org, 475 Riverside Dr. (between 72nd and 155th).* ❶ ❷ ❸ *to 72nd St.*

Learn about everything from human biology and evolution to geology and Afr
mammals. Make sure to walk on over to the attached Rose Center for E
and Space. *79th St. and Central Park West, 212-313-7278,amnh.org. Hours: 1C
5:45pm Admission: Adults $14, Children (2-12) $8, Students/Seniors $10.50.*
81st, ❶ *to 79th St.*

WHERE TO EAT

A *French / Caribbean*

French and Caribbean flavors intertwine in this tiny dining room. Bring a b
of your favorite red and put your faith—and your hunger—in the deft hand
the cooks. Expect to wait in the bar next door, where an ice-cold Red Stripe
make you dream of Spring Break. *947 Columbus Ave. (at 106th St.), 212-531-1
Cash Only.* ❸ ❸ *to 110th St.-Central Park North.* **$$**

Alouette *French*

An anomaly for the Upper West Side, this intimate bi-level French bistro se
up savory and inventive cuisine in a rich, warm atmosphere. The red velvet c
ery and lace-curtained windows create a romantic setting while the prices
great, considering the culinary and atmospheric decadence. *2588 Broadway
97th and 98th Sts.), 212-222-6808, alouettenyc.com.* ❶ ❷ ❸ *to 96th St.* **$$**

Ayurveda Café *Indian*

Upper Westsiders swear by this quaint Indian restaurant with a daily prix
menu. The food is vegetarian and based on the Hindu philosophies of Ayur
That boils down to simple, healthful, holistic food that satisfies without overstu
706 Amsterdam Ave. (bet 94th and 95th Sts.), 212-932-2400. ❶ ❷ ❸ *to 96th*

Bettola *Italian*

The décor is centered around the woodburning oven—clearly the focus o
restaurant. The ingredients are fresh and simple, the service is attentive, and
desserts are heavenly. From singles to seniors, this restaurant is popular
everyone in between. Check out Isola and Acqua, the owner's other prope
serving solid northern Italian fare. *412 Amsterdam (at 80th St.), 212-787-1*
❶ *to 79th St.* **$**

Bruculino Italian *Seafood*

Sicilian seafood cooked to perfection, served in the soothing wood and
interior of this West Side treasure. Dishes are inventive and colorful and out
seating is available on the terrace. Try the specials of the evening and leave r
for coffee and dessert. *225 Columbus Ave. (at 70th St.), 212-579-3966.* ❸
72nd St. **$$**

Café Des Artistes *French*

You'll feel glamorous at this classic New York restaurant. Don't get addicted tc

H&H Bagels

feeling though, because visiting this romantic rendezvous too often will clean out your wallet as seductively as it filled you up. *1 W. 67th St. (bet. Columbus Ave. and Central Park West.), 212-877-3500, cafényc.com.* **❶** *to 66th St.-Lincoln Center.* **$$$**

Café Mozart *German*

A slice of Europe on the Upper West Side, this café is perfect after a show or for late morning paper perusal. Watch for awkward Columbia students going on even more awkward first dates at this casual but just-romantic-enough café. It's far enough from campus to make your date think you have some class without shelling out for cab fare, plus, there's live music once a week. *154 W. 70th St. (at Broadway), 212-595-9797, cafémozart.com.* **❶ ❷ ❸** *to 72nd St.* **$$**

'Cesca *Italian*

An elegant setting and a relaxing atmosphere make 'Cesca an unique Italian eatery on the Upper West Side. The food is interesting and flashy and served by a helpful and attentive staff. Make sure to try the innovative and delicious pastas. *164 W. 75th St. (at Amsterdam Ave.), 212-787-6300, cescanyc.com.* **❶ ❷ ❸** *to 72nd St.* **$$$**

Crepes on Columbus *French*

Brick walls and ten small mahogany tables create an intimate atmosphere in an unlikely location. Aside from a wide selection of delectable dinner and desert crepes, the menu offers soups, salads, and sandwiches and a complete breakfast to fill any craving, all at a reasonable price. The somewhat slow service gives youample time to sit back and inhale the interesting smells seeping from the kitchen. *990 Columbus Ave. (bet. 108th and 109th Sts.), 212-222-0259, crepesoncolumbus.com.* **❶ Ⓑ Ⓒ** *to 110th St.-Cathedral Pkwy.* **$**

Gabriel's *American*

Among the *crème de la crème* of the bevy of restaurants around Lincoln Center, the combination of casual and class here is just about perfect. Beautiful decor, an astonishing seasonal menu (try the delectable butternut squash ravioli in the summer), and a refined yet informal staff all account for why this is one of New York's hottest spots for dinner. Come after 7:45pm to avoid the pre-concert crowd. *11 W. 60th St. (bet. Broadway and Columbus Ave.), 212-956-4600.* **Ⓐ Ⓑ Ⓒ Ⓓ ❶** *to 59th St.- Columbus Circle.* **$$$**

Gennaro *Italian*

Native Italian chef Gennaro Picone graced several upscale Manhattan eateries before opening his own place where he serves unpretentious, authentic Italian dishes in a tiny, unassuming space. The décor may seem a little rough around the edges, but the food is not—try the gnocchi. The prices are so reasonable that they impose a $20 minimum, but be warned: the waits are long and the space is cramped. *665 Amsterdam Ave. (bet. 92nd and 93rd Sts.), 212-665-5348.* **❶ ❷ ❸** *to 96th St.* **$$**

Gray's Papaya *American*

Gray's resembles its low-brow cousin Papaya King, offering lots of cheap
dogs, papaya juice and other heartburn-inducing fare. A hit with bankers sl
ming it during lunch hour, to penniless students, to out-of-work types, Gray's
New York institution. Don't expect Julia Child, but for $3 you too can fill up
mediocre dogs. *2090 Broadway (at 72nd St.) 212-799-0243. Cash only.*  ❶ ❷
to 72nd St. **$**

H&H Bagel *Delis*

H&H's are the iconic, stereotypical, world-famous New York Bagels. Some pe
swear by them, but others know that the NY bagel train has left H&H sta
The poppy and everything varieties go quickly, but the basic plain sourdou
something special, too. At H&H you must buy in bulk, fix your own bagel,
put up with pretentious, harried employees—but if that's your bag so be it.
1-800-NY-BAGEL to have mail orders delivered anywhere in the world. Qu
comes at a price. *2239 Broadway (at 80th St.), 212-595-8003, hhbagel.com. (
only.* ❶ *to 79th St.* **$**

Jacques-Imo's NYC *International*

Jacques-Imo's is a Cajun oasis on a street filled with overpriced Upper V
Side snob-factories. The food tends towards creative twists on Cajun classics
original dishes like shrimp, alligator cheesecake, and succulent carpet-bagger s
make Jacques-Imo's truly shine. It's also one of the few places in the city
offers fruity-fresh Abita Purple Haze beer. And they stir up some serious N
lins cocktails, like the Hurricane, Cajun-tini, and a Bloody Mary so good tha
decorated with an entire shrimp salad. The vibrant Bayou murals, colored s
lights, and Spanish moss on the rafters might make Jacques-Imo's seem ou
place, but it's an excellent choice for a post-Museum meal or lively celebra
366 Columbus Ave. (at 77th St.), 212-799-0150, jacquesimonyc.com. ❶ *to 79th*

Gray's Papaya

Le Pain Quotidien

Josie's Restaurant *American*

Josie's Restaurant caters to vegans and vegetarians with creative entrees like their All Veggie Meatloaf or Seared Asian Tofu Stir-fry. Their warm apple pie topped with soy ice cream is sure to please the most discerning veggie-head. Josie's also serves plenty of meat and fish, like the Peppercorn-crusted Rare Yellow fin Tuna, to satisfy more mainstream appetites. The atmosphere is friendly and casual, and the service is pleasant if slightly disorganized. *300 Amsterdam Ave. (at 74th St.), 212-769-1212, josiesnyc.com.* ❶ ❷ ❸ *to 72nd St.* **$$**

Le Pain Quotidien *French*

The earthy golden décor and menu holders (made of bread) complement the delicate upscale versions of provincial fare that this restaurant-bakery serves so well. The sandwiches and desserts are culinary works of art. Come for a meal or spend hours in a quiet corner sipping a warm, delicious cup of coffee. Either way, do not leave without tasting what might be the best mozzarella in New York. *50 W. 72nd St. (bet. Central Park W. and Columbus Ave.), 212-712-9700.* ❸ ❹ *to 72nd St. Additional locations throughout Manhattan.* **$**

Nonna *Italian*

Nonna's stucco and exposed brick create a romantic vibe that smacks of Tuscany, despite the Upper West Side bustle just outside. The refreshing cocktails, like the blood orange martini ($10), make the perfect beginning to a solid meal. The $28.95 tasting menu lets you sample five of the chef's favorites without going broke. The pannacotta (and other deserts) make the outing worthwhile; they're neither too sweet nor too rich. Just like grandma used to make! *520 Columbus Ave. (at 85th St.), 212-579-3194.* ❶ *to 86th.* **$$**

Ollie's *Chinese*

Efficiency is king at this substandard Chinese restaurant located in supra-standard locations, next to Columbia University and Lincoln Center, for instance. There are rumors of health code violations and complaints about bad service, but Ollie's looks good, and the food sure comes fast. Occasionally you'll hit a gem, like the General Tso's shrimp. *1991 Broadway (at 68th St.), 212-595-8181,* ❶ *to 66th St Lincoln Center. Additional locations throughout Manhattan.* **$$**

Pampa *Steakhouse*

This Argentinean steakhouse features a succulent bacon wrapped filet mignc and wide array of juicy meats, South American style. Pop down to Pampa for a empanada, filled with diced beef or warm caprese. Their steaks pair with Arge tinean wines made from the Malbec grape, hard to find in most stores. If there one thing Argentines like more than steak (which there isn't), it's caramel; try th saccharine panqueques con dulce de leche—luckily, it comes with a bit of vani ice cream for balance. There's a $30 minimum for dinner and Pampa accepts ca only—truly the Argentine way. *768 Amsterdam Ave (bet. 97th & 98th Sts.) 21 865-2929. Cash only, $30 minimum.* ❶ ❷ ❸ *to 96th St.* **$$$**

ISN'T THIS THAT PLACE...FROM THAT MOVIE?

You could probably spend hours perusing the extensive menu at **CAFÉ LA** which features everything from wine to cheese to gourmet salads. This charmi cutesy café has a definite French flair and simply decadent desserts. The hard part is choosing one of the dozens of delicious offerings. Unfortunately, wheth it's because of the yummy food or that scene from *You've Got Mail* that w filmed here, Lalo can get pretty crowded—so prepare your sweet tooth fo bit of a wait. *201 West 83rd St. (bet. Amsterdam and Broadway), 212-496-60 cafélalo.com. Hours: M-R 8am–2am, F 8am–4am, Sa 9am–4am, Su 9am–2am to 79th St.* **$**

Popover Café *American*

New England charm meets New York savvy at this convivial spot, one of the m popular brunch venues in the neighborhood. Feast upon gourmet omelets excellent griddle specialties—and don't forget the popovers! *551 Amsterdam A (at 87th St.), 212-595-8555, popovercafé.com.* ❶ *to 86th St.* **$$**

Rikyu *Japanese*

The freedom to choose can be mind-boggling for early-birds taking advantag the $9.95 prix fixe, especially with Rikyu's 17 dinner options. You can't go wr with remarkably fresh sushi or any combination involving tempura, teriyak cooked fish. *483 Columbus Ave. (bet. 83rd and 84th Sts.), 212-799-7847.* ❶ ❸ *to 72nd St.* **$**

Sarabeth's *American*

This cheerful yellow café is brimming with old-fashioned goodness. Sarab serves up hearty breakfasts and light, sophisticated lunches. For a special drop in for afternoon tea between 3:30pm and 5:30pm. You'll feel like the Qu of England as you sip tea and nibble on finger sandwiches, cookies, and sc Check out their Upper East Side location on Madison Ave. Cheers, dahling! Amsterdam (bet. 80th and 81st Sts.), 212-496-6280, sarabeth.com.* ❶ *to 79th S*

Tamarind *Indian*

This brightly-decorated Upper West Side restaurant offers authentic Indian eats at very reasonable prices. There are nearly a dozen vegetarian entrées to complement the meat-oriented cuisine, and the wide selection of breads like naan, roti, paratha, kulcha and puri are not to be missed. The Chicken Tikka appetizer is a little dry, especially considering that most other dishes are doused in special sauces. If you want a little spice in your life, try a generous portion of lamb vindaloo in a sharp and pungent red curry sauce. *424 Amsterdam Ave. (at 80th St.), 212-712-1900.* ❶ *to 79th St.* **$**

Tavern on the Green *American*

In New York, it's all about location: set smack-dab in Central Park, the rustic idyll that is Tavern may not be all it's cracked up to be, but it's cool nonetheless. Some diners complain of slow service, mediocre fare, and exorbitant prices; and yet, tourists (and affluent locals, mainly grannies) can't help but be impressed by the natural grace and top-notch wine list of this storybook restaurant. Don't miss the truly strange bar upstairs, where velvet chairs, a jukebox, and a large glass window panel depicting a female lion-rider smacks of Graceland. A once-in-a-lifetime experience; but for many, once is enough. *Central Park West (at 67th St.), 212-873-3200, tavernonthegreen.com.* ❸ ❹ *to 72nd St.* **$$$**

Time Café *American*

Around mealtimes there are rarely free tables in this vast, lofty space. That's no wonder, because Time Café is one of the better places filling the niche between greasy coffee shop and fancy restaurant. Health-conscious organic food and an extensive menu with selections like fancy tuna sandwiches and pan roasted penne are sure to satisfy nearly any craving. *2330 Broadway (at 85th St.), 212-579-5100, timecafényc.com.* ❶ *to 86th St.* **$$**

Turkuaz *Middle Eastern*

With the restaurant's artistically-draped fabric ceiling that evokes a breezy Ottoman tent, and the waiters' red satin balloon pants, you might think you've stepped into a tale from the *Arabian Nights*. Enjoy the traditional Turkish dishes and desserts the almond pudding is especially good. Skip the drinks. *2637 Broadway (at 100th St.), 212-665-9541, turkuazrestaurant.com.* ❶ *to 103rd St.* **$$**

Zanny's Café *American*

Why Zanny's is not teeming with Columbia students is a mystery. A brightly-lit café with a funky alt-rock soundtrack and free Wi-Fi should be the hangout spot of choice. Whether you're in need of caffeine, looking for a fresh and fast healthy meal, or into meeting new people during one of their Wednesday movie nights, take advantage of this neighborhood café. The "Putin" and "Sumo" sandwiches are must-tries, and the breakfast wraps are delicious. *975 Columbus Ave. (at 108th St), 212-316-6849, zannyscafé.com.* ❸ ❹ *to 110th St.* **$**

NIGHTLIFE

The All-State Café *Bar*

Once the Upper West Side's best singles bar, the All-State is still a great p'
to grab a steak or a beer. The menu features hearty American offerings, and
draughts run cool with several good ales. The regular clientele is a mixed ba
young professionals and old-timers. *250 W. 72nd St., (bet. West End Ave. and Brc
way), 212-874-1883.* ❶ ❷ ❸ *to 72nd St.*

Bourbon Street *Bar*

Show up here to find athletic women dancing on the bar (especially Friday
Saturday nights) and kick back. Lots of neighborhood sport teams love to
quent this bar and take in a few brews. Make sure to have a potent frozen h
ricane or two. *407 Amsterdam Ave. (at 79th St.), 212-721-1332, bourbonstreet
com.* ❶ *to 79th St.*

Dive Bar *Bar*

Sure, it's got dive written all over it but this haunt is actually quite tame. Even
resident pool sharks won't intimidate. Chug till 4am every day and don't over
a strong menu. *732 Amsterdam Ave. (at 96th St.), 212-749-4358.* ❶ ❷ ❸ ❶
to 96th St.

Dublin House *Pub*

While not a traditional Irish bar, the Dublin House is nevertheless a blessin
the Upper West Side. Its unpretentious atmosphere and straight-up bar at
the authentic old-timer and college student alike. Even the ex-pat Irish c
here. *225 W. 79th St. (bet. Broadway and Amsterdam Ave.), 212-874-9528.*
Only. ❶ *to 79th St.*

The Evelyn Lounge *Lounge*

This spacious bar is crowded most days of the week. It's almost romantic,
fireplaces and comfortable chairs and couches in the back rooms. On the o
hand, it's kind of cheesy. Evelyn is a singles scene with men outnumbering wo
about 3 to 1. There is live music several nights a week, but not enough roo
dance. *380 Columbus Ave. (at 78th St.), 212-724-5145, evelyn-lounge.com.*
79th St.

Fez (Time Café) *Music*

Originally the site of Sticky Mike's, a Warhol hangout, now housing hip singer-s
writers like Ellis Paul, Peter Mulvey, and Jennifer Kimball. Though they've move
place uptown, it still has that same vibe. This unique room has mirrored colu
and sparkly vinyl booths, and every so often the room vibrates from the sub
train passing underneath. Full menu, full bar. With acoustic, comedy, jazz, rock
singer-songwriter shows. *2330 Broadway (at 85th St.), 212-579-5100, time
nyc.com. Cover: $8-$20.* ❶ *to Broadway-86th St.*

The P&G

Jake's Dilemma *Bar*

This bar steals attention from other watering holes along the Amsterdam bar strip in the West 80s. With three levels, a young, hip crowd, pool tables, and good looking bartenders, Jake's only dilemma is what drink to order next. Ladies' Night on Thursday features $1 margaritas for the female clientele. Happy hour lasts until 8pm. *430 Amsterdam Ave. (bet. 80th and 81st Sts.), 212-580-0556.* ❶ *to 79th St.*

The P&G *Bar*

You may know the P&G from its cameo roles in *Taxi Driver, Seinfeld*, or *Donnie Brasco*, but it's still an unassuming place. An old neighborhood bar dating back to the 1940s, the P&G is the real deal, filled with locals and old-timers drinking to tunes from the classic rock jukebox. *279 W. 73rd St. (at Amsterdam Ave.), 212-874-8568.* ❶ ❷ ❸ *to 72nd St.*

Raccoon Lodge *Bar*

You'll get just what you'd expect from a bar with this name – it's a dive. The patrons are not your typical Westsiders; men with cowboy hats and motorcycles frequent this bar. Maybe it's the video and electronic poker games. There is little seating and what there is resembles picnic tables. But hey, the alcohol is cheaper than average for the neighborhood. *480 Amsterdam Ave. (at 83rd St.), 212-874-9984.* ❶ *to 86th St.*

Shark Bar *Bar*

A well-known, upscale hangout. Low lighting and polished wood accents make this hideaway a romantic alternative to other more raucous nightspots. You might need to ward off the post-collegiate singles hovering around the bar. *307 Amsterdam Ave. (bet. 74th and 75th Sts.), 212-874-8500.* ❶ ❷ ❸ *to 72nd St.*

Time Out *Sports Bar*

For the true sports fanatic: know your stats and be ready to talk some serious trivia. The crowd of cheering, jeering, 30-something men ignores the pool table in favor of the 23 televisions. This is New York's home to the Celtic's soccer porter club, so know what you mean when asking about the "football" game. *Amsterdam Ave. (bet. 76th and 77th Sts.), 212-362-5400.* ❶ *to 79th St.*

Yogi's *Bar*

An old-fashioned country saloon like this one provides a stark contrast to new age eateries and standard pubs that line Broadway and Amsterdam in 70s. Bras dangle behind the bar and the jukebox is stacked with hits by Crede Willie Nelson, Johnny Cash, and Dolly Parton. Enjoy $8 pitchers of Bud und big American flag and a bear's head, alongside shouting sports fans. *2156 Br way (bet. 75th and 76th Sts.), 212-873-9852. Cash only.* ❶ ❷ ❸ *to 72nd St.*

ARTS

Avery Fisher Hall *Music*

Over a hundred virtuosos led by Kurt Masur play Western classics, with an phasis on European standards and American innovations. Home to the New Philharmonic. *10 Lincoln Center Plaza (bet. 64th and 65th Sts.), 212-875-5 lincolncenter.org.* ❶ *to 66th St.*

The Julliard School *Music*

Prodigies from all over the world converge at Lincoln Center to study with illu ous faculty and soak up the influence of the inspiring professional talent on di there. Naturally, the performers need an audience, and New Yorkers are an ap priately attentive, discriminating bunch. Modern dance and music of every kin on the bill most nights, and recitals are often free. Who knows? Maybe the str virtuoso cellist you watch now is the next Yo-Yo Ma. *60 Lincoln Center Plaz Broadway and 66th St.), 212-799-5000, juilliard.edu.* ❶ *to 66th St.-Lincoln Ce*

Metropolitan Opera *Music*

When the Carnegies were the nouveau riche, Old Money's monopoly or city's theater boxes frustrated the family so much that they went and built own opera house. Though the original Met was further downtown, its curren cation retains a historic stodginess. A safely classical though consistently outs ing repertory. *Lincoln Center (at Broadway and 66th St.), 212-362-6000, meto family.org* ❶ *to 66th St.-Lincoln Center.*

New York City Opera *Music*

Renews and redefines the soul of opera through stellar, innovative performa of both forgotten and familiar classics. NYCO is world-renowned for its risk ing World Premiere Festival, which introduces opera-goers to works they cou see anywhere else. The New York State Theater is smaller and less overwhel than the Met's, and the ticket prices are more affordable. *New York State Th at Lincoln Center (at Broadway and 66th St.), 212-870-5570, nycopera.com. 66th St.-Lincoln Center.*

The Metropolitian
Opera House

New York Philharmonic *Music*

Over a hundred virtuosos, led by Kurt Masur, play Western classics, with an emphasis on European standards and American innovations. *Avery Fisher Hall, 10 Lincoln Center Plaza, 212-875-5900, nyphil.org.* ❶ *to 66th St.-Lincoln Center.*

American Ballet Theatre *Dance*

This dance giant, once led by legends such as Lucia Chase, Oliver Smith, and Mikhail Baryshnikov is now headed by former Principal Dancer Kevin McKenzie. ABT continues to stage staggering performances at its home at Lincoln Center. Classical ballet had its first renaissance here, and famous composers such as Balanchine, Antony Tudor, and Agnes de Mille have commissioned new works specifically for the company. Call for schedules. *Metropolitan Opera House, Lincoln Center. (at Columbus Ave. and 64th St.), 212-362-6000, abt.org.* ❶ *to 66th St.-Lincoln Center.*

New York City Ballet *Dance*

Co-founded in part by George Balanchine after WWII, this top-notch company, currently directed by Peter Martins, produces a particularly breathtaking Nutcracker with champagne galore and lots of three-year-olds made up like dolls. In residence at the $30 million New York State Theater, the ballet has the largest repertory of any company, and performs for 23 weeks each year. *New York State Theater at 20 Lincoln Center Plaza (63rd St. and Columbus Ave.), 212-870-5570, nycballet.com.* ❶ *to 66th St.-Lincoln Center.*

Lincoln Plaza Cinemas *Film*

Down the street but still in the shadow of its titan neighbor Loews, this smallish theater doesn't want to do the big-budget Hollywood shtick, instead favoring foreign and independent film festival standouts (along with a few surprises). *1886 Broadway (bet. 62nd and 63rd Sts.), 212-757-2280, lincolnplazacinema.com.* ❶ *to 66th St.-Lincoln Center.*

SHOPPING

Citarella *Groceries*

With humble beginnings as a small fish market, this gourmet supermarket r
boasts a full range of fresh fish, meat, and pastas. Best known for its exten
selection of fresh local and imported seafood, Citarella also carries a samplin,
foie gras, caviar, and cheeses for all your dinner party needs. *2135 Broadway*
75th St.), 212-874-0383, citarella.com. ❶ ❷ ❸ *to 72nd St. Additional location*
Manhattan at 1313 Third Ave. and 424 Sixth Ave.

Gryphon Bookshop *Books*

A heaven for book addicts, where crowded shelves of used books climb almos
the ceiling and are piled upon the floor. You'll find many books here that are
available anywhere else in Manhattan. Given those stacks all over the place, le
extra time to browse. *2246 Broadway (at 80th St.), 212-362-0706.* ❶ *to 79t*

Murder Ink *Books*

This specialty bookstore, named after the Lanksy-Siegel crew, is every wanr
sleuth's dream. Featuring new and used mystery fiction, their stock includes m
classic whodunits as well as novels filled with espionage and suspense. A me
for the city's mystery buffs, this shop has frequent book-signings that draw sc
big names. Plus, the staff members really know their stuff. *2486 Broadway*
92nd St.), 212-362-8905, murderink.com. ❶ ❷ ❸ *to 96th St.*

Olive and Bette's *Clothing : Boutiques*

With merchandise that is almost always dead-on trend, this shop strives tc
ahead of the fashion pack. The store is cramped with a sizeable selection of
tops and t-shirts. Brands like Diesel, Seven, Juicy and three dots attract a follov
of native New York women who don't mind dropping extra bucks for casual c
ity. By far the best splurge is the boutique's bright-patterned rain boots. *252*
lumbus Ave. (at 72nd St.), 212-579-2178, oliveandbettes.com. ❶ ❷ ❸ *to 72nc*

The cheese counter
at Zabar's

Zabar's *Groceries*

A name with impressive cachet in uptown circles, this longtime Upper West Side institution is the prime source for gourmet meats, cheese, breads, and produce. Upstairs you'll find an equally well-stocked kitchenware department featuring at least 30 kinds of whisks. Heads up: The store can be shoulder-to-shoulder on the weekends and during the holidays. *2245 Broadway (at 80th St.), 212-787-2000, zabars.com.* ❶ *to 79th St.*

LASSES AND WORKSHOPS

Life in Motion

Members can take classes at any of the studio's various locations in NYC and Brooklyn. A variety of classes including Hatha, Vinyasa, Pre-Natal, Jivamukti and Pilates are offered 7 days a week. *2744 Broadway, 212-666-0877, lifeinmotion. com.* ❶ *to 103rd St.*

Manhattan Motion Dance Studios

Brush up on dance styles such as salsa, tap, belly dancing and the foxtrot in a fun, relaxed environment. The studio even offers wedding dance choreography for fiancés with two left feet. Three classes cost $35, and a variety of membership packages are available. *215 W. 76th St., Fourth Floor (at Broadway.), 212-724-1673, manhattanmotion.com.* ❶ ❷ ❸ *to 72nd St.-Broadway.*

ORTS AND LEISURE

Claremont Riding Academy

The only Manhattan option, Claremont Riding is conveniently located, and is the oldest continually operated stable in the United States. Primarily a riding school, the stable horses are also available for hire for bridle path rides in Central Park. *175 W 89th St., 212-724-5100, potomachorse.com.* ❶ ❷ ❸ Ⓐ Ⓑ Ⓒ Ⓓ *to 96th St.*

ExtraVertical Climbing Center

This beginner-friendly 50-ft track is the city's tallest 'outdoor' wall. Adult day passes are $20, but student rates are available, and the staff is both knowledgeable and helpful. *61 W. 62nd St. (at Broadway), 212-586-5718, extravertical.com.* ❶ *to 66th St.*

OTELS AND HOSTELS

Central Park Hostel

As the newest hostel in Upper West Side, the Central Park Hostel is newly renovated and offers sunny and bright rooms that house up to eight beds. Private two-person rooms are also available that offer a bathroom en-suite, but the shared bathrooms per floor are well maintained. Just a block away from Central Park, this hostel combines good location with great price, perfect for students and in-

ternational travelers. *19 West 103rd Street near Central Park West, 212-678-0*
centralparkhostel.com. Rooms are $29-$149. Cash only. ❸ ❻ *to 103rd St.*

Days Hotel

A comfortable 250-room hotel with fitness and business centers and a fant
location. Right next to the 96th Street express subway stop, you can quickly
easily get anywhere in the city while still benefiting from staying in the rela
quiet of the UWS. Within walking distance to restaurants, shopping, Central P
and only one mile to Lincoln Center. Free WiFi and a great location make th
convenient vacation and business stop. *215 W. 94th St. 800-834-2972. Rooms*
$110-$170. ❶ ❷ *to 96th St.*

Hotel Newton

This no-frills uptown gem located near Columbia University is conveniently c
to the subway, placing many tourist attractions within reach. It boasts an upt
more residential New York experience. Although a budget hotel, the rooms
clean and relatively spacious. Bathrooms are usually shared, but a minor comp
considering the savings. *2528 Broadway (bet. 94th and 95th Sts.), 888-HOTEL*
or 212-678-6500, thehotelnewton.com. Rooms are $120-$160. ❶ *to 96th St.*

International Student Center

This youth hostel located on the Upper West Side near Central Park offer
beds in dormitory-style housing.amenities include free linens, full kitchen, h
speed Internet, TV lounge, and a summer garden. Being a hostel, proper pre
tions should be taken with personal belongings, but other than that, the st
friendly along with the other guests. For the price and its location, this hoste
good choice. *38 W. 88th St., 212-787-7706, nystudentcenter.org. $30/night.* ❶
❸ ❻ ❶ *to 86th St.*

Upper East Side

WOODY ALLEN IMMORTALIZED IT, Tom Wolfe parodied it, *Sex and the City* reveled in it, and the tell-all book *The Nanny Diaries* scandalized it. The Upper East Side is the first and last word in old money, style and aristocracy.

The neighborhood's galleries are among the city's most esteemed, offering Picassos, Braques and Chagalls to a public that can actually afford them. Here is the picturesque "good life" that you thought existed only in movies. On shaded streets and in red-carpeted lobbies you will find brightly buttoned doormen hailing cabs, nannies taking the kids out for a stroll, and personal shoppers delivering the goods from Saks and Bergdorf's.

Of course, an area as large as the Upper East Side could not be so homogenous; sprawling over nine avenues and almost 40 blocks, the neighborhood includes both palatial luxury apartments and cramped studios. The scenery varies between Fifth Avenue duplexes with views of Central Park and the bars, burrito-joints, and high-rises that line Second, Third, and Lexington avenues—but the two extremes are blended to a remarkable degree.

These qualities might not sound like they would attract many tourists, but the Upper East Side is indisputably a cultural destination. Museum Mile, a section of Fifth Avenue home to nine museums, is here; so is the prestigious Frick Collection and Whitney Museum of American Art, not to mention a beautiful stretch of Central Park. Residents

from other parts of the city bump elbows with international visitors
a chance to eat at some of New York's better restaurants and shop
high-end Madison Avenue boutiques.

Central Park, the city's biggest patch of green, is a favorite of locals and
tourists alike. During warm weather, the lawns fill up with picnic blanks
and the wait for boat rentals can be over an hour long. The Central Park
Reservoir stretches 1.6 miles across the middle of the park and is accessible from both east and west. The path surrounding it is a popular spot
for jogging and surveying the architecture. The Guggenheim is visible
over the tops of the trees, as is a pyramidal structure by I. M. Pei, similar
to the one he designed for the Louvre. The roof of the Metropolitan
Museum of Art also provides some spectacular views of both the Park
and Fifth Avenue. So don't let the gated community feeling intimidate
you: the only thing you need to appreciate the artistic splendor of
Upper East Side is a pair of eyes.

HISTORY

>>AS WITH MOST OF UPPER MANHATTAN, there wasn't much to see until
Central Park opened to the public in the 1860s. Back then, omnibuses and horse
cars transported park goers uptown, where much of the landscape resembled
affluent countryside.

The eastern section of the region developed quickly as the Second and Third
Ave. elevated lines, completed in 1879, eased transportation between the urban
center and the outlying regions; this attracted Irish and German immigrants who
settled in the brownstones and tenements lining the streets of an area that came
to be known as Yorkville.

The development that would earn the Upper East Side its elite reputation, however, was construction to the west along Fifth, Madison, and Park avenues. From
Astor to Tiffany, New York's wealthiest barons erected mansion after mansion facing
the new park. Although most were later demolished, the Carnegie and Frick mansions were reincarnated as art institutions—the Cooper-Hewitt Museum and the
Frick Collection, respectively.

Park Avenue's reputation as a glamorous address developed after the New York
Central Railroad buried its aboveground tracks and elegant apartment build-
lined the newly cleared blocks. In the 20th century, the Upper East Side cemented
its reputation for both ethnic diversity and upscale living. Even the formerly work-
ing-class, immigrant-packed Yorkville area became desirable after the demolition of
the Third Avenue elevated line in 1956 and the construction of high-rise buildings.

The Upper East Side is home to its own folksy traditions. Like the one begun
by the like the Mayor of Central Park, Alberto Arroyo, who, with the help of an
enviable moustache, inaugurated the trend of jogging around the Central Park Reservoir.

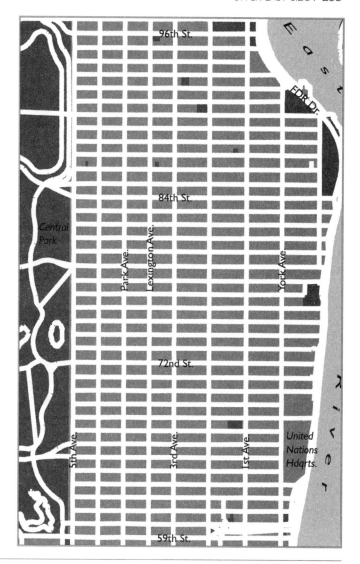

WHAT TO SEE

Carl Schurz Park

This well-kept East Side secret offers one of the best views of Queens, the Triborough and Queensboro Bridges in the city. The park runs along the East River, on a path above the FDR Drive; and not only is it beautiful, with gardens, recreational areas and a playground, but it also has celebrity status: at the north end you can see Gracie Mansion, the New York mayor's residence. *E. 84th to E. 90th St. (bet. East End Ave. and East River).* ❹ ❺ ❻ *to 86th St.*

The Carlyle

A long-time landmark of New York glamour, this swanky hotel is famous for ing the frequent of the city's most stylish visitors. Its distinguished guests incl Princess Diana and JFK (who is rumored to have met up with Marilyn Mon here). The stage of the hotel's Café Carlyle has been occupied by the likes Woody Allen. Ludwig Bemelmans, illustrator of *Madeline*, lived here, and his ta is displayed in the murals that decorate the hotel's more casual Bemelmans *35 E. 76th St. (at Madison Ave.), 212-744-1600, thecarlyle.com.* 🄶 *to 77th St.*

Temple Emanu-El

Built in 1928-29, this gorgeous place of worship is the world's largest form Jewish synagogue, seating 2,500 people. The building displays a méla of architectural influences, combining Romanesque, Byzantine, Moorish,

{Stop Right There!}

CENTRAL PARK

>> CENTRAL PARK WAS BUILT in the 1800s as a grassy oasis inside New York's foliage-starved urban sprawl. To this day, the Frederick Law Olmstead-designed park serves as a playpen for families, weekend warriors and couples. Bordered by 59th street in the south and 110th street in the north, the park offers 843 acres of uninterrupted greenery in the center of Manhattan.

Admission is always free, as are many of the events organized by the **CENTRAL PARK CONSERVANCY.** The Conservancy provides walking tours (T-Sa, call 212-360-2726 for more information), and rents sports equipment out of the **NORTH MEADOW RECREATION CENTER** (mid-park at 97th St, 212-348-4867), both free of charge. A rock-climbing wall, tai chi classes, and numerous basketball, baseball, and soccer fields are also available at the recreation center.

Ever the gracious host, the park is the site for many city event fixtures, including a summer concert series (summerstage.org) and the popular Shakespeare in the Park (publictheater.org). While tickets to star-studded Shakespeare performances are free, they do go fast, so make sure to get yours early.

The **CHARLES A. DANA DISCOVERY CENTER** (212-860-1370) is located at 110th street, and is re-sponsible for many of the park's family-oriented programs. The Center is located on the North shore of the Harlem Meer, one of the park's numerous and beautiful man-made lakes—the huge Reservoir, located in the center of the park, being the largest example.

Other park highlights include two outdoor skating rinks which operate from November through March, **THE CONSERVATORY GARDEN** at 105th street, **THE WILDLIFE CENTER AND CHILDREN'S ZOO** (212-439-6500), and the always-popular **SHEEP'S MEADOW,** a massive open field which serves as the perfect setting for a picnic or as an ideal spot to toss a Frisbee or football.

Whether taking a romantic carriage ride at night (available carriages line up at the Southeast corner of the park) or finding an open field to play some softball with friends, Central Park is the perfect destination for tourists and natives alike. *For more information on Central Park, visit centralparknyc.org or call 212-310-6600.*

*The Model Boat Pond
in Central Park*

art deco styles. The interior is filled with colorful mosaics and stained-glass windows. Enter at 5th Ave. through bronze doors that display the symbols of the twelve tribes of Israel. *1 E. 65th St. (at 5th Ave.), 212-744-1400, emanuelnyc.org. Sabbath services F 5:15, Sa 10:30; weekday services Su-R 5:30. Open daily 10-5pm Museum open Su-R 10am-4:30pm ⑥ to 68th St.–Hunter College.*

TOY BOAT,
TOY BOAT…YOU
KNOW THE REST

The airy space surrounding the **CONSERVATORY WATER,** easily accessible from the park's E. 72nd Street entrance, is the perfect place to relax in the sun. Popularly known as "Model Boat Pond," both the Model Yacht Club and amateurs enjoy racing boats on the water. A nearby café makes for good lounging and people-watching. One of the best attractions is the bronze Alice in Wonderland statue, introduced in the 1960s; come any day and you're almost guaranteed to see at least one kid climbing up and sitting on her lap. ⑥ *to 68th St.–Hunter College.*

WHERE TO EAT

Candle 79 *Vegetarian*

A must for every health-nut, Candle 79 is one of the best vegan restaurants in the city. The place works exclusively with natural, organic ingredients and even offers a gluten-free menu. If you're a vegan virgin, try the Seitan Piccata and the Chimichurris. Brooke Shields and Woody Harrelson come here for good reason. *154 E 79th Street (between Lexington and 3rd Ave), 212-537-7179, candlecafé.com.* ④ ⑥ *at 77th St.–Lexington Ave.* **$$**

Daniel *French*

One of New York's finest and most exclusive restaurants. Chef Daniel Boulud prepares haute, seasonal French cuisine in a beautiful setting, and, of course, prices to match. If you feel like acting entitled for a day, spring for the $96 three course prix frix and enjoy the one-of-a-kind meal. Just don't be intimidated by the incomprehensible menu. *60 E. 65th St. (bet. Park and Madison Aves.), 212-288-0033, danielnyc.com.* ⑥ *to 68th St.–Hunter College.* **$$$**

David Burke at Bloomingdale's *American*

Celebrity chef David Burke's 50s-style diner caters to a mélange of Bloomingda
le's shoppers, faithful Upper East Siders, and annoying tourists. The menu feature
modest twists on classic deli staples like the "Big Pretzel Panini" and "Pastrami To
pedo," but the appetizers are more interesting; Burke spins classics like dumpling
or shrimp tempura into not-so-customary morsels. The highlight of the meal
Burke's cheesecake lollipop tree with bubblegum whipped cream. It's unusual t
find a dessert that tastes better than it sounds, but this is definitely one of ther
Although an annoying beep rings out every time a shopper walks out of Bloomy
with a security tag on an overpriced bag, it's still is a pricey respite from a prici
bout of buying. *150 E. 59th St. (bet. Lexington & Third Ave.), 212-705-3800, burkei
thebox.com.* ❹ ❺ ❻ Ⓝ Ⓡ Ⓦ *to 59th St-Lexington Ave.* **$$**

DTUT *Café*

Ever want to hang out in Central Perk? Here's your chance to get as close
possible. With deep couches, delicious coffee, and yummy goodies, you can sper
hours chatting with your airhead, beautiful, neurotic, nerdy, promiscuous, or aw
ward pals at this Upper East Side café. Be sure not to miss the do-it-yourse
s'mores. *1626 Second Ave. (bet. 84th and 85th Sts.), 212-327-1327, dtut.com.*
❺ ❻ *to 86th St.* **$**

Fondue Lounge *Desserts*

Just don't call this place cheesy. Fondue, conveniently named, attempts to of
a modern spin on an old European tradition. Under new ownership, this Upp
East Side hangout dishes out creamy cheeses melted over vegetables, meats, a
other goodies. The real attraction is the chocolate fondue, which lets you fu
your lifelong fantasy of covering everything you eat with chocolate. For those r
so young of heart, the impressive wine pairings offers more mature enterta
ment. Movies on the back screen complement happy dipping, and be sure
check it out once Fondue starts showcasing local artists. *303 E. 80th St. (bet.
and 2nd Aves.), 212-772-2390.* ❻ *to 77th St.* **$**

Garden Court Café *Asian Fusion*

In the Asia Society Museum, Garden Court Café is an island of delicious cuisi
The flora is a welcome change of scenery from the concrete city, and ba
boo shoots straight through the floor toward the natural light falling on patro
through the Café's sunroof. And the food is as bright and refreshing as the atn
sphere, with light yet hearty Asian-inspired dishes, such as sushi and a scintillatir
spicy Chicken Curry with Coconut Rice. Wash it all down with one of Gard
Court Café's incredible effervescent tea blends, steeped right before your ey
725 Park Avenue (at 70th St.), 212-570-5202, asiasociety.org-visit-café.html. ❺
to 59th. **$$**

Gobo *Vegetarian*

There's vegetarian dining, and then there's Gobo. This organic, Pan-Asian rest rant rooted in what they call Zen compassion really will appeal to your five senses. The chakra rolls are a must-order, and even non-veggies will enjoy the varied menu—the smoked Beijing-style seitan with Chinese vegetables looks like its duck counterpart and is just as flavorful. Try the organic smoothies and don't shy from the vegetables—the taste will pleasantly surprise you. *1426 Third Ave. (bet. 80th & 81 Sts.), 212-288-5099, goborestaurant.com.* 🚇 *to 77th St.* **$$**

MOST DELICIOUS
OXYMORON

Famous for its frozen hot chocolate and Garden of Edenambiance, **SERENDIPITY III** is the Upper East Side's (and perhaps the city's) favorite dessert destination. After being featured in the John Cusack romance *Serendipity*, the already famous sweet haven skyrocketed in popularity. Come in on any night, and after waiting over an hour for a table, watch couples gaze lovingly at each other and kids fight over banana splits while you scarf down a hugely delicious dessert. *225 E. 60th St. 9bet. 2nd and 3rd Aves.), 212-838-3531, serendipity3.com.* 🚇 🚇 🚇 🚇 🚇 🚇 🚇 *to 59th St.-Lexington Ave.* **$$**

Mainland *Chinese*
Find your land-legs and a fine meal at this extravagant restaurant bar in New York's Upper East Side The Asian-chic decor is as bright and flavorful as the creative drinks coming from the bar. Mainland has one of the last remaining classic Asian duck-roasters in New York City—the extra care and effort really come through when you bite into the succulent, crispy Peking Duck. But don't count your quackers before they hatch, because the Seared Ahi Tuna is a real show-stealer. *1081 3rd Ave (At 64th Street), 212-888-6333.* 🚇 🚇 🚇 🚇 🚇 🚇 *to 59th St.* **$$$**

Mañana Restaurant *Mexican*
Delicious and reasonably-priced Mexican food lingers behind this otherwise unassuming First Ave. facade. The atmosphere is cute, if a little cheesy, but the main draw here is the food. Everything is good across the board, but the Yucatan-style carnitas are worth a trip all by themselves. *1136 First Ave. (bet. 62nd and 63rd Sts.), 212-371-8023.* 🚇 🚇 🚇 🚇 🚇 🚇 *to 59th St.* **$**

Serendipity III

NIGHTLIFE

Amsterdam Billiard Club Bar
More genteel than most pool halls, the ABC is the kind of place that's full of
men and rich mahogany. Weekends can get feisty, but the scene is mostly laid-b
with lots of regulars, including director-actor-owner Paul Sorvino. *344 Amster*
Ave. (bet. 76th and 77th Sts.) 212-496-8180, Amsterdambilliardsclub.com. ❹ ❺
to 86th St.

Lexington Bar and Books Bar
This pricey, high-class cigar bar offers great ambience and fantastic martinis. I
nice place to pretend you're all grown up with the white-collar types. Obvio
proper attire is required. Live jazz on Fridays and Saturdays. *1020 Lexington*
(at 73rd St.), 212-717-3902. ❻ *to 77th St.*

Loeb Boathouse Bar
It's the only place to get a cocktail in Central Park, and luckily, a gorgeous
Come and pass an afternoon at one of the outside tables while watching
slickers plying the oars on rental dinghies. Hours vary with the season (
weather), but rarely extend past nine, so be sure to call ahead. The adjacent
serves food, too. *Central Park Lake (bet. 74th and 75th Sts..), 212-517-2233,*
centralparkboathouse.com. ❽ ❾ *to 72nd St.*

Mo's Caribbean Bar and Grill Bar
With twelve beers on tap and a monster 50-oz. margarita on the drink menu,
clear that Mo's is a place for serious partiers. The tropical decor lights up Sec
Ave., and the inside is equally vibrant with large-screen televisions, video ga
and neon-colored drinks straight out of a Jimmy Buffett song. Don't miss
pseudo-spring-break parties that are thrown at all times of the year. *1454 Sec*
Ave. (at 76th St.), 212-650-0561, nycbestbars.com. ❻ *to 77th St.*

Subway Inn Bar
It's right across the way from Bloomingdale's, but you'll seldom see shoppers
a load off their Manolos at this perfect dive bar. Dark, smelly, dirty, and cheap, S
way is heroically antithetical to the glittering retail stores surrounding it. Drin
and then tumble down the conveniently located subway entrance while cur
the Upper East Side squares. *143 E. 60th St. (bet. 3rd and Lexington Ave.), 212-2*
8929. ❻ ❼ ❽ ❾ ❹ ❺ ❻ *to 59th St.*

ARTS

Asia Society Cultural Centers
Asia Society includes ceramics and Japanese folding screens owned by the R
erfeller family. First floor exhibits detail the history of Rockefeller's acquisitio
the artworks and showcases the pieces themselves, ranging from Chinese cer

ics to Japanese wood-block prints. Vivid colors are a visual reflection of Asia's rich history: literary figures, prophets, and poets hang memorialized on sixteenth-century Chinese and Japanese scrolls. On the third floor, contemporary art with a technological bent suggests with humor some of the ways that modern Asian artists conceive of their cultural heritage. *725 Park Ave. (at 70th St.), 212-288-6400, asiasociety.org. Hours: T-Su 11am-6pm, F 11am-9pm Admission $5 for students, $10 nonmembers, free on Friday from 6pm-9pm* ❻ *to 68th St.*

Goethe-Institut *Cultural Centers*

Standing just across from the Met, this center for Germanic culture is the New York contingent of a global network that provides programs for learners and lovers of the German language. A stately staircase leads you to the second floor gallery where art depicts the First World War, brutal Nazi occupations, and photos of revolutionary leaders. German films are screened on Thursdays at six (for $5). *1014 Fifth Ave. (at 83rd St), 212-439-8700, goethe.de, Hours: T-Fr 10am-7pm, Sa-Su 12pm-5pm. Admission free.* ❻ *to 77th St, M3-M4.*

PARK VIEW FOR
N-MILLIONAIRES

During the summer, the **ROOF GARDEN AT THE MET** puts you on top of Central Park's gorgeous green canopy. Sip some wine, listen in on the ritzy pick-up scene, or just admire the view. *1000 Fifth Ave. (bet. 79th and 84th Sts.), 212-535-7710, metmuseum.org.* ❹ ❺ ❻ *to 86th St.*

Neue Galerie *Museums*

Inspired by its Vienna namesake, this stately Fifth Avenue landmark houses turn-of-the century German and Austrian fine and decorative arts from Bauhaus to Brücke. Follow the live music and delicious smells to the classic Viennese café that's as well decorated as the museum itself—and as well-stocked with strudel and Linzertorte as the city it salutes. *1048 Fifth Ave. (at E. 86th St.), 212-628-6200,*

{Stop Right There!}

ROOSEVELT ISLAND

>> IF MANHATTAN IS THE MOTHER of all islands, then Roosevelt Island is the cutest baby imaginable. This delightful, 147-acre island is nestled between Manhattan and Queens, and accessible via the ❻ train, the Queensboro Bridge and the celebrated **TRAMWAY** (2nd Avenue between 59th and 60th streets...remember from the *Spiderman* movie?).

Populated mostly by families, it's not immediately clear why one would go there, and not many do. But with a lighthouse on its northern tip—built by convict labor (from the Island's Blackwell Penitentiary days, 1821-1935) and designed by James Renwick, Jr. (who also did St. Patrick's Cathedral)—not to mention parks and cobblestone streets, Roosevelt Island boasts something that few places in NYC can claim: peace and quiet. *For more information, visit roosevelt-island.ny.us.*

neuegalerie.org. Hours: M R Sa Su 11am-6pm, F 11am-9pm Students pay $10
❹ **❹** **❺** **❻** *to 86th St.*

PAY NOTHING,
SEE EVERYTHING

Most of **MUSEUM MILE** has at least one "pay what you wish" night per week,
if getting in for free is your wish, it's their command. Schedules change, so loo
museum web sites for details. The Guggenheim has a suggested admission Frid
from 6-8pm, and the long lines that wrap around the building on those nights
flect this. At the Met, tickets are always "suggested admission," and it's a suggest
the penniless are free to decline.

Gagosian *Galleries*

A vast gallery filled by established artists who are often eager to take adv
tage of the space. As such, large paintings, three-dimensional pieces, and sculpt
dominate. Even when the physical potential isn't utilized, the art is usually wo
checking out. *980 Madison Ave. Sixth Fl. (at 76th St.), 212-744-2313, gagosian.c
Hours: T-Sa 10am-6pm* **❻** *to 77th St.*

Leo Castelli *Galleries*

Don't want to take a risk? The next best thing to playing it safe at a big muse
is found here. The art is by people who have made a name for themselves, ei
in the art world or culture at-large. In 1958, Castelli hand-picked Jasper Johns
a one-man show, thus launching pop art and minimalism. They even show so
Picassos. *18 E. 77th (bet. Madison and 5th Ave.)., 212-249-4470, castelligallery.c
Hours: M-F 10am-5pm* **❻** *to 77th St.*

SHOPPING

Barney's *Department Stores*

Power dressers and chic shoppers put dents in their bank accounts at this
beautiful legend that still holds its head high despite the closing of its orig
Chelsea location. The men's department is solid, but shoe-holics go crazy o
the women's collection on the fourth floor. Head to the CO-OP on the top
floors for the lowest prices and casual wear. New Yorkers wait in line for ho
and fight like cats every February and September at Barney's Warehouse Sale
score stellar stuff at up to 70 percent off. *660 Madison Ave. (at 61st St.), 212-8
8900, barneys.com. Hours: M-F 10am-8pm, Sa 10am-7pm, Su 11am-6pm* **❻** **❻**
Fifth Ave. or **❹** **❺** **❻** *to 59th St.-Lexington Ave. and Lexington Ave.-63rd St.*

Bergdorf Goodman *Department Stores*

Tour the museum-quality merchandise, worthy of its chandelier and marble
roundings, in this home of high fashion. Bergdorf is notorious for mixing est
lished designers with cool downtown brands, scorching price tags, and the
lavender salon-spa on the top floor. All cash and credit card transactions occu
a "back room" whose doors blend with the walls. When money isn't an obsta
this is as good as it gets. But if you're not rolling in dough, head to the fifth f
for moderately priced casual looks. Or just go straight to the lower level

one of the city's best makeup and beauty collections. FYI: window displays here are among Fifth Avenue's finest and are also worth a trip, especially during the holidays. *754 Fifth Ave. (at 58th St.), 212-753-7300, bergdorfgoodman.com. Hours: M-F, Sa 10am-7pm, R 10am-8pm, Su 12am-6pm* **N** **R** **W** *to Fifth Ave.-59rd St.*

Calvin Klein *Clothing : Designer*

Pay tribute to the commercial master who made a young American public hunger for androgyny. Along with its refined, simple men's and women's wear, this flagship megastore boasts roomfuls of classically styled home accessories and a full staff of predictably trendy, long-limbed sales specimens. *654 Madison Ave. (at E. 60th St.), 212-292-9000, calvinklein.com. Hours: M-W, F-Sa 10am-6pm, R 10am-7pm, Su 12pm-6pm* **N** **R** **W** *to Fifth Ave.,* **4** **5** **6** *to 59th St.-Lexington Ave.*

Crate and Barrel *Housewares*

For the last minute housewarming party, this "upscale IKEA" delivers a rare combination of style and value, ready to equip the urban warrior with all the bare necessities—from crème brulée ramekins to martini glasses. *650 Madison Ave. (at 59th St.), 212-308-0011, crateandbarrel.com. Hours: M-F 10am-8pm, Sa 10am-7pm, Su 12pm-6pm* **N** **R** **W** **4** **5** **6** *to 59th St.-Lexington Ave.*

Dolce & Gabbana *Clothing : Designer*

This flagship boutique that's worshipped by the wealthy carries the latest sports line in all its raw vibrancy. The two unisex floors feature a variety of styles in colors like fuchsia, lime green, and azure blue. For the tamer soul, there is also conservative wear like black pants and khaki blazers. If you are looking for accessories, they also have their own line of belts, bags, and shoes. Younger (and cheaper) styles can be found at the D & G store on West Broadway. *825 Madison Ave., 212-249-4100, dolcegabbana.it.* **6** *to 68th St.*

One of four locations scattered throughout the city, **SHAKESPEARE & CO.** bookstore offers a diverse selection of books along with the soul of an independently run business that you won't find at Barnes and Nobles. Come and enjoy the relaxed atmosphere while perusing some of the naughtier books found in the sex section. *939 Lexington Ave. (at 68th St.), 212-570-0201. Hours: M-F 9am-8pm, Sa 10am-7pm, Su 11am-6pm.* **6** *to 68th St.-Hunter College.*

ST BOOKSTORE
ABOVE 14TH
STREET

Dylan's Candy Bar *Miscellaneous*

Need a sugar boost before Bloomingdales? Head across the street and check out the candy store launched by Ralph Lauren's daughter, Dylan. One look at the giant chocolate bunny at the top of the stairs should tell you that they take candy very seriously. Pick from cases of every kind of confection as you listen to the store's soundtrack, while exclusively features songs that include the words "sugar" or "candy." For weirdos that only like blue M&M's or popcorn-flavored Jelly Bellies, some candy is even separated by color. Its location has made it into a tourist trap, so beware of the high prices and swarms of city visitors. *1011 Third Avenue, 646-*

735-0078, dylanscandybar.com. ❹ ❺ ❻ Ⓝ Ⓡ Ⓦ to Lexington Av.-59th St.

Gucci Clothing : Designer
Tom Ford's looks find their home in this ultra-modern Fifth Avenue showc
The leather goods are of excellent quality, and the clothes upstairs are sleek.
store that caters to "the beautiful people," be prepared for some high-end
high-attitude sales help. Walking away with that Gucci bag will make most fee
a million bucks. 685 Fifth Ave. (at 54th St.), 212-826-2600, gucci.com. Hours: M-
10am-6:30pm, R Sa 10am-7pm, Su 12pm-6pm. ❺ Ⓝ Ⓡ Ⓥ to Fifth Ave.

Nicole Farhi Clothing : Designer
An emporium from the Turkish-French designer, whose London base makes i
felt in her well-cut, muted, and detailed pieces for men, women, and home. F
likes solid construction paired with the harder flavors like fringe, ruche, and
patterns in familiar places. This makes for stylish clothes that don't play to tre
but still feel in-the-moment, and are fairly affordable compared with Mad
Avenue counterparts. There's also a respectable restaurant in the downstair
those who want to make a day of it. 10 E. 60th St. (at Fifth Ave), 212-223-8
nicolefarhi.com, Hours: M-F 10am-6pm, Sa 11am-6pm, Su 12pm-5pm Ⓝ Ⓡ Ⓥ
Fifth Ave.-59th St., ❹ ❺ ❻ to 59th St.

So maybe you can't afford to buy a purse on Madison Ave. That shouldn't
you from accessorizing at **TENDER BUTTONS**, where the selection numbe
the thousands and the materials range from silver to leather to crystal to g
old plastic. 143 E. 62nd St. (bet. Lexington and Third Aves.), 212-758-7004. Ⓝ Ⓡ
CHIC AND CHEAP   ❹ ❺ ❻ to 59th St.

Zara Clothing : National Chain
This well-priced and attractive Spanish chain is a favorite of the internati
crowd. Although the carbon-copy designer looks have been called "scandal
by fashion's inner circle, shoppers tend to find the low prices far more shoc
From one-season staples to everyday standbys, this chain is sure to please.
Lexington Ave. (at 59th St.), 212-754-1120, zara.com, Hours: M-Sa 10am-8pm
12pm-7pm ❻ Ⓝ Ⓡ Ⓦ ❹ ❺ ❻ to 59th St.-Lexington Ave. Additional locatio
Manhattan at 39 34th St., 689 Fifth Ave., 101 Fifth Ave., 580 Broadway.

CLASSES AND WORKSHOPS

92nd Street YMCA
One of New York's most valuable cultural resources serves as an umbrella or
zation for a multitude of classes and workshops, as well as a speaking and rea
series. The reading series is by far the city's most star-studded, drawing natio
and internationally renowned poets and authors. Tickets run around $5-$7
students. 1395 Lexington Ave. (at 92nd St.), 212-415-5500, 92y.org. Hours:
9am-7pm ❹ ❺ ❻ to 96th St.

Alliance Française

Brush up on the language of love at Tuesday's $8 ($6 for students) screenings of French flicks. Dance classes and more than 200 language courses are also available. Members enjoy free films, food and wine tastings, travel seminars, art excursions, discounts on French performances around the city, and use of the multimedia library. *22 E. 60th St (bet. Madison and Park Aves.), 212-355-6100, fiaf. org. Hours: M-R 9:30am-7:30pm, F 9:30am-6pm, Sa 9am-2pm* ❶ ❻ ❿ ❷ ❹ ❺ ❻ *to Lexington Ave-59th St.*

America's Society

Inter-American policy issues come up for debate at the conferences and study groups organized by the Society's Western Hemisphere Department. The Cultural Affairs department offers an extensive arts library, lectures in conjunction with special exhibits, and concerts with receptions for the wine-sipping crowd. *680 Park Ave. (at 68th St.), 212-628-3200, counciloftheamericas.org. Hours: T, R-Sa 12-6pm, W-Su 12pm-6pm Cash Only.* ❻ *to 68th St.-Hunter College.*

China Institute in America

America's oldest bicultural organization focusing on China promotes awareness of Chinese culture, history, language, and arts through semester-long classes. Offerings include Mandarin, Cantonese, Tai Chi, calligraphy, cooking, and painting. Seminars, lecture series, and film screenings with Chinese and Chinese-American themes are also regularly scheduled. *125 E. 65th St. (bet. Lexington and Park Aves.), 212-744-8181, chinainstitute.org. Hours: M W F 10am-5pm, T R 10am-8pm Admission: $5.* ❻ *to 68th St.-Hunter College.*

New York Society Library

George Washington, James Fenimore Cooper, Henry Thoreau, and Herman Melville all frequented the oldest circulating library in New York, founded in 1754. Nowadays you'll have to fork over $135 ($90 for students) for the privilege of perusing literature in the luxurious reading rooms. Non-members are accommodated in the ground floor's reference room. *53 E. 79th St. (bet. Madison and Park Aves.), 212-288-6900, nysoclib.org. Hours: M W F 9am-5pm, T R 9am-7pm, Sa 9am-5pm, Su 1-5pm Cash only.* ❻ *to 77th St.*

The Spanish Institute

Exhibitions acquaint visitors with various forms of Spanish culture. Semester-long language classes are offered, and allow access to both the reference collection and reading room with current publications. *684 Park Ave. (bet. 68th and 69th Sts.), 212-628-0420, spanishinstitute.org. Call for schedule. $60 per membership.* ❻ *to 68th St.-Hunter College.*

Urasenke Chanoyu Center

This Kyoto-based organization dedicates itself to the "chado," or The Way of Tea, a strictly scripted ceremony infused with serenity, order, and calm. The New York

chapter is one of five U.S. branches of the Urasenke organization and it c
traditional Japanese tea ceremonies that are open to the public. Call ahea
dates and times as they usually change every season. *153 E. 69th St. (bet. Lexir
and Third Aves.), 212-988-6161, urasenke.or.jp.* ⑥ *to 66th St.-Hunter College.*

HOTELS AND HOSTELS

The De Hirsch Residence

In this dormitory-style residence hall, you can stay by the day (minimum
stay) or apply to stay by the month for up to one year. The activities ava
at the 92nd St. Y are open to De Hirsch residents. *1395 Lexington Ave. (c
92nd St. YMCA), 212-415-5650, dehirsch.com. Rooms are $35/doubles (per pe
$49/singles.* ⑥ *to 96th St.*

The Franklin

This quaint, charming hotel has a European feel. Rooms are furnished with E
tian cotton sheets, flat panel televisions, and bathrooms with Aveda proc
Complimentary newspapers are offered at breakfast and a complimentary
night shoeshine is offered daily. Beautiful chandeliers and lovely mosaics ador
lobby, and its small but welcoming rooms transport you to another world
while the city awaits outside the hotel's doors. *164 E. 87th St. (Btw Lexingtor
Third Ave.), 877-847-4444 or 212-369-1000, franklinhotel.com. Rooms are $
$225.* ④ ⑤ ⑥ *to 86 St.*

Morningside Heights

MORE THAN ANY OTHER New York neighborhood, Morningside Heights is shaped by the academic institutions that call it home. While New York University manages to more or less blend in with its Village surroundings, the colleges of Morningside exert an undeniable influence on the neighborhood. Throughout the school year, throngs of students from Columbia University, Barnard College, the Jewish Theological Seminary, Union Theological Seminary, Bank Street College of Education, and the Manhattan School of Music crowd the local bars and restaurants in between study sessions. And while the majority of students leave campus during the summer, the area always plays host to eager volunteers, prospective students and lifetime academics.

With the neighborhood's inextricable link to Columbia, the limits of Morningside should no doubt be defined, at least colloquially, as the places where Columbia students live, learn, and let their hair down. Bounded by Riverside Park to the west and Morningside Park to the east, the neighborhood peters out after about 122nd Street to the north and 110th Street to the south. Despite the unflagging college-town feeling, Morningside Heights does manage to retain its link with neighboring Harlem as countless area residents, many in rent-controlled apartments, have seen wave after wave of idealistic students come and go over the past several decades.

Morningside Heights is constantly in the throes of change. Some of the transformations are cosmetic, like famed Beat Generation bar (and Columbia undergrad staple) The West End, which recently tra formed from a beloved dive pub to a Cuban restaurant. Other char have a more serious impact: Columbia's proposed expansion plan nearby Manhattanville is polarizing those on both sides of the schc walls, casting a spotlight on this otherwise quiet neighborhood.

HISTORY

>>THE BATTLE OF HARLEM HEIGHTS took place around what is now I and Broadway, on September 16, 1776. That day, the Yankees pushed the Br back, before soon abandoning the city to the Brits. The battlefields remained al fields until 1818, when the Bloomingdale Asylum took up residence and hou its director in Columbia's present-day Maison Française/Buell Hall. (Contrar mythology, the ever-unpopular Columbia undergrad dorm Wien Hall was actually a part of the original asylum.) The Leake and Watts Orphan Asylum over the site in the 1840s only to follow Bloomingdale up to Westchester Co in the 1890s. After outgrowing Lower Manhattan, Columbia chose a more urban setting and made its way to its current uptown location. The domina Low Library, built in 1895, and the steps leading up to it above College Walk \ modeled after the Roman Pantheon.

The area remained a backwater through the turn of the century, but the pa of area roads and the promise of subway accessibility encouraged developn The Anglican church began construction of the world's largest gothic cathe St. John the Divine, which remains unfinished to this day. The landmark's biz hybrid of architectural styles reflects the various visions of several designers a century.

President Ulysses S. Grant and his wife were re-buried in Grant's Tomb, structed in 1897. Soon, Columbia was joined by sister, all-women's Bar College and the Jewish and Union Theological Seminaries. Within 20 years modern institutions were all in place, and although the neighborhood is no ger considered an isolated backwater, reminders of its open fields, orphans, lunatics linger on in its grassy campuses and diverse student bodies.

WHAT TO SEE

Grant's Tomb

This national monument, which overlooks the Hudson River in Riverside is well worth a visit. When it opened in 1897, it was a more popular tourist than the Statue of Liberty. The towering granite tomb of the famous Civil general Grant, engraved with the words "Let Us Have Peace" from his speec the Republican Convention during his Presidential nomination, remains the la mausoleum in Northamerica. *Riverside Dr. and W. 122nd St., 212-666-1640, gov/gegr. Hours: 9am-5pm.* ❶ *to 125th St. Free 20-minute tours on the hour.*

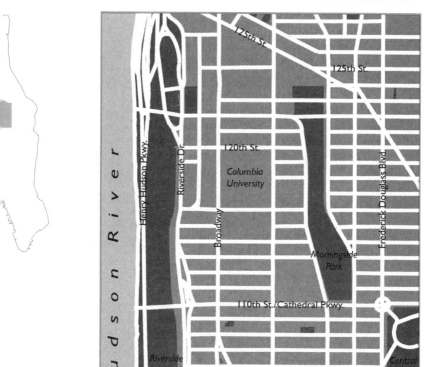

Barnard College

Located across the street from Columbia University, this women's college was established in 1889 as one of the former Seven Sisters. Famous graduates include Suzanne Vega, Laurie Anderson, Martha Stewart, Erica Jong, Zora Neale Hurston, and Joan Rivers. *Broadway and W. 117th St. 212-854-2014, barnard.edu.* ❶ *to 116th St.*

Cathedral Church of St. John the Divine

This colossal church, the largest Gothic Cathedral in the world, truly stands out on Amsterdam. Its 601-foot long nave can accommodate a whopping 5,000 worshippers, and the 162-foot-tall dome could house the Statue of Liberty. The Great Rose Window, made from more than 10,000 pieces of glass, is the largest stained-glass window in the country. Perpetually unfinished, the church is also home to many construction crews. *1047 Amsterdam Ave. (at W. 112th St.), 212-316-7540, stjohndivine.org. Hours: M-Sa 7am-6pm Su 7-7, July and August church closes at 6 on Sun. Tours T-Sa at 11am, Su at 1pm Su services at 8, 9, 9:30, 11, 6.* ❶ *to 110th St.*

Barnard College

Riverside Church

This Gothic-style church, modeled after the French cathedral of Chartres built in 1904. Take the elevator to the top of the 22-story, 365-foot bell towe a spectacular view of the Hudson River, New Jersey Palisades, and the Ge Washington Bridge. *490 Riverside Dr. (bet. W. 120th and W. 122 Sts.), 212-6792, theriversidechurchny.org. Visitor Center Hours: Tu 10:30am-5pm, W 10:3 7pm, R-F 10:30am-5pm, Su 9:45am-10:45am and 12:15pm-3pm Service 10:45am ❶ to 116th S*

WHERE TO EAT

Amsterdam Restaurant
& Tapas Lounge *American*

As one of the latest stops on the Morningside gentrification express, "AmC cheap beer and greasy burgers have disappeared, only to be replaced wit phisticated yet unsatisfying steaks and the pinnacle of New York trendy snob tapas. Without its college-town charm, only local grad students and profe care enough about the new menu to come. *1207 Amsterdam Ave. (at 120t 212-662-6330, amsterdamrestaurant.com. ❶ to 116th St. $$*

Awash *International*

The walls of this comfortable neighborhood fave are covered with bright, g paintings of Ethiopia's emperors. When the food arrives on its injera plate springy, sour bread which you use in lieu of cutlery), it's just as colorful. The almost overwhelmingly pungent, is a bright toxic green but tastes great, and are numerous vegetarian options as well. Bring your date. There's something sual about eating with your hands that just begs people to feed each other *Amsterdam Ave. (at 106th St.), 212-961-1416, awashnyc.com. ❶ to 110th S*

Bistro Ten 18 *French*

This ritzy restaurant is a rarity in Morningside Heights. It presents some wonderful culinary combinations (the scallops and roasted apples make a delicious pair), and the regular favorites like New York strip steak and linguine with marinara are stand-outs as well. Enjoy the view of the Cathedral of St. John the Divine from the front windows and the firelit back room in winter. *1018 Amsterdam Ave. (at 110th St.), 212-662-7600, bistroten18.com.* ❶ *to 110th St.* **$$**

Café Fresh *Mediterranean*

Café Fresh is a nice alternative to the many greasy brunch options in the area. They serve some interesting salads with a Mediterranean theme, but the roasted stuffed pepper is the star of any meal. They take the little things seriously at Café Fresh, from the international array of fine coffees, to home baked cakes and breads, to the inspiring wall paper. Fresh should soon become a Columbia/Manhattan School of Music staple, so bring a book and stay for a while. And it's cheap, too! *431 W 121st St (at Amsterdam Ave). 212-222-6340.* ❶ *to 125th Street.* **$**

Caffe Pertutti *Italian*

Bright and breezy, with a hard-tiled floor and marble-topped tables, this neighborhood café hosts intellectual tête-à-têtes while serving up well-prepared Italian standards alongside inventive pasta dishes, but don't expect anything too innovative. The dessert selection is huge, and the cakes, when fresh, taste as good as they look. *2888 Broadway (bet. 112th and 113th Sts.), 212-864-1143.* ❶ *to 110th St.* **$$**

Camille's *Italian*

Named after the owner's mother, this cozy Columbia magnet is reliably good – think mom's cooking. Pizzas are a bargain at $4.25, and the hearty pasta dishes are topped with light and flavorful sauces. It's difficult to eat this well for less money; breakfast is a particularly cheap alternative to the bacon 'n egg grease-pits at area diners. *1135 Amsterdam Ave. (at 116th St.), 212-749-2428.* ❶ *to 116th St.* **$**

Famous Famiglia's *Pizza*

Come for the photos of celebrities on the wall, the jocular service, and the delicious and greasy pizza. The Heights's finest garlic twists and the pizza's garlicky tomato sauce will keep the vampires away. While the pizza's not perfect, "Famig's" will sop up all that alcohol that Columbians drink on Saturday night. *2859 Broadway (at 111th St.), 212-865-1234, famousfamiglia.com.* ❶ *to 110th St.* $

Hamilton Deli *Delis*

The true New York deli experience awaits at this popular Columbia University spot. Hefty heroes with names like "The Lewinsky" are served up dripping with onions and mustard by a whirlwind staff of no-nonsense locals. Grab a bagel, yogurt, muffin, drink or candy bar from the convenience store in the back, and you're ready to go. *1129 Amsterdam Ave. (at 116th St.), 212-749-8924.* ❶ *to 116th St.* **$**

The Heights Bar & Grill *American*

This slick restaurant-bar has a rooftop garden which is heated in the cooler (mer) months. Potent margaritas, fresh salsa with tricolored chips, and an e waitstaff make this a favoriteamong Columbia students. Start early by slu $2.50 margaritas at happy hour between 5pm-7pm and 11pm-1am week 11:30pm-12:30am weekends. *2867 Broadway (at 111th St.), 212-866-7035. 110th St.-Cathedral Pkwy.* **$**

The Hungarian Pastry Shop *Desserts*

The café's enduring reputation as Columbia University's intellectual hangou excellence has suffered somewhat since the citywide smoking ban. It's sti place of choice, however, to ostentatiously discuss Wittgenstein or write dissertation while sipping chamomile tea and nibbling on a linzer torte.*103C sterdam Ave. (bet. 110th and 111th Sts.), 212-866-4230.* ❶ *to 110th St.-Cath Pkwy.* **$**

Jerusalem Restaurant *Middle Eastern*

Step off the grungy street and into Jerusalem's Arab quarter in this small M Eastern hot spot.amidst the cook's frantic Arabic exclamations and the music, you'll find some of Manhattan's best shawarma and falafel, guarante be a sumptuous meal. *2715 Broadway (bet. 103rd and 104th Sts.), 212-865-* ❶ *to 103rd St.* **$**

Kitchenette *American*

As their slogan says, Kitchenette serves up "comfort food at its best" for b fast, lunch, and dinner. In the front take-out counter, there is a wonderful b with delicious coffee and cakes, while the back houses a comfortable sit-section with quirky country-kitchen décor. It's packed for weekend brunch, prepared to wait twenty minutes or more for a table, but the pancakes with preserves are worth it. Dinner is great too, and the special multi-course pri is a steal.*1272 Amsterdam Ave. (bet. 122nd and 123rd Sts.), 212-531-7600, enettenyc.com.* ❶ *to 125th St. Additional location at 80 W. Broadway (at Warre 212-267-6740.* ❶ ❷ ❸ *to Chambers St.* **$**

La Rosita *Latin*

For years, New Yorkers have sworn that this place serves a great cup of c The service is paced so that food usually arrives as you're about to crac devouring your meal is always worth the wait. This place probably has the authentic cooking and definitely some of the best Spanish food in the neig hood. *2809 Broadway (bet. 108th and 109th Sts.), 212-663-7804.* ❶ *to 110t*

Le Monde *French*

Le Monde does not make culinary history with its take on the traditional F brasserie, but it does a commendable job of imitating the real thing. The Col crowd comes here to escape from the more mediocre eating in Mornir

Le Monde

Heights. The décor of vintage posters and too many mirrors is true to the French name, and the waitstaff is appropriately snooty. *2885 Broadway (bet. 112th and 113th Sts.), 212-531-3939.* ❶ *to 110th St.-Cathedral Pkwy.* **$$**

Max Soha *Italian*

At Max Soha, a ten-spot will buy you the city's best bowl of lamb ragu. For another eight bucks, a glass of Montepulciano will complete your meal in style. While waiting for your table, walk two doors down to their café and enjoy a drink on one of the plush vintage sofas. *1274 Amsterdam Ave. (at 123rd St.), 212-531-2221, maxsoha.com.* ❶ *to 125th St.* **$$**

Mama Mexico *Mexican*

During evenings, this always-packed restaurant showcases a giant mariachi band blaring boleros to hungry (but not for long) diners. Ask for a tequila shot, and you'll think an alarm went off in the back of the restaurant. Service suddenly picks up, and a couple of shots later the owner is pouring booze down your throat. Expect long waits for the decent (and somewhat pricey) food and booze. *2672 Broadway (at 102nd St.), 212-864-2323, mamamexico.com.* ❶ *to 103rd St.* **$$**

Metro Diner *American*

Unique to the world of diners, this veggie-friendly establishment offers all the standard diner fare—only fresh!—with a splash of Mediterranean dishes including a variety of salads and vegetarian plates. Grab a booth and soak in its streamlined train car decor. A great post-movie hangout. *2641 Broadway (at 100th St.), 212-866-0800.* ❶ *to 103rd St.* **$$**

The Mill Korean Restaurant *Korean*

The food here is solid, with a large variety of noodles, rice casseroles, barbecued meats, and pickled veggies. The Mill consistently pulls in a native Korean crowd,

which bodes well for the quality and authenticity of the food. Korean food
spicy, and at the Mill, they will bring you a pitcher of hot sauce to pour over
(already) steaming dish. Vegetarian options are lacking. The service is great, bu
assertive when asking for the check. Be sure to take in the untraditional bathro
a throne to the Evil Empire with a large old-fashioned typewriter attached to
wall. *2895 Broadway (between 112th and 113th Sts.), 212-666-7653.* ❶ *to 1*
St.-Cathedral Pkwy. **$$**

Miss Mamie's Spoonbread Too *Soul Food*

How do you want your soul food: barbecued, blackened, deep-fried, or sm
ered in sauce? It's all here. Save room for some banana bread pudding, coc
pineapple cake, or sweet potato pie. The laid-back staff, who can take just
enough to make you appreciate your meal, will be more than happy to serve
any of the above. Some dishes are greasy—what do you expect with deep-
food?—though most are great. *364 W. 110th St. (bet. Columbus and Manh*
Aves.), 212-865-6744, spoonbreadinc.com. ❸ ❶ *to 110th St.-Cathedral Pkwy.*

Nussbaum & Wu *Delis*

This isn't your ordinary coffee stop—a Chinese pastry shop and Jewish deli ¤
usually collide. With its good lighting and great wrap-around counter, you
may decide to stay a while. Fresh sandwiches and yummy pastries, both ¤
and non, are available here, not to mention bagels and, of course, coffee. Rec
Nussbaum has been doing a booming business in a make-your-own salac
around the back of the shop. Try the Asian Sesame Ginger dressing and
never go back to Italian. *2897 Broadway (at 113th St.), 212-280-5344.* ❶ *to 1*
St.-Cathedral Pkwy. **$**

Royal Kabab and Curry *Indian*

Inexpensive, but not cheap, Indian food on the Upper West Side. Over the
decorations and deep wall-to-wall red evoke a sense of Indian vertigo. Foo
ies: though served piping hot, some dishes are over-spiced while others lac
excitement they deserve. Be prepared for a long wait; otherwise satisfy yo
with some of the better options this neighborhood contains. *2701 Broadw*
104th St.), 212-665-4700. ❶ *to 103rd* **$$**

Saji's Kitchen *Japanese*

This hole-in-the-wall is one of Morningside Heights' hidden gems. Behind ¤
counter blaring rock music lies uptown's best Japanese food atamazingly
prices. This is mainly a take-out/delivery place, but the food is so good that
anywhere else seems like a waste. *256 W. 109th St. (at Broadway), 212-749-*
❶ *to 110th St.-Cathedral Pkwy.* **$**

Silver Moon Bakery *Bakery*

On a quiet Sunday morning, there is no better place to sip a frothy cappu
nibble a pumpkin muffin, and tackle the *Times* crossword puzzle. The freshly b

breads are magnificent, and the atmosphere rivals that of the coziest Parisian cafés. On Fridays, they churn out batches of challah, and for those with dietary restrictions, they make surprisingly tasty wheat-free treats. *2740 Broadway (at 105th St.), 212-866-4717, silvermoonbakery.com.* ❶ *to 103rd St.* **$**

Terrace in the Sky *French*

The restaurant, as romantic as it is appetizing, floats majestically above the Manhattan skyline and is best enjoyed at dusk or on a starry night. Red roses, candles, an inviting fireplace, and beautiful harp music create a warm and opulent atmosphere. The hand roasted foie gras and vanilla crème brulee are highly recommended. *400 W. 119th St. (bet. Amsterdam and Morningside Dr.), 212-666-9490, terraceinthesky.com.* ❶ *to 116th St.* **$$$**

Tomo *Japanese*

Enjoy good sushi and Japanese fare in this upbeat Morningside Heights eatery. The place tends to fill up quickly, and the tables are packed close together, but the prices are reasonable. *2850 Broadway (bet. 110th and 111th Sts.), 212-665-2916.* ❶ *to 110th St.-Cathedral Pkwy.* **$$**

Tom's Restaurant *Diners*

Once you push through the occasional crowd from a Kramer's Reality tour (the southern façade served as the exterior for Seinfeld's diner), you'll question what all the fuss is about. Though recent renovations have jacked prices up, the huge platters and thick "Broadway" shakes (half coffee, half chocolate) are standard, but still keep kids coming back to this greasy spoon. *2880 Broadway (at 112th St.), 212-864-6137.* ❶ *to 110th St.-Cathedral Pkwy.* **$**

Turquoise Grill *Mediterranean*

That this amazing restaurant has yet to be overrun by hungry Morningside Heights residents is nothing short of criminal. Don't let the often-empty dining room fool you. This is one of the best spots in the area. The low cost is happily incongruous with the generous portions, and the delicious, fresh food. Avoid the temptation to split an order of zucchini pancakes with your dining partner—they're so addictive, everyone will want their own. *1270 Amsterdam Ave. (at 123rd St.), 212-865-4745.* ❶ *to 125th St.* **$**

GHTLIFE

1020 *Bar*

1020 is just a bar, and quite content to stay that way. During the week, come with a good friend to throw back a few in peace. On the weekends, watch the artsy kids take their first fumbling steps towards skankiness at a nascent pick-up scene. The pool table in the back can get crowded very quickly. The drinks are okay and prices are friendly. *1020 Amsterdam Ave. (bet. 110th and 111th Sts.), 212-531-3468.* ❶ *to 110th St.*

The pool table at 1020

Abbey Pub *Pub*

Both the food and the atmosphere are comforting at this ideal neighbor
bar where older locals mingle easily with the collegiate (and younger) crow
perfect spot to meet for beers and a shared basket of fish 'n chips. *237 W.*
St. (bet. Broadway and Amsterdam Ave.),212-222-8713. ❶ *to 103rd St.*

Lion's Head *Bar*

Lion's Head prides itself on being a college bar. The late-night kitchen make
place a neighborhood favorite, as well as $10 all-you-can-drink beer night ar
draft beer night. Look out for darts as you're walking through the tiny bar
and play some of your favorite tunes on the jukebox. *995 Amsterdam Av*
110th St.), 212-866-1030. ❶ *to 110th St.*

Nacho's Kitchen *Bar*

Large numbers of college students gather to drink, grope, and be merry. Na
offers decent drinks at decent prices, and their frozen margaritas are perfect
sultry summer night. Be warned, the surly bouncers occasionally forget they
Morningside Heights. *2893 Broadway (bet. 112th and 113th Sts.), 212-665-*
❶ *to 110th St.-Cathedral Pkwy.*

Inquiring minds have conjectured that the slices of pizza to be purchas
KORONET'S got to be so big by eating smaller and weaker slices of pizza.
satisfactory flavor attests to this as well. Happily triple your cholesterol for
$2.75. Koronet is open late, making this a great place to stop by after a nig
the town. *2848 Broadway (bet. 110th and 111th Sts.), 212/222-1566.* ❶ *to*
St.-Cathedral Parkway. **$**

BEST
POST–PUB PIZZA

Smoke *Music*

This is the classiest bar in the neighborhood, and one of the best places for
intimate jazz. Smoke made a name for itself with jazz acts like George Col
Slide Hampton, Cecil Payne, Leon Parker, Eric Alexander, and a legendary c

by George Benson. Don't miss Wednesday Blues night or Latin Jazz on Sundays. 2751 Broadway (bet. 105th and 106th Sts.), 212-864-6662, smokejazz.com. Cover: $15 ($10 drink minimum). 1 to 110th St.

Tap-a-Keg *Bar*

As one of Morningside Heights's true "neighborhood joints," Tap-a-Keg is a fun and relaxed classic beer hall. Cheap beer and a low-key atmosphere make it the ideal place to hang out with friends on any night of the week. They offer a pool table, video games, a dartboard, a friendly and engaging staff, and most importantly, an extensive selection of quality beers. *2731 Broadway, (bet. 104th and 105th Sts.) 212-749-1734.* ❶ *to 103rd St.*

The West End *Bar*

Hanging out at the West End is a rite of passage for Columbia freshmen with bad fake IDs. Now half-converted into a Cuban accented restaurant (complete with terrific empenadas and mojitos), it's gone downhill since the days when Kerouac and Ginsberg made this their haunt, now attracting a loyal clientele of frat boys in too much cologne. College Night on Saturday is complete with beer pong tournaments in the back, and parties downstairs in the dingy lounge. If you go to school in this area, you'll inevitably wind up here at least once. *2911 Broadway (bet. 113th and 114th Sts.), 212-662-8830.* ❶ *to 116th St.*

TS

Manhattan School of Music *Music*

See prodigies perform at one of the country's most prestigious conservatories, usually for free. Call ahead for scheduled performances and times. *120 Claremont Ave. (at 122nd St.), 212-749-2802, msmnyc.edu. Cash Only.* ❶ *to 125th St.*

Miller Theater *Music*

With some of the lowest ticket prices in the city and huge discounts for students, this theater generally draws a young and casual audience from the surrounding neighborhood. The programming is centered on cutting-edge classical music and the heart of the offerings is the Composer Portrait Series, which showcases the works of a single composer. The theater also runs a series of early music concerts in sacred spaces on or around the Columbia University campus. See listing for St. Paul's Chapel. *Broadway and 116th St. (at Columbia University), 212-854-7799, millertheater.com.* ❶ *to 116th St.-Columbia University.*

St. Paul's Chapel

Music Before 1800 *Music*

In Morningside Heights' Corpus Christi Church on certain Sunday afternoons, it's easy to slip back a few centuries. In the church's austere nave, the group Music Before 1800 resurrects songs of Medieval and Renaissance Europe on authentic instruments and hosts visiting groups that specialize in music from specific epochs or regions. The audience is mostly filled with the senior citizens and students from nearby Columbia University and the Manhattan School of Music. Season passes available. *529 W. 121st St. (bet. Broadway and Amsterdam Aves.), 212-666-(mb1800.org.* ❶ *to 125th St.*

St. Paul's Chapel *Music*

The Music at St. Paul's Program at St. Paul's Chapel, located on the Columbia versity campus, is co-sponsored by Miller Theater (see listing) and showcase cred music outside the context of worship service, as well as setting-approp secular chamber music. The concerts, which include chamber works, organ p and non-instrumental vocal recitals, generally take place on Tuesday evening are free and open to the public. *1116 Amsterdam Ave. (at 117th St., Columbia versity), 212-854-6625. Cash only.* ❶ *to 116th St.-Columbia University.*

CREEPIEST
SETTING FOR
COOL MUSIC

Located in the basement of St. Paul's Chapel on the Columbia University ca and seating only 50, the **POSTCRYPT COFFEEHOUSE** is one of the most u rooms in the city. No electronic equipment is allowed on the stage and the lighting is from candles stuck in wine bottles and chandeliers. Suzanne Vega p her first gig here when she was a student at Barnard College across the s Call for details and performance schedule. *St. Paul's Chapel at Columbia Univ (at 117th St. and Broadway)* ❶ *to 116th St.-Columbia University.*

Miriam and Ira D. Wallach Art Gallery *Galleries*

Columbia University's resident gallery presents traveling exhibitions throug the year, curated by professors and students who ensure an academic tilt t line-up. Lectures and receptions are often sponsored in conjunction with ex *Columbia University, Schermerhorn Hall, Eighth Floor (116th St. and Amsterdam 212-854-7288, www.columbia.edu/cu/wallach. Hours: W-Sa 1pm-5pm* ❶ *to St.-Columbia University.*

SHOPPING

Columbia University Bookstore *Books*

Not just for students. Despite its abundance of textbooks, this Barnes & N run store provides one-stop shopping for all the accoutrements of the er astic collegian, from sweatshirts to pennants. Prepare for mark-ups. *Columbi versity Campus, entrance at 2922 Broadway and 115th St., 212-854-4131, colu bkstore.com. Hours: M-Su 9am-9pm, Summer hours M-F 9am-7pm, Sa-Su 11am Summer hours may vary.* ❶ *to 116th St.-Columbia University.*

Hoshi Coupe III *Salons*

This Japanese owned and operated salon is great for a dose of Tokyo hipster with Asian pop music blaring and Vogue Nippon lying around. Along with the fu cuts, the stylists will also throw in a head massage (and that New York rarity, a st discount). English really is a second language here, so beware of special reque though it's probably worth the risk. *2801 Broadway (at 108th St.), 212-663-04 to 100th St.-Cathedral Pkwy. Additional locations at 214 E. 9th St. and 259 W. 1*

Kim's Mediapolis *Music*

This newest installment of the Kim's stores boasts videos, DVDs, music, and books. Here you'll find an enormous collection of Hollywood and indie movies, and rentals are cheaper than bigger video chains. Beware the late fees—they can cost you the family farm. It's very hip, and the staff knows their stuff. If you're planning a move and you've pre-paid for rentals (a good way to save off already low rental prices), you better get renting; Kim's doesn't give it back, and doesn't let you use it for purchases. *2906 Broadway (bet. 113th and 114th Sts.), 212-864-5321, mondokims.com. Hours: M-Su 9am-12am* ❶ *to 116th St.-Columbia University. 6 St. Marks Pl. (at Third Ave.), 212-505-0311, Hours: M-Su 10am-12am* ❻ *to Astor Pl.,* ❶ *to Third Ave.*

Kim's Mediapolis

Labyrinth Books *Books*

Professors and students alike applaud this addition to Morningside Heights' healthy population of bookstores. Relying on a strong selection of academic titles rather than coffee bars and comfy furniture, Labyrinth is a haven for hard-core biblio-philes. *536 W. 112th St. (at Broadway), 212-865-1588, labyrinthbooks.com. Hours: M-F 9am-10pm, Sa 10am-8pm, Su 11am-7pm* ❶ *to 110th St.-Cathedral Pkwy.*

BEST STREET VENDORS

Forget the bookstores. Your wallet will be much happier if you fill your bookshelf from the **USED BOOK TABLES ON BROADWAY** between 110th and 114th Sts. Sweet deals and great reading can be had here at any time. ❶ *to 110th or 116th.*

Milano Market *Groceries*

This gourmet Italian deli and grocery store is stocked from floor to ceiling. In ad-dition to countless sandwich combinations, the store has a pastry counter full of cakes and cookies, a gourmet cheese counter, a sushi counter, a fresh fruit stand, and every-day grocery items. Beware: Most items are slightly more expensive

than their grocery store counterparts. *2892 Broadway (at 112th St.), 212-6*
9500. Hours: M-Su 6am-1am ❶ *to 110th St.-Cathedral Pkwy.*

Morningside Bookshop *Books*

This mid-sized bookstore has been a mainstay of Morningside Heights for c
40 years. Recent renovations lend the store a modern look, and the selec
ranges from literary fiction to global politics. Almost half of the books are u
and a bargain table sits in front of the store. The staff is helpful, and owner F
Soder is almost always on hand to offer fantastic suggestions. Great for ecle
tastes and low prices. The store features 5 monthly events and 20 percent of
new hardcover books (year-round). *2915 Broadway (at 114th st), 212-222-3.*
Hours: M-F 10am-10pm, weekends 11am-9pm with extended summer hours. ●
116th St.

Possibilities at Columbia *Miscellaneous*

Located a few blocks from campus, this card and trinket store is good for l
minute gifts. From greeting cards to mugs, it's filled with items that contain insp
tional quotes. *2871 Broadway (at 112th St.), 212-865-1510. Hours: M-Sa 9am-9*
Su 10am-8pm ❶ *to 110th St.-Cathedral Parkway.*

Scott J *Salons*

The Columbia crowd pampers itself with professional cuts and excellent mak
or waxing at this convenient location. Service can be expensive for a stud
but you get what you pay for. *292 Broadway (bet. 114th. And 115th Sts.), Sec*
Fl., 212-666-6429. ❶ *to 116th St.*

CLASSES AND WORKSHOPS

Test Prep New York

One-on-one test preparation classes tailored to meet individual student nee
127 W. 106th St. Apt. B. 917-805-6015, testprepny.com. ❶ *to 103rd St,*

HOTELS AND HOSTELS

New York International House

Visitors can stay in large ten-to-twelve-person bedrooms, while members g
better deal. Maximum stay is one week. *891 Amsterdam Ave. (at 103rd St.),*
932-2300, ihouse-nyc.org. Rooms are $27/$24 (members). ❶ *to 103rd St.*

Union Theological Seminary's
Landmark Guest Rooms

These uptown guestrooms are sublimely nestled into the walls of the Sem
which is listed in the National Register of Historic Places. The interesting Go

style accommodations offer private baths, cable televisions and complimentary continental breakfasts (on weekdays only) for all rooms. The idyllic garden next door is perfect for rest and relaxation. *3041 Broadway (at 121st St.), 212-280-1313, uts.columbia.edu. Rooms start at $130.* ❶ *to 125th St.*

New York International House

Harlem

HARLEM'S FAMOUS 1920'S Renaissance may have faded into romance of history and cultural memory, but a second Renaiss is alive today. The last ten years have seen a revitalization of Har housing, business, and cultural capital. In this diverse neighborh rundown commercial storefronts give way to stunning, leafy streets, and sometimes all it takes to go from Spanish to French walk across the street. One of Harlem's main drags, 125th Stre well worth a stroll. Keep an eye out for the famous Apollo The you may even catch a glimpse of Bill Clinton, whose office isn away.

While you're enjoying Harlem's unaffected sense of commu keep in mind that the area's recent rise is rife with political co versy. Although safer streets, new restaurants, and the restoratic many buildings have proven positive byproducts of the recent b the impact of further gentrification has yet to be seen. Some fear rising rents and an influx of chain stores may force many long residents and their businesses out of the area.

Regardless of its future, Harlem is and has always been a pla lively change and possibility. Seventy years ago, Langston Hughes "Harlem is a place where I like to eat, sleep, drink, and be in love to work, read, learn, and understand life." Spend some time str through Harlem and you'll soon understand why his take on the still applies today.

HISTORY

>>HARLEM HAS ALREADY SEEN its share of prosperity and decline. Since the Dutch settled the area in the mid-17th century, Harlem's borders, population, and character have shifted more than once. Spatially, this remains Manhattan's largest neighborhood, stretching from the East River to the Hudson, and from the north edge of Central Park to 155th Street; it's also possibly its most historically diverse. Waves of new immigrants have taken advantage of falling property values: The English replaced the Dutch at the end of the 17th century, then the Irish moved in during the late 19th century. New Jewish immigrants adopted Harlem until the outbreak of World War I, followed by the Italians for much of the first half of the 20th century.

The migration of African-Americans to Harlem was accomplished almost single-handedly by the real estate entrepreneur Philip Payton, Jr., who moved his company into the area when property values fell at the turn of the last century. Racial strife and a handful of race riots drove many African-Americans from lower Manhattan up to Harlem, and many more moved there from the South. By 1920, Central Harlem was an almost exclusively African-American neighborhood; it spawned the development of the pre-eminent artistic, literary, and musical talent of the Harlem Renaissance, including Langston Hughes, Zora Neale Hurston, Duke Ellington, Bessie Smith, and Jean Toomer. By 1930, Harlem had nearly grown into its current boundaries. Since then, the area has been a study in paradoxes, seeing its share of affluence and poverty, publicity and abandonment, crime and community.

WHAT TO SEE

The Apollo Theater

This legendary venue, opened in 1934, has launched the careers of luminaries such as Ella Fitzgerald, James Brown, The Jackson Five, and Lauryn Hill.amateur Night, the landmark series that began many careers, is still alive and well today every Wednesday night at 7:30. The performance schedule continues to be impressive—check out the web site for details. *253 W. 125th St., 212-749-5838, apollotheater.com.* **A B C D 2 3** *to 125th Street.*

Apollo Theater

Strivers' Row

These1890s row houses sit on 138th and 139th, between Adam Clayton Powell and Frederick Douglass Blvd. When their Caucasian inhabitants began to abandon Harlem, African-American professionals, "strivers," moved in to these gawk-worthy spaces boasting truly elegant architecture. Designed by David King, also responsible for Madison Square Garden. **B C** *to 135th St.*

CONVENT AVENUE and HAMILTON TERRACE, while easily missed, are two of the loveliest streets in Manhattan. Take a stroll down the leafy lanes, admire the architecture, and chat with the stoop-sitters. Don't miss the house on the South-

east corner of Convent and 144th—you'll recognize it from the movie *The Ro*
Tenenbaums. **A** **C** **D** **B** *to 145 St.*

WHERE TO EAT

Amy Ruth's *Soul Food*

Tongue-in-cheek menu offerings like the Rev. Al Sharpton Chicken and W
special give new meaning to the concept of soul food. The atmosphere is fun
the traditional Southern food is decent. Hearty portions ensure you won't l
hungry. The honey-dipped fried chicken alone is worth a trip. *113 W. 116t*
(bet. Seventh and Lenox Aves.), 212-280-8779. **2** **3** *to 116th St.* **$$**

Dinosaur Bar-B-Que *Barbecue*

Carnivores, unite! This NYC branch of the ever-increasingly popular chain
satisfy every meat craving you've ever had—and even ones you didn't even k
to exist. Hearty combo dishes like the Tres Hombres piled high with pulled p
brisket, and tender ribs will make you adjust that belt buckle another notch
two. Dinosaur is a great place to bring a big group of friends and share ju

wings, all cooked home-style. The extensive beer list with 20 some varieties will leave you wide-eyed. Leave the knife and fork at home—fingers make it all the more fun. *646 W. 131st St. (at 12th Ave.), 212-694-1777, dinosaurbarbque.com/nyc.* ❶ *to 125th St.* **$$**

Londel's *Soul Food*
Owner Londel Davis greets customers at the door of his sophisticated new Strivers Row supper club, a harbinger of gentrification in this quickly changing neighborhood. Harlem's hottest restaurant serves delicious, painstakingly prepared Southern food like smothered pork chops and pan-seared red snapper to the neighborhood's most estimable. *2620 Frederick Douglass Blvd. (bet. 139th and 140th Sts.), 212-234-6114, londelsrestaurant.com.* ❸ ❸ ❷ ❸ *to 135th St.* **$$**

Make My Cake *Desserts*
Though quite small—there are only two tables in inside—this cupcake, cake, and pie shop is so simple it's superb. The cake designer will draw almost anything on a special-order cake, and the staff is super-friendly. Once you try a Red Velvet slice, you'll return so often that they'll get to know you by name. *103 W. 110th St. (at Lenox Ave.), 212-932-0833, makemycake.com.* ❷ ❸ *to 110th St.-Central Park North.* **$**

Miss Maude's *Soul Food*
Newly opened by the owners of Miss Mamie's on W. 110th Street, Miss Maude's is the bigger and better of the two: you can't find better soul food for a lower price. Come summertime, as it's a great place to sip lemonade and get fat; when winter rolls around, it's a great place to sip something warmer and stay fat. *547 Lenox Ave. (bet. 137th and 138th Sts.), 212-690-3100, spoonbreadinc.com.* ❷ ❸ *to 135th St.* **$$**

MOST
ATURAL NOSH

In the middle of soul food city, **RAW SOUL**—an organic juice bar and deli raw foods restaurant—is an unexpected surprise. Delicious juice combinations, smoothies, and munchies abound here. The restaurant is open on Thursdays and Saturdays, and Sunday for brunch. Classes in food preparation are also offered. *348 W. 145th St. (bet. St. Nicholas Ave. & Edgecombe), 212-491-5859, rawsoul.com.* Ⓐ Ⓑ Ⓒ Ⓓ *to 145 St.* **$**

Playing it Safe...

>>HARLEM STILL HASN'T FULLY shed its stigma as a gang-ridden, dangerous neighborhood—but rest assured, it is home to many, many people who safely live there. As with any unfamiliar neighborhood, visitors should still approach the area with care and respect; concerns about safety in Harlem aren't much different than those anywhere in New York City. Most of Harlem is perfectly safe to explore during the day. The region east of St. Nicholas Avenue and north of 135th is probably the least safe part of Harlem, and be especially careful when you're north of 145th at night—the streets are less populated and not as well-lit. Harlem's well-inhabited 125th Street feels safe almost all the time, and areas near subway stops tend to be safer than dark side streets.

Perk's Fine Cuisine *Soul Food*

"Every third person's a gangsta and the other two are yuppies," said one l◼
about this Harlem hangout. Savor succulent baby back ribs while vocalist Rob◼
Fox serenades the ladies with his super-slick renditions of "Me and Mrs. Jo◼
and other R&B standards. They have a terrific bar menu and gracious wait sta◼
a plush, expensive, and comfortable dining room downstairs. *553 Manhattan*
(at 123rd St.), 212-666-8500, perksfinecuisine.com. **Ⓐ Ⓑ Ⓒ Ⓓ** *to 125th St.* **$◼**

Revival *Soul Food*

Well worth the trip to Harlem for the shockingly good soul food creations
modest but impeccable service. Go for the great happy hour deals, then stay f◼
fabulous feast in this stylish, casually elegant and intimate restaurant. Some of t◼
best dishes are the spicy butter shrimp, crusted Chilean sea bass, sizzler lob◼
tail with scallops and LA Lamb Rack. Dinner will leave you completely satis◼
The food has an international flare as well as the traditional elements of soul◼
portions with lots of flavor. Be sure to check out the full-page martini menu. *2.*
Frederick Douglass Blvd. (Corner of 127th St. and Eighth Ave.), 212-222-8338. **Ⓐ**
Ⓒ Ⓓ *to 125th St.* **$$**

CHILLEST
COFFEE HOUSE

SUGARHILL JAVA & TEA LOUNGE is a cozy little hole-in-the-wall coffee hous◼
an excellent place to go when you need to read, write, or catch up with an◼
friend. Offerings include tea, coffee drinks, baked goods, and lunch items, the◼
service is top-notch. *344 W. 145th St. (bet. St. Nicholas Ave. & Edgecombe), 2◼*
281-3010, sugarhilljavatea.com. **Ⓐ Ⓒ Ⓓ Ⓑ** *to 145 St.* **$**

Settepani *Café*

Quell your pastry cravings at this bright and airy café-plus-bakery in Har◼
where you'll find a wide variety of cookies, chocolates, and pastries to be ea◼
right away or perhaps taken to Marcus Garvey Park, a block away. They also se◼
a good (and reasonably-priced) lunch, which you can top off with gelato or ◼
of the unique cakes. Also check out their Williamsburg location. *196 Lenox Ave◼*
120th St), 917-492-4806, settepanibakery.com. **❷ ❸** *to 116th St.* **$**

Slice of Harlem *Pizza*

Darn they're good, and they know it. Hailed as some of the best pizza in N◼
York, Slice offers innovative combinations, lots of toppings, and prices a n◼
above Domino's. Try the veggie pizza: even the most passionate broccoli-ha◼
will be impressed. *308 Lenox Ave. (bet. 125th and 126th Sts.), 212-426-740◼*
❸ *to 125th St.* **$**

Sylvia's *Soul Food*

Although the most venerable soul fod restaurnat in New York, Sylvia's succe◼
on more than reputation alone. The crispy and flavorful fried chicken is good,◼
some of the sides could use reviving. Come Sunday for the after—church go◼
brunch, and don't forget t leave space for socrumptious sweet potato pie. ◼
Lenox Ave. (bet. 126th and 127th Sts.), 212-996-0660. **❷ ❸** *to 125th St.* **$$**

NIGHTLIFE

elevated subway overpass on 125th street

Cotton Club *Cabaret*

A Harlem legend since before you were born, the Cotton Club is still kicking. Show times vary widely and you must call for reservations. The "don't miss" $25 gospel brunches are served every weekend. Full Southern menu and full bar. *656 W. 125th St. (at Twelfth Ave.), 212-663-7980, cottonclub-newyork.com. Cover $15-$30.* ❶ *to 125th St.*

Lady Luci's Cocktail *Lounge*

This spacious neighborhood lounge brings in an older crowd with live jazz most nights. Monday nights are the best, when a 17-piece big band takes the stage and offers an especially entertaining performance. *2306 Frederick Douglass Blvd. (corner of 124th St.), 212-864-8760.* ❷ ❸ ❹ ❺ *to 125th St.*

Lenox Lounge *Lounge*

There's live jazz most nights, and, with recent renovations, it looks as cool as it sounds. *288 Lenox Ave. (bet. 124th and 125th Sts.), 212-427-0253, lenoxlounge. com.* ❷ ❸ *to 125th St.*

TAKE THE ❹ TRAIN

A favorite local watering hole, **ST. NICK'S PUB** also features some of the best live music in the city. Instead of spending a fortune at the Village Vanguard or the Blue Note, slip into St. Nick's, grab a beer, and let local jazz take you away. *773 St. Nicholas Ave. (at 149th St.) 212-283-7132, stnicksjazzpub.com.* ❹ ❻ ❹ ❸ *to 145 St.*

Showman's *Music*

Everything is satisfactory at this laidback haunt, at least, according to the Copasetics, a brotherhood of tap dancers, which headlines at this popular club. Come for the live jazz. Wednesday through Saturday. *375 W. 125th St. (bet. Morningside and St. Nicholas Aves.), 212-864-8941. Two-drink minimum.* ❶ *to 125th St.*

ARTS

Boys Choir of Harlem *Music*

Founded in 1968, this legendary choir has evolved from a small church group to an internationally-acclaimed phenomenon. They perform classical, contemporary, spiritual, and jazz music at their year-round world-wide performances. *2005 Madison Ave. (bet. 127th and 128th Sts.), 212-289-1815, boyschoirofharlem.org. Cash only.* ❹ ❺ ❻ *to 125th St.*

National Black Theatre *Theater*

Family values are the focus of this company, founded in 1968 by Broadway star Barbara Ann Teer. Performances take place year-round and acting workshops are also offered. *2031-33 Fifth Ave. (bet. 125th and 126th Sts.), 212-722-3800, nationalblacktheatre.org.* ❷ ❸ *to 125th St.*

Lenox Lounge

Dance Theatre of Harlem *Dance*

This world-renowned, neo-classical company was founded in 1969 as a sche
and remains one of the country's most competitive. They dabble in a bit of
erything: jazz, tap dance, modern ballet, and several subgenres. Students of
ages and all levels perform in a monthly open house, usually with accompany
performances by guest artists. *466 W. 152nd St. (bet. St. Nicholas and amsterd
Aves.), 212-690-2800, dancetheatresofharlem.com.* **B** **C** **D** *to 155th St.*

SHOPPING

Fairway *Groceries*

"Like no other market" reads the awning. Indeed, this is the largest, lowest-pri
and most popular produce and gourmet market on the West Side. A full
counter offers prepared hot and cold dishes, the cheese department stocks
array of imports and the bakery sells over a million bagels every year. *2328 Twe
Ave. (at 133rd St.), 212-234-3883, fairwaymarket.com. Hours: M-Su 8am-11pm
to 125th. St.*

Hue-Man Bookstore *Books*

One of the largest and best-known African-American bookstores in the cou
Hue-Man Bookstore boasts such esteemed guests as Maya Angelou, Toni I
rison, and Bill Clinton. As a major force in the cultural life of Harlem, the store
great place to peruse the vast array of African-American literature. *2319 Fred
Douglass Blvd. (bet. 124th and 125th Sts.), 212-665-7400. huemanbookstore
Hours: M-Sa 10am-8pm, Su 11am-7pm* **A** **B** **C** **D** *to 125th St.*

Jimmy Jazz *Clothing : Trendy Basics*

This men's clothing store has a great stock of upscale hip-hop gear. Going bey
mainstream brands like Phat Farm and FUBU, this shop sells names like Pepe
Mecca that are harder to find in New York City. Also home to a good sele
of footwear, you can stock up on Tims or Nikes here. *239 W. 125th St., 212-
2827. M-F 9am-7:30pm, Sa 9:30am-8pm, Su 11am-6:30pm* **A** **B** **C** **D** *to 125*

Old Navy *Clothing : National Chain*

Those catchy commercials don't lie. Old Navy has a lot to offer for men, women, boys, and girls. Their styles are often simple, yet take their inspiration from the more expensive fashion trends at a fraction of the cost. *300 W. 125th St. (at Frederick Douglass Blvd.), 212-531-1544, oldnavy.com. Hours: M-Sa 10am-9pm, Su 11am-8pm* **Ⓐ Ⓑ Ⓒ Ⓓ** *to 125th St.*

Strawberry *Clothing : Discount*

While Manhattan fashionistas may consider this store passé, there are many bargains to be had at this reasonably-priced staple. Trendy is mixed with frumpy, but shoppers can find stylish looks with small price tags if they look hard enough. *226 W. 125th St., 212-663-4677. Hours: M-Sa 10am-8pm, Su 12am-6pm* **❷ ❸** *to 125th St.*

Washington Heights

CONTRARY TO POPULAR BELIEF, life does indeed exist near M
hattan's extreme upper boundaries, where demographics chang
rapidly as the weather and diverse cultures mesh in a refreshingly
back way. Contrast the tranquility of the Cloisters with the chee
pandemonium of the main shopping districts on Dyckman, 181st,
207th Sts., or the wild recesses of Inwood Hill Park with the kara
chaos at Coohan's Bar, the city's only Latin-Irish hangout. In Wash
ton Heights, august educational institutions—Yeshiva University
Columbia-Presbyterian Medical Center—tower over blocks of p
tenements, while doctors live in ocean-view apartments only min
away.

The story of Washington Heights and Inwood began with the
tension uptown of the old IRT and BMT subway lines in the e
20th century. Now, as then, the neighborhood houses immigrants
the original Irish-Jewish mix has been superseded by a predomina
Hispanic population in recent years. On hot weekends and afternc
the streets pulse with salsa and merengue rhythms as the area's
minican residents flock to the many grassy parks.

With gentrification on the rise, this neighborhood is anything
static. Lured by airy and affordable apartments and lush parks, stud
artists, musicians, and families are moving here in droves. Reside
love the area's generally easygoing "vibe," one comfortably remc
from the aggressive urban grit many associate with Manhattan.

>>AFTER THE IRT SUBWAY was built at the start of the 20th century, Washington Heights developed rapidly, with the Polo Grounds, Presbyterian Hospital, and Yeshiva University all appearing soon after. It was at the same time that many Greek and Irish immigrants began to call the area home.

As Jews fled European oppression, many settled in the Heights, but were soon disappointed when ethnic tensions erupted: right-wing groups and Irish gangs vandalized synagogues and assaulted young Jews during the '30s and '40s, causing many immigrants to become disenchanted with the neighborhood; by the '60s, the area was largely abandoned by the Irish and Jewish populations. Soon after, the neighborhood housed a predominantly African-American, Puerto Rican, and Cuban population. The 1965 assassination of Malcolm X in the Audubon Ballroom was simultaneously a reminder of earlier conflict and a harbinger of the crime wave that would hit the area in the '80s and '90s—accompanied by an upswing in drugs, poverty, and overcrowding.

Dominicans soon came to outnumber other residents during this period; by 1990, there were more Dominicans in Washington Heights than in any other community in the United States. District lines were eventually redrawn to offer residents better government representation, and in 1991 Guillermo Linares became a councilman and the country's first elected official of Dominican descent. Still, such representation has done little to ease growing tension between residents and police. In the summer of 1992 a police officer fatally shot a drug dealer, and the neighborhood erupted in riots that lasted for several days. Currently the violence and racial tensions have become nearly nonexistent, although poverty still plagues much of the area.

HAT TO SEE

Inwood Hill Park

Once inhabited by the Lenape Indians, Inwood Hill Park remains one of the oldest historic areas in Manhattan. The 200-acre park is home to the last surviving forest and salt marsh in New York City. Plaques throughout the park display the famous exchange between Peter Minuit and the Lenape Indians that resulted in the purchase of Manhattan for trade goods valued at less than $25. Also preserved for display are tools, artifacts, and miscellaneous remains of prehistoric life in the area. Volunteer life is rich in the park, with adults and schoolchildren working together to restore and maintain the beautiful marshes so particular to the area. **Ⓐ** *to 207th St. or* **❶** *to 215th St. and walk northwest to the park entrance on 218th.*

George Washington Bridge

Not only is this bridge practical and necessary (it's the only bridge connecting the Garden State to the Big Apple), it's also a sight to see. Famed architect Le Corbusier called it the most beautiful bridge in the world, even though Othmar H.ammann's original plans to use granite sheathing for the bridge had to be changed as a result of financial limitations from the Great Depression. **Ⓐ** to 175th St.

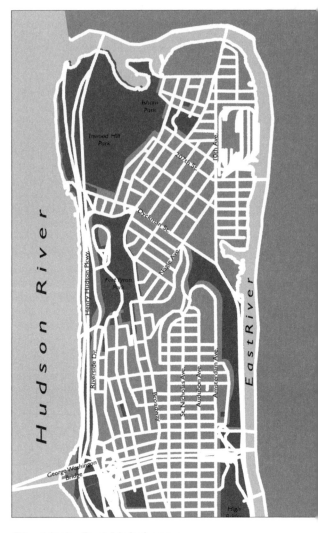

The Little Red Lighthouse

Originally made famous by *The Little Red Lighthouse and the Great Gray Brid[e]*, children's book published in 1942, this bright red beacon is part of Fort Wash[ing]ton Park and sits on the Hudson River beneath the George Washington Br[idge]. It was in use as a navigational aid until 1947, when the Coast Guard decom[mis]sioned it and put it up for sale. In protest, children who had made the lighth[ouse] part of their bed-time story repertoire sent in their piggy bank savings to ke[ep it] in place. In 1951, the New York City Department of Parks and Recreation [took] ownership and preserved it in its location where it now stands as a landmark[. Fort] *Washington Park, 178th St. 212-304-2365.* **Ⓐ** *to 175th St.*

*The George Washington
Bridge and the
Little Red Lighthouse*

WHERE TO EAT

BLEU Evolution *American*

The food and setting will justify the trek uptown. There's a lovely garden to eat in and a lounge that stays open long after the kitchen closes. Despite its out-of-the-way location, this Washington Heights mainstay is undeniably hip. *808 W. 187th St. (at Fort Washington Ave.), 212-928-6006, metrobase.com/bleu.* ❶ *to 191st St.* **$$**

CHEAPEST
SALVADORIAN
FOOD

If you're in the mood for Latin cuisine, stop by **EL RANCHITO** and try the pupusas, a kind of quesadilla with pork. Their chicken is also tasty and moist, all for less than a $10 meal. Good luck finding a comparable deal in midtown. *4129 Broadway (at W. 174th St.), 212-928-0866.* ❹ *to 175th St.*

Carrot Top Café *Café*

The unbelievable carrot cake at Carrot Top Café makes it easy to follow mom's advice and eat all the veggies on your plate. *3931 Broadway (bet. 164th and 165th Sts.), 212-927-4800.* ❶ *to 168th St.* **$**

NIGHTLIFE

Coogan's *Pub*

This upscale pub has a layout that reminds us of *Cheers*; generally Coogan's hosts a bustling after-work crowd from Columbia-Presbyterian Medical Center, as well as a loyal and mixed (mostly Latino and Irish) neighborhood clientele. The atmosphere is always festive, especially on karaoke nights (Saturday and Tuesday). As far as food goes, the shell steak, shrimp scampi, French onion soup, and roast beef au jus come highly recommended. *4015 Broadway (at 168th St.), 212-928-1234, coogans.com.* ❹ ❻ ❶ *to 168th St.-Washington Hts.*

Irish Brigade *Pub*

A feisty female bartender serves a much older crowd interested in letting loose.

Beers start at $1.50, pitchers at $6. Sometimes, as a special treat, there's a *4716 Broadway (at Arden St.), 212-567-8714.* Ⓐ *to Dyckman St.-200th St.*

Rose of Kilarney Bar

This dive is beloved by Columbia med students for its friendly, down-to-earth mosphere and starving-student prices. *1208 St. Nicholas Ave. (bet. 170th and 17 Sts.), 212-928-4566.* Ⓐ Ⓒ ① *to 168th St.-Washington Hts.*

ARTS

The Cloisters Museums

This subsidiary of the Metropolitan Museum of Art boasts the world's prem collection of art and architecture from Medieval Europe. Overlooking the H son River in northern Manhattan's Fort Tryon Park, the building itself is a pi of art, incorporating elements from five medieval French monastic cloisters. collection is based in the Gothic and Romanesque periods, and suppleme the six thousand pieces already on view at the Met's main location.among interesting pieces at the museum are the Unicorn Tapestries (which fill an en room), stained glass panels, and various sculpted tombs. In the summer mor the museum offers Medieval music concerts in the outdoor garden and café. *Tryon Park, 212-923-3700, metmuseum.org.* Ⓐ *to 190th St. or M4 Bus to Fort Tr Park-the Cloisters.*

The Cloisters in Fort Tyron Park

Morris-Jumel Mansion Museums

Visit the Morris-Jumel Mansion for a taste of the American Revolution, wh General George Washington housed his Manhattan troops in October and S tember of 1776. Built in 1765, the mansion is also Manhattan's oldest exis house. Get a glimpse of life before indoor plumbing and start counting y newfangled blessings. *65 Jumel Terrace (at 160th St.), 212-923-8008, morrisju org.* Ⓒ *to 163rd St.-Amsterdam Ave.*

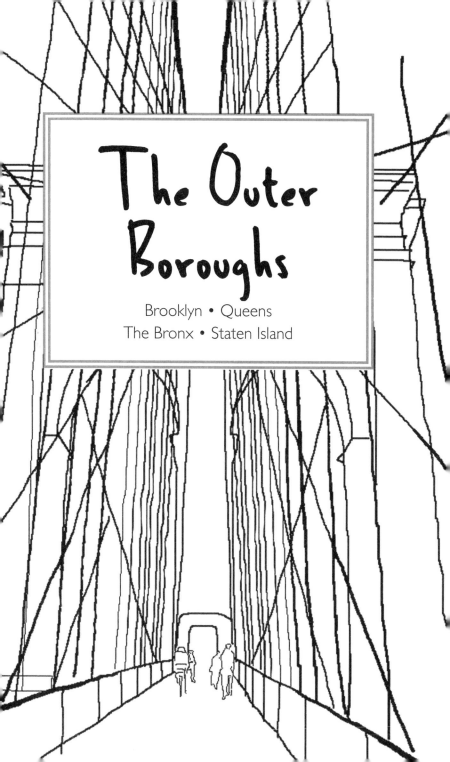

The Outer Boroughs

Brooklyn • Queens
The Bronx • Staten Island

Brooklyn

>>

HOME TO THE CITY'S leafiest streets, best pizza, and oldest bridge other borough inspires as much pride among its residents as Brook Just ask the borough's president, Marty Markowitz, whose love for borough and campaign to convince New York (and the rest of world) that Brooklyn is in fact worlds better than that famous isl across the river is both obsessive and passionate.

Throughout its history, Brooklyn has been defined by the domir ethnic and immigrant groups residing in its many enclaves—Boro Park, Orthodox Jewish; Bensonhurst, Italian-American; Greenpo Polish; and Brighton Beach, Russian—creating insular commun whose distinct flavors and eccentricities are still detectable today.

As is the case with the rest of the city, however, Brooklyn is chang Fast. Chinese restaurants replace Italian bakeries; luxury condos o up near housing projects; espresso bars arrive and rents skyrocket. previously gritty and dangerous area around Atlantic Avenue has b graced with a new mall and a slew of development deals. Fairway cently opened in the soon-to-be-chic Red Hook and there's no st ping Williamsburg's hipster scene from spreading eastward. South Brooklyn, just you wait. Expansion and gentrification abound, cau longtime residents to be displaced in favor of trendy boutiques, rest rants, and new development projects.

Despite these challenges, Brooklyn, sometimes referred to as ' bedroom of New York," continues to remain largely residential. With its array of recreational and cultural institutions, tree-lined streets and cheaper rents, it's easy to see why nearly 2.6 million New Yorkers call this place home. As a traffic sign posted by the 2006 borough administration proclaims, Brooklyn is "Home to Everyone from Everywhere!"

HISTORY

>> BROOKLYN, LIKE MANHATTAN, was originally settled by Dutch explorers. The name "Brooklyn" likely comes from "Brueckelen," the Dutch word for "broken land," though the settlers in effect consolidated several villages after "buying" land from the Canarsie Native Americans in 1642.

Brooklyn remained mostly rural until the 1800s, when a large number of immigrants began to settle in the area. By 1814, Robert Fulton's steamboat service established regular transportation to Manhattan and helped develop stronger commercial links between the two island communities.

In 1833, Brooklyn was asked to join Manhattan in forming a city, but refused and instead incorporated itself as a separate city the following year. It remained independent even after the opening of the Brooklyn Bridge in 1883, an event that stimulated a great wave of residential and industrial development. Brooklyn finally became part of NYC in 1898, a decision that writer Pete Hamill once termed "The Great Mistake."

Various embarrassments ensued, including the transformation of many stylish neighborhoods into slums, the closing of the award-winning newspaper *The Daily Eagle*, and perhaps the most maddening of all, the move of the Brooklyn Dodgers to Los Angeles in 1958.

If Brooklyn were itself a city, it would be the fourth largest in the United States. Though it remains the most populous of the five boroughs, Brooklyn still maintains its own spirit

BROOKLYN HEIGHTS

>> NEAR THE BROOKLYN BRIDGE lies a tree-lined neighborhood with distinguished townhouses and grand gardens so peaceful you might forget that Manhattan is just minutes away. But a stroll along the Promenade of Brooklyn Heights brings the Big Apple back into sharp focus, yielding unimpeded views of the Manhattan skyline. Perhaps that is why this neighborhood has appeared as a backdrop in so many films. Gaining the status of an historic district in 1965, "the Heights" has maintained many of the original brownstones and buildings of the affluent families that populated it for decades. Although today's Brooklyn Heights tends to attract more professionals than artists, in the past some of America's most lauded renegade writers such as Walt Whitman, Norman Mailer, and Truman Capote called it home.

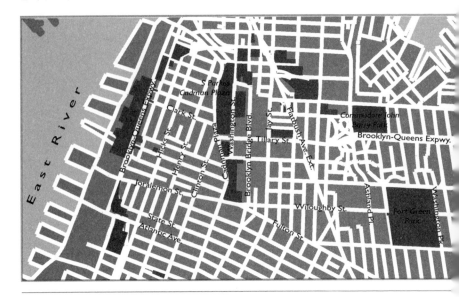

WHAT TO SEE

Brooklyn Heights Promenade

Bring your camera. This shoreline promenade from Remsen to Cranberry Stre offers majestic views of the Manhattan skyline, the Statue of Liberty, Ellis Islar The Brooklyn Bridge, and Governor's Island from across the water. The Brook industrial waterfront and expressway below provide an interesting contrast.

❷ ❸ *to Clark St.,* ❹ *to High St.*

WHERE TO EAT

Pete's Downtown *Italian*

Pete's Downtown opened its doors and began dishing up Italian fare long, lo ago—back when Brooklyn was its own city. Located at the foot of the Brook Bridge, the building remains a landmark in itself. Inside, diners can devour menu vorites like veal parmesan and lemony baked clams while savoring a spectacular vi of the Manhattan skyline. Three roomy seating areas and a friendly waitstaff m Pete's especially great for groups. Reservations are only necessary on weekend *Water St. (at Old Fulton St.), 718-858-3510, PetesDownTown.com.* ❸ *to High St.*

Toro *Asian Fusion*

Spanish and Asian? Sangria and sake? Fusion cuisine is not a gimmick at T where a team of multicultural chefs creates innovative, exquisite twists on e nic favorites. Several new French- and Italian-inspired additions, like honey-sw scallops over asparagus, blend in seamlessly alongside hand rolls and sashimi. appetizers, artistically presented, could count as meals themselves. Located in up-and-coming Fulton Landing neighborhood, this is a great place to bring visiting friends to prove you've broadened your horizons beyond Manhattan. *Front Street (at Old Fulton Street), Fulton Landing, 718-625-0300.* to High Street, ⑤ to Jay Street. **$$**

BEST LUNCH
WITH A VIEW

Montague Street and the Brooklyn Promenade feature an abundance of quaint shops and cafés. Many locals stroll leisurely, soaking in the stunning views of the Manhattan skyline and window-shopping. If all that strolling makes you hungry, stop in for lunch at **LASSEN & HENNINGS**. This gourmet market has been around since 1940, and offers wraps, salads, and fresh-baked bread in a variety of earthy flavors, including walnut sage and pumpernickel. The long lines at lunchtime are unavoidable but well worth it. *114 Montague Street, 718-875-6272, lassencatering.com.* Ⓐ Ⓒ ⑤ to Jay Street. ② ③ ④ ⑤ to Clark St/Borough Hall. **$**

NIGHTLIFE

Frank's Lounge *Lounge*
In this part of Brooklyn, Frank's is known as the friendly neighborhood lounge. Come in and you'll be greeted with smiles and the sounds of smooth DJing. The place does get crowded on weekends, but you can always expect to see regulars and enjoy quality mixed drinks. *660 Fulton St. (at S. Eliot St.), 718-625-9339.* Ⓒ to Lafayette St., G to Fulton St., ② ③ ④ ⑤ to Nevins Ave.

Last Exit *Lounge*
Last Exit is an oasis of cool in the sometimes-stuffy nightlife wasteland that is Brooklyn Heights. This low-key lounge serves delicious martinis and strong mixed drinks to a young, fresh clientele. A friendly staff, comfy couches, and unpretentious crowd await. *136 Atlantic Ave. (bet. Henry and Clinton Sts.), 718-222-9198.* Ⓝ Ⓡ Ⓦ ② ③ ④ ⑤ to Borough Hall, ⑤ Ⓖ to Bergen St.

ARTS

New York Transit Museum *Museums*
Housed in an historic 1936 IND subway station in Brooklyn Heights, and easily accessible by subway, the New York Transit Museum is the largest museum in the United States devoted to urban public transportation history, and one of the premier institutions of its kind in the world. The Museum explores the development of the greater New York metropolitan region through the presentation of exhibitions, tours, educational programs and workshops dealing with the cultural, social and technological history of public transportation. Visit the web site for details of current exhibits and programs, or to shop the online store. *Boerum Place and Schermerhorn Street. Brooklyn Heights, 718-694-1868, mta.info/mta/museum. Hours: T-F 10am-4pm, Sa-Su 12pm-5pm.* ② ③ ④ ⑤ to Borough Hall, Ⓜ Ⓡ to Court Street, Ⓐ Ⓒ Ⓖ to Hoyt-Schermerhorn St. Ⓐ Ⓒ ⑤ to Jay Street–Borough Hall.

The American Numismatic Society *Museums*

This is a chance to see what you may have had if you'd only stuck with or those penny-collecting books as a kid. Numismatics, the study of coins and me has been practiced in these hallowed halls since 1858, and their library main over 70,000 volumes. *96 Fulton St. (at William St.), 212-571-4470, numism org. Hours: T-F 9am-5pm Admission free.* **A C J M Z 2 3 4 5** to Fu Broadway-Nassau.

SPORTS AND LEISURE

Yoga People

157 Remsen St., 718-522-9642, yoga-people.com.

DUMBO

Though some call it "the new SoHo" for attracting the latest wave of artists musicians to its cobbled streets, Down Under the Manhattan Bridge Over is an area that offers some of the most luxurious and expensive condos lofts in any of the five boroughs. Hardly a place for a starving artist to reside neighborhood offers a truly cutting-edge arts scene. A multitude of galleries, grocery stores, cafés, and bars make this once largely-industrial neighbor thoroughly livable.

WHAT TO SEE

Brooklyn Bridge State Park and Empire-Fulton Ferry State Park

Adjacent to one another, these parks stretch between the Manhattan and Br lyn bridges. Don't miss Brooklyn Bridge State Park's amazing Summer Film S

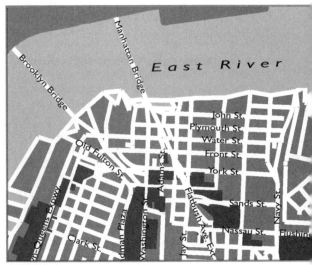

BB Park: entrance at top of Main St. EFF Park: 26 New Dock St. 718-858-4708, bbpc. net. **Ⓐ** **Ⓒ** *to High St.,* **Ⓕ** *to York St.*

HERE TO EAT

Brooklyn Ice Cream Factory *Desserts*
Some say the flavors at Brooklyn Ice Cream Factory could use revamping, but we say there's nothing better than eating ice cream while overlooking the waterfront on a hot summer day. They don't offer samples, so stick with the classics, like butter pecan or strawberries and cream. *1 Water St., Fulton Ferry Landing Pier (at Old Fulton St.), 718-246-3963. Hours: 12pm-10pm, cash only.* **Ⓒ** *to High St.* **$**

Rice *Asian Fusion*
It doesn't take a genius to guess the main ingredient of almost every dish at Rice. This eclectic offshoot of the original SoHo restaurant incorporates elements of Asian, Latin American, and Italian cuisines. The vegetarian meatballs are particularly tasty. *81 Washington St. (bet. Front and York Sts.), 718-222-9880, riceny.com. Hours: Daily 12pm-12am. Cash only.* **Ⓐ** **Ⓒ** *at High St.,* **Ⓕ** *to York St.* **$**

T MEMORABLE
SLICE

According to many Brooklynites, **GRIMALDI'S PIZZERIA** serves up the best brick coal oven pies in the city. That's why a long line of locals (and in-the-know visitors) can be seen waiting outside the restaurant's bright green storefront at almost every hour of the day. The red and white checkered table establishment maintains a strictly "No Delivery, No Credit Cards, No Slices" policy, but with expertly prepared thin-crust pies steaming with fresh mozzarella right out of the oven, no one seems to mind. *19 Old Fulton St. under the Brooklyn Bridge 718-858-4300* **Ⓐ** **Ⓒ** *to High St.* **$**

RTS

D.U.M.B.O. Art Center *Galleries*
Located on the Brooklyn waterfront, the gallery's surrounding neighborhood is home to thousands of artists who gain free membership to the D.U.M.B.O. Art Center. The Center collaborates with other arts organizations to organize festivals and promote experimentation within the local art community. In particular, the Art Under the Bridge Festival in October encourages local studios and galleries to open their doors to the public. *30 Washington St. (bet. Plymouth and Water Sts.), 718-694-0831, dumboartscenter.org. Hours: R-M 12pm-6pm.* **Ⓐ** **Ⓒ** *to High St.*

ARROLL GARDENS & COBBLE HILL

Carroll Gardens was named after Charles Carroll, the only Roman Catholic signer of the Declaration of Independence. A long-time Italian-immigrant enclave, the neighborhood boasts great brownstones set off of the street by about 30-40 feet, creating space for narrow, gated front yards and quaint gardens otherwise unusual in the borough. Carroll Gardens shares a northern border with Cobble Hill,

which, in addition to having its share of land-marked buildings, is home to a vit
Middle-Eastern community, especially along Atlantic Avenue. Gentrification
hit the big avenue in recent years, and its new boutiques and younger resid
reflect this change. Area historians are quick to point out that Cobble Hill wa
birthplace of Winston Churchill's mother, Jenny Jerome, in 1854.

WHAT TO SEE

Smith Street

Located on the eastern side of Cobble Hill and Carroll Gardens, this stree
enjoyed a growing status as a restaurant and shopping district, and has bec
one of Brooklyn's hottest destinations. ❻ *to Bergen or Carroll.*

WHERE TO EAT

Bedouin Tent *Middle Eastern*

Bedouin Tent, a family business, has been around for 17 years in various form
but still serves up delicious Middle Eastern cuisine at affordable prices. Po
dishes include lambajin, a lamb pizza, and harira, a Moroccan stew. *405 Atlant*
(bet. Bond and Nevins Sts.), 718-852-5555. Cash only. ❷ ❸ ❹ *to Nevins St,*
❺ *to Hoyt-Schermerhorn.* **$**

Cube 63 *Seafood*

The Brooklyn location of the LES sushi restaurant Cube 63 may be slightly bigger, but the menu is mostly the same. The bold blue walls and bright plastic chairs signal something out of the ordinary, and the cuisine confirms that this is not your typical sushi dive. If you like innovative dishes, try the Tahiti, which incorporates caviar, eel and avocado. It's strictly B.Y.O.B., but that can be more economical anyhow. *234 Court St. (at Baltic St.), 718-243-2208.* **F** **G** *to Bergen St.* **$**

IGHTLIFE

Boat *Bar*

Great jukebox, good drinks, friendly staff, as well as a nice design and layout—what more could you want of a neighborhood bar in Brooklyn? Located just off the **F** train, this local-friendly Cheers-type place is usually buzzing early in the week, and attracts the nightcap crowd on the weekends. *175 Smith St. (bet. Wyckof and Warren Sts.), 718-254-0607.* **F** **G** *to Bergen St.*

ORTS AND LEISURE

Yoga Center of Brooklyn

Two free classes are offered per week (donations accepted). This studio recently re-opened in a larger space. *474 Smith St. (bet. Huntington and 9th Sts.), 718-834-6067, brooklynyoga.com.* **F** **G** *to Smith-9th Sts.*

ARK SLOPE & PROSPECT PARK

If you ever need an escape from the hustle and flow of Manhattan, let the **F** train whisk you away to 7th Avenue, where you'll emerge in the heart of Park Slope, a Brooklyn oasis. The 1880s and 90s construction boom saw the rise of the gorgeous brownstones and row houses that still characterize the area today. Stretching from Prospect Park West to the Avenue, and from Park Place to the Prospect Expressway, this architecturally stunning neighborhood is packed with charming restaurants, cute boutiques, low-key locals, a bustling coffeehouse scene, and a bevy of baby carriages. The young and the hip continue to thrive in this family-oriented neighborhood, but the 1990s Park Slope boom, and the Manhattanesque rents that ensued, made it difficult for the immigrant and working class population—once so prevalent in the area—to stay.

HAT TO SEE

Prospect Park Bandshell

Prospect Park serves up amazing sounds in the summer with its Celebrate Brooklyn! Performing Arts Festival, where acts run the gamut from indie rock to reggae to modern dance. Recently renovated for $3 million, the bandshell now attracts hundreds of thousands of arts lovers each year. Though concerts are free, a $3

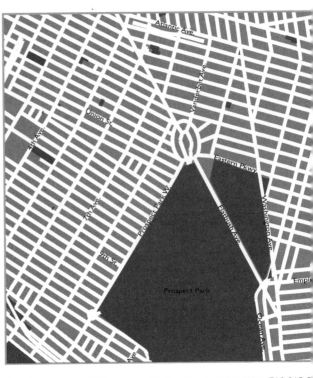

*Brooklyn
Museum of Art*

donation is suggested. *Entrance on 9th St at Prospect Park West, 718-965-8* *prospectpark.org.* ❻ *to 7th Ave.*

Brooklyn Botanic Garden

The most popular botanic garden in greater Manhattan is also the most beau
Spend an afternoon strolling in Brooklyn Botanic Garden's lovely 52 acres for
than $5. Be sure not to miss the Cherry Blossom Festival in May, with fea
more than 200 cherry trees in full bloom, or the 1,200 species of blooming r
in June. *900 Washington Ave between Eastern Pkwy and Empire Blvd., 718-*
7200, bbg.org. $5 adults, $3 students & seniors, free for under age 16, seniors
and everyone T & Sa from 10am-12pm. ❸ ⓪ *to Prospect Park*

Brooklyn Museum of Art

Gorgeously renovated and rarely, if ever, as crowded as the Met, BMA is e
art-lover's dream. Its impressive European sculpture and paintings collectic
showcased gracefully under skylights in the new Beaux Arts Court. On the
Saturday of each month, the museum hosts a gigantic (and free!) party:
5pm-11pm, musicians rock the house as a diverse group of Brooklynites sip
and beer and dance in the courtyard. An affair not to be missed. *200 Ea*
Parkway, 718-638-5000, brooklynmuseum.org. Donations suggested. ❷ ❸ *to Ea*
Parkway.

Prospect Park

A design by Frederick Law Olmstead, architect of Central Park, Prospect Park features the "Long Meadow," the longest uninterrupted stretch of meadow in any U.S. park. Other notable features include the Audubon Center, the Prospect Park Zoo, the Lefferts Historic House, a trolley system for easy transportation, and ice skating during the winter. Don't forget to take an electric boat tour of the park's 60-acre lake, and stay late on summer nights for the Celebrate Brooklyn! series. *718-965-8954, prospectpark.org.* ❶ *to 7th Ave,* ❷ ❸ ❿ ❺ *to Prospect Park.*

HERE TO EAT

Beast *Mediterranean*

Though winged gargoyles, dangling chandeliers and heavy velvet curtains give Beast a dark goth vibe, this culinary star in Prospect Heights will brighten your night. Careful accents like wine served in quartino carafes and bewitchingly good charred salted flatbread set the stage for tapas that are as eclectic as the customers and as big as other restaurants' entrees. Lighter dishes like deftly seasoned lentils topped with smoked mozzarella or a ricotta and onion tart flanked by spiced pears whet the appetite for the heartier seared scallops with squash puree and fried leeks. For dessert, the homemade pistachio ice cream atop grilled baby bananas or the specialty sticky toffee cake will leave your smile as wide as the creepy pot-bellied gargoyles across the room. *638 Bergen St. (at Vanderbilt Ave.), 718-399-6855.* ❷ ❸ *to Bergen St.,* ❿ *to Seventh Ave.* **$**

Blue Ribbon Brooklyn *American*

At first, Blue Ribbon Brooklyn looks like it could be your local family restaurant; the interior is cozy and the tables are filled with couples and families with noisy Park Slope kids. But when you see what people are eating, you'll realize this is no ordinary diner. Tables are covered in trays sporting oysters on ice and smoked trout salad, Paella Magdalena, chicken sausage and utterly tender organic beefsteaks. Don't tell Bubbe, but the matzo ball soup is even better than hers, and the whole roast garlic tastes better than it sounds—and will keep the vampires away for days. For dessert, the chocolate cake and bread pudding are absolute musts. The waitstaff nails the delicate balance of friendly and professional and they cater to the late-night crowd looking for a 3am meal worth the substantial money they'll spend. *280 5th Ave. (bet. 1st St. and Garfield Pl.), 718-840-0404, blueribbon-restaurants.com.* ❶ *to 9th St.* **$$**

Cocoa Bar *Café*

Cocoa Bar is a snug little shop that will certainly satisfy your sweet tooth. Here, scores of delectable chocolate-based treats await your taste buds, along with a formidable selection of award winning coffee and wine. A cozy, unpretentious back room is perfect for the laptop-oriented student, and the seasonal patio is a great spot for a conversation. *228 Seventh Ave. (between 3rd and 4th Sts.), 718-499-4080, cocoabarnyc.com.* ❶ *to Seventh Ave.* **$**

BEST FOOD ON
FLATBUSH

In the 1950s, Flatbush Avenue was known more for its saloons and rowdy ors than its cheap eats. But these days, the Avenue is lined with tasty, afford ethnic fare, minus the belligerent seamen. **CHRISTINE'S BAKERY** (334 Flatb Ave at Sterling Place, 718-636-9746) is known for its aromatic Jamaican tries, and **EL GRAN CASTILLO DE JAGUA** (345 Flatbush Ave. at Park Pl., 7 622-8700) offers Cuban sandwiches for under $5 dollars a pop, in additio tropical milk shakes and other Latin American delicacies. ❷ ❺ *to Flatbush* ❶ ❶ *to 7th Ave.* **$**

Miriam *Middle Eastern*

This small Brooklyn restaurant takes Israeli food beyond 3 dollar falafel into realm of fine dining. The usual plates of hummus, chicken shwarma, and Med ranean salad are certainly on the menu, but Miriam's specialty dishes go a and beyond the standards, such as marjoram crusted wild striped bass and seared scallops. .The traditional Middle Eastern flavors are still here, but the p are artfully assembled in elegant presentations. *79 Fifth Ave. (at Prospect Pl.), 622-2250, miriamrestaurant.com.* ❶ ❶ ❶ ❷ ❹ *to Pacific St.* **$$**

Stone Park Café *American*

When did Brooklyn eats get so good? Situated in a long line of fabulous Slope bars, lounges, and gourmet restaurants, Stone Park Café bests not most of its formidable Brooklyn neighbors, but also competes with Manhat elite. Much of their New American fare is a little fatty, but as soon as you it, you'll understand why—and won't care. Their ample use of succulent belly bacon (like with their tender quail schnitzel) and their gourmet twis American favorites (chicken soup with ginger and chicken dumplings) add a rich selection of delicious comfort classics with the variation that makes S Park's rich flavors come alive. For such an intimate restaurant, they have an a selection of wines and, as a bonus, their quiet Brooklyn digs makes sitting ou more pleasant than in grubby Manhattan. *324 Fifth Ave. (3rd St.) 718-369-0 stoneparkcafé.com.* ❶ *to Union St.* **$$**

NIGHTLIFE

The Carriage Inn *Sports Bar*

Home away from home for Park Slope's cable-deprived in need of a Knicks our basic sports bar, that also offers karaoke on Saturday nights. Pool tables in the back. Amuse yourself at the pool table or come by on karaoke night *Seventh Ave. (bet. 7th and 8th Sts.), 718-788-7747.* ❶ *to Seventh Ave.*

SHOPPING

Community Book Store and Café *Books*

Although this little haunt can sometimes be crowded (especially on w ends), the charm of the Community Bookstore is undeniable. No matter your reading interests are, this place will charm you—and the staff is unfa helpful. Papered with fliers for local events and populated by people who often know each other, this bookshop does a fine job of living up to its name. *143 Seventh Ave. (at Garfield Carroll St.), 718-783-3075.* **B** **Q** *to Seventh Ave.*

Founded in 1973, the **PARK SLOPE FOOD CO-OP** is much beloved in the community and remains the largest member-owned-and-operated food co-op in the country today. Although you must become a member to shop here, the Co-Op's events remain open to everyone. *782 Union St. (between 6th and 7th Ave.), 718-622-0560, foodcoop.com.* **B** **Q** *to 7th Ave,* **2** **3** *to Grand Army Plaza.*

HOP AND SHARE

?ORTS AND LEISURE

Kate Wollman Rink in Prospect Park
East Dr. (near Parkside and Ocean Ave. entrance), 718-287-6431. Open: Nov-March. Ice Skating Adults $5, Children and Seniors $3. Skate Rentals, $5. **Q** **B** **S** *to Prospect Park.*

St. John's Recreation Center
1250 Prospect Pl. (bet. Troy and Schenectady Aves.), 718-771-2787. Hours: M-F 9am-10pm, Sa 7am-5pm **3** **4** *to Utica Ave.*

Xramps
159 20th St., 718-840-0430, xramps.com. **M** **R** *to Prospect Ave.*

Devi
873 Union St. (bet. 6th and 7th Ave.), 718-789-2288. **M** **R** *to Prospect Ave.*

Park Slope Yoga
792 Union St., 718-789-2288, parkslopeyoga.com. **B** **Q** *to 7 Ave.*

?RT GREENE

Just four stops into Brooklyn on the **C** train is Fort Greene, one of the borough's most diverse neighborhoods. Once home to filmmaker Spike Lee (rumor has it that he modeled *Do The Right Thing*'s pizza joint after local landmark Not Ray's), this predominantly African-American enclave draws many a hip-hop artist shooting their next music video at the ominously named Meat Market on the corner of Lafayette and South Portland. In the last decade or so, the neighborhood has absorbed a new wave of Fort Greeners: hipsters, musicians, writers and academics who've fled Manhattan in search of that ever-elusive bargain apartment or brownstone. While these newbie residents come for the long, canopied streets, good subway access, and proximity to the Park, day-trippers will love Fort Greene's top-notch bars and restaurants and its generally relaxed atmosphere.

WHAT TO SEE

Fort Greene Park

The park's focal point is a 145-foot high Doric column, a monument to the 11,0 men who died on British prison ships in Wallabout Bay during the Revolution War. Once dangerous even in daylight, Fort Greene Park is now a great place relax under a big ole tree and contemplate the universe—or where you'll go dinner. Long-time Fort Greene resident, Spike Lee, featured the park in his w known film, *She's Gotta Have It. DeKalb Ave (at Washington Park), 718-222-1 fortgreenepark.org.* 🅁 🄾 🄱 🄼 *to DeKalb Ave.*

WHERE TO EAT

Habana Outpost *Latin*

The Brooklyn baby of SoHo's Café Habana, Habana Outpost takes up the con lot at South Portland and Fulton. Eco-friendly and open only in summer, th the perfect place to grab a tasty cob while browsing through clothing and jew made by local artists. *755-757 Fulton St, 718-230-8238, habanaoutpost.com. H R-F 4pm-12am, Sa-Su 12pm-12am Cash only.* 🄲 *to Lafayette St.,* 🄶 *to Fulton.* $

Madiba *International*

This South African restaurant is modeled on African speakeasy-style social called shebeens. Madiba is decorated with quirky tribal crafts and Nelson N

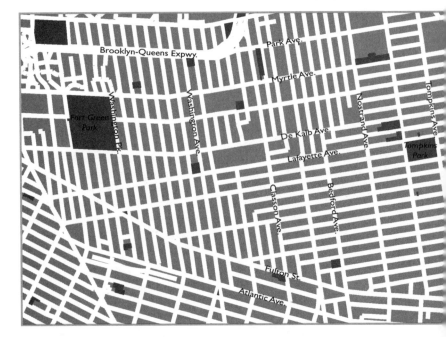

dela paraphernalia. A coke bottle chandelier (made by blind African orphans) completes the funky, informal dining room. Madiba's links to Africa are apparent everywhere, from the condiments and candy sold in the anteroom, to the South African singer playing acoustic guitar. Water served in milk bottles and exotic drinks in jam jars add to the friendly thrown-together vibe. The spicy food is creative and exotic (like the ostrich carpaccio), if not thoroughly impressive, but Madiba's friendly vibe and social conscience are enough to make you love this little slice of Africa in Fort Greene. *195 DeKalb Ave. (at Carlton Ave.), 718-855-9190, madibarestaurant.com.* ❶ ⓡ *to DeKalb Ave.* **$$**

Not Ray's Pizza *Pizza*

Opposite Habana Outpost, Not Ray's Pizza is a legend around these parts. It's big, it's greasy, and it's the classic New York slice. Only problem? It's not open when we need it most—after a night on the town. *690 Fulton St, 718-855-8206.* ⓒ *to Lafayette St.* **$**

RTS

BAM (Brooklyn Academy of Music) *Music / Dance / Theater*

Whether you're in the mood for a good movie (they play three contemporary films at a time, as well as frequent retrospectives) or some highbrow culture (Ibsen's *Hedda Gabler* starring Cate Blanchett was the big hit of 2006), the Brooklyn Academy of Music is most definitely the jewel in Fort Greene's crown. *Corner of Lafayette Ave. and Ashland, bam.org.* ❷ ❸ ❹ ❺ Ⓑ ⓞ *to Atlantic Ave. BAM Harvey Theater bet. Ashland Pl. and Rockwell Pl.* ❷ ❸ ❹ ❺ *to Nevins,* ⓖ *to Fulton.*

MoCADA *Museums*

MoCADA (The Museum of Contemporary African Diasporian Arts) is New York's first and only museum with a focus on the art, culture and history of African Americans and the African Diaspora at large. *80 Hanson Place (South Portland), 718-230-0492, mocada.org. Hours: W-Su 11-6pm Suggested admission $4.* ⓒ *to Lafayette,* ⓖ *to Fulton St.*

BEST LOCAL
STAR SEARCH

Want to see the next big thing? The BAMcafé's **NEXT NEXT** series is sure to be a hit with music lovers, showcasing fresh-faced performers of all musical persuasions in the space above the lobby in the Brooklyn Academy of Music. Most shows take place on weekends; check the site for details. *30 Lafayette Ave. (bet. Ashland Pl and St. Felix St.), 718-636-4100, bam.org.* ❷ ❸ ❹ ❺ Ⓑ ⓞ *to Atlantic Ave.*

BAM Rose Cinemas *Film*

The extraordinary cinema located in the Brooklyn Academy of Music's (BAM) building benefits from being located in a growing urban arts center. The unique four-screen theater opened in 1998, and devotes one screen to BAMcinematek classic movies. Worth both the money and the trip, as one can watch old and new movies while supporting a non-profit institution that helps to expose young

children to the arts. *30 Lafayette Avenue. (at Flatbush Ave.), 718-636-4100, bam*
M **N** **R** **W** *to Pacific St.,* **2** **4** **5** *to Atlantic Ave.*

SHOPPING

Jelly Accessories

This Brooklyn shop stocks a well-edited variety of eclectic shoes and access
for both men and women. From ties to jewelry, the store deals in all things vib
youthful, and loud. Prices range widely. Though nothing is truly inexpensive,
supplies most goods for less money than its Manhattan counterparts. If you
what you see, check out the clothing at sister store Butter just up the stre
407 Atlantic Avenue. *389 Atlantic Ave. (bet. Hoyt and Bond Sts.), 718-858-821*
3 **4** **5** *to Nevins St.*

SPORTS AND LEISURE

Hot Yoga People

659 Fulton St., 718-237-2300, yoga-people.com. **2** **3** **4** **5** *to Nevins St.*

WILLIAMSBURG

This area is to new millennium hipsters what Haight-Ashbury was to the hip
of the 1960s. A mecca for indie music and fashion, the 'burg remains a virtua
of white iPod earbuds snaking out of shaggy haircuts, as beautiful people in im
sibly tight jeans float from one hot bar to another to discuss bands still scu
under the radar of mass taste. Bedford Ave., conveniently the first stop on th
train heading to Brooklyn from Manhattan, is home to many of the area's bu
bars and cafés, including the inimitable Peter Luger Steakhouse (178 Broa
bet. Bedford and Driggs Aves.). Perhaps an indication of how chic this neigh
hood has become, rapper Busta Rhymes recently acquired a $10 million d
apartment here at 60 Broadway.

WHAT TO SEE

Brooklyn Brewery

New York's closest thing to a hometown beer is brewed here, and on w
ends they open the place up. That means free brewery tours, beer tastings
merchandise for sale. They've recently begun using the brewery as a gallery
performance space as well. *N. 11th St., (bet. Barry and Wyeth Sts.), 718-486-7*
brooklynbrewery.com. **L** *to Bedford Ave.*

GO AHEAD,
PIG OUT

Don't miss **BROOKLYN PIGFEST**, presented by The Brooklyn Brewery. Loca
up this annual spring festival, where cold suds, tangy barbeque, and live r
converge for the ultimate down-home pig-out. *1 Brewers Row, 79 North 11*
718-486-7422, brooklynbrewery.com. **L** *to Bedford Ave.*

BARC's Annual Dog Show and Fair

Every fall, playful pups parade in costume and compete for awards like Best Kisser. *Wythe Ave at North 1st St to McCarran Park, 718-486-7489, barcshelter.org.* 🚇 *to Bedford Ave.*

HERE TO EAT

Monkey Town *American*

Part video-installation showcase, part eclectic restaurant, it's all monkey business at Monkey Town. In the front room, munch on dishes like grilled pistachio-encrusted striped bass or tender braised short ribs over fried oatmeal cakes; you can also take the party to the screening room in the back, where four giant projection screens show an assortment of films—sometimes at one-third the normal speed. *58 N. Third St. (bet. Kent & Wythe Aves.), 718-384-1369, monkeytownhq.com.* 🚇 *to Bedford Ave.* **$$**

Relish *American*

Don't let the 50's-era diner or the hamburgers, mac and cheese, and banana splits fool you—this is no greasy spoon. Beautifully restored, mixing influences from North Africa to Long Island, the flavors at Relish are as eclectic as its Williamsburg patrons. Enjoy glazed salmon with lentils and spinach in the dining car's banquets, sip a Singapore Sling in the "Gold Room," or perch on a counter stool for a

brunch of scrambled eggs with coriander chutney. In the summer, you can
among the roses in one of Williamsburg's most spacious and beautiful restau
gardens (the smoking section is an inviting strip of lawn presided over by a s
Madonna). Be sure to make a reservation for groups of 6 or more. *225 Wyth*
North 3rd), 718-963-4546, relish.com. ● *to Bedford Ave.* **$$**

NIGHTLIFE

Black Betty *Music*

Black Betty dishes up cool live music and North African cuisine to a young cr
of new Brooklynites seven days a week. The jazz, world music, and trip-hop
booked by the "Professor" have helped to make this one of Williamsburg's
popular nightspots. Be sure to call ahead for reservations. *366 Metropolitan*
(at Havemeyer St.), 718-599-0243. ● *to Bedford Ave.,* ● *to Metropolitan Ave.*

FRESHEST BEATS

Though the hip-hop haven known as **TRIPLE CROWN** has been around
2004, it continues to offer up fresh beats from some of the industry's ho
megastars. Triple 5 Soul, Jazzy Jay and Rob Swift have all performed here, alon
a host of rotating DJs. *108 Bedford Ave (at North 11th St.), 718-388-8883, tr*
rownpage.com. ● *to Bedford Ave.*

Pete's Candy Store *Music*

Only locals, cool Brooklynites, and "those who know" visit this venue, which c
an eclectic mix: bingo on Tuesdays, Quiz-O on Wednesdays, and jazz quarte
Thursdays, with DJs and a neighborhood band filling the rest of the week. To
panini accompanies a drink list packed with dark and stormy "Mac Daddys,"
all the usual cocktail suspects. *709 Lorimer St. (bet. Frost and Richardson Sts.),*
302-3770, petescandystore.com. ● *to Metropolitan Ave.,* ● *to Lorimer St.*

ARTS

Momenta Art *Galleries*

The neighborhood's most grown-up gallery still floats beyond the orbit o
conventional. The focus is on group shows featuring works by many artists re
ing a central, provocative theme, and the execution ranges from compete
brilliant. *72 Berry St. (bet. 9th and 10th Sts.), 718-218-8058, momentaart.org. H*
M-F 12pm-6pm. ● *to Bedford Ave.*

Pierogi 2000 *Galleries*

The name reflects the way the traditional Polish flavor of the community r
with the influx of forward-focused artists. Like most Williamsburg gallerie
art here is as far outside of the mainstream as the location. The gallery serv
everything from an outlet for resurrections of art treasures unseen for yea
a center for lots of the neighborhood's resident artists, many of whom ca
found hanging out on its stoop. *177 N. 9th St. (bet. Bedford and Driggs Aves.),*
599-2144, pierogi2000.com. Hours: F-M 12pm-6pm. ● *to Bedford Ave.*

Galapagos Art Space *Performance Space*

Priced out of solo ownership, artists got together to buy this almost impossible to categorize venue. Part bar/theater/cinema/gallery/concert venue, only its cavernous size reveals that it was once a mayonnaise factory. It now creates emulsions of a different kind, as resident artists collaborate on their various projects. The directors take no grants, so the whole experiment relies on putting together high-quality, innovative programming that will draw and impress audiences. Numerous festivals run here, creative non-profits of all kinds rent it out for their own shows, and DJs are glued to their turntables until well into the wee hours, keeping people in the mood for cutting-edge art. *70 N. 6th St. (bet. Kent and Whythe Aves.), 718-782-5188.* ● *to Bedford Ave.*

Williamsburg Art Nexus *Galleries*

This gallery, theater, and rehearsal space aims to cultivate a supportive environment for contemporary artists in all media while fostering a love of art in the community. WAX features a one-room gallery space and a white-walled black-box theater available for rent to local artists and performers. *251 N 8th St., 718-599-7997, wax205.com.* ● *to Bedford Ave.*

HOPPING

Beacon's Closet *Clothing : Vintage & Consignment*

A wide assortment of used clothing fills the racks in this Williamsburg shop, and it doesn't take too much hunting to find something really nice like a suede jacket or a pair of perfectly worn boot-cut Wranglers. The prices are slightly expensive for Brooklyn but are still a fraction of what you'd pay in Manhattan. Plus, they'll buy your unwanted clothes or take them in for store credit. Check out the other Beacon's Closet in Park Slope. *88 North 11th St. (at Berry St.), 718-486-0816, beaconscloset.com, Hours: M-F 12pm-9pm, Sa-Su 11am-8pm* ● *to Bedford Ave. Park Slope. 220 Fifth Ave. (near Union St.), 718-230-1630.* ⓜ ⓡ *at Union St.*

PORTS AND LEISURE

Metropolitan Pool and Fitness Center

261 Bedford Ave. (at Metropolitan Ave.), 718-599-5707. ● *to Bedford Ave.*

Go Yoga

218 Bedford Ave., 718-486-5602, goyoga.ws. ● *to Bedford Ave.*

GREENPOINT

In the 19th century, Greenpoint was a center of shipbuilding and commerce, surrounded by waterways on three sides. These water-borne industries were made up of hardworking immigrants, whose homes and places of work lined the streets that became Greenpoint's Historic District, listed today on the National Register

of Historic Places. The neighborhood is sometimes referred as "Little Poland," a
has attracted a large population of Polish immigrants, especially in the past th
to four decades. Though not as chic (yet) as its southern neighbor, Williamsb
this enclave offers a wealth of hidden gastronomic gems on the bustling Manl
tan Avenue.

WHAT TO SEE

McCarren & Monsignor McGolrick Parks

McGolrick Park is a beautiful European-style square, but McCarren Park is re
"where it's at." Pet owners love the convenience of the dog run and the Anl
Animal Show and Parade at McCarren, while the rest of us can enjoy the Pa
running track, handball courts, and baseball fields, and continue to wish the g
swimming pool (capacity 6,500) were reopened for more than just concerts.
Carren: Nassau Ave. (bet. Bayard and N. 12 Sts.), *to Bedford Ave.,* **G** *to Nassau*
McGorlick: Driggs St. (bet. Russell and Monitor) **L** *to Bedford Ave.,* **G** *to Nassau*

WHERE TO EAT

Greenpoint's Restaurant Row

The Polish and Thai restaurants that line Manhattan Avenue between Greenp
and Driggs Ave. are particularly endearing, often serving up entire meals for ur

$10. Try Lomzynianka *(646 Manhattan Ave. bet. Nassau and Norman Aves, 718-389-9439)* or Polonia *(631 Manhattan Ave. at Bedford Ave., 718-383-9781)* for authentic Polish home cooking, with entrees as low as $5.50, including all the fixings. Moon Shadows *(643 Manhattan Ave. at Bedford Ave., 718-609-1841)* and Amarin Café *(617 Manhattan Ave. bet. Driggs and Nassau Aves., 718-349-2788)* offer spicy curries that satisfy without burning a hole in your wallet. **G** *to Nassau Ave.* **$**

NIGHTLIFE

Mugs Ale House *Bar*

Baffled by so many good beers on tap, most people never investigate their vast selection of bottled imports. The colorful local contingent and a decent jukebox explain why Manhattanites schlep all the way out here for a drink. Join 'em. *125 Bedford Ave. (at N. 10th St.), 718-486-8232.* **L** *to Bedford Ave.*

Teddy's Bar and Grill *Bar*

The best bar food in Brooklyn. Try a burger or go for dessert and then wash it down with a bevy of good drinks. Teddy's is one of the few places offering pitchers of really good beer. *96 Berry St. (at N. 8th St.), 718-384-9787.* **L** *to Bedford Ave.*

CONEY ISLAND & BRIGHTON BEACH

After the Civil War, Coney Island became a wildly popular resort easily reachable by railroads and the Coney Island & Brooklyn Railroad Streetcar. An ideal spot for escaping summer heat in the city, Coney Island offered amusement parks, horse racing, gambling and plenty of hotel space, attracting a multitude of visitors. Though little remains of its former glory—except the formidable Cyclone roller-coaster, which was built in 1927—Coney Island is an interesting, if slightly seedy, destination. West of the Boardwalk is Brighton Beach, sometimes called "Little Odessa" for its large Russian community. A recently revived area, the beach is slightly cleaner and less chaotic than that of Coney Island, and the restaurants on Brighton Beach Avenue are certainly worth a try for lavish Russian cuisine and revelry.

WHAT TO SEE

Coney Island Museum

For just 99 cents, this has got to be the best bargain in Brooklyn for a rainy afternoon, as well as the best way to relive the Island in its heyday. *1208 Surf Ave (at W. 12th) 718-372-5159, coneyisland.com.* **D** **F** **N** **Q** *to Stillwell Ave-Coney Island.*

The New York Aquarium

Located just off the boardwalk, the Aquarium is a great stop between riding the Cyclone and eating lunch. Huge tanks replicate reef and wetland ecosystems with

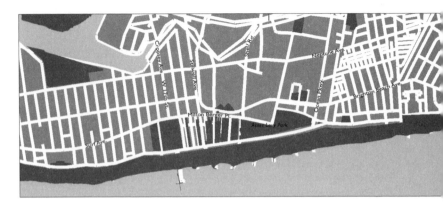

endangered species, and there are traditional sea lion shows and shark tank
well. Don't miss the jellyfish—requiring unique care, they swim in lit cylinders
extend from ceiling to floor, lighting the otherwise dark exhibit. An underw
exhibit features penguins and even an octopus. *Brooklyn. Surf Ave. and W. 8t
718-265-FISH; nyaquarium.com. Hours: Summer, M-F 10am-6pm, Sa-Su 10am-7
Otherwise, M-F 10am-5pm, Sa-Su 10am-5:30pm Adults $12, Children & Seniors*
🅳 *to Stillwell,* 🅕 🅠 *to W. 8th St. in Coney Island.*

BETCHA CAN'T
EAT JUST ONE

The original **NATHAN'S FAMOUS** hot dog stand opened here in 1916, anc
serves up the delectable all-American treat. A hot dog eating contest held
annually is not for the weak of heart…or stomach. *1310 Surf Ave. (bet. 15th St
Stillwell Ave.), 718-946-2202, nathansfamous.com. Hours: Daily 8am-1am.* 🅳 🅕
🅠 *to Coney Island-Stillwell Ave.* **$**

*The ferris wheel at
Coney Island*

Queens

HOME TO OVER 100 DIFFERENT ethnic groups and over 120 linguistic groups, Queens is one of the most ethnically diverse spots in the world. In neighborhood after neighborhood, new residents form tight communities with fellow immigrants and residents. Forest Hills and Kew Gardens have long been predominantly Jewish and Italian, while Woodside, Rockaway Beach, and Long Island City house the Irish. Astoria is a little Greece, while Jamaica, Far Rockaway and Elmhurst hosts the borough's largest black population, and Jackson Heights mostly consists of Latin American and South Asian communities.

Despite its reputation as the ignored stepchild of the five city boroughs, Queens has plenty to brag about. Few areas can beat its ethnic and cultural diversity, museums, parks, and amazing food. Still, perhaps because Queens is home to both of NYC's major airports, many people are content to simply pass through. Or maybe they're just boggled by the Byzantine street grid—Queens is notorious for interspersing its Roads, Avenues, and Streets with no discernable logic. But some of the madness can be decoded: Queens addresses contain two numbers separated by a dash; the first refers to the closest cross street, while the second names the actual address. The address 34-21 42nd Street, for example, is on 42nd Street, closest to 34th Avenue. Got it? Good. Now that you know how to get around, here are some reasons to stay a while.

HISTORY

>>WHEN QUEENS WAS MERGED into New York in 1898, much of it wa
fenced off into farms, and, in the eastern section of Queens, there was little as
tion to become a city. A non-binding referendum introduced to voters in
found Flushing, Hempstead, and other outlying areas solidly opposed to cor
dation. This lack of a distinct borough community was mitigated by the sece
of far eastern areas toward Nassau County as well as increasing urbanizatior
much of the original identity crisis remains today. By the 20's and '30s, Queens
beginning to develop its current character, with tree-lined rows of modest
and wood-frame houses.

Queens was already developing when the 1939 World's Fair solidified its
as New York's primary locale for recreation, arenas, and beautiful parks. Prep
tion for the Fair converted Flushing Meadows/Corona Park from a dumpsi
the city's second-largest landscaped recreation area. Queens has become
borough of choice for the latest influx of immigrants, a place where newcor
can solidly establish themselves at arm's length from big-city pressures.

ASTORIA & LONG ISLAND CITY

>> If you've ever taken the elevated 🅝 🅦 or 🕖 train to Queens and spott
gigantic sign reading Silvercup, then you've seen Long Island City, the closest
of Queens to Manhattan. Silvercup, a huge former bakery reborn as a movie
dio, has filmed scenes for *The Sopranos* and *Sex and the City*. The studio's indu
past and artistic present provide an apt metaphor for the neighborhood's ec
cism, where abandoned factories alternate schizophrenically between gall
and museums.

The population of Long Island City has long been a mix of the working clas
artists in search of reasonable rent. Hugging the East River is Gantry Plaza
Park, where the area's award-winning designers paid homage to the City's ir
trial history by integrating old train gantries into the park's architecture. From
park's sculpted piers, visitors can take in one of the most breathtaking view
Manhattan's east side. With the recent construction of several luxury water
condos, Long Island City is set to undergo some major changes in the co
years. Its oddly beautiful industrial stretches, as well as its affordability to a
may soon be things of the past.

Astoria, which borders Long Island City, is often thought of as "Little Gre
but it also houses Brazilian, Italian, Croatian, Colombian, and Egyptian immig
to name a few. A walk down Steinway Street (named for Henry Steinway, w
famous piano factory is still in full working order at the street's end) lea
signs in Arabic, hookah bars aplenty, and mouth-watering Egyptian food. Like
Island City, Astoria has a rich cinematic history. It boasts its own landmark n
studio, Kaufman-Astoria Studio (which also doubles as a Cineplex), which st
across the street from the Museum of the Moving Image. Ditmars, Astoria's
dominantly Greek region, lies at the very end of the elevated 🅝 🅦 line a
home to numerous Greek restaurants, a Bohemian beer garden, and Astoria

HAT TO SEE

Gantry Plaza State Park

Come here for the best view of the Chrysler Building, the U.N., and the Empire State Building. An enormous, vintage Pepsi-Cola sign, which used to sit atop the company's now-defunct Queens bottling plant, glows neon red from inside the park. *50-50 2nd Street, Long Island City, 718-786-6385.* **7** *to Vernon-Jackson.*

Socrates Sculpture Park

A former waterfront dumpsite transformed into a quirky public art space, the sculpture park has also been known to welcome the occasional amateur traveling circus. *Vernon Boulevard (at Broadway), Long Island City, 718-956-1819, socratess-culpturepark.org.* **N** **W** *to Broadway.*

Astoria Park

A grassy waterfront oasis crisscrossed by the majestic Triborough and Hell Gate Bridges, this park hosted the 1936 Olympic swimming trials in its pool. *21st Street (at Hoyt Avenue), Astoria, 718-626-8621.* **N** **W** *to Ditmars Blvd.*

HERE TO EAT

Agnanti *Mediterranean*

A Greek-Turkish restaurant with affordable prices and quick service, Agnanti has plenty of meze (small plates), so you can sample several platters and not miss out on something great. *Astoria, 19-06 Ditmars Boulevard (at 19th St.), 718-545-4554, agnantimeze.com.* **N** **W** *to Ditmars Blvd.* **$**

Butcher Brothers Steakhouse *Steakhouse*

Butcher Brothers Steakhouse is the fifth establishment opened by the esteemed Redzic brothers. The steakhouse is a welcome addition to brothers Dino and Johnny's Italian ristorante Amici Amore I. Though the two restaurants share an entrance, the space is divided between the Italian restaurant and the upscale steakhouse, each of which offers its own menu. The restaurants boast the most extensive wine list in all of Astoria, and the brothers' dedication to the quality of their establishment is evident in the impressive, customized wall of over 4,000 red wines. The oysters are excellent, and the porterhouse, while expensive, is worth every morsel. *Astoria, 29-33 Newtown Ave., 718-267-2771, amiciamore1.com.* **N** *to 30th St.* **$$$**

Café Bar *Café*

This is one of those places that will become a favorite the first time you walk in. The laidback atmosphere make it a good place to spend hours over coffee, dessert, or a drink. It's especially good for people-watching on Friday and Saturday nights, when the old country locals mix with club kids. *Astoria, 32-19 36th Ave. (bet. 32nd and 33rd Sts.), 718-204-5273.* **G** **R** **V** *to Steinway St.,* **N** **W** *to Broadway.* **$**

TEA TO A T

The bright, airy café known as **COMMUNITEA** offers free wi-fi and an impres
selection of green, black, and white teas. Customers with laptops abound in
low-key alternative to Starbucks. *47-02 Vernon Blvd. (at 47th Ave.), Long Island*
718-729-7708, *to Vernon-Jackson.* **$**

Fatty's Café *Café*

An always-bustling spot, Fatty's Café is a small eatery with Latin flavor an
young crowd. Menu highlights include the jalapeno turkey burger and the cub
sandwich. *2501 Ditmars Boulevard, Astoria, 718-267-7071, fattyscafényc.com.* **N**
to Ditmars Blvd. **$**

Freeze Peach *Café*

Freeze Peach is an independent internet-equipped coffee shop that also h
various group meetings (Vegastorians, an Astoria vegan organization, is one).
toria, 22-00 29th St. (at Ditmars Blvd. and 29th St.), freezepeach.org. **N** **W** *to Ditr*
Blvd. **$**

Mombar *Egyptian*

Mombar is an eye-catching Egyptian restaurant, covered by chef/artist Mous
Rahman's fascinating mosaics, paintings, and re-imagined objects (including pi
hammers and a vintage U.S. Mail chute). Good food and moderate prices top
this unique atmosphere. *25-22 Steinway St. (bet. 25th and 38th Aves.), Astoria, 7*
726-2356. **N** **W** *to Astoria Blvd.* **$**

NIGHTLIFE

Irish Rover *Pub*

The Irish Rover pours a mean pint of Guinness and makes a pretty good sh
herd's pie for its mostly local clientele. As one might guess, the regulars are mo
Irish, but the crowd is always mixed. Occasional live performances liven up
joint. *Astoria, 37-18 28th Ave. (bet. 38th and 37th Sts.), 718-278-9372.* **G** **R**
to Steinway St.

BEST FLOWER-FREE
GARDEN

Hundreds of beer gardens used to populate New York City. Now, only the
HEMIAN HALL AND BEER GARDEN remains, having survived development
Prohibition. In this walled-in space full of Pilsner and picnic benches, it's eas
forget you're in the city. It's also a great place to learn Czech. *21-19 24th Ave*
Astoria, 718-274-4925, bohemianhall.com. **N** **W** *to Astoria Blvd.*

Krash *Club*

No doubt its parent club in San Juan would be proud of the Latin music this
ernous dance emporium serves up Mondays, Thursdays, Fridays, and Saturday
definitely worth the ride if you crave a night of mesmerizing beats. *Astoria, 3*
Steinway St. (at 35th Ave.), 718-937-2400, krashnyc.com. Cover: $1-$10. **G** **R**
to Steinway St.

RTS

Isamu Noguchi Garden Museum *Museums*

The perfect place to escape the summer heat, this museum is devoted to Isamu Noguchi, a sculptor and Columbia dropout, showcasing his art in cool gardens and dark interior spaces. *Long Island City. 9-01 33rd Road (at Vernon Blvd.), 718-545-8842, noguchi.org.* ⓝ ⓦ *to Broadway,* ⓕ *to Queensbridge-21st St.*

Museum of the Moving Image *Museums*

Devoted to the history of film and TV, this space is full of moving image memorabilia, including the original Yoda puppet and a hand-wound projector screening silent films. The museum's attached theater often hosts intimate screenings with famous directors. *Astoria, 35th Avenue (at 36th St.), 718-784-0077, ammi.org.* ⓡ ⓥ ⓖ *to Steinway St.*

P.S. 1 Contemporary Art Center *Museums*

This unique art venue is housed in a Romanesque revival building (a former elementary school, hence the name) and its shows feature exciting, up-and-coming artists. Check out the Warm Up music series in the summer, and bring your moves, as everyone dances. *22-25 Jackson Avenue (at 46th Ave.), Long Island City, 718-784-2084, ps1.org.* ⓥ ⓔ ⓖ *to 23rd Ely,* ⓻ *to 46th Road-Courthouse Square.*

ACKSON HEIGHTS

Marketed as a "garden community" in the early 20th century, Jackson Heights is nestled beneath the elevated ⓻ train and accessible by many other trains. Near the 74th Street-Broadway transit hub, a vibrant, glittering stretch of sari shops, Indian jewelry stores, South Asian grocery stories, and Indian restaurants provides evidence of Jackson Heights' largest ethnic groups; Indian and Bangladeshi immigrants have arrived here in droves over the past 30 years. Jackson Heights is also home to a sizable Latin American community along Roosevelt Avenue, including Colombians, Argentineans, and Ecuadorians. Proof of their presence is the famous "Arepa Lady," Maria Piedad Cano, who can be found selling her delicious, piping-hot corncakes on late-night weekends near the entrance to the 82nd Street-Jackson Heights stop on the ⓻ train. The Jackson Heights Historic District comprises a number of "garden apartments," a term invented by neighborhood officials, some of which were designed by the planners of Central Park. Most of Jackson Heights' green space is private, but bike trails along 80th and 81st streets link the neighborhood to Flushing Meadows-Corona Park.

HERE TO EAT

The Delhi Palace *Indian*

The Delhi Palace serves up original and traditional Indian cuisine, and features walls decorated with colorful murals. Mouth-watering food, reasonable prices, and a lively atmosphere make Delhi Palace a favorite for locals. Check ou attached sweet shop for dessert. *37-33 74th Street, 718-507-0666.* ❼ *to St.- Broadway;* ❸ ❸ ❹ *to Roosevelt Avenue-Jackson Heights.* **$$**

**MOST WELCOME
MISNOMER**

Swap the standard burgers and milkshakes for aloo gobi and mango las **JACKSON DINER,** a huge Indian restaurant with deliciously affordable wee buffet specials. *37-47 74th Street, 718-672-1232, jacksondiner.com.* ❼ *to 74t Broadway.* ❸ ❸ ❹ ❹ *to Roosevelt Avenue-Jackson Heights.* *$*

SHOPPING

Butala Emporium *Marketplaces*

A field day for browsers, the colorful Butala Emporium in Jackson Heights everything from Sanskrit comic books to Indian jewelry, all at affordable p *37-46 74th St. (at 37th Rd.), 718-899-5590, butalaemporium.com.* ❼ *to 74t Broadway,* ❸ ❸ ❹ ❹ ❹ *to Roosevelt Avenue-Jackson Heights.*

Mita Jewelers *Jewelry*

Mita Jewelers, an Indian jewelry store, glitters with a blinding assortment of necklaces, earrings, and bracelets. *37-30 74th Street (near 37th Rd.), 718-507-* ❼ *to 74th St.- Broadway,* ❸ ❸ ❹ ❹ ❹ *to Roosevelt Avenue-Jackson Heights*

Patel Brothers *Specialty Foods*

Patel Brothers, a warehouse-sized supermarket, stocks plenty of imported S Asian fruits, vegetables, and spices, among many other products. *37-46 74th S 718-899-5590, patelbrothersusa.com.* ❼ *to 74th St.-Broadway;* ❸ ❸ ❹ ❹ Roosevelt Avenue-Jackson Heights.

ARTS

The Eagle Theater *Film*

Colorful posters decorate this theater which features movies hailing from lywood, replete with songs and English subtitles. *73-07 37th Road near 73rd S 718-205-2800.* ❼ *to 74th St.- Broadway,* ❸ ❸ ❹ ❹ ❹ *to Roosevelt Av Jackson Heights.*

FLUSHING MEADOWS

>> A former dumpsite described by F. Scott Fitzgerald in *The Great Gats* a "valley of ashes" Flushing Meadows received a complete makeover wh hosted the World's Fair in 1939-40 and then again in 1964-65. Older reside the neighborhood have fond memories of the fairs, whose booths predicted sons-like future and showcased artifacts from different countries around the g Though the World's Fairs may not have gotten their visions of the future right—we're not riding around on hovercrafts (yet)—their World Pavilio manage to mirror Flushing's eventual transformation into a global mixing gr

These days, you're more likely to hear Korean, Cantonese, or Mandarin than English spoken on the streets of Flushing. Numerous Korean and Chinese restaurants reflect the current population, which is fifty-five percent Asian-American.

Flushing Meadows-Corona Park was built on the site of the departed World's Fair, which lives on in the enormous metal Unisphere, visible from many blocks away. Other remnants of the fairs, such as a scale model of the five boroughs, can be observed in the Queens Museum of Art. Flushing is also home to Shea Stadium, where the New York Mets play, and Flushing Cemetery, where Louis Armstrong and Dizzy Gillespie are buried. The area is also home to the National Tennis Center, which hosts the U.S. Open for two weeks near the end of the summer. Most attractions in Flushing are accessible by the ❼ train.

WHAT TO SEE

Shea Stadium

Sure, this major-league ballpark built in 1964 is far from user-friendly, but Shea is home to the New York Mets—and these die-hard Queens fans won't let you forget it. *Roosevelt Avenue off Grand Central Parkway, 718-507-8499, nymets.com. ❼ to Willets Point/Shea Stadium.*

Queens Botanical Gardens

Those craving herb and bee gardens alike can find themselves in this serene space, which includes an arboretum and 39 acres of gardens. Like many sights in the area, it was built for the 1939-40 World's Fair. *43-50 Main Street, Flushing, 718-886-3800, queensbotanical.org. ❼ to Main Street-Flushing.*

WHERE TO EAT

Ocean Jewels *Chinese*

A mainly Cantonese restaurant across the street from Flushing Mall, the newly refurbished Ocean Jewels specializes in seafood of all shapes and sizes. *133-30 39th Avenue, 718-359-8600. ❼ to Main Street-Flushing.* **$$**

Corona Park, site of the 1964 World's Fair

Kum Gang San *Korean*

Kum Gang San, a Korean restaurant, offers a variety of barbeque dishes and ditional fare, as well as lunch specials. *138-28 Northern Boulevard, 718-461-0 kumgangsan.net.* ❼ *to Main Street-Flushing.* **$**

Spicy and Tasty *Chinese*

Some of the best and most inexpensive Sichuan in all of Queens can be fo at Spicy and Tasty, where no type of chili pepper is ignored. *39-07 Prince St., (at 39th St.), 718-359-1601. Hours: Daily 11am-11pm. Cash Only.* ❼ *to Main Flushing.* **$**

ARTS

Colden Center for the Performing Arts *Theater*

The Colden Center at Queens College Theater holds classical, pop, jazz, the opera, and children's events weekly. *Flushing, 65-30 Kissena Blvd., 718-793-8 coldencenter.org.* ❼ *to Main St.*

Louis Armstrong House Museum *Museums*

Opened to the public in 2003, this modest two-story home in Queens was first house Armstrong owned and is now a National Historical Landmark. Tho it only cost $3,500, after Louis and his wife Lucille moved in 1943, they took decorations and renovations to the max. The house is so full of fascinating sto the guided tour can sometimes last over an hour. *Corona, 34-56 107th St., 478-8274, satchmo.net. T-F 10am-5pm, Sa-Su 12pm-5pm $8 adults, $6 stude seniors-children.* ❼ *to 103rd St.-Corona Plaza.*

Queens Museum of Art *Museums*

While largely devoted to contemporary art, the museum is best known the Panorama, a scale model of the five boroughs constructed for the 196 World's Fair. It's still updated periodically to reflect changes to the NYC la scape. *Flushing Meadows-Corona Park, 718-592-9700, queensmuseum.org.* ❼ *Willets Point–Shea Stadium.*

The New York Mets

{Meet the Mets}

>>WHEN NEW YORKERS AREN'T SHOUTING AT THE TV as their favorite team wins or loses, while eating a slice, sipping Long Island Iced Tea, or listening to Billy Joel, they're out having fun in the only way that makes sense: confusing newcomers by talking about "The Met," without saying which one.

Let the visitor beware: between the Met Opera, Metlife insurance, and the Mets, there is vast room for confusion.

Just to be clear: the **METROPOLITAN OPERA,** established in 1880, with its first performance in 1883, became the centerpiece of Lincoln Center (66th Street and Broadway) when it moved there in 1966. One of the world's most acoustically perfect opera stages, this Met has begun to add to its conservative roots with world premiers of such modern operas as *Mourning Becomes Electra* by Marvin David Levy (1967) and *The Voyage* by Phillip Glass and David Henry Hwang (1992). Long known for the luxuriant sets of Franco Zeffirelli *(Romeo and Juliet, Tea with Mussolini)*, this Met has since expanded to the modern touches of Frank Philipp Schlössman and others, sometimes successfully, sometimes not.

THE METROPOLITAN MUSEUM, a neoclassical colossus that yawns across several blocks of Central Park Real estate (main entrance 83rd Street and 5th avenue), is one of the largest comprehensive art museums in the world. Unlike its rivals, the Louvre and the Vatican Museum, *this* Met boasts a sampling of art from every continent and most every epoch. One suite of rooms features gold jewelry from Incan empire, while the modern art suite showcases the modernist chaos of the Chilean, Matta (1911-2002).

The **"MIRACLE METS"** are an expansion team that has played Major League Baseball out of Queens since 1962. They are now home to such stars as Tom Glavine of the Braves' winning 1995 World Series combination and Pedro Martinez of the Red Sox' winning 2004 combination, as well as Jose Reyes, who led the National League in stolen bases last year, and Julio Franco who, as a 47-year-old pinch hitter, became the oldest player to smack a home run.

METLIFE is an insurance company whose principle advertiser is Snoopy, the dog (not the doggy-dog) and benighted pilot of Sopwith Camels, whose tragic pursuit of the Red Baron would probably raise his premiums, were dogs to pursue life insurance too.

The Bronx

THANKS TO TOM WOLFE and *The Bonfire of the Vanities*, drove
tourists and naïve locals have been avoiding the Bronx since l
After all, no one in their right mind would visit a crime-ridden s
teeming with would-be murderers—except that the Bronx hardly
that description. Sure, the area has some neighborhoods you'd do
to avoid visiting alone or late at night, but the same can be said at
every borough in New York City. Luckily, many people are capab
separating fact from fiction, and plenty of visitors can attest to the
that Wolfe's Bronx no longer exists—if it ever did in the first plac

Home values rule in this neighborhood. The communities are
ten tight-knit and child-centric. That 1950s Hollywood version of N
York—the one where kids play stickball in the streets while
mothers sit on building steps and dish the local dirt while folding l
dry—is alive and well in some areas of the Bronx. And, of cou
nothing boosts local pride like living near Yankee Stadium, espe
when the boys of summer are in the throes of a winning streak.

In Riverdale, the wealthy locals spend their weekends in the gar
of Wave Hill. In Mott Haven, locals enjoy the transformation of bu
out city blocks into livable homes, and on City Island, the landscap
best compared to a New England fishing village—which is, of cou
what most people think of when they think of the Bronx. There
also several colleges, the New York Botanical Garden and a fan

zoo, just in case you felt like something was missing.

Between urban blight and placid city parks, it may seem that the Bronx has seen it all, but in the only borough on the mainland continent of North America, there's always more to see.

HISTORY

>> IN 1841, THE NEW YORK and Harlem Railroad was built, connecting the rural region now known as the Bronx to the bustling metropolis of Manhattan. Over the next few decades, a new system of rails ushered in hundreds of thousands of wealthy Manhattanites and first and second-generation immigrants, all looking for a peaceful alternative to the big city. It wasn't long, however, before the Bronx became rather crowded itself.

Officially declared a part of New York City in 1898, the Bronx continued to undergo rapid urbanization; Jewish, Italian, and Irish immigrants arrived in large numbers to find prosperity in a borough that was on the move. The buildings along the Grand Concourse were decorated with lavish architectural flourishes, and an entrepreneurial spirit prevailed throughout the growing middle class with more changes to come.

In the postwar era, many of the Bronx residents who could afford to leave flocked to the northern suburbs, and the Latino and African-American population that followed faced severe housing shortages, high crime rates, and indifference on the part of government and financial institutions. Drug trafficking, arson, and poverty took root in the South Bronx in particular. But now, things are changing in the Bronx. Through the work of relentless community organizations, new visions are being implemented to turn the borough into an even more sustainable and pleasant place to live.

WHAT TO SEE

The New York Botanical Garden

More than just a pretty walk, these fifty acres of forest and fabulous rose and rock gardens are a botanist's delight. In fact, this place is one of the major players in worldwide botany research. Through the Bronx Green-Up program, the Garden provides plants and horticultural wisdom to community gardens throughout the borough. *200th St. and Kazimiroff Rd., Bedford Park, 718-817-8700, nybg.org. Hours: Apr-Oct T- Su 10am-6pm, Nov.-Mar. T-Su 10am-5pm $3, free Sa 10am-12pm and W.* ⓓ ❹ *to Bedford Park Blvd. Metro-North to Botanical Garden.*

The Bronx Museum of the Arts

Like the borough it represents, this contemporary Art Museum offers exhibitions and collections that are culturally diverse and artistically dynamic. The Museum specializes in artists who have lived or worked in the Bronx. *1040 Grand Concourse (at 165th St.), 718-681-6000, bronxmuseum.org. Hours: W 12pm-9pm, R-Su 12pm-6:00pm, Suggested Admission $5 Adults, $3 kids.* ❸ ⓓ *167th St–Grand Concourse.*

Yankee Stadium

The Bronx Zoo

Matched by few other zoos, the sheer number of wildlife exhibits and activ
here is enough to merit an entire day of exploration. Make sure to wear cc
walking shoes and be choosy with where you spend your time, lest you miss y
favorite animal. Never mind the summer crowds, the distance between ex
its, and the rather hefty admissions price—none of it detracts from the ov
beauty and educational value of this place. The expanded admissions optic
well worth the extra money since it includes access to Congo (the gorilla exh
which is easily the best attraction, as well as a number of other activities and ri
*Entrances on Bronx Park S. Southern Blvd., and E. Fordham Rd., 718-330-1234, br
zoo.com. Hours: M-F 10am-5pm, Sa-Su 10am-5:30pm Parts closed Nov-Apr. A
$12, Children & Seniors, $9.* ❷ ❺ *to East Tremont Ave.–W Farms Sq.*

The Loew's Paradise Theater

An emblem of the Bronx's own historical trajectory, this theater hosts many ty
of events. It was built along the Grand Concourse in 1929 during a time of we
and impressive architecture. The theater fell into disrepair in the early '90s,
to have its majestic interior restored in 2005 when it reopened for busine
tickets are too pricey, you might just opt for a building tour. *2413 Grand Conco
718-220-6143, theparadisetheater.com. $6.* ❸ ❿ *to Fordham Rd*

BEST STEP
FORWARD

In collaboration with numerous organizations like Sustainable South Bronx
the Bronx Museum of the Arts, the **POINT COMMUNITY DEVELOPMENT C
PORATION** provides educational counseling, artistic opportunities, and commu
development programs to young people in the Hunts Point neighborhood. T
also put on the Annual Fish Parade and Street Festival, great for families
anyone who enjoys street fairs. *940 Garrison Avenue, 718-542-4139, thepoin
❻ to Hunts Point Ave.*

The Writer's Bench

The bench located toward the back of the uptown platform at the 149th St
and Grand Concourse station may not look like much, but it was once kne
as The Writer's Bench—and, prior to the city's clean trains initiative, it forr
the central meeting place for graffiti artists (vandals, if you must) who used
spot to sign black books and admire the graffiti on passing trains. ❷ ❺ *to 1
St–Grand Concourse*

Orchard Beach

A marvel of engineering as well as a popular summertime destination am
Bronx's residents, this 1.1 mile long "Bronx Riviera" was built in the 1930s
public works project by Parks Commissioner Robert Moses. It remains a pop
recreation area for activities such as tennis and basketball, as well as a pop
meeting place for locals. It is also the site of the Tropical Music Festival, which t
place every Sunday in July and August. ❻ *to Pelham Bay*

WHERE TO EAT

Bellavista *Italian*

Riverdale abounds in good restaurants, but this moderately priced Italian joint is a favorite haunt among locals. The humble yet charming atmosphere goes well with the style of food: simple but satisfying. Think pizza, pasta, and heavenly lasagna served up by a friendly staff. *Riverdale, 554 W. 235th St. (bet. Oxford and Johnson Aves.), 718-548-2354.* ❶ *to 231st St.* **$$**

BEST TASTE OF
IRELAND

AN BEAL BOCHT CAFÉ is Gaelic through and through, right down to its name. They serve up scrumptious Irish food in the daytime, and deliver pints of lager by night. Groceries are also available. Entertainment includes live Irish folk music and poetry readings which happen almost every night of the week. *445 W. 238th St. (bet. Greystone and Waldo Aves.), 718-884-7127, anbealbochtcafé.com. Hours: M-Su 10am-4am* ❶ *train to 238th St.* **$$**

Café al Mercato *Italian*

In this heavily ethnic Belmont neighborhood populated by Italians and Albanians, Café al Mercato is a great place nestled in the active market considered the Little Italy of the Bronx. This Italian eatery serves a variety of Sicilian entrees from pizza to chicken pizziola served with garlicky broccoli rabe. Along with many of its neighbors on Arthur Avenue, this restaurant evolved from a cook with a pushcart to a cultural mainstay. *2344 Arthur Ave., 718-364-7681.* ❸ ❹ *to 182-183rd Sts.* **$$**

Jimmy's Bronx Café *Café*

After just four years in the Bronx, this "Latin Restaurant and Entertainment Complex" has become the nucleus of nightlife in the borough's Latino community. Upstairs, seafood is served into the early-morning hours as patrons watch boxing and baseball on large TVs. Downstairs, the dance floor resembles a hotel ballroom, built for high capacity. As at other area clubs, there's no such thing as overdressing, though casual dress seems prevalent. *Fordham, 281 W. Fordham Rd. (at Major Deegan Expressway), 718-329-2000, jimmysbronxcafé.com.* ❶ *to 207th St.* **$$**

Le Refuge Inn *French*

You'll be tempted to stay the night at this bed and breakfast once you taste its delicious French food and great service. *City Island, 620 City Island Ave. (at Sutherland St.), 718-885-2478, lerefugeinn.com.* ❻ *to Pelham Bay Park.* **$$$**

Lobster Box *Seafood*

Though not what it used to be, the Lobster Box still provides an amazing view of the Bay. The pride of the place is the view and the lobster, but the fish is underwhelming. A fun place to go with family, or when you have that all-consuming lobster craving. *City Island, 34 City Island Ave. (bet. Belden and Rochelle Sts.), 718-885-1952, lobsterbox.com.* ❻ *to Pelham Bay Park.* **$$$**

View of Manhattan from City Island

Mario's *Italian*

After visiting the Botanical Gardens, amble over to this Arthur Ave. institut
that's been around since 1919. Here, a near oppressive amount of tourists ming
with locals, but the pasta is well worth the hassle. *East Tremont, 2342 Arthur* ₳
(bet. 184th and 186th Sts.), 718-584-1188. ❷ ❺ *to Pelham Pkwy. $$*

SHOPPING

Casa Amadeo *Music*

Casa Amadeo arrived in the Longwood neighborhood in 1941 and is now
oldest Latin music store in the Bronx. For the past 55 years, it has remained a
spot for musicians and aficionados of music from the Hispanic Caribbean.
Prospect Ave. (at Macy Pl.), 212-328-6896, casaamadeo.com. ❷ ❺ *to Prospect*

The Hub *Clothing : Bargain*

One of the borough's oldest and most popular shopping strips, the Hub is the i
place for bargain hunting. Rumor has it that clothing designers visit the Hub to
cover the newest in urban street style, create clothes accordingly, and then ma
them to the suburbs. *Third Avenue (at E. 149th St.).* ❷ ❺ *to Third Ave.-149*

Staten Island

WHEN ASKED WHAT there is to do on Staten Island, most residents reply with a look that says, "Do you really want to know?" This self-deprecating attitude is characteristic of a borough not always comfortable alongside its bigger-name neighbors.

The history of New York's greenest borough is perhaps prophetic of its future. The site of Giovanni da Verrazano's "discovery" of North America proper in 1524, the island was won by Manhattan as a prize in a boat race sponsored by the Duke of York in 1687. Today, Staten Island is rarely awarded an equal place among the city's other boroughs: perpetually snubbed by its urban neighbors for its telltale accents and legendary big-haired residents, the most suburban of the five boroughs has the smallest population and the least representation in City Council. Adding insult to injury, for many years the city sent its garbage to the island's Fresh Kills landfill.

Staten Island is largely residential and content to remain as such. Communities are small and no one is a stranger for long. Although the Indian and Latino populations are growing rapidly, Staten Island is still predominantly Italian, and when asked about El Capo di Tutti Capi, the house where *The Godfather* was filmed, one local replied: "Films like *Goodfellas* and *The Godfather* are treated like documentaries here."

While Staten Island boasts many attractions—like the Jacques Marchais Center of Tibetan Art and the Staten Island Botanical Gar-

den—for some residents, none of these outweigh the lure of the B
City, which is just a ferry ride away. On a late-afternoon ride out, a grou
of high school kids sit at the front of the boat, watching Manhattan ge
closer and closer. As soon as the gangplank is down, they whiz out o
rollerblades and skateboards, soon lost in the bustle of taxis and wear
commuters. At night, they'll return to the suburbia other kids came
New York to forget: green lawns, driveways, and quiet streets, which, f
the older generations, are the reasons it's worthwhile to stick around.

HISTORY

>> HENRY HUDSON GAVE Staaten Eylandt its original name in 1609, wh
he sailed into the bay now bearing his name. In 1639, the Dutch opened Stat
Island to colonization, but the area remained difficult to settle due to confli
with native inhabitants; there were constant skirmishes, and the Dutch and Nat
Americans attempted to reach a peace agreement five times.

Staten Island became a province of New Jersey after the British took cont
of New York in 1664. From then on, the island was known as Richmond Cou
after the Duke of Richmond, son of Charles II.

Largely known as a secluded place for fishing and farming—or years, reacha
only by boat—Staten Island remained isolated until 1713, when a public ferry
gan carrying passengers to New York. Staten Island became officially incorpora
into New York City in 1898. Staten Island's independent streak remains to
which may seem surprising since the 1964 construction of the Verrazano-N
rows Bridge, connecting the island to Brooklyn. Fed up with garbage dumps fi
largely with trash from elsewhere, the citizens of Richmond voted overwhelmi
in 1993 to secede from the city, though the vote was only symbolic. The Fr
Kills landfill was closed in 2002, but to many, Staten Islanders remain ambiva
participants in New York City.

WHAT TO SEE

Jacques Marchais Center of Tibetan Art

This museum "was founded in 1945 to encourage interest, study, and researc
the art and culture of Tibet and the surrounding regions." Hey, the Staten Is
Ferry is way cheaper than a plane ticket to Lhasa. *338 Lighthouse Ave., 718-*
3500, tibetanmuseum.org. SX15, S54, S74, S84, Staten Island Railway to Oak
Heights.

Staten Island Botanical Garden

A botanical garden in the middle of suburbia is not as jarring and unexpecte
one in more urban environs such as Brooklyn, but that doesn't make this gar
any less delightful than its big-city siblings. *1000 Richmond Terrace, 718-273-8*
sibg.org. S40, S90, Staten Island Railway to St. George.

BEST OF
OLDEN DAYS

The exhibit at **RICHMOND TOWN** documents local history and includes, among other historic buildings, the oldest surviving elementary school in America. Volunteers dress in 18th-century costume to reenact everything from candle-making to declarations of war. *441 Clarke Ave., 718-351-1611, historicrichmondtown.org. Hours vary seasonally. S74 bus from Whitehall Ferry.*

The Staten Island Ferry

The only way to get between Staten Island and Manhattan without driving, this ferry carries 70,000 passengers a day between St. George and Whitehall Street in Lower Manhattan. The 5-mile, 25-minute ride is a scenic one, giving panoramic views of the Statue of Liberty on Ellis Island and the downtown Manhattan skyline. The best part? It's absolutely free. The 50-cent fare established in 1990 (previously it was a nickel in 1897, and then a dime in 1975) was eliminated altogether in 1997. *1 White Hall St. in Manhattan, 1 Bay St. in Staten Island. Staten Island Railway to St. George.*

ASHIEST PLACE
IN THE CITY

Before it gets converted into the largest park in New York City, catch a glimpse of **FRESH KILLS LANDFILL,** which is three times bigger than Central Park and rumored to be visible from space. Check it out while it's still fresh.

The Staten Island Zoo

An alternative to the always crowded Bronx Zoo, take a stroll through the smaller (and cheaper) Staten Island Zoo. Wednesdays are free. *614 Broadway (bet. Clove Rd., Broadway, and Forest Ave.), 718-442-3100, statenislandzoo.org. Cash Only. Admission: $2-$3. Hours: M-Su 10am-4:45pm*

HERE TO EAT

Ralph's Ices *Desserts*

From the traditional lemon to more exotic flavors like honeydew, the ices at Ralph's Ices are the perfect summer weather treat. *501 Port Richmond Ave., 718-273-3675, ralphsices.com.* **①** *to South Ferry, Staten Island Ferry to S44.* **$**

Ruddy & Dean *Steakhouse*

This steakhouse's convenient location near the ferry terminal makes it a great pick for Manhattanites wanting to escape for a night. Patrons can enjoy a great view of the city skyline from the outside patio while enjoying the bar's wide selection of beer and vodka. *44 Richmond Terrace (bet. Day and Wall Sts.), 718-816-4400.* **④ ⑤** *to Bowling Green, then Staten Island Ferry at South Ferry Terminal.* **$$**

Quick Reference

DINING

Turkuaz **225**

ARTS

Insider Notes

Advertisers

49 Grove	Life in Motion
apexart	Magnet Theater
Blue Man Group	Mandolin Brothers
Campustickets.net	Mill Korean Restaurant
Columbia Bartending	New Special Car Service
Condomania	Nikki Midtown
CU Bookstore	NY Fertility Institute
CU Career Education	NY Philharmonic
CU Health Services	NYC Ballet
CU Opthalmology Consultants	Ontological Theater
Days Hotel	P &W Sandwich Shop
DiningFever.com	Planned Parenthood
Domino's	The Princeton Review
Eastside Gynecology	The Producers
eFundraise.org	Performance Space 122
EventiQue	*Putnam County Spelling Bee*
Evil Dead	Sharebooks.com
Excelsior Hotel	Solutions for Writers
The Fantasticks	Sotheby's International Realty
Fotorush	STOMP
GGMC Parking	SusanSez NYC Walkabouts
Guitar Man	*Sweeney Todd*
Hairspray	Tap-A-Keg
Havana Central	Taqueria y Fonda la Mexicana
Horse Trade Theater Group	Tekserve
Hotel Belleclaire	Test Prep NY
Hotel Excelsior	TheaterLab
Hudson Moving & Storage	Tonic
Hungarian Pastry Shop	Tuck-It-Away
Irish Repertory Theatre	Velocity Design
Jewtopia	Village Copier
Katra	West Way Café
Landmark Guest Rooms	The Writers Studio

Eating out in NYC?

Save at NYC's Hottest Restaurants with

Hot Restaurants. Hot Deals.

Exclusive dining discounts available
only on DiningFever.com !

Whether you are looking for fine dining establishments,
casual restaurants, fast food places or takeout/ delivery
options, **DiningFever.com** is your ultimate source for
amazing dining deals at NYC's most exciting eateries.

Check out today's hottest dining deals at
www.DiningFever.com

It's FREE, SIMPLE, & SMART

Plus, sign up for DiningFever's Top Deals
e-newsletter today, so you don't miss out on
New York's top dining deals!

WEST WAY Café

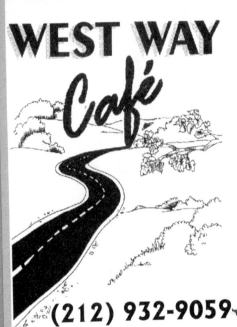

Prompt Delivery

Breakfast - Lunch Dinner - Smoothies Fresh Juice Bar

2800 BROADWAY (corner of 108th)

(212) 932-9059

TAP-A-KEG

2731 BROADWAY
BET. 104th & 105th STS

INTERNET JUKEBOX
POOL TABLE   DARTS
12 BEERS ON TAP

WE HAVE NO KITCHEN SO BRING YOUR OWN OR HAVE IT DELIVERED
HAPPY HOUR EVERDAY 12 NOON UNTIL 7PM
OPEN 7 DAYS FROM 12 NOON TO 4AM
212-749-1734

Domino's...
Pizza and a whole lot more!

Get the door. It's Domino's.™

HOURS OF OPERATION
365 Days a Year
11AM - 2AM

222-2000

965 Amsterdam Avenue (108th Street)

Order online at: www.dominos.quikorder.com

Above 122nd St. Call **280-3200** 409 W. 125th St.

Make it a Meal!

Buffalo Chicken Kickers (10)	$6.49
Buffalo Wings .... (10) $6.49 .... (50)	$26.99
Breadsticks (8)	$2.99
Cheesy Bread (8)	$4.49
Cinna Stix (8)	$3.99
Amazin' Greens Garden Fresh Salad	$4.99
Amazin' Greens Grilled Chicken Caesar Salad	$4.99

Coke, Diet Coke or Sprite:
20-Oz. Bottle **$1.30**   2-liter bottle $2.25

Pizza Toppings: Pepperoni, Ham, Beef, Italian Sausage, Fresh mushrooms, Onions, Green Peppers, Black Olives, Pineapple, Cheddar, Extra Cheese

Venue	:	Katra
Address	:	217 Bowery
Contact	:	Chris Collins
Phone	:	212-473-3113
Fax	:	212-473-3336
Website	:	www.katranyc.com
Email	:	info@katranyc.com

Katra incorporates intimate dining and cocktails amidst a unique and authentic décor. With one of a kind light fixtures and rich furnishings imported from Morocco, Katra's surroundings stimulate the senses and create a warm and dramatic environment for any event.

Katra's menu fuses the flavors and spices of traditional Middle Eastern/Moroccan dishes with French cuisine. Your experience continues with Katra's signature cocktail menu, blending aromatic ingredients with creative flair. Every detail is carefully executed and all elements come together for an experience that blends the old world with the new world.

Venue size	: 5,000 sq. ft.
Capacity	: 400
Number of ppl. cocktail	: 350
Number of ppl. seated	: 150
On-site Catering	: Yes
Outside Catering Permitted	: Yes
Live Music/DJ/Sound System	: Yes

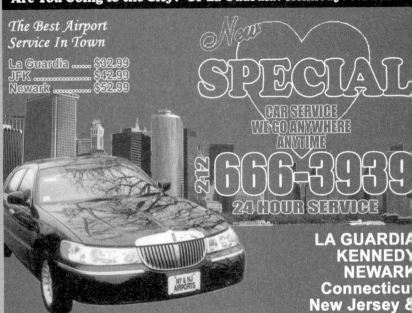

The Princeton Review

Small Group Tutoring

Review à Trois for the GMAT, LSAT, or GRE

Many students want the structure of our prep courses combined with the flexibility of a personal tutor, so we've created *Small Group Tutoring*—a new way to prepare for grad school entrance exams. This program groups three students with an experienced tutor in a course that's built around you.

To learn more or to enroll in a *Small Group Tutoring* program call **800-2Review** or visit **PrincetonReview.com**.

Start with a Mac.

NIKKI
MIDTOWN

It is here that you will find a unique blend of gorgeous people from all parts of the globe sharing languid afternoons and endless nights. Nikki Beach Midtown is world renowned for its surreal beauty and ambiance. It is one of the few places on the planet that serves contemporary European delights & mood enhancing tunes.

Designed in simplistic elegance, all the venues contain the same elements that bring nature into this luxury lifestyle. Nikki Midtown invites guests to completely let loose by feeling the energy that Nikki Beach is famous for in South Beach, Europe, Latin America and the Caribbean. The signature white linens, throw pillows and plush beds will adorn the 6,000 sq. ft venue that will transform from simple New York cool to South Beach chic and trendy. Nikki Midtown is the place where the modeling world meets the business world as an array of high level business professionals and models drink, dance and dine together. Our 2nd level offers a private refuge for Nikki VIP Members featuring the most exclusive service and amenities. Nikki Midtown offers an array of international cuisine combines with an amazing spin on service.

Nikki Midtown, located between Lexington Avenue and 50th Street, is the new offspring of Nikki Beach International. Nikki Midtown will bring the luxury leisure lifestyle to New York City.

OPEN: Monday - Saturday: 5:00pm • HAPPY HOUR: Monday - Friday: 5:00pm - 8:00pm
51 East 50th Street • New York, NY 10022 • 212.753.1144 • www.nikkibeach.com/newyork

Health Services at Columbia is part of the University's Student Services division on the Morningside Campus, and provides integrated and accessible services and programs that support the well-being of the campus community, and the personal and academic development of students. We are comprised of more than 100 individuals: medical providers, nutritionists, disability specialists, health educators, therapists, psychiatrists, peer counselors, student personnel, support staff, and administrative professionals.

www.health.columbia.edu

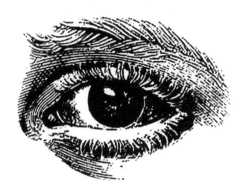

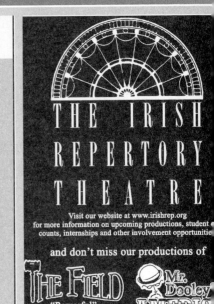

"RIOTOUSLY FUNNY AND REMARKABLY INGENIOUS."
- The New York Times

A New Musical Comedy

The 25th Annual Putnam County
SPELLING BEE

A limited number of $25 tickets
are available by lottery
prior to the performance.

TELECHARGE.COM: (212) 239-6200 Groups: (212) 398-838

CIRCLE IN THE SQUARE THEATRE
50th St. bet. Broadway & 8th Ave.
SpellingBeetheMusical.com   Original Broadway Cast Album on Ghostlight Records

GOLD CARD EVENTS PREFERRED SEATI
800-292-946
BROADWAY.YAHOO.CO
RESTRICTIONS APPLY

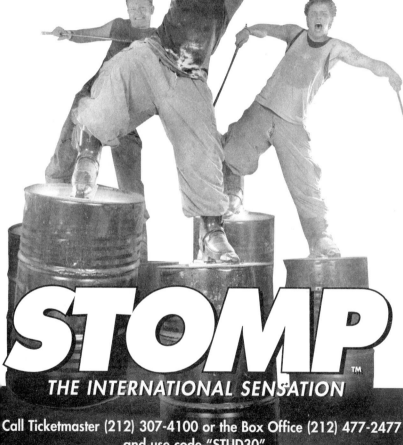

NOT YOUR TYPICAL
BOY MEETS GIRL MEETS DEMON COMEDY
EVIL DEAD
THE MUSICAL
STUDENT
PRICING
AVAILABLE
TELECHARGE.COM OR 212-239-6200
EVILDEADTHEMUSICAL.COM
myspace.com
a place for comedy
OFFICIAL FAN SITE: MYSPACE.COM/EVILDEADTHEMUSICAL
340 West 50th St.
btwn 8th and 9th Aves
NEW WORLD STAGES

"SEE THIS SHOW!"

—*E! Entertainment News*

BLUE MAN GROUP

SHOW SCHEDULE
Tue–Thu 8pm,
Fri 7+10pm, Sat 4,7+10pm,
Sun 2,5+8pm
Schedule subject to change.

TICKET INFORMATION
Box Office 212.254.4370
ticketmaster 212.307.4100
ticketmaster.com
Group Sales 212.260.8993

LOCATION
Astor Place Theatre
434 Lafayette Street NY
1.800.BLUEMAN
blueman.com

Student Rush Tickets $25 day of performance

Tickets available one hour before showtime for all performances except Friday and Saturday at 7pm. Must
have valid student ID. Subject to availability. Limit one ticket per ID. $1.00 theatre restoration fee applies.

INSIDE NEW YORK
can serve both your informational and promotional needs.

ADVERTISE WITH US.

Reach over 50,000 students and young professionals in the NYC area.

INY reaches potential customers upon their arrival in New York City and remains with them for their entire academic and professional careers.

Advertising with us is a great way to gain exposure for your brand or business among the important 18-35 year-old demographic.

SCHOOL/CORPORATE SALES

Orient new students, employees, or clients to the world's greatest city with the ultimate "under 30" guidebook. For years, local area schools and companies have distributed our guids for:

- Orientation materials
- Employee gifts
- Event giveaways
- Client/customer appreciation

Over 30 colleges and dozens of businesses purchase INY for all of their new members.

Bulk discounts make INY affordable for any organization.

Customized editions are also available (e.g. XYZ's Guide to New York), with your logo on the cover.

For more information on Ad Sales and Book Sales, check out **www.insidenewyork.com**, contact **adsales@insidenewyork.com** or **sales@insidenewyork.com**.

Phone: (212) 854-2804
Fax: (212) 663-9398

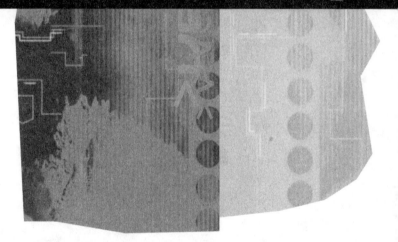

Sharebooks.com --

The Bookstore alternative for used books.

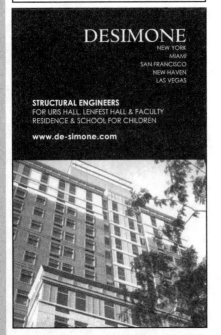

WELCOME
CLASS OF 2010!